IB DIPLOMA PROGRAMME

English A1

Course Companion

Elizabeth Druce
Hannah Tyson

Heard melodies are sweet, but those unheard
Are sweeter; therefore, ye soft pipes, play on;
Not to the sensual ear, but, more endear'd,
Pipe to the spirit ditties of no tone:
Fair youth, beneath the trees, thou canst not leave
Thy song, nor ever can those trees be bare;

OXFORD

UNIVERSITY PRESS

OXFORD
UNIVERSITY PRESS

Great Clarendon Street, Oxford OX2 6DP

Oxford University Press is a department of the University of Oxford.
It furthers the University's objective of excellence in research, scholarship, and education by publishing worldwide in

Oxford New York

Auckland Cape Town Dar es Salaam Hong Kong Karachi
Kuala Lumpur Madrid Melbourne Mexico City Nairobi
New Delhi Shanghai Taipei Toronto

With offices in

Argentina Austria Brazil Chile Czech Republic France Greece
Guatemala Hungary Italy Japan Poland Portugal Singapore
South Korea Switzerland Thailand Turkey Ukraine Vietnam

First published 2007

British Library Cataloguing in Publication Data

Data available

ISBN: 978-0199151479

10 9 8 7 6

Printed by Bell and Bain Ltd., Glasgow

Acknowledgements
The authors and publisher are grateful for permission to reprint the following copyright material:
Simon Armitage: 'I Say, I Say, I Say' from *The Dead Sea Poems* (1995), copyright © Simon Armitage 1995, reprinted by permission of the publishers, Faber & Faber Ltd and of David Godwin Associates on behalf of the author. **Margaret Atwood:** extracts from *The Handmaid's Tale* (Jonathan Cape, 1986, Virago, 1997), copyright © O. W. Toad Ltd 1985, reprinted by permission of Curtis Brown Ltd, London, Houghton Mifflin Company, and McClelland and Stewart Ltd, The Canadian Publishers; 'Postcard' from *True Stories* (Jonathan Cape, 1982), reprinted by permission of Curtis Brown Ltd, London, also from *Selected Poems II: Poems Selected and New 1976–1986*, copyright © Margaret Atwood 1987, reprinted by permission of the publishers, Houghton Mifflin Company. All rights reserved. **Iain Banks:** extract from *The Crow Road* (Abacus, 1992), copyright © Iain Banks 1992, reprinted by permission of Little, Brown Book Group Ltd. **Laurence Binyon:** 'For the Fallen (September 1914)' from *Collected Poems 1869–1943*, 2 vols. (Macmillan, 1931), reprinted by permission of The Society of Authors as the Literary Representative of the Estate of Laurence Binyon. **Rupert Brooke:** letter to Katharine Cox from *The Letters of Rupert Brooke* edited by Geoffrey Keynes (1968), reprinted by permission of the publishers, Faber & Faber Ltd. **Gwendolyn Brooks:** 'The Bean Eaters' from *The Bean Eaters* (Blacks, 1991), reprinted by consent of Brooks Permissions. **Italo Calvino:** *Six Memos for the Next Millennium* (Harvard University Press, 1988), copyright © Italo Calvino 1988, reprinted by permission of the Wylie Agency, Inc. **Albert Camus:** extract from *The Outsider* translated by Joseph Loredo Penguin Books, 1989), translation copyright © Joseph Loredo 1982, reprinted by permission of Penguin Books Ltd. **J M Coetzee:** extracts from *Waiting for the Barbarians* (Secker & Warburg, 2000), reprinted by permission of the Random House Group Ltd. **Lorna Crozier:** 'The Spirit Fox' from *What the Living Won't let Go* (McLelland & Stewart, 1999), copyright © Lorna Crozier 1999, reprinted by permission of the publisher. **E E Cummings:** 'anyone lived in a pretty how town' from *Complete Poems 1904–1962* edited by George J Firmage, copyright © 1991 by the Trustees for the E E Cummings Trust and George J Firmage, reprinted by permission of W W Norton & Company. **W H Davies:** 'Leisure' from *Collected Poems of W H Davies* (Jonathan Cape, 1928), reprinted by permission of the Trustees for Mrs H M Davies and the Estate of W H Davies. **Anita Desai:** extract from 'Studies in the Park' from *Games at Twilight* (Penguin, 1982), copyright © Anita Desai 1978, reprinted by permission of the author c/o Rogers, Coleridge & White Ltd, 20 Powis Mews, London W11 1JN. **Imtiaz Dharker:** 'Blessing' from *Postcards from God* (1997), reprinted by permission of the publishers, Bloodaxe Books Ltd. **Margaret Drabble:** extract from 'Hassan's Tower' in *Winter's Tales* (Macmillan, 1966), copyright © Margaret Drabble 1966, reprinted by permission of PFD on behalf of Margaret Drabble. **Carol Ann Duffy:** 'Mean Time', 'Havisham', 'Confession', 'First Love', and 'Stuffed' from *Mean Time* (Anvil Press Poetry, 1993), reprinted by permission of the publisher. **Nissim Ezekiel:** 'Night of the Scorpion' from *Poverty Poems* (OUP, India), reprinted by permission of Oxford University Press India, New Delhi. **Carolyn Forché:** extract from 'The Colonel' from *The Country Between Us* (HarperCollins, 1980), copyright © Carolyn Forché 1980, 1987, first published by Women's International Resource Exchange (WIRE), reprinted by permission of HarperCollins Publishers and William Morris Agency, LLC on behalf of the author. **E M Forster:** extracts from *A Passage to India* (Edward Arnold, 1924), reprinted by permission of the Provost and Scholars of King's College Cambridge and The Society of Authors as the Literary Representatives of the Estate of E M Forster. **Robert Francis:** 'Glass' from *Robert Francis: Collected Poems 1936–1976*, copyright © 1976 by the University of Massachusetts Press, reproduced by permission of the publishers, University of Massachusetts Press via Copyright Clearance Center. **Brian Friel:** extract from *Making History*, copyright © 1989 by Brian Friel, reprinted by permission of the publishers, Faber & Faber Ltd and of William Morris Agency, LLC on behalf of the author. All rights reserved. Enquiries concerning rights should be addressed to the Authors' agent, William Morris Agency, LLC, Attn: Jack Tantleff. *Making History* was first produced at Guildhall, Derry, Ireland in 1988. **Paul Fussell:** extract from introduction to *The Bloody Game: An Anthology of Modern War*, edited by Paul Fussell (Scribners, London 1991), reprinted by permission of Little, Brown Book Group Ltd; also from *The Norton Book of Modern War* by Paul Fussell, copyright © 1991 by Paul Fussell, reprinted by permission of W W Norton & Company, Inc. **Eduardo Galeano:** extract from *The Book of Embraces* translated by Cedric Belfrage with Mark Schafer (W W Norton, 1991), copyright © 1989 by Edward Galeano, English translation copyright © 1991 by Cedric Belfrage, reprinted by permission of the author and W W Norton & Company, Inc. **Dana Gioia:** 'Planting a Sequoia' from *The Gods of Winter* (Graywolf Press, 1991), copyright © 1991 by Gina Gioia, reprinted by permission of Graywolf Press, Saint Paul, Minnesota. **Nadine Gordimer:** extract from *The Pickup* (Penguin, 2001), copyright © Felix Licensing B V 2001, reprinted by permission of Farrar, Straus & Giroux, LLC, Penguin Group (Canada), a Division of Pearson Canada Inc, and Bloomsbury Publishing Plc. **Rahila Gupta:** 'A Gift', first published in *Don't Ask Me Why: An Anthology of Short Stories by Black Women* edited by Da Choong, Olivette Cole Wilson, Sylvia Parker and Gabriela Pearse (Black Woman Talk, 1991), reprinted by permission of the author. **Donald Hall:** 'My Son. My Executioner' from *White Apples and the Taste of Stone: Selected Poems 1946–2006* (Houghton Mifflin, 2006), copyright © 2006 by Donald Hall, reprinted by permission of Houghton Mifflin Company. All rights reserved. **Joanne Harris:** extract from *Chocolat* (Black Swan, 2000), copyright © Joanne Harris 1999, reprinted by permission of The Random House Group Ltd and Viking Penguin, a division of Penguin Group (USA) Inc. **Seamus Heaney:** 'Churning Day' from *Death of a Naturalist* (1966), copyright © Seamus Heaney 1966, 1991, reprinted by permission of the publishers, Faber & Faber Ltd; and from *Opened Ground: Selected Poems 1966–1996*, copyright © Seamus Heaney 1998, reprinted by permission of the publishers, Farrar, Straus & Giroux, LLC. **Ernest Hemingway:** extract from 'Indian Camp' from *The Short Stories of Ernest Hemingway* (Scribner Paperback Fiction/ Jonathan Cape), copyright 1925 by Charles Scribner's Sons, renewed © 1953 by Ernest Hemingway, reprinted by permission of Scribner, an imprint of Simon & Schuster Adult Publishing Group, and The Random House Publishing Group Ltd. **Susan Hill:** extracts from 'Missy' from *A Bit of Singing and Dancing* by Susan Hill, (Long Barn Books), copyright © Susan Hill 1973, reprinted by permission of Sheil Land Associates Ltd. **Ted Hughes:** 'Swifts' from *New Selected Poems 1957–1994*, (1995) copyright © Ted Hughes 1995, reprinted by permission of the publishers, Faber & Faber Ltd; and from *Selected Poems 1957–1981*, copyright © Ted Hughes 2001, reprinted by permission of the publishers, Farrar, Straus & Giroux, LLC. **Evan Jones:** 'Song of Banana Man' from *The Penguin Book of Caribbean Verse* selected and edited by Paula Burnett (Penguin 1986); copyright holder not traced. **Franz Kafka:** 'An Imperial Message' from *The Complete Stories of Franz Kafka* edited by Nahum N Glatzer (Secker & Warburg, 1971), copyright 1946, 1947, 1948, 1949, 1954, 1958, 1971 by Schocken Books; and extracts from 'Metamorphosis' from *Metamorphosis and Other Stories* translated by Willa and Edwin Muir (Martin Secker & Warburg), copyright 1948 by Schocken Books, copyright © renewed 1975 by Schocken Books, both reprinted by permission of The Random House Group Ltd and Schocken Books, a division of Random House, Inc. **Brian Keenan:** extract from *An Evil Cradling* (Hutchinson, 1992), reprinted by permission of The Random House Group and Elaine Steel on behalf of Brian Keenan. **Philip Larkin:** 'Naturally the Foundation Will Pay Your Expenses' from *Collected Poems* (1988), copyright © the Estate of Philip Larkin 1988, 1989, reprinted by permission of the publishers, Faber & Faber Ltd and Farrar, Straus & Giroux, LLC. **Felicia Hardison Londré:** extract from 'A streetcar running fifty years' in *The Cambridge Companion to Tennessee Williams* edited by Matthew C Roudané (Cambridge University Press, 1997), reprinted by permission of the publisher. **Earl Lovelace:** extract from *The Dragon Can't Dance* (Andre Deutsch, 1979), reprinted by permission of Capel & Land Ltd for the author. **David Malouf:** extract from *Remembering Babylon* (Chatto & Windus, 1994), reprinted by permission of the Random House Group Ltd. **David Mamet:** extracts from *Three Uses of the Knife* (Columbia University Press, 1998), copyright © David Mamet 1998, reprinted by permission of International Creative Management, Inc. **R. A. K. Mason:** 'On the Swag' from *Collected Poems* (Victoria U Press, 1971), reprinted by permission of the copyright holder, the Hocken Librarian, Hocken Collections, University of Otago, Dunedin, New Zealand. **Pablo Neruda:** 'Ode to Clothes' translated by W S Merwin from *Neruda: Selected Poems* edited by Nathaniel Tarn (Jonathan Cape, 1970), reprinted by permission of the Random House Group Ltd. **Grace Nichols:** 'Hey There Now!' from *The Fat Black Woman's Poems* (Virago Press, 1984), copyright © Grace Nichols 1984, reprinted by permission of Curtis Brown Ltd, London, on behalf of Grace Nichols. **Michael Ondaatje:** extract from *Running in the Family* (Vintage, 1982), copyright © 1982 Michael Ondaatje, reprinted by permission of W W Norton & Company, Inc. **George Orwell:** extract from *Nineteen Eighty Four* (Martin Secker & Warburg, 1949), copyright © George Orwell 1949, copyright © Harcourt, Inc 1949, renewed 1977 by Sonia Brownell Orwell, reprinted by permission of A M Heath & Co Ltd on behalf of Bill Hamilton as the Literary Executor of the Estate of the late Sonia Brownell Orwell, and of Harcourt, Inc. **Wilfred Owen:** letter to Susan Owen from *Wilfred Owen: Collected Letters* edited by Harold Owen and John Bell (1967), copyright © Oxford University Press 1967, reprinted by permission of Oxford University Press. **Sylvia Plath:** 'Blackberrying', 'Mirror', 'Metaphors' and line from 'Frog Autumn' from *Collected Poems* edited by Ted Hughes (1981), copyright © Ted Hughes 1981, reprinted by permission of the publishers, Faber & Faber Ltd; 'Blackberrying', 'Mirror,' and 'Metaphors' also reprinted from *Crossing the Water* (1971), copyright © Ted Hughes 1971 by permission of HarperCollins Publishers, Inc; line from 'Frog Autumn' also reprinted from *The Colossus and Other Poems*, copyright © 1962 by Sylvia Plath, reprinted by permission of Alfred A Knopf, a division of Random House, Inc. **Theodore Roethke:** 'The Storm (Forio D'Ischia)', copyright © 1961 by Beatrice Roethke, Administratrix of the Estate of Theodore Roethke, from *The Collected Poems of Theodore Roethke* (1966), reprinted by permission of the publishers, Faber & Faber Ltd and Doubleday, a division of Random House, Inc. **Anne Sexton:** extract from 'Snow White and the Seven Dwarves' from *Transformations* (Houghton Mifflin, 1990), copyright © Anne Sexton 1971, reprinted by permission of SLL/Sterling Lord Literistic, Inc. **Wistawa Szymborska:** 'Notes from a Nonexistent Himalayan Expedition' from *Poems New and Collected 1957–1997* translated by Stanislaw Baranczak and Claire Cavanagh (Harcourt, 1998), copyright © 1998 by Harcourt, Inc, reprinted by permission of the publishers, Faber & Faber Ltd and Harcourt, Inc. **Alexander Solzhenitsyn:** extract from *One Day in the Life of Ivan Denisovich* translated by Ralph Parker (Victor Gollancz Ltd, 1963), reprinted by permission of the Orion Publishing Group Ltd. **Wole Soyinka:** 'Season' from *Idanre and Other Poems* (Methuen, 1967), copyright © 1967, 1995 by Wole Soyinka, and lines from 'Samarkand' from *Samarkand and Other Markets I Have Known* (Methuen, 2002), copyright © 2002 by Wole Soyinka, reprinted by permission of Methuen Publishing Ltd and Melanie Jackson Agency, LLC. **John Updike:** 'Winter Ocean' from *Telephone Poles and Other Poems* (Deutsch, 1963), copyright © John Updike 1959, 1963, reprinted by permission of Penguin Books Ltd and Alfred A Knopf, a division of Random House, Inc. **John Wain:** extract from 'A Message from the Pig-Man' first published in *Nuncle and Other Stories* (Macmillan, 1960), reprinted by permission of the Executors of J B Wain. **Tennessee Williams:** extracts from *A Streetcar Named Desire* (New Directions), copyright © 1947,1953 by Tennessee Williams, renewed 1975, 1981 by The University of the South, reprinted by permission of New Directions Publishing Corp. and Methuen Publishing Ltd on behalf of The University of the South, Sewanee, Tennessee. **Judith Wright:** extract from 'In the Park' from *The Nature of Love* (ETT Imprint, Sydney, 1998), reprinted by permission of the publishers.

We are also grateful to the authors' students for allowing us to use their responses as examples.

and to the following for use of images:
P12 General Photographic Agency/Getty Images; **p24** Ashley Cooper/Corbis; **p40** Hulton Archive/Getty Images; **p92** Wikimedia; **p127** Colin McPherson/Corbis; **p156** Oxford University Press; **p216** Ulf Anderson/Getty Images.
Cover image: Digital Vision and Ingram.

We have tried to trace and contact all copyright holders before publication. If notified the publishers will be pleased to rectify any errors or omissions at the earliest opportunity.

Consultants
Boyd Roberts for international-mindedness
Manjula Salomon for Theory of Knowledge

Mixed Sources
Product group from well-managed forests and other controlled sources
www.fsc.org Cert no. TT-COC-002769
© 1996 Forest Stewardship Council

Course Companion definition

The IB Diploma Programme Course Companions are resource materials designed to provide students with extra support through their two-year course of study. These books will help students gain an understanding of what is expected from the study of an IB Diploma Programme subject.

The Course Companions reflect the philosophy and approach of the IB Diploma Programme and present content in a way that illustrates the purpose and aims of the IB. They encourage a deep understanding of each subject by making connections to wider issues and providing opportunities for critical thinking.

These Course Companions, therefore, may or may not contain all of the curriculum content required in each IB Diploma Programme subject, and so are not designed to be complete and prescriptive textbooks. Each book will try to ensure that areas of curriculum that are unique to the IB or to a new course revision are thoroughly covered. These books mirror the IB philosophy of viewing the curriculum in terms of a whole-course approach; the use of a wide range of resources; international-mindedness; the IB learner profile and the IB Diploma Programme core requirements; theory of knowledge; the extended essay; and creativity, action, service (CAS).

In addition, the Course Companions provide advice and guidance on the specific course assessment requirements and also on academic honesty protocol.

The Course Companions are not designed to be:

- study/revision guides or a one-stop solution for students to pass the subjects
- prescriptive or essential subject textbooks.

IB mission statement

The International Baccalaureate aims to develop inquiring, knowledgable and caring young people who help to create a better and more peaceful world through intercultural understanding and respect.

To this end the IB works with schools, governments and international organizations to develop challenging programmes of international education and rigorous assessment.

These programmes encourage students across the world to become active, compassionate, and lifelong learners who understand that other people, with their differences, can also be right.

The IB learner profile

The aim of all IB programmes is to develop internationally minded people who, recognizing their common humanity and shared guardianship of the planet, help to create a better and more peaceful world. IB learners strive to be:

Inquirers   They develop their natural curiosity. They acquire the skills necessary to conduct inquiry and research and show independence in learning. They actively enjoy learning and this love of learning will be sustained throughout their lives.

Knowledgable   They explore concepts, ideas, and issues that have local and global significance. In so doing, they acquire in-depth knowledge and develop understanding across a broad and balanced range of disciplines.

Thinkers   They exercise initiative in applying thinking skills critically and creatively to recognize and approach complex problems, and make reasoned, ethical decisions.

Communicators   They understand and express ideas and information confidently and creatively in more than one language and in a variety of modes of communication. They work effectively and willingly in collaboration with others.

Principled   They act with integrity and honesty, with a strong sense of fairness, justice, and respect for the dignity of the individual, groups, and communities. They take responsibility for their own actions and the consequences that accompany them.

Open-minded   They understand and appreciate their own cultures and personal histories, and are open to the perspectives, values, and traditions of other individuals and communities. They are accustomed to seeking and evaluating a range of points of view, and are willing to grow from the experience.

Caring   They show empathy, compassion, and respect towards the needs and feelings of others. They have a personal commitment to service, and act to make a positive difference to the lives of others and to the environment.

Risk-takers   They approach unfamiliar situations and uncertainty with courage and forethought, and have the independence of spirit to explore new roles, ideas, and strategies. They are brave and articulate in defending their beliefs.

Balanced   They understand the importance of intellectual, physical, and emotional balance to achieve personal well-being for themselves and others.

Reflective   They give thoughtful consideration to their own learning and experience. They are able to assess and understand their strengths and limitations in order to support their learning and personal development.

A note on academic honesty

It is of vital importance to acknowledge and appropriately credit the owners of information when that information is used in your work. After all, owners of ideas (intellectual property) have property rights. To have an authentic piece of work, it must be based on your individual and original ideas with the work of others fully acknowledged. Therefore, all assignments, written or oral, completed for assessment must use your own language and expression. Where sources are used or referred to, whether in the form of direct quotation or paraphrase, such sources must be appropriately acknowledged.

How do I acknowledge the work of others?
The way that you acknowledge that you have used the ideas of other people is through the use of footnotes and bibliographies.

Footnotes   (placed at the bottom of a page) or endnotes (placed at the end of a document) are to be provided when you quote or paraphrase from another document, or closely summarize the information provided in another document. You do not need to provide a footnote for information that is part of a 'body of knowledge'. That is, definitions do not need to be footnoted as they are part of the assumed knowledge.

Bibliographies should include a formal list of the resources that you used in your work. 'Formal' means that you should use one of the several accepted forms of presentation. This usually involves separating the resources that you use into different categories (e.g. books, magazines, newspaper articles, Internet-based resources, CDs and works of art) and providing full information as to how a reader or viewer of your work can find the same information. A bibliography is compulsory in the extended essay.

What constitutes malpractice?

Malpractice is behaviour that results in, or may result in, you or any student gaining an unfair advantage in one or more assessment component. Malpractice includes plagiarism and collusion.

Plagiarism is defined as the representation of the ideas or work of another person as your own. The following are some of the ways to avoid plagiarism:

- Words and ideas of another person used to support one's arguments must be acknowledged.

- Passages that are quoted verbatim must be enclosed within quotation marks and acknowledged.
- CD-ROMs, email messages, web sites on the Internet, and any other electronic media must be treated in the same way as books and journals.
- The sources of all photographs, maps, illustrations, computer programs, data, graphs, audio-visual, and similar material must be acknowledged if they are not your own work.
- Works of art, whether music, film, dance, theatre arts, or visual arts, and where the creative use of a part of a work takes place, must be acknowledged.

Collusion is defined as supporting malpractice by another student. This includes:

- allowing your work to be copied or submitted for assessment by another student
- duplicating work for different assessment components and/or diploma requirements.

Other forms of malpractice include any action that gives you an unfair advantage or affects the results of another student. Examples include, taking unauthorized material into an examination room, misconduct during an examination, and falsifying a CAS record.

Contents

Introduction

This book has been written to help both standard and higher level students with the English A1 course. English A1 is a literature course for mother-tongue speakers, and that is the standard by which it is assessed. In International Schools many students study English A1 even though English is not their first language. This does not matter as long as they remember that they will be judged in the same way as those whose mother language is English. Higher Level and Standard Level candidates are expected to learn the same skills. The differences lie in the number of books read and the level of achievement that is expected. English A1 is not designed to be an academic study only. Being able to write and speak effectively and think clearly are skills that are obviously invaluable in everyday life, but it is also hoped that you will derive pleasure from reading and from visiting cinemas and theatres.

Although the approach of this book is fairly general (so that techniques can be applied to any text) it is also necessary to give specific examples to illustrate more clearly how to read, write and analyse. Many of these examples come from authors who are popular in IB schools around the world, such as Dickens, Conrad, Camus and Soyinka. Sometimes poems and extracts have been chosen because they effectively illustrate specific skills or techniques. There are also examples of students' work so you can gain some idea of the standards that are expected. Almost all courses in English are primarily skill-based rather than content-based, and English A1 is no exception. The book is therefore organized around acquiring the skills of literary analysis, essay writing, close reading and the achievement of clarity in both written and spoken communication.

Part 1 deals with learning about the literary analysis of poetry and prose. This is directed towards skills needed to write a commentary on an unseen poem or prose passage. Part 2 is concerned with writing about the works you have studied in Part 3 of the syllabus, all of which will be from the same genre.

The next section of the book (Part 3) is about studying your World Literature texts and about writing the World Literature assignments. This is the coursework part of the course. Part 4 helps to prepare you for oral assessments. The IB is unusual in that it expects students to do oral work, which is assessed by the school. Finally, Part 5 has three chapters, one on writing essays for the exam, another about the Extended Essay and a third on Theory of Knowledge.

English is a subject that overlaps readily with Theory of Knowledge. Both are concerned with linguistics, aesthetics and ethics. While using this book, you will be expected to discuss with others the texts and your ideas; it is easier to learn English through writing, reading and discussion, rather than through being told what to do by teachers or textbooks. Discussions normally range in scope from analysis of the texts to the ideas contained within them, so it is easy to move into areas covered by Theory of Knowledge.

We would like to thank the many teachers and students who have both directly and indirectly contributed to this book. We are equally indebted to Steven Croft and Helen Cross, who wrote the original version of this book which we have revised.

Elizabeth Druce and Hannah Tyson

Approaching literary criticism

Objectives
- To establish a strategy for approaching unseen texts
- To practise close reading of poetry and prose texts
- To look at style and structure in literary criticism

To what degree can writers choose to make words mean more than one thing? What is meant by "meaning"? Though they may not be quite as arbitrary as Humpty Dumpty, writers will often stretch the meaning of words to considerable lengths, or even invent words to try to convey an idea or concept as accurately as possible. Literary criticism is concerned with looking very closely at not just the meanings of words, but also their associations. All words have denotations (the meaning found in the dictionary) and connotations, which are associations connected with that word. For example, the first definition of "milk" in *The Concise Oxford Dictionary* is: "Opaque white fluid secreted by female mammals", but the connotations you have for milk will depend on whether you like to drink it or not.

> "'When I use a word,' Humpty Dumpty said, in a rather scornful tone, 'it means just what I choose it to mean – neither more nor less.'
>
> 'The question is,' said Alice, 'whether you can make words mean so many different things.'
>
> 'The question is,' said Humpty Dumpty, 'which is to be master – that's all.'"
>
> Lewis Carroll

Activity

What are the words that come to your mind when you see the word "milk"? Ask other students what they associate with the word. You will be surprised at how much the connotations vary. See the end of this chapter for some suggested connotations. Look at some other words, for example, "light", "cats", "energy" and "environment" and list their associations.

You will often see in newspapers or hear on the television words used by politicians and public relations people who are following the Humpty Dumpty approach. They manipulate language to make their message more appealing.

Activity

1 Look at the following pairs of synonyms and discuss with a partner the differences in connotation between them.

freedom fighter	terrorist
tall	gangling or lanky
rich man	fat cat
persistent	stubborn
economical	stingy
economical with the truth	lying

2 Write two brief descriptions of the room you are in, the first using words that make it seem attractive, and the second using words that convey a negative impression.

Literary criticism

Literary criticism is another name for what is known in the IB Language A1 programme as "commentary". It is an essential skill for you to acquire for your Language A1 examinations, as it appears in three parts of the assessment system:

- Paper 1, where you are required to write a commentary on an unseen passage or poem
- the internal assessment, where you have to give an oral commentary on a passage taken from a work you have studied
- the second assignment for World Literature, where you can choose from several options to write a commentary on a passage from a text you have studied.

A commentary is a literary analysis, which is essentially a close study of the elements that contribute to the success, or otherwise, of a work of literature. As well as understanding the connotations of words, you need to examine structure, imagery, diction and a wide range of literary devices. In a commentary you need to:

- understand the text
- be able to identify and comment on the literary features of the text
- be able to organize your findings into a coherent piece of writing.

The Language A1 Paper 1 exam consists of two unseen texts, one a poem and the other a prose passage. You have to choose one of them and write a commentary on it, in two hours for Higher Level and in one-and-a-half hours for Standard Level.

In this unit you will be given the opportunity to discuss strategies for developing your commentary skills in order to respond to the kinds of unseen literary texts you will encounter in Paper 1. Being able to analyse texts will not only help you in your exams but it is also an important skill to acquire for other reasons:

- it enables you to appreciate the skills involved in writing and therefore enhance your appreciation of literature
- it will help improve your own writing style when you recognize that you can use a wide range of techniques
- you become more aware that language shapes meaning and can be used for manipulation. All the time we are bombarded with information from a wide range of sources; being able to evaluate the messages and where they are coming from enables you to make your own decisions.

What is a written commentary?

In Paper 1 of the English A1 examination, as mentioned above, you will be given an "unseen" paper. This means that the texts on the paper will be ones that you have not studied or seen before. The paper will contain **two** unseen texts. One of the texts will be a poem and the other may be an extract from a novel, a short story, an essay, a biography, or a journalistic piece of writing "of literary merit". The texts for commentary may either be complete pieces of writing, or extracts from larger pieces. You select only **one** of the two pieces on which to write your commentary and to do this you must apply the "techniques of literary criticism". At Higher Level there will be no accompanying questions or guidelines – you will simply be asked to write your commentary. At Standard Level there will be three or four guiding questions or prompts which are intended to direct you to significant aspects of the text. You do not have to respond directly to these questions if you do not wish to, but, if you use them, your responses must be integrated into the main body of your commentary. You must not simply answer them as individual questions.

What are the techniques of literary criticism?

A commentary involves literary criticism. The term "criticism" may be misleading here, for it suggests some kind of fault-finding, or looking for the negative sides of a text. In literary terms, however, it means assessing the quality of a piece of writing, examining how it has been written and deciding on the effects created by the writer's choices.

The terms **literary appreciation** or **literary analysis** describe the process more accurately. The techniques you employ are the methods with which you approach your analysis and the way you present it.

Your own response to a text is important too and the best pieces of literary analysis are those which blend a personal response with an objective examination. The objective analysis will look at aspects such as the content, theme, style, language, and structure of the text. A personal response does not mean gushing comments where you identify with a character or a situation in the text. It means that you become involved in the critical process so that you give your own individual reading, which may be similar to that of others, but which will be stamped with your own perceptions and arise from your own experiences.

You can help yourself prepare for the unseen exam by reading as widely as possible, so that you can feel at ease with as many different styles of writing as possible.

Close reading

Not many people will agree with the opinion of Logan Pearsall Smith quoted here, but being able to read closely is essential for the understanding of literature in general; it is especially important when you are writing a commentary. Whenever you encounter a literary text for the first time – whether it is a text you are reading for class, or a poem or passage you have been asked to analyse in an examination – all the skills of close reading that you have learned will enable you to discover more about the text. "Close reading" is the art of reading very carefully, paying great attention to details of language, in order to understand what the author is trying to convey. It can also be called "reading between the lines", as sometimes it is what the author does *not* say that is interesting.

Here is an example of what is meant by close reading. The last line of Gerard Manley Hopkins's poem, *Felix Randal* is:

> Didst fettle for the great grey drayhorse his bright and
> battering sandal!

This can be paraphrased very simply as: "[you] made the horseshoes for the large grey horse". But this paraphrase leaves out many of the implications of the poem. Felix Randal was a blacksmith who had just died, someone who could be regarded as just an ordinary workman. The poem, however, especially the last lines, elevates his status by the choice of slightly archaic diction as in "didst" and "fettle", while the use of the word "sandal" instead of "shoe" suggests an earlier, classical period; Greek and Roman soldiers wore sandals. It also makes the line onomatopoeic. If you read the words aloud you will hear the noise of the horse's hooves in "bright and battering sandal". The word "shoe" would not create the same effect. The alliteration and assonance in "great grey drayhorse" help to emphasize the size of the horse, as one has to say the words slowly. A dray is a cart for carrying heavy loads so a drayhorse has to be large and strong. We are left with the impression that Felix Randal was a smith for the horses of gods and heroes: a mighty man.

"People say that life is the thing, but I prefer reading."
Logan Pearsall Smith

Thus one can see how a poet can transform an ordinary person into a hero by the choice of diction. Like Humpty Dumpty, a poet can make words mean what he or she wants them to mean.

Samarkand, and other Markets I have Known

A market is a kind haven for the wandering soul

Or the merely ruminant. Each stall

Is shrine and temple, magic cave of memorabilia.

Its passages are grottoes that transport us,

Bargain hunters all, from pole to antipodes, annulling

Time, evoking places and lost histories.

Wole Soyinka

> **Activity**
>
> Read closely these lines from Wole Soyinka's *Samarkand, and other Markets I have Known*. Discuss what you think they mean with other members of your class.

Did you find this exercise difficult? Unusual words such as "ruminant" and "antipodes" may have stumped you. If so, you need to realize that it is vital to increase your knowledge of vocabulary by reading widely and having recourse to the dictionary when you do not understand a word.

Developing your skills

The best way to develop your ability to read closely is to practise, by reading carefully as wide a variety of texts as you possibly can. Here are some of the skills you need to develop:

- to read and make sense of a text so that you can recognize its most important features quickly – a kind of instant "research" where you have to think quickly
- to apply your own literary insights rather than depend on ideas that you have read about or been taught
- to be able to analyse style and structure
- to understand how writers use language to create different effects according to audience and purpose
- to organize your ideas into a coherent and persuasive piece of writing.

Many students find literary texts intimidating and find literary analysis very difficult. There are fields, however, where you are already an expert at this kind of analysis. Most students have very little difficulty in understanding both the obvious and the hidden messages of films, television programmes, advertisements and cartoons.

It is likely that for most of your life you have looked at advertisements. You may even think you are immune to them because you know how they are trying to influence you. It has been said that advertisements appeal to the attractiveness of at least one of the seven deadly sins: pride, sloth, anger, envy, lust, avarice and gluttony.

> *"Promise, large promise, is the soul of an advertisement."*
> Samuel Johnson

It may not be obvious, but most newspapers have some kind of political bias that affects the way they report events or issues.

You are likely to be able to contribute usefully to discussions on cartoons, advertisements and newspaper articles. Just remember that commenting on literary texts relies on similar skills.

Approaching unprepared texts
Some students feel happier if they have some kind of method to apply when they are reading a text they have not seen before. First, it is important not to be daunted by a poem or a prose extract you are given to analyse. There will be good reasons why a particular piece has been chosen, and with close reading you will be able to discover them.

Once you have the text in front of you, it is helpful to have a strategy that will enable you to examine it in detail. First read the poem or passage through at least twice. Then make annotations. either on the page or on a separate piece of paper. Here is a suggested checklist of the aspects you need to consider.

1 **What** is the text about? This may seem obvious, but it provides a broad starting point. Look at the title; sometimes that gives you a way in, but be careful, because some titles can be deceptive. You should also look at the writer's name and the date of publication, as they may also be helpful.
2 **Where** is it set? What country? Is it set inside or outside? In a town or in the country?
3 **When** is it set? Is it in the present, the future or the past? The date of publication can help, but the text could be set in a different period, so be careful.
4 **Who** is the speaker? Is the speaker the same as the writer? Are there other characters in the text? Who are they?
5 **Why** has it been written? What are the underlying themes or messages?
6 **Structure:** What is the overall structure of the piece? How many paragraphs or stanzas? Does each one deal with a different aspect? Are layout and meaning closely related? If it is a poem, is it written in a recognizable form such as a sonnet? Look at the sentence structure. Are the sentences long or short? If it is a poem, are there caesuras or enjambment? How do they contribute to the overall meaning?
7 **Vocabulary or diction:** What do you notice about the words that the writer has chosen? Is the diction simple or complex? Are technical or scientific or archaic words used? Are there words, or types of word, that recur? Are there words that are unexpected or seem out of place?
8 **Imagery:** Does the writer use similes or metaphors? How do they affect the meaning of the text? Are there patterns of images? For example, are there words that suggest darkness or light?
9 **Other literary features:** These include rhyme, rhythm, assonance, alliteration, repetition and many more, but understanding how a literary technique works is more important than knowing its name. If the text is a poem, does it have a rhyme scheme, and what is its effect? (Beware of describing

Activity

Bring some advertisements into class or describe ones you have seen on television and decide whether they are appealing to human weaknesses. If so, which ones? For example, why are so many cars sold in association with beautiful women?

Activity

Working with a partner, choose a controversial topic and find two articles from two different newspapers on that topic. Discuss the way the articles have been written and then decide if either of them has a hidden political agenda.

a rhyme scheme without going on to say why you think the poet has chosen it and how far this aim has been achieved.) Alliteration (or head rhyme) is sometimes used in place of end rhymes and it can also be used for creating sound effects or for emphasis. Rhythm can be important in prose as well as poetry. Is the rhythm smooth or jerky? Does it change at any point in the text? Sometimes the sound of the words or the use of assonance can suggest or reinforce the meaning of a line.

10 **Tone and atmosphere:** It is often very difficult to decide on the tone, mood or atmosphere of a text. It requires considerable experience and it may be better to wait until you have read enough before trying to decide. Sometimes the tone may be so obvious that it is worth identifying, but if you are not sure, leave it out.

This is just a checklist and should not be used as a basis for organizing your commentary. Nor is it enough just to identify any of the above features. You must also discuss their effects, otherwise you are merely showing that you can recognize literary features. You need to explain how each particular feature influences or enhances the meaning of the text.

> **Activity**
>
> Read Wilfred Owen's poem, *Anthem for Doomed Youth*, and apply the checklist to it.

Anthem for Doomed Youth

What passing-bells for those who die as cattle?
   Only the monstrous anger of the guns.
   Only the stuttering rifles' rapid rattle
Can patter out their hasty orisons.
No mockeries now for them; no prayers nor bells,
   Nor any voice of mourning save the choirs, –
The shrill, demented choirs of wailing shells;
   And bugles calling for them from sad shires.

What candles may be held to speed them all?
   Not in the hands of boys, but in their eyes
Shall shine the holy glimmers of good-byes.
   The pallor of girls' brows shall be their pall;
Their flowers the tenderness of patient minds,
And each slow dusk a drawing-down of blinds.

Wilfred Owen 1917(?)

Your notes may look like the following:

What? The poem is about the fact that soldiers who died during the First World War had no proper funerals.

Where and when? In France during the First World War. Owen is a well-known war poet who died just before the war ended.

Who? The speaker is presumably the poet but is not identified in the poem. Other characters are the dead soldiers and those who mourn for them.

Why? The word "doomed" in the title highlights the appalling numbers of young men who died during the war. Owen is protesting against these deaths by showing that these young soldiers do not even have proper funerals; they are buried without any of the normal funeral ceremonies.

Structure: The form of the poem is that of a standard Petrarchan sonnet with 14 lines divided into two stanzas of 8 and 6 lines respectively. The first stanza deals with the substitutes for bells, prayers and choirs (guns, rifles and shells) while the second refers to those who are mourning for the young men at home.

Diction: Many words refer to church services ("bells", "orisons", "choirs", "candles", "holy"), and to military matters ("guns", "rifles", "wailing shells", "bugles").

Imagery: The soldiers' deaths are compared to the deaths of cattle in the first line, implying that they are regarded as being of no more worth than animals. Both the guns and the rifles are personified by giving them human characteristics of anger and "stuttering", as if the weapons were more important than the soldiers. The shells are said to be "shrill, demented choirs" – there is no harmony, only madness on the battlefield. The line "The pallor of girls' brows shall be their pall" associates the pale faces of the girls who mourn for their brothers, husbands or friends with the palls that will not be used to cover the dead bodies.

Other literary features: Alliteration: "rifles' rapid rattle", which suggests the sound of the rifles as do words such as "stuttering" and "patter"; "sad shires" slows the pace and emphasizes the sorrow those left at home will feel; "each slow dusk a drawing-down of blinds" again slows the pace and contributes to the slow movement, like a funeral.

The rhyme scheme is *ababcdcd effegg*. The rhythm is basically iambic pentameter with significant changes that emphasize certain words such as "only" in lines 2 and 3. It conforms to the schemes used in a sonnet, and ties the images and ideas closely together.

Tone: Both the pace and the tone of the poem are suitable for a funeral: solemn, sad, and slow.

You will probably have a slightly different set of comments. Far more features could be found in this very complex poem; the above is just a sample of what you could do, and these notes are just the beginning of the literary analytical process. Individual features and the impact of the whole poem need to be analysed further; the above notes are mainly descriptive.

Never organize your commentary according to the checklist. The checklist is just an aid to discovering the elements of the poem.

Using evidence from the text effectively

Once you have done some thinking about and annotation of the text, you will have established the main points that you will want to convey in your commentary, and perhaps you will even feel you know what the text is about. However, as you write, it is essential that you provide some good reasons and evidence to support what you say. Evidence in this context means examples and quotations from the text. It is not useful to write that a poet "uses a great deal of alliteration" in a poem. All this demonstrates is that you can recognize alliteration and that you know the technical term for it. Nor is it useful to state that every stanza has four lines. This merely demonstrates that you can count. General statements need to be supported with examples and from there you need to go on to analyse the example and comment on the effects that have been created.

Broadly speaking, literary comment has three stages.

1 State the point you wish to make.
2 Follow this with your quotation, making sure that the context of the quotation is clear, by briefly explaining the situation, or identifying the speaker. Quotations should be presented in speech marks or clearly differentiated from the rest of your writing by indenting and/or smaller print.
3 Analyse the quotation in detail, commenting on individual words or phrases and explaining how and why they are used and to what effect.

For example, in *Anthem for Doomed Youth*, Owen states that there will be no proper prayers for the dead soldiers; all that will be heard is the sound of rifles firing. Owen mimics the sound of the rifles in his choice of the words "stuttering", "patter" and "rattle" in lines 3 and 4 by the repetition of the "t" as it echoes the sound of the rifles. The words "stuttering", "patter" and "hasty" also suggest that if any "orisons" (prayers) were said they would be skimped, muttered quickly and even mangled, for the person saying them would be too fearful to say them with reverence. In other words, the soldiers are not given the proper funeral rites, and instead are treated as if they were "cattle".

It cannot be emphasized enough that the two most common difficulties students have when writing commentaries are setting quotations in context and analysing the examples they have given.

Structuring a commentary essay

There is no single structure that will work for every commentary. Each will demand a slightly different approach, as the following guidelines illustrate.

● **Introduction**
  Briefly outline the subject of the essay. Sometimes it can be useful to give a very concise introduction to the text you are writing about. This might include one or two sentences to establish the context of the piece, for example in terms of theme or setting. Do not describe what the poem or prose piece is about

at great length, but do not be so brief as to be enigmatic. In the introduction you should deal with the text as a whole.

● **Main section**
Discuss the separate elements of the text. If you have already thought about how to approach the text and made a plan, then set about working through the various aspects that you wish to cover. Sometimes, especially with some poems, the best way is to comment line by line or stanza by stanza in the order they appear on the page. Whatever your method of organization, make sure that there is a clear, connected line of argument running through your writing. Use conjunctions such as "however", "although", or "on the other hand" to help you make transitions from one paragraph to the next.

When you present your ideas make sure you always support them with evidence from the text, commenting on the various elements analytically.

● **Conclusion**
Once you have explored all the ideas you want to mention and feel that your analysis of the text is complete, finish by explaining what conclusion you have reached and/or summing up the most important points you have made. Do not just repeat what you have stated in your introduction. It is sensible to begin by discussing the whole text and then to end with comments on the whole text but the conclusion should show deeper levels of understanding and evaluation.

Good commentaries often conclude by suggesting other possible interpretations or making personal comments on the impact of the piece. Try to express your conclusion clearly. An otherwise good commentary can be marred by a weak ending.

Writing in a formal manner

When you are talking to friends you speak informally, but if you talk to someone in authority you speak more formally. Instead of "Hi!" you are more likely to say "Good morning". The same applies when you write. You write much more informally to friends than you would to your doctor. When writing formally you avoid slang, dialect words and abbreviations. Numbers up to 100 are usually written in letters, and both vocabulary and syntax are likely to be more sophisticated.

Avoid over-using the first person ("I"). Instead of writing "I think Louisa is over-imaginative" it is better to write "It seems that Louisa allows her imagination to obscure her judgement". This does not mean that you should never use "I". The occasional use of it can be very effective, especially in your conclusion.

It is also common for literary criticism to be written in the present tense. This is because the text itself, no matter what the genre, always exists in the same way. But it is even more important to be consistent; if you do use the past tense, continue to do so throughout your essay.

"True ease in writing comes from art, not chance, As those move easiest who have learned to dance."
Alexander Pope

Activity

Read the following two statements:

The writer of this poem has a very laid-back attitude to the little kids she is looking at.

The writer's portrayal of the young girls is very objective.

In what ways is the second sentence more formal than the first?

Here is a sample of critical writing to give you an example of an appropriate tone and style and to demonstrate the use of quotations. It is an extract from an essay on Tennessee Williams's play A *Streetcar Named Desire* by an American scholar, Felicia Hardison Londré, in which she comments on Scene 3 of the play.

On *The Poker Night*

Scene 3 stands out from the others in several ways. It has its own title, 'The Poker Night'. Its pictorial atmosphere of 'lurid nocturnal brilliance, the raw colors of childhood's spectrum' is inspired by a picture of Van Gogh's of a billiard parlour at night, which Henry I. Schvey has identified as *All Night Café* (1888). It is one of the few ensemble scenes in a play composed largely of two- or three-character sequences. And most importantly, it is the scene in which Blanche and Stanley truly begin to see each other as a threat. The opening line, spoken by one of the men at the card table, serves as a pointer: 'Anything wild in this deal?'

Stanley has been losing at cards and displays a volatile irritability even before Stella and Blanche come in. Mitch sets himself apart from the other card-players by his anxiety over his sick mother. The association with sickness and the dread of loneliness in his comment that 'I'll be alone when she goes' convey a subtle thematic linkage with Blanche, to whom he is introduced by Stella. Blanche quickly senses that Mitch is a prospective conquest. When she changes out of her dress, she deliberately stands in the light so the men can see her through the portieres. When Stella exits into the bathroom, Blanche turns on the radio and sits in a chair… as if confident of her power to attract Mitch to her. First, however, it is Stanley who crosses to the bedroom and turns off the radio, but 'stops short at the sight of Blanche in the chair. She returns his look without flinching', and he returns to the poker table. Thus with great economy of means, by a simple dramatic gesture, Williams demonstrates the staking out of territory.

Mitch soon leaves the card game to chat with Blanche. He shows her the inscription on his silver cigarette case, given to him by a girl who knew she was dying. Blanche homes in on his vulnerabilities: 'Sick people have such deep, sincere attachments.' She asks him to cover the light bulb with a paper lantern she bought on Bourbon Street: 'I can't stand a naked light bulb, any more than I can a rude remark or a vulgar action.' Her equation of the naked bulb with vulgarity implies its opposite: the soft glow of filtered light as the refined sensibility by which she identifies herself. It recalls her comment to Stanley in Scene 2: 'I know I fib a good deal. After all, a woman's charm is fifty per cent illusion…' Blanche's desire for illusion in opposition to the harsh realities that surround her is probably the play's most obvious thematic value. It is significant that Mitch is the one who both installs the paper lantern and, in Scene 9, removes it, for these actions define the period during which he sees Blanche as she wants him to see her, under the spell of an illusion she creates... Blanche... is an artist who dramatizes herself as if she were a stage character, playing roles detached from the reality of her situation, costuming herself from the trunk containing fake furs and costume jewellery, designing the lighting effects that will show her to advantage. With Mitch as her enthralled audience, she adds musical underscoring: she turns on the radio and 'waltzes to the music with romantic gestures'.

The radio galvanizes Stanley into aggressive action, though the actual source of his action undoubtedly lies deeper. Here in his own home, where he is cock of the roost and host of the poker party, the intruder Blanche has lured both his wife and his best friend into her orbit. She has appropriated his radio for her kind of music. In a drunken rage, he throws the radio out of the window.

Felicia Hardison Londré

Activity

Working on your own or with a partner, compare Londre's analysis with the following extract from a student who has written about the same scene. The student's style needs to be improved. Redraft it, so that is becomes more acceptable. Don't worry if you do not know the text. It is not necessary for the purpose of this activity. If, however, you do know the text you might want to change some of the student's judgements. For example, is Mitch sensitive, or just under the thumb of his mother?

Commentary
In the scene of the poker night the men and women were presented very differently. Stanley seems to me to be presented in a very macho style character. This is shown in the way that Stanley gets very drunk and this is seen to be the manly thing to do. Also the way he mocks Mitch about having to go home and see his Mam. Stanley says "Hurry back and we'll fix you a sugar-tit." He's also shown as a hard and nasty character when he hits Stella because she wants them to stop playing poker. This shows Stanley to be a harsh and hard character because he hits his wife because she asks him to stop playing poker.

Whereas in contrast with the other 3 men, Mitch is shown to be a very sensitive and understanding person. This is shown in the fact that he goes home early to see his Mam because she's ill. Mitch says, "I gotta sick mother. She don't sleep until I come in at night. She says, go out, so I do, but I don't enjoy it. I just keep wondering how she is." I think this shows Mitch is sensitive and caring and thinks about his mother a lot.

Mitch also shows his sensitivity when after Stanley had hit Stella he said, "This is terrible. Poker should not be played in a house with women." This showed Mitch felt very sorry and awful about what had happened to Stella.

The craft in your writing
As your study of literature progresses, you will develop an awareness of the variety of ways in which writers use language.

You will begin to think of writing as a "craft", something to which good writers devote a great deal of care and attention. They are concerned with every detail and may spend hours deciding on the correct word to choose for a specific effect. This is particularly true of poets, who do not always sit down and write "in a fine frenzy", as Theseus says in *A Midsummer Night's Dream*. If you ask writers how often they are inspired to write spontaneously, they are likely to echo Thomas Edison's definition of genius. Their results arise from "one per cent inspiration, ninety-nine per cent perspiration".

To improve your own writing keep in mind the following suggestions.

- Think carefully about the vocabulary you use. Choose the most appropriate word, not the one that springs immediately to mind. Do not keep repeating the same word.
- Try out different lengths and types of sentences, such as passive constructions. To give a very simple example: as well as "the cat chased the mouse", you can say "the mouse was chased by the cat".
- Remember that each paragraph should deal with only one topic and that a paragraph needs to be linked to the one preceding it.
- Always aim for clarity. Sometimes students become so enamoured of complex writing that they forget that the reader has to understand their ideas. Sophistication does not mean impenetrability.

Some fortunate people – usually those who have read widely – seem to have an innate sense of how to write appropriately for different purposes. Most of us only develop a sense of style with practice. It is always important to consider who will be your readers, as your style should be adjusted to suit them. Apart from reading widely, the only way to improve is to practise, practise, practise.

Activity

1 Look at one of your recent essays and decide on your strengths and weaknesses as a writer. Try to improve on a different weakness each time you write an essay.

2 Working with a partner, or in a group, exchange essays and write comments about them. Consider whether they are easy to understand, written in an appropriate style, organized effectively and contain analysis as well as description. Make positive comments as well as negative ones. Look at the IB assessment criteria for Paper 1 (the topic areas are shown below) and discuss them with the writer of the essay.

Assessment criteria for the commentary paper

A Understanding of the text
- How well has the candidate understood the thought and feeling expressed in the text?

B Interpretation of the text
- How relevant are the candidate's ideas about the text?
- How well has the candidate explored those ideas?
- How well has the candidate illustrated claims?
- To what extent has the candidate expressed a relevant personal response?

C **Appreciation of literary features**

- To what extent is the candidate aware of the presence of literary features in the text, such as diction, imagery, tone, structure, style and technique?
- To what extent does the candidate appreciate the effects of the literary features?
- How well has the candidate supported claims about the effects of literary features?

D **Presentation**

- How well has the candidate organized the commentary?
- How effectively have the candidate's ideas been presented?
- To what extent are supporting examples integrated into the body of the commentary?

E **Formal use of language**

- How accurate, clear and precise is the language used by the candidate?
- How appropriate is the candidate's choice of register and style, for this task? (Register refers, in this context, to the candidate's sensitivity to elements such as the vocabulary, tone, sentence structure and idiom appropriate to the task.)

"Milk"

Words associated with "milk" can be: comforting, healthy, white, pure, nauseating, horrible, cold, school. There are of course many others.

2 Analysing poetry

Objectives

- To establish a strategy for approaching unseen poetry texts
- To practise close reading of poetry texts
- To look at examples of commentaries on poems

Writing about poetry

In Chapter 1 we looked at how to approach the commentary and literary analysis in general. In this chapter we will look at ways of examining specific poems, together with giving examples of students' commentaries on some of these poems. First, it is worth reminding yourself of the things you should do when you have to write about a poem or when you are sitting the Paper 1 examination.

- Read the poem through very carefully several times before starting to write about it.
- Avoid rushing into hasty judgements on it – this is not easy under exam conditions, but thinking before you write is essential.
- When you are with other students their comments can help you find a way into the poem, but in an exam only further close reading will help you.
- Having read the poem, make notes by marking lines, underlining words, and so on. In an exam, or if you have a photocopy, you can annotate the poem on the page. Twenty minutes spent making notes will pay dividends when you finally start writing your commentary.
- When writing under exam conditions, remember that you are not in a race. It is not quantity but quality that will gain you marks. The examiner will be aware of the time constraints that you are working under and will take them into account.
- Do not write down your comments in a haphazard fashion; try to organize your ideas under one main approach, depending on what you feel is the most important aspect of the poem.

> "'Sir, what is poetry?'
> 'Why Sir, it is much easier to say what it is not. We all know *what light is; but it is not easy to* tell *what it is.*'"
> Samuel Johnson

Swifts

Fifteenth of May. Cherry blossom. The swifts
Materialize at the tip of a long scream
Of needle. 'Look! They're back! Look!' And they're gone
On a steep

Controlled scream of skid
Round the house-end and away under the cherries. Gone.

Activity

Working alone or with a partner, read the poem *Swifts* by Ted Hughes carefully, making notes under each of the headings given on pages 22–24.

Suddenly flickering in sky summit, three or four together,
Gnat-whisp frail, and hover-searching, and listening

For air-chills – are they too early? With a bowing
Power-thrust to left, then to right, then a flicker they
Tilt into a slide, a tremble for balance,
Then a lashing down disappearance

Behind elms.
They've made it again,
Which means the globe's still working, the Creation's
Still waking refreshed, our summer's
Still all to come –
And here they are, here they are again
Erupting across yard stones
Shrapnel-scatter terror. Frog-gapers,
Speedway goggles, international mobsters –

A bolas of three or four wire screams
Jockeying across each other
On their switchback wheel of death.
They swat past, hard fletched,
Veer on the hard air, toss up over the roof,
And are gone again. Their mole-dark labouring,
Their lunatic limber scramming frenzy
And their whirling blades
Sparkle out into blue –
Not ours any more.
Rats ransacked their nests so now they shun us.
Round luckier houses now
They crowd their evening dirt-track meetings,

Racing their discords, screaming as if speed-burned,
Head-height, clipping the doorway
With their leaden velocity and their butterfly lightness,
Their too much power, their arrow-thwack into the eaves.

Every year a first-fling, nearly-flying
Misfit flopped in our yard,
Groggily somersaulting to get airborne.
He bat-crawled on his tiny useless feet, tangling his flails

Like a broken toy, and shrieking thinly
Till I tossed him up – then suddenly he flowed away under
His bowed shoulders of enormous swimming power,
Slid away along levels wobbling

On the fine wire they have reduced life to,
And crashed among the raspberries.
Then followed fiery hospital hours
In a kitchen. The moustached goblin savage

Nested in a scarf. The bright blank
Blind, like an angel, to my meat-crumbs and flies.
Then eyelids resting. Wasted clingers curled.
The inevitable balsa death.
Finally burial
For the husk
Of my little Apollo –

The charred scream
Folded in its huge power.

Ted Hughes

Here are notes for one interpretation of Hughes"s poem. Remember, however, that this is just one interpretation. As long as they can be supported by the text itself, a number of different ideas may be valid.

What is the text about? As the title tells us, the poem is almost entirely devoted to describing and "capturing" in writing the appearance, movements, and behaviour of swifts (they are fast-moving, fork-tailed birds related to swallows and martens).

Where and **when**? Although the setting is not obvious in the poem, the fact that swifts arrive in England in the summer and Hughes is an English poet suggests that the poem is set in England at the beginning of summer: "Fifteenth of May", to be precise. From the words, "Look! They're back! Look!" one can assume that their arrival is welcomed as the sign of the summer "Still all to come".

Who is the speaker? In this case it is probably safe to say it is the poet, Ted Hughes, himself. It is written in the first person and addresses the reader directly. One feels that Hughes wants us to share his excitement and fascination with these remarkable birds.

Why has it been written? This is an example of a poem where there does not seem to be a deep, hidden meaning. The swifts are themselves, not a metaphor for anything else. Hughes wishes to celebrate their amazing flying skills and their vulnerability ("Rats ransacked their nests"). Young birds can fail to fly successfully, and when that is the case no human care can save them. Anyone who has tried to save an injured bird will empathize with the burial of the bird, "my little Apollo". Apollo is the Greek god of youth, beauty, poetry and music. The comparison to Apollo highlights Hughes's admiration and respect. But the burial also reminds us that there may be little point in interfering with nature. The rule of the survival of the fittest would ensure that a weak bird would not live long. The poem also mentions the cycles of the seasons. "They've made it again,/ Which means the globe's still working, the Creation's/ Still waking refreshed". The poem is about the inexorable processes of the natural world as well as being about the swifts in particular.

Structure and form. For the most part, four-line stanzas are used, but rather freely. Line lengths vary from two words to 11 and are frequently broken by caesuras (such as in the line "Nested in a scarf. The bright blank"). There are many run-ons from one line to the next (enjambment) as in lines 1 and 2, 2 and 3, and 3 and 4. The erratic nature of the form suggests the free, jagged, erratic nature of the flight of these birds.

Vocabulary, language, diction. As this is a descriptive poem it is not surprising that the poem is full of words that convey movement and sound: "scream of skid", "toss up over the roof", "crashed among the raspberries", to give just a few examples. Many words describe the flying skills of the birds, with Hughes often borrowing the language of speeding vehicles to convey the speed and thrust of their movement.

Imagery. There is hardly a line in the poem which does not convey meaning through metaphor. As already mentioned, many words and phrases suggest the flight of planes or of speedway motoring. For example, "On a steep/ Controlled scream of skid"; and "with a bowing/ Power-thrust to left, then to right, then a flicker they/ Tilt into a slide…". These are phrases that could be used of an air display. So too are words such as "switchback", "whirling blades", and "Shrapnel-scatter terror", which also acknowledge their aggression and ability to frighten.

But as well as making the swifts sound powerful and dangerous, Hughes draws attention to their delicacy: they "flicker" and "tremble" and are "Gnat-whisp frail". He frequently uses paradox to contrast their speed, which can seem blundering and uncontrolled, a "lunatic limber scramming frenzy", with their small size and controlled grace. They have both a "leaden velocity" and "butterfly lightness". Another aspect that Hughes captures is the way the swifts' cries combine sound and movement. It is as if the birds are faster than the sounds which they leave trailing behind them like wires: "A bolas of three or four wire screams". When they come into view, they: "Materialize at the tip of a long scream/ Of needle…" The word "needle" conveys the sharp, piercing quality of the scream. A "bolas" is a small round mass which can be used as a weapon. The damaged bird is an "Apollo" but also a "moustached goblin savage", suggesting something mischievous or even malevolent. It is also "like an angel" and its "inevitable balsa death" could refer to the lightweight balsa-wood coffin the bird is buried in. Balsa wood is light and brittle, so the word encapsulates the feel of the tiny bird's body, little more than feather and bones. The words "fiery hospital hours" and "Nested in a scarf" indicate the care and attention paid to the bird when the poet is nursing it.

Other literary features include alliteration, as in "The bright blank/ Blind…" emphasizing the lack of response of the bird to the attempts at feeding it; onomatopoeia, as in "long scream of needle" and "shrieking thinly", where Hughes conveys the high pitch of their cries, and "first-fling, nearly-flying/ Misfit flopped in our yard", where the repetition of the "fl" sound suggests the floundering and fluttering of the bird. There is no rhyme scheme to the poem, but the varying length of the lines and the rhythmic pattern emulate the darting movements of the birds.

Tone and atmosphere. Much of the poem has a tone of excitement and hurry. The short, broken first five lines reflect the way the swifts dart in and out of sight. The poem has a breathless quality, reinforced by repetitions of "gone" and "here they are". The latter part of the poem is quieter and sadder, when there is mourning for the dead bird. But movement is always accompanied by a feeling of speed and danger.

This is a long poem and you will realize that many lines have not been examined in the above notes. Under examination conditions there is rarely time to comment on all aspects of a poem, so you have to select. From the notes above you could write a reasonable analysis of the poem in essay form. It is important to emphasize that the notes are *not* an essay. You need to organize them into a coherent analysis and explanation of the poem.

Commentary

Ted Hughes begins the poem by describing the time and one aspect of the natural surroundings associated with that time when the birds return:

"Fifteenth of May. Cherry blossom."

The poet also shows how excited he is to see the returning swifts. This is shown by the use of exclamation marks and the repetition of the word "Look!" Almost immediately the poet goes on to discuss the speed of the swifts. He does this by saying that by the time a step has been taken the swifts are out of sight. This is a sign of the tone of the poem; the most striking feature is that of the way the poet describes the speed with which the swifts fly. The speed of the swifts is also shown by the poet by the way the different stanzas are written. The sentences are fragmented as they use exclamation marks, dashes, commas, and question marks. This gives the poem a sense of pace which is reflected by the way the swifts fly.

The language the poet uses in the first stanza shows how the swifts use power and agility to fly. This is best described in the lines:

"Power-thrust to left, then to right, then a flicker they
Tilt into a slide."

The swifts manage to use both power and agility to fly, which is something that man-made machines fail to achieve. A rocket has power but agility is reserved for machines such as gliders.

The poet also uses metaphors of nature to explain how the swifts arrived:

"They've made it again.
Which means the globe's still working."

This gives the connotation that the arrival of the swifts signifies that nature will continue to develop as long as they arrive after their winter break.

In the next few stanzas sporting metaphors are used and this helps again to highlight the speed at which the swifts fly. Examples of these are "Speedway goggles", "jockeying", and "Veer on the hard air". These are used because of the speed associated with them – speedway for fast motorbikes, jockeying as

in jockeying for a position in a race, and veering hard as in some other form of motor sport. These all help to give a sense of realism to the reader who may be unfamiliar with the sight of a swift flying.

The poet feels saddened when they have gone. He tries to find something to blame. In this case it is the rats who have destroyed their nests. The poet seems jealous that the swifts have gone. This is shown in the line that says they are "Round luckier houses now".

This also shows the fondness which the poet has for the birds.

The next stanza best highlights the speed of the swifts. Again dashes are used in the sentence structure, which adds to the sense of speed. The way the poet describes how the swifts are "clipping the doorway" shows that the birds are flying so quickly that there is hardly any margin for error. They try to take short-cuts to reach their destination quicker and this could prove fatal.

The final few stanzas show the youth of the swift and how frail and vulnerable they can be. This is in great contrast to the agility and power with which they are described early in the poem.

The poet describes how in the early days, swifts, like any other birds, find it hard to fly. He uses language which again is in contrast to the language used earlier. Words such as "crawled", "useless feet", and "tangling" are in vast contrast with the sure and certain movements such as "erupting" and veering. These also show the power the young swift has to come.

The poet also describes how he once found a swift that had "crashed among the raspberries". He attempted to care for it in his kitchen but the bird died. The poet describes the death of the swift as "The inevitable balsa death".

This shows both the benefits and drawbacks of being, as balsa wood is when used for model planes, swift and light through the air but also frail.

The life the swifts lead is best described by "the fine wire".

This shows that they live on the edge, risking their life by flying so quickly through the air.

It is not always easy to detect patterns or repetition in a poem. One way is to try colour-coding. Using a range of different-coloured pens or pencils, go through a poem marking the same ideas, images, diction and any form of repetition you can find with one colour. For example, you could mark words such as "scream", indicating sounds, in green. Words indicating movement could be marked with yellow. This will show you the extent of one type of imagery or feature and thus help focus on what the poem is illustrating.

Activity

Read carefully the following poem, *Blessing* by Imtiaz Dharker, and make your own notes on it. When you have finished your notes compare your ideas with those that follow, which have been written by a student. You could also write out a copy of the poem and try to colour code it.

Blessing

The skin cracks like a pod.
There never is enough water.

Imagine the drip of it,
The small splash, echo
in a tin mug,
the voice of a kindly God.

Sometimes, the sudden rush
of fortune. The municipal pipe bursts,
silver crashes to the ground
and the flow has found
a roar of tongues. From the huts,
a congregation: every man woman
child for streets around
butts in, with pots,
brass, copper, aluminium,
plastic buckets,
frantic hands,

and naked children
screaming in the liquid sun,
their highlights polished to perfection,
flashing light,
as the blessing sings
over their small bones.

Imtiaz Dharker

Commentary

1 Content: The poem tells about how the "blessing" of water is received in a land where rainfall is sparse. The opening line of the poem "The skin cracks like a pod" suggests that this is a place with a hot climate, the image of "skin cracking" showing the effects on a dry, parched land where there is "never enough water".

The poem goes on to relate how people celebrate during the times of heavy rainfall and how everyone is affected by the "blessing". We are told that all the people in the place present themselves with all different kinds of pots to collect some water and that "naked children" scream "in the liquid sun".

The poem concludes with the reiteration of the idea of rainfall being a "blessing": "as the blessing sings/ over their small bones". However, this positive sentiment is accompanied by the inclusion of the image of "small bones", which presents an idea of fragility.

2 Structure: The structure of the poem is very interesting as the length of the initial three stanzas reflects the amount of rainfall being received. For instance, in the first stanza only two lines are used to describe life without water. This succeeds in giving the poem an initial slow pace which suggests what life is like during a drought period. This pace increases a little in the second, four-lined, stanza, which asks us to imagine the sound of a "small splash" of water echoing "in a tin mug". We see much excitement and activity in the third stanza, which is reflected in the eleven lines. The pace here is very quick, which supports the idea of the activities described. The final stanza has six lines, which suggests that the excitement and pleasure from receiving such a "blessing" is slowing down and that a return to lack of rainfall is inevitable.

3 Mood: Initially the poem has a mood of desperation. However, by the third stanza a celebratory mood is evident as the place with the drought receives a "sudden rush of fortune" and there is so much water that "The municipal pipe bursts". This injects a degree of energy into the poem, which is lacking initially.

4 Imagery: The opening image of "skin cracking" through lack of water can have two meanings which adds to its power within the poem. It could relate to the cracking of the parched earth or indeed the skin of the people themselves. Both interpretations present negative images in relation to the lack of water. When the rain does arrive in abundance, positive images of "children/ screaming in the liquid sun" present a picture of children dancing in puddles which are bright and golden as they reflect the hot sun's rays. However, at the conclusion of the poem their vulnerability is suggested in the words "small bones". There is a pattern of religious imagery in the poem beginning with the title "Blessing". Water is seen as a gift from God, like a blessing; the sound of it splashing is like the voice of God. When there is water the people are a "congregation" who rush for the water as they might rush to church for salvation.

5 Language/vocabulary: The language used in the poem is supportive of the sentiments expressed within it. The preciousness of the long-awaited rainfall is reflected in its description as "silver". The "roar of tongues" suggests fire and heat and we get the impression that the rainfall's presence will quench a great thirst of both the people and the land. When a little water is available in stanza 2, the word "echo" as the drips fall into the bottom of a "tin mug" suggests emptiness. The word "frantic", which is used to describe hands which try to contain water, is powerful and suggests the energy involved in the activity.

6 Rhythm: Devices used to increase the rhythm of the poem when the rainfall comes are effective in increasing the pace. For example, the use of commas towards the end of the third stanza speeds up the pace in line with the activity being described: "every man woman/ child for streets around/ butts in, with pots,/ brass, copper, aluminium,/ plastic buckets/ frantic hands". This quickened pace is slowed by the end of the poem as the poet uses longer line lengths. This succeeds in emphasizing a sense of relief at the rain's eventual return and suggests a tapering off of the rainfall itself.

7 Poetic devices: The opening line contains the simile "cracks like a pod". This induces a feeling of destruction through lack of water – the "pod" indicating the effect on crops and therefore food sources. When there is limited water available in stanza 2, the onomatopoeic "drip" is effective in that its repetition could indicate the passing of time. This idea is emphasized in the inclusion of the alliterative "small splash" used to describe the water as it falls into the mug. The onomatopoeic word "crashes" used to describe the heavy rainfall in stanza 3 adds a degree of power and sound which enhances the life-giving force of water.

Activity

Now write a commentary on the poem using both your own notes and the notes provided here.

Metaphors

I'm a riddle in nine syllables,
An elephant, a ponderous house,
A melon strolling on two tendrils.
O red fruit, ivory, fine timbers!
This loaf's big with its yeasty rising.
Money's new-minted in this fat purse.

I'm a means, a stage, a cow in calf.
I've eaten a bag of green apples,
Boarded the train there's no getting off.

Sylvia Plath

Activity

Even if Sylvia Plath had not entitled her poem *Metaphors*, you would still have realized that this riddling poem is packed with them. Count the lines and the number of metaphors and then decide what the answer to the riddle is. All the metaphors are concerned with a particular state and when carefully analysed reveal Plath's attitude to this state. Discuss with one or two other students the implications of each metaphor and then decide whether she is happy with her state or not. For example, compare the discomfort of eating "green apples" with the promised riches of money "new-minted".

The poem is an example of an extended metaphor with every line concentrating on one idea. Try writing a poem of your own in which you use an extended metaphor. Suggestions for topics could be: an animal, elastic, a flirt, snow, music or any other ideas of your own. When you have finished ask someone else to read it and comment on its effectiveness.

The Flower-fed Buffaloes

The flower-fed buffaloes of the spring
In the days of long ago,
Ranged where the locomotives sing
And the prairie flowers lie low:–
The tossing, blooming, perfumed grass
Is swept away by the wheat,
Wheels and wheels and wheels spin by
In the spring that still is sweet.
But the flower-fed buffaloes of the spring
Left us, long ago.
They gore no more, they bellow no more,
They trundle around the hills no more:–
With the Blackfeet, lying low,
With the Pawnees, lying low,
Lying low.

Vachel Lindsay

Part 1 The commentary

Activity

Understanding Vachel Lindsay's poem also depends on understanding the implications of the metaphors although, unlike Plath's poem, it does not contain an extended metaphor. It depends on ambiguity, which is often used by poets to compress several layers of meaning into a few words. What is Lindsay's attitude to the disappearance of the buffalo? Is he glad they have gone? Sad about it? Or does he present an objective view? To answer the question one needs to look very carefully at diction and imagery. Here are some questions to consider.

- Why are the buffaloes eating flowers rather than grass?

- Why are locomotives singing and not screaming or clanging?
- Why is the spring still "sweet"?
- What is the effect of the repetition of "wheels", "long ago" and "lying low"?
- What is the effect of the following words all directly describing the buffaloes: "flower-fed", "gore", "bellow", "trundle" and "lying low"?

The Blackfeet and the Pawnees are Native American tribes. Why are they, like the buffaloes, "lying low"? "Lying low" is the most obvious example of ambiguity in the poem. How many different meanings can you think of for this phrase?

Parody

A parody is an imitation of someone else's style of writing which is deliberately exaggerated in order to amuse the reader, or sometimes to satirize the content or the author. Not only writing, but music, painting and a variety of other activities can be parodied, as many comedy shows illustrate. The writer of a parody may concentrate on the diction of the original, the syntax, the content, or the rhyme and rhythm if it is a poem. Poems that have a very marked rhyme and rhythm are usually easy to parody. In Lewis Carroll's *Alice in Wonderland*, the Mad Hatter parodies the first verse of a poem called *The Star* by Jane Taylor. You probably know it.

> Twinkle, twinkle, little star,
> How I wonder what you are!
> Up above the world so high,
> Like a diamond in the sky.

Here is the Mad Hatter's parody:

> Twinkle, twinkle, little bat!
> How I wonder what you're at!
> Up above the world you fly,
> Like a tea-tray in the sky.

You can see and hear that the rhyme and rhythm are the same, with four beats to a line and a rhyme scheme of *aabb*. The humour arises from changing "star" to "bat". Everyone regards stars as beautiful and inaccessible, while a bat can be considered as rather ugly (it is certainly not the most prepossessing of creatures), while a "tea-tray" is undoubtedly far less valuable than a "diamond" (though in shape, a bat could be likened to a tea-tray). The humour arises from bathos, which means the effect of descending from the sublime to the mundane.

A pastiche is very like a parody, but a pastiche is not meant to be funny. In a pastiche the writer tries to copy the original without exaggeration or mockery. It is very difficult to write a successful pastiche. A well-known example of a pastiche is Sir Walter Raleigh's reply to Christopher Marlowe's poem *The Passionate Shepherd to his Love*, which begins:

Come live with me and by my Love,
And we will all the pleasures prove
That hills and valleys, dales and fields,
Or woods or steepy mountain yields.

"Prove" means test or try. Raleigh's poem *Her Reply* begins:

If all the world and love were young,
And truth in every shepherd's tongue,
These pretty pleasures might me move
To live with thee and be thy Love.

To get a real feeling for a writer's style it is worth trying to parody it. This can be particularly useful for those who find it hard to detect the rhythm of a poem.

Leisure

What is this life if, full of care,
We have no time to stand and stare?

No time to stand beneath the boughs
And stare as long as sheep or cows:

No time to see, when woods we pass,
Where squirrels hide their nuts in grass:

No time to see, in broad daylight,
Streams full of stars, like skies at night:

…

A poor life this if, full of care,
We have no time to stand and stare.

W.H. Davies

Activity

Try to write a parody of an easy target first, such as *Leisure* by W.H. Davies.

On the swag

His body doubled
   under the pack
   that sprawls untidily
   on his old back
   the cold wet deadbeat
   plods up the track.

The cook peers out:
   'oh curse that old lag –
   here again
   with his clumsy swag
   made of a dirty old
   turnip-bag.'

Activity

Henry Wadsworth Longfellow's *Hiawatha* is another fairly easy poem to parody, as are most nursery rhymes. Try to parody Vachel Lindsay's poem on page 28, or to imitate the style of New Zealand poet R.A.K. Mason's poem *On the swag*. A swag is the bag or bundle that tramps in Australia and New Zealand carried their belongings in.

'Bring him in cook
    from the grey level sleet
    put silk on his body
    slippers on his feet,
    give him fire
    and bread and meat.

Let the fruit be plucked
    and the cake be iced,
    the bed be snug
    and the wine be spiced
    in the old cove's nightcap:
    for this is Christ.'

R.A.K. Masons

Activity

When you have written a parody
and discussed the results with a
partner, write a commentary on
the poem you have parodied, or
on R.A.K. Mason's poem.

Activity

Write a commentary on the following poem. It is not compulsory for you to
respond directly to the guiding questions provided below, but it is a good
idea to use them as starting points for your commentary.

- What impression do you gain of the mother's experiences? How does
  the poet convey those impressions?
- How are the reactions of people around the mother conveyed by the
  poet?
- What is the role of the scorpion in the poem?
- Comment on the last three lines.

Night of the Scorpion

I remember the night my mother
was stung by a scorpion. Ten hours
of steady rain had driven him
to crawl beneath a sack of rice.
Parting with his poison – flash
of diabolic tail in the dark room –
he risked the rain again.
The peasants came like swarms of flies
and buzzed the name of God a hundred times
to paralyse the Evil One.
With candles and with lanterns
throwing giant scorpion shadows
on the mud-baked walls
they searched for him: he was not found.
They clicked their tongues.
With every movement that the scorpion made
his poison moved in Mother's blood, they said.
May he sit still, they said.

May the sins of your previous birth
be burned away tonight, they said.
May your suffering decrease
the misfortunes of your next birth, they said.
May the sum of evil
balanced in this unreal world
against the sum of good
become diminished by your pain.
May the poison purify your flesh
of desire, and your spirit of ambition,
they said, and they sat around
on the floor with my mother in the centre,
the peace of understanding on each face.
More candles, more lanterns, more neighbours,
more insects, and the endless rain.
My mother twisted through and through,
groaning on a mat.
My father, sceptic, rationalist,
trying every curse and blessing,
powder, mixture, herb and hybrid.
He even poured a little paraffin
upon the bitten toe and put a match to it.
I watched the flame feeding on my mother.
I watched the holy man perform his rites
to tame the poison with an incantation.
After twenty hours
it lost its sting.

My mother only said
Thank God the scorpion picked on me
and spared my children.

Nissin Ezekiel

Activity

First read the poem *Planting a Sequoia* by Dana Gioia several times.
Then read the commentary on it written by a student. A sequoia is a huge
coniferous tree in California, often known as a giant redwood.

Planting a Sequoia

All afternoon my brothers and I have worked in the orchard,
Digging this hole, laying you into it, carefully packing the soil.
Rain blackened the horizon, but cold winds kept it over the Pacific,
And the sky above us stayed the dull gray
Of an old year coming to an end.

In Sicily a father plants a tree to celebrate his first son's birth –
An olive or a fig tree – a sign that the earth has one more life to bear.
I would have done the same, proudly laying new stock into my father's orchard,
A green sapling rising among the twisted apple boughs,
A promise of new fruit in other autumns.

But today we kneel in the cold planting you, our native giant,
Defying the practical custom of our fathers,
Wrapping in your roots a lock of hair, a piece of an infant's birth cord,
All that remains above earth of a first-born son,
A few stray atoms brought back to the elements.

We will give you what we can – our labor and our soil,
Water drawn from the earth when the skies fail,
Nights scented with the ocean fog, days softened by the circuit of bees.
We plant you in the corner of the grove, bathed in western light,
A slender shoot against the sunset.

And when our family is no more, all of his unborn brothers dead,
Every niece and nephew scattered, the house torn down,
His mother's beauty ashes in the air,
I want you to stand among strangers, all young and ephemeral to you,
Silently keeping the secret of your birth.

Dana Gioia

Commentary: The unity of man and nature

The cycle of life requires both human and nature's input. A tree cannot grow even with the help of the Earth's natural resources, water and light, without a man initially planting the seed. The poem "Planting a Sequoia" written by Dana Gioia unites man and nature. The death of a man becomes the birth of a tree.

Creating a grave and planting a tree requires the same action, digging a hole. The first stanza of the poem introduces a person, the narrator, digging a "hole, laying you into it, carefully packing the soil". This refers to both planting a tree, and burying a man. The weather is dark and cold which introduces a sad and harsh tone to the poem. The narrator than continues and describes a tradition in Sicily, where planting of a tree represents the birth of a child, because the earth has "one more life to bear". The narrator claims that he would have followed this tradition. However instead he is in the cold on his knees planting the sequoia, the native tree of California. With the tree he plants a lock of hair and an infant's umbilical cord. Only now in the middle of the poem does the narrator express that he is burying his son and reconnecting him with the elements of nature. After the planting of the tree, the reader is told how nature and man will work together to raise this tree. The men will give labour and soil while nature provides water and light. This tree will live longer than any of the family members and forever "stand among strangers".

Unlike the life of a tree, human life is not forever. However, through the simple act of planting a tree a person's life is forever remembered. A father is burying his first-born son. By burying hair and the umbilical cord with the tree, the tree becomes the son. This unification of man and nature becomes the pattern and running theme through the poem. The unification is presented through personification. The literal meaning of the poem, the tree, is referred to throughout the poem as "you". This creates a human connotation and establishes a personal relationship between the figurative you, represented in the tree, and the speaker. This supports the idea of a father burying his son.

Death is natural. Throughout this poem the natural theme is supported through natural imagery, "Rain blackened the horizon", "Nights scented with the ocean fog", and "days softened by the circuit of bees". However, a father burying his son is unnatural. Unnatural imagery, like "We plant you in the corner of the grave", "Digging this hole", "packing the soil" and "We will give you… Water drawn from the earth when the skies fail" supports the unnatural tragic event of a child dying before his father. The death of a child is the reason the father is "Defying the practical custom of our fathers". He is going against tradition like nature has gone against the tradition of a father dying before his son.

The pain, sadness, and grief for the tragic death of a son is represented within the imagery of the first stanza in the poem. The dark and cold weather sets a gloomy tone to the poem. This creates an expectation within the reader for a dark and sad poem. This expectation is supported by the alliteration of the harsh "k" sound. This is an unpleasant sound which provokes feelings of pain and hurt. However within the first sentence a reference to "orchard" is made. Orchard has the connotation of beauty, life and growth. Towards the end of the first stanza there is the foreshadowing of rain; however the "cold winds kept it over the Pacific, and the sky above us stayed the dull gray". There was a natural force which kept the rain away. The tree is the natural force which reduces the mourning for the death of the child. The mourning and tragic grief is replaced by the tree, which represent life, beauty and growth like the orchard. There is a sense of hope as well as sadness which rises within the poem from the first stanza.

Birth, "A promise of new fruit in other autumns", also provides a sense of hope in life. Therefore within the poem an allusion to another culture and tradition is made. This comparison shows how a tradition which creates hope for a joyful event has been used to change grief into hope and a celebration of life, not to those who are new to life but for those who will be remembered for their life and have died. The difference between the boy who has died and the newborn baby is symbolized through the use of different trees. The dead boy is represented as a giant native sequoia. This tree represents age, experience, strength, development and beauty, all the aspects which a "green sapling" or "apple boughs" still need to develop just like newborn babies.

While the "native giant" sequoia stands tall and strong, the rest of the family is going to be scattered in the air when they die. The tree will forever be a representation of the dead son. This death was the reason the tree was born. However the last line of the poem, "Silently keeping the secret of your birth", indicates that the reason for the tree and the actual planting of the sequoia was the intimate and private moment for the father in order to be at peace with the death of his son. Therefore it was a secret and shall remain a secret. The quiet alliteration of the sound "s" provides a sense of calmness which closes the poem with a tone and mood of serenity and rest. The secret of the birth of the tree will always remain between the father and the tree. Therefore the relationship between father and son will remain forever.

Not only does the poem show a relationship between nature and man but also between father and son. This is evident through the structure of the poem. The lack of rhythm and rhyme presents the poem as a private monologue from a father to his son. The reader is invited to listen and experience the unification of a man and nature as well as the everlasting tie between father and son.

The father created a way to have the memory of his son live on forever. By planting a tree man and nature worked together to create life. Through the use of natural and unnatural imagery, personification, diction and symbolism man and nature were unified within this poem. Either through having a symbolic tree, being buried or scattered everyone unifies with nature after death. This is the natural cycle of life.

Activity

List what you think are the positive and the negative aspects of the student's commentary. Now read an examiner's comments and see if you agree with them.

Examiner's comments

This commentary contains examples of two common faults. The first is a tendency for students to start writing before they have really understood the poem, but then to gradually arrive at a better interpretation as they write. The second is to make an overall interpretation and then to maintain it without further questioning. Perhaps this accounts for the fact that this literary analysis contains a mixture of perceptive and slightly off-beat interpretations.

The first sentence is not promising. Is it even true? Trees grew long before human beings arrived on earth. Is it relevant to the poet's message? Only to a certain extent. Also, the poem is about the death of a child, not a man.

The second paragraph, however, gives a satisfactory outline of what happens in the poem, while the third paragraph discusses the ambiguity of "We will give you what we can" where the "you" is both the child and the tree.

There is some confusion between the meanings of "natural", "unnatural" and "nature", and the examples of unnatural imagery are not explained convincingly. It is not unnatural to dig a hole except in this particular situation. It is against tradition to plant a tree for a dead child, just as it is against tradition and nature for a child to die before his father; but can these events be called unnatural or just unusual? In writing about this, the student misquotes "grove" as "grave" in paragraph 4.

The discussion of the effects of the weather on the tone is valid, as is the significance of the use of the sequoia to represent the dead child. Unfortunately, the language and syntax used in paragraphs 5 and 6 tends to obscure rather than clarify what the student is trying to say. The next paragraph, beginning "While the 'native giant' sequoia…", is very good as the student shows that he has grasped the central idea of the poem. It is a pity that at the end, the commentary reverts to the earlier idea of the poem being about the unification of man and nature. This is a patchy performance which is sometimes marred by faulty and confusing writing.

Activity

Write a commentary on the following poem.

The Storm

Against the stone breakwater,
Only an ominous lapping,
While the wind whines overhead,
Coming down from the mountain,
Whistling between the arbours, the winding terraces;
A thin whine of wires, a rattling and flapping of leaves,
And the small streetlamp swinging and slamming against the lamp-pole.
Where have the people gone?
There is one light on the mountain,
Along the sea-wall a steady sloshing of the swell,
The waves not yet high, but even,
Coming closer and closer upon each other;
A fine fume of rain driving in from the sea,
Riddling the sand, like a wide spray of buckshot,
The wind from the sea and the wind from the mountain contending,
Flicking the foam from the whitecaps straight upwards into the darkness.
A time to go home!
And a child's dirty shift billows upward out of an alley;
A cat runs from the wind as we do,
Between the whitening trees, up Santa Lucia,
Where the heavy door unlocks
And our breath comes more easy.
Then a crack of thunder, and the black rain runs over us, over
The flat-roofed houses, coming down in gusts, beating
The walls, the slatted windows, driving
The last watcher indoors, moving the cardplayers closer
To their cards, their Lachryma Christi.
We creep to our bed and its straw mattress.
We wait, we listen.
The storm lulls off, then redoubles,
Bending the trees halfway down to the ground,
Shaking loose the last wizened oranges in the orchard,
Flattening the limber carnations.
A spider eases himself down from a swaying light bulb,
The bulb goes on and off, weakly.
Water roars in the cistern.
We lie closer on the gritty pillow,
Breathing heavily, hoping –
For the great last leap of the wave over the breakwater.
The flat boom on the beach of the towering sea-swell,
The sudden shudder as the jutting sea-cliff collapses
And the hurricane drives the dead straw into the living pine-tree.

Theodore Roethke

3 Analysing prose

Objectives
- To establish a strategy for approaching unseen prose texts
- To practise close reading of prose texts
- To look at examples of commentaries on prose texts

Analysing prose is not so very different from analysing poetry. In both you have to look at literary techniques, at choice of language, imagery, structure and so on, but these may be used in different ways to achieve different effects in prose. You may have to read even more carefully when studying prose passages as the techniques used may not be so readily detected.

Most of the prose passages you will be asked to analyse will be extracts from longer pieces of work, rather than complete texts, although occasionally very short essays or stories are set which are complete.

When writing your commentary on a prose text you will need to examine closely the writer's style in order to analyse the way the language is used. You will need to be aware of the features to look for and the ways in which the author's choice of style can influence meaning and effect.

"A writer's personality is his manner of being in the world: his writing style is the unavoidable trace of that manner."
Zadie Smith

Examining writers' styles

Throughout this book you are being asked to think not only about what writers are saying – the content of their work – but also about *how* they write. This means examining the particular combination of literary devices, structures, and vocabulary which a writer uses and which go together to form that writer's individual "style". From your own reading you will know that some writers' work is easy to recognize immediately because they have a distinctive "style". However, it can be more difficult to explain exactly which characteristics make a writer's style recognizable.

As a student of literature, you will need to develop the ability to analyse and write about style. One shortcoming noted by examiners is that students fail to take account of this and do not engage in enough detailed analysis of how texts are written. It is easier to concentrate on the writer's use of language when studying poetry, but it can be tempting, when writing about novels or other longer prose works, to focus on the content or the ideas and neglect to examine other features that make up the writer's style.

The following are aspects of prose that you need to examine:

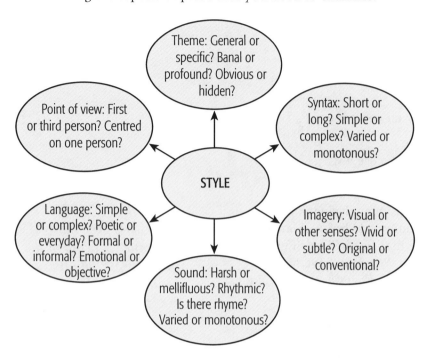

Thinking or feeling

"Style" can also be viewed as the expression of a writer's personality and preoccupations. The ways in which writers experience the world and the things which are most important to them are bound to affect how and what they write. Most writing involves thinking but it is not just a cerebral activity. Although all good writers "craft" their work carefully, even when they wish to convey emotional or sensual experiences, there can be unconscious influences, especially for writers who use more intuitive or free-ranging techniques, allowing their words to flow without controlling them too carefully.

> **Activity**
>
> D.H. Lawrence writes extensively about the emotional reactions of his characters but he does not always reveal their characters directly; instead, he uses imagery and actions to suggest hidden aspects of personalities and relationships. In the following extract from *Sons and Lovers*, identify the images and try to find out what they tell us about the characters. Discuss with a partner how Lawrence uses these images.
>
> In this extract Paul Morel, the protagonist, is just getting to know Miriam Leivers. On the basis of their reactions in this extract, what do you think their relationship will be like?

Sons and Lovers

'It's a treat of a swing,' he said.

'Yes.'

He was swinging through the air, every bit of him swinging, like a bird that swoops for joy of movement. And he looked down at her. Her crimson cap hung over her dark curls, her beautiful warm face, so still in a kind of brooding, was lifted towards him. It was dark and rather cold in the shed. Suddenly a swallow came down from the high roof and darted out of the door.

'I didn't know a bird was watching,' he called.

He swung negligently. She could feel him falling and lifting through the air, as if he were lying on some force.

'Now I'll die,' he said, in a detached, dreamy voice, as though he were the dying motion of the swing. She watched him, fascinated. Suddenly he put on the brake and jumped out.

'I've had a long turn,' he said. 'But it's a treat of a swing – it's a real treat of a swing!'

Miriam was amused that he took a swing so seriously and felt so warmly over it.

'No; you go on,' she said.

'Why, don't you want one?' he asked, astonished.

'Well, not much. I'll have just a little.'

She sat down, whilst he kept the bags in place for her.

'It's so ripping!' he said, setting her in motion. 'Keep your heels up, or they'll bang the manger-wall.'

She felt the accuracy with which he caught her, exactly at the right moment, and the exactly proportionate strength of his thrust, and she was afraid. Down to her bowels went the hot wave of fear. She was in his hands. Again, firm and inevitable came the thrust at the right moment. She gripped the rope, almost swooning.

'Ha!' she laughed in fear. 'No higher!'

'But you're not a *bit* high,' he remonstrated.

'But no higher.'

He heard the fear in her voice, and desisted. Her heart melted in hot pain when the moment came for him to thrust her forward again. But he left her alone. She began to breathe.

'Won't you really go any farther?' he asked. "Should I keep you there?'

'No; let me go by myself,' she answered.

He moved aside and watched her.

'Why, you're scarcely moving,' he said.

She laughed slightly with shame, and in a moment got down.

'They say if you can swing you won't be sea-sick,' he said, as he mounted again. 'I don't believe I should ever be sea-sick.'

Away he went. There was something fascinating to her in him. For the moment he was nothing but a piece of swinging stuff; not a particle of him that did not swing. She could never lose herself, so, nor could her brothers. It roused a warmth in her. It was almost as if he were a flame that had lit a warmth in her whilst he swung in the middle air.

D.H. Lawrence

Activity

Write character studies of Paul and Miriam based on what you have learned from the above extract. Include a consideration of how their different reactions to the swing could foreshadow the nature of their relationship.

1–2–4 method

When you are first learning how to write commentaries, an extract or a poem can be very daunting. You may read it through and think of nothing to say. It is much easier, at this stage, to work with others. The 1–2–4 method is very useful. For this exercise you need at least four people.

Stage 1 Each person, on his or her own, writes down three points about the extract (or poem) to be analysed. These points can be very obvious (for example, there are three paragraphs), or they can be put in the form of a question. It does not matter as long as you write down three comments.

Stage 2 In pairs, look at the six statements you have made between you and try to put them in order of importance.

Stage 3 Now form a group of four. On the basis of the two lists you have, decide what are the key points you wish to make about the extract. For example: What is it about? What is the point of view? In what style is it written? And so on. By this stage you will find that you are very likely to have a good understanding of the passage, as well as being able to make pertinent comments about the way it is written.

Activity

Read the passage that follows, taken from Nathaniel Hawthorne's *The Scarlet Letter*, and use the 1–2–4 method to understand what it is about and make comments on how it is written. After your discussions you will find it is easier to write your own commentary on the passage.

The Scarlet Letter

When the young woman – the mother of this child – stood fully revealed before the crowd, it seemed to be her first impulse to clasp the infant closely to her bosom; not so much by an impulse of motherly affection, as that she might thereby conceal a certain token, which was wrought or fastened into her dress. In a moment, however, wisely judging that one token of her shame would but poorly serve to hide another, she took the baby on her arm, and, with a burning blush, and yet a haughty smile, and a glance that would not be abashed, looked around at her townspeople and neighbours. On the breast of her gown, in fine red cloth, surrounded with an elaborate embroidery and fantastic flourishes of gold thread, appeared the letter A. It was so artistically done, and with so much fertility and gorgeous luxuriance of fancy, that it had all the effect of a last and fitting decoration to the apparel which she wore; and which was of a splendor in accordance with the taste of the age, but greatly beyond what was allowed by the sumptuary regulations of the colony.

The young woman was tall, with a figure of perfect elegance, on a large scale. She had dark and abundant hair, so glossy that it threw off the sunshine with a gleam, and a face which, besides being beautiful from regularity of feature and richness of complexion, had the impressiveness belonging to a marked brow and deep black eyes. She was lady-like, too, after the manner of feminine gentility of those days; characterized by a certain state and dignity, rather than by the delicate, evanescent, and indescribable grace, which is now recognized as its indication. And never had Hester Prynne appeared more lady-like, in the antique interpretation of the term, than as she issued from the prison. Those who had before known her, and had expected to behold her dimmed and obscured by a disastrous cloud, were astonished, and even startled, to perceive how her beauty shone out, and made a halo of the misfortune and ignominy in which she was enveloped. It may be true, that, to a sensitive observer, there was something exquisitely painful in it. Her attire, which, indeed, she had wrought for the occasion, in prison, and had modelled much after her own fancy, seemed to express the attitude of her spirit, the desperate recklessness of her mood, by its wild and picturesque peculiarity. But the point which drew all eyes, and, as it were, transfigured the wearer, – so that both men and women, who had been familiarly acquainted with Hester Prynne, were now impressed as if they beheld her for the first time, – was that SCARLET LETTER, so fantastically embroidered and illuminated upon her bosom. It had the effect of a spell, taking her out of the ordinary relations with humanity, and inclosing her in a sphere by herself.

'She hath good skill at her needle, that's certain,' remarked one of the female spectators; 'but did ever a woman, before this brazen hussy, contrive such a way of showing it! Why, gossips, what is it but to laugh in the faces of our godly magistrates, and make a pride out of what they, worthy gentlemen, meant for a punishment?'

'It were well,' muttered the most iron-visaged of the old dames, 'if we stripped Madam Hester's rich gown off her dainty shoulders; and as for the red letter, which she hath stitched so curiously, I'll bestow a rag of mine own rheumatic flannel, to make a fitter one!'

'O, peace, neighbours, peace!' whispered their youngest companion, 'Do not let her hear you! Not a stitch in that embroidered letter, but she has felt it in her heart.'

Nathaniel Hawthorne

Activity

Read the following passage from the opening of a novel by Iain Banks.
Working with a partner, make notes on the passage in preparation for writing
a commentary on it. You might like to think about how character is conveyed
through use of detail; what Banks's style is like; how humorous effects are
created; the relationship between the protagonist/narrator and his family.

The Crow Road

It was the day my grandmother exploded. I sat in the crematorium, listening to
my Uncle Hamish quietly snoring in harmony to Bach's Mass in B Minor, and I
reflected that it always seemed to be death that drew me back to Gallanach.

I looked at my father, sitting two rows away in the front line of seats in the cold,
echoing chapel. His broad, greying-brown head was massive above his tweed
jacket (a black arm-band was his concession to the solemnity of the occasion). His
ears were moving in a slow oscillatory manner, rather in the way John Wayne's
shoulders moved when he walked; my father was grinding his teeth. Probably he
was annoyed that my grandmother had chosen religious music for her funeral
ceremony. I didn't think she had done it to upset him; doubtless she had simply
liked the tune, and had not anticipated the effect its non-secular nature might
have on her eldest son.

My younger brother, James, sat to my father's left. It was the first time in years
I'd seen him without his Walkman, and he looked distinctly uncomfortable,
fiddling with his single earring. To my father's right my mother sat, upright and
trim, neatly filling a black coat and sporting a dramatic black hat shaped like a
flying saucer. The UFO dipped briefly to one side as she whispered something to
my father. In that movement and that moment, I felt a pang of loss that did not
entirely belong to my recently departed grandmother, yet was connected with her
memory. How her moles would be itching today if she was somehow suddenly
reborn!

'Prentice!' My Aunt Antonia, sitting next to me, with Uncle Hamish snoring
mellifluously on her other side, tapped my sleeve and pointed at my feet as she
murmured my name. I looked down.

I had dressed in black that morning, in the cold high room of my aunt and uncle's
house. The floorboards had creaked and my breath had smoked. There had
been ice inside the small dormer window, obscuring the view over Gallanach in
a crystalline mist. I'd pulled on a pair of black underpants I'd brought especially
from Glasgow, a white shirt (fresh from Marks and Sparks, the pack-lines still
ridging the cold, crisp cotton) and my black 501s. I'd shivered, and sat on the
bed, looking at two pairs of socks; one black, one white. I'd intended to wear the
black pair under my nine-eye Docs with the twin ankle buckles, but suddenly I
had felt that the boots were wrong. Maybe it was because they were matt finish...

The last funeral I'd been to here – also the first funeral I'd ever been to – this gear
had all seemed pretty appropriate, but now I was pondering the propriety of the
Docs, the 501s, and the black biker's jacket. I'd hauled my white trainers out of

the bag, tried one Nike on and one boot (unlaced); I'd stood in front of the tilted full-length mirror, shivering, my breath going out in clouds, while the floorboards creaked and a smell of cooking bacon and burned toast insinuated its way up from the kitchen.

The trainers, I'd decided.

So I peered down at them in the crematorium; they looked crumpled and tea-stained on the severe black granite of the chapel floor. Oh-oh; one black sock, one white. I wriggled in my seat, pulled my jeans down to cover my oddly-packaged ankles. 'Hell's teeth,' I whispered. 'Sorry, Aunt Tone.'

My Aunt Antonia – a ball of pink-rinse hair above the bulk of her black coat, like candy floss stuck upon a hearse – patted my leather jacket. 'Never mind, dear,' she sighed. 'I doubt old Margot would have minded.'

'No,' I nodded. My gaze fell back to the trainers. It struck me that on the toe of the right one there was still discernible the tyre mark from Grandma Margot's wheelchair. I lifted the left trainer onto the right, and rubbed without enthusiasm at the black herring-bone pattern the oily wheel had left. I remembered the day, six months earlier, when I had pushed old Margot out of the house and through the courtyard, past the outhouses and down the drive under the trees towards the loch and the sea.

Iain Banks

Commentary

The extract from the novel "The Crow Road" by Iain Banks is rather unusual. The passage describes his family at his grandmother's cremation in his home town of Gallanach. The piece is unusual as it is written in a jovial style which is not often connected with death except in black comedy. However, this is not a comedy so it is unusual. The opening sentence, "It was the day my grandmother exploded" is so surprising when put in context with the rest of the passage.

The narrator does not dwell on the grief of losing a member of his family, but more so on his isolation from his parents. In a movement his mother makes to his father he feels "a pang of loss that did not entirely belong to my recently departed grandmother".

The fact he has had to stay at his aunt and uncle's house and is sitting with them shows his isolation from his parents. The narrator does not seem to "fit in" with the rest of his family. His clothes are different and his whole attitude towards the funeral is distracted.

This distraction of the narrator is shown in his digressions from the funeral. He notices his father's ears move, as he grinds his teeth, like "John Wayne's shoulders when he walks". He notices his brother James is not wearing his Walkman for the first time in years and that his mother's dramatic hat is shaped like a UFO. There do not seem to be many emotions shown by the narrator, nor any of the other characters. He remarks how his father is probably angry his grandmother had chosen religious music for her funeral ceremony instead of secular, as he would have wanted. His Uncle Hamish has fallen asleep and is snoring "in harmony to Bach's Mass in B Minor"; he is obviously oblivious or uncaring of the situation around him.

The narrator tries to create a cold atmosphere, one traditionally associated with death. They are sitting in the cold "echoing chapel" which emulates a feeling of emptiness and loss. The cold temperature of his bedroom, however, which the author embellishes upon, seems to be more related to his isolation from his family. The fact he is not in his parents' home shows how they have excluded him from their lives. Also that they do not sit with him at the chapel. The atmosphere is not maintained as the author makes comical asides which are more light-hearted, for example the references to John Wayne and the UFO and the fact his boots didn't look right because they had a matt finish. Also, how he has odd socks on and his description of his Aunt Antonia being like "candy floss stuck upon a hearse".

From this passage, the narrator shows himself to be a young man who has moved away from his home town, possibly without his parents' blessing as they have become disassociated. The narrator shows that he did love his grandmother Margot as he describes a fond memory of her at the end of the passage, yet shows no real signs of grief.

This passage is quite effective as the opening of a novel as it makes me want to read on. It provides details of what are, presumably, the main characters (his family) and it would be interesting to find out what happens next. His jovial style is easy to read and understand, being quite light-hearted.

Examiner's comments

The student provides a clear introductory paragraph, giving enough information to put the passage in context without wasting time on paraphrasing.

She describes the style as "jovial". This may be a good way to describe it, but she will need to clarify what she means by explaining fully later in the essay. Perhaps a more accurate word to express what she means would be "humorous". The reference to black comedy is very useful. Again she needs to pick out examples of this later, even though she has stated that the passage as a whole is not comedy.

She comments on the surprising first sentence in relation to the rest of the passage. A fuller analysis would improve this. For example, she could point out the strangely matter-of-fact tone of the sentence and the shocking effect of the word "exploded" when applied to a "grandmother".

Her point in paragraph 3 about the narrator seeming isolated from his parents is a good one. We have to be careful, though, not to speculate too far. From this extract, we do not know that the whole family were not staying with the aunt and uncle! It's best to keep to points for which you can find evidence in the passage. However, within the extract, there is a sense of his distance from his parents.

The student has pointed out that the narrator's clothes are different, but could expand on this. What do the details of his clothes tell us about him? They could suggest an image or stereotype: "Nine-eye Docs, 501s and the black biker's jacket".

She makes a good point about the narrator's "digressions" in paragraph 4, giving examples of how his attention wanders to dwell on the people around him. Again, she could comment more analytically about these, on what they tell us about the members of his family and also, through his choice of words, about himself. For example, the similes he uses, referring to John Wayne and UFOs, suggest the popular culture of film stars and science fiction, which contrasts with the sombre music his grandmother has chosen. It seems that his brother, too, with his earring, but without his Walkman, has made concessions for the occasion.

In paragraph 5, the student's remarks on atmosphere are apt, the quotation is helpful, and she has added some further comment. She could also go on to say something about the use of colour in the passage. Repeated "black" and "white" are appropriate for cold and death. Having mentioned the aunt's pink hair, she could go on to explain why this is humorous: its inappropriateness among all the black, which is captured by the candy-floss/hearse image.

The penultimate paragraph is disappointing. The student is rather too concerned with inventing theories about the young man's background at the expense of paying close attention to the details that are provided.

This highlights a broader point. The texts chosen for the commentary are specially selected so that there is as little chance as possible that students will have already read them or be familiar with them. However, if you are familiar with the whole text from which the extract has been set, although your previous knowledge of the text may help you to understand it and the way it is written more readily, you will need to avoid letting your wider knowledge distract you from focusing on and making deductions from the details of the passage itself. Remember, the whole focus on the commentary is only on the text you are given on the exam paper.

The student begins to explore the narrator's reference to his grandmother at the end; however, we are not given any evidence in the extract that the memory is a "fond" one, as she claims.

The passage has obviously captured the student's interest, and her final paragraph provides a fair summing up of her response, but overall the paragraphing and general organization of the commentary could have been improved.

However, there is more to notice about the young man in relation to his family and the scene at the crematorium. Here are some suggestions:

- His outward "style" and image, which suggest rebellious youth, could lead to his being labelled uncaring. It contrasts with the conventional dress of his older relatives. As the student's commentary above points out, he does not overtly declare his emotions or much sense of loss, although we do not detect much emotion in the other characters either.

- In opposition to this is his painful preoccupation with "getting it right". He is very concerned that his dress should be appropriate, so he does care. In a strange sense, what seemed inappropriate is in fact fitting: the white trainers carry the mark of his grandmother's wheelchair, and serve as a record of their last meeting, and of his having shown his care of her. The adults, on the other hand, may be dressed more conventionally, but seem, if anything, to be less involved in the proceedings.

Activity

Now look at another student's commentary, which has different qualities. Read it carefully, noting its strengths and suggesting how it could be improved. In particular look at:

- major points the student has noticed about the passage

- how well his ideas are supported with evidence

- the appropriateness of quotations from the text

- his analysis of the writer's style

- how well is it written; is it well-organized?

- technical accuracy: punctuation, paragraphing, and spelling.

Commentary

This passage is an effective opening to the novel, as the first sentence "It was the day my grandmother exploded" grabs the reader's attention instantly. This opening line also establishes the mood of the piece, a quite darkly humorous style – the various family members present at the crematorium are described in a lot of detail – the images created of them are expanded upon (the narrator's mother is said to be wearing a hat that looks like a flying saucer – this is furthered when we are given the image of it "dipping" to the side when she talks). There is a very sarcastic tone to the passage in places, such as when the narrator tells us his father is probably "annoyed that my grandmother had chosen religious music for her funeral ceremony", and the constant references to Uncle Hamish snoring in the background – this style of humor fits in quite well with the proceedings as it isn't (for want of a better term) "Har-de-har-har" humor – it is subtle, and certain points about it are written in such a way, that they could just be taken as extra description of the events (the flashback to the narrator getting dressed is a good example – with him rattling off precise descriptions of his clothes, and where they are from). The atmosphere, despite the humor, is retained: the formal mood is (kind of) still there, and there are references to the cold atmosphere to add to this (although this refers to the morning, it still has an effect on the scene at hand). Also, a lot of the comments from the narrator (who seems to be taking the event as a sort of "family reunion" – or a freak show, depending) are linked with death, even if in an obscure way such as referring to somebody as looking like candy floss stuck on a hearse – which in itself, is mixing something associated with fun & something associated with death – much like the whole passage.

PS – is the "smell of cooking bacon & burned toast" line a really sick reference to the cremation taking place?

> ### Activity
>
> Now read carefully the following extract from *The Dragon Can't Dance*, written by Earl Lovelace in 1979. Make notes on the key elements of the passage that you would wish to include in a commentary. Use whatever approach you think suitable.

The Dragon Can't Dance

Up on the Hill Carnival Monday morning breaks upon the backs of these thin shacks with no cock's crow, and before the mist clears, little boys, costumed in old dresses, their heads tied, holding brooms made from the ribs of coconut palm leaves, blowing whistles and beating kerosene tins for drums, move across the face of the awakening Hill, sweeping yards in a ritual, heralding the masqueraders' coming, that goes back centuries for its beginnings, back across the Middle Passage, back to Mali and to Guinea and Dahomey and Congo, back to Africa when Maskers were sacred and revered, the keepers of the poisons and heads of secret societies, and such children went before them, clearing the ground, announcing their coming to the huts before which they would dance and make their terrible cries, affirming for the village, the tribe, warriorhood and femininity, linking the villagers to their ancestors, their Gods, remembered even now, so long after the Crossing, if not in the brain, certainly in the blood; so that every Carnival Monday morning, Aldrick Prospect, with only the memory burning in his blood, a memory that had endured the three hundred odd years to Calvary Hill felt, as he put on his dragon costume, a sense of entering a sacred mask that invested him with an ancestral authority to uphold before the people of this Hill, this tribe marooned so far from the homeland that never was their home, the warriorhood that had not died in them, their humanness that was determined not by their possession of things. He had a desire, a mission, to let them see their beauty, to uphold the unending rebellion they waged, huddled here on this stone and dirt hill hanging over the city like the open claws on a dragon's hand, threatening destruction if they were not recognized as human beings.

But this Carnival, putting on his costume now at dawn, Aldrick had a feeling of being the last one, the last symbol of rebellion and threat to confront Port of Spain.* Fisheye was under orders not to misbehave, Philo had given up on his own calypsos of rebellion to sing now about the Axe Man. Once upon a time the entire Carnival was expressions of rebellion. Once there were stickfighters who assembled each year to keep alive in battles between themselves the practice of a warriorhood born in them; and there were devils, black men who blackened themselves further with black grease to make of their very blackness a menace, a threat. They moved along the streets with horns on their heads and tridents in hand. They threatened to press their blackened selves against the well dressed spectators unless they were given money. And there were the jab jabs, men in jester costumes, their caps and shoes filled with tinkling bells, cracking long whips in the streets, with which they lashed each other with full force, proclaiming in this display that they could receive the hardest blow without flinching at its coming, without feeling what, at its landing, must have been burning pain. Suddenly they were all gone, outlawed from the city or just died, gone, and he felt alone. The dragon alone was left to carry the message. He felt that now, alone, with even Philo and Fisheye gone, it was too great to carry. It would be lost now among the clowns, among the fancy robbers and the fantasy presentations that were steadily entering Carnival; drowned amidst the satin and silks and the beads and feathers and rhinestones. But bothering him even more than this was the thought that maybe he didn't believe in the dragon any more.

Earl Lovelace

*The capital of the Caribbean island of Trinidad

Commentary

1 Content: This extract from "The Dragon Can't Dance" describes what the Carnival is like in Trinidad from the view of Aldrick Prospect who wears a dragon costume on Carnival Monday. He not only describes the present-day carnival but also what it used to be like in times when the Carnival was a symbol of rebellion. It is very detailed, listing all the different types of people who participate in it.

2 Structure: The passage is divided into two paragraphs. The first describes the boys who sweep the streets and connects them to earlier rituals carried out in African countries where their ancestors came from. These rituals assert their warriorhood and humanity and now their rebellion against their loss of status as independent people.

The second paragraph mourns the loss of the old customs of carnival, when men put black grease on themselves and intimidated the crowd into giving them money, and when others whipped themselves to show that they could endure pain. Some of these men had died and some of the practices had been made illegal. Aldrick feels that he is the only one left to carry on the traditions and that maybe even he does not believe in it any more.

The sentence structure is unusual. There are only two sentences in the first paragraph. The length suggests the long trailing procession of the carnival; like the sentence it goes on and on. In the second paragraph the sentences are shorter as here they are listing the elements that have disappeared and each one needs to be highlighted.

3 Point of view: The scene is described from Aldrick Prospect's point of view. As he is a participant, not a spectator we are given an insider's view. He describes what he sees, and what he has seen as well as letting us know his feelings about the Carnival. His descriptions are both celebratory and nostalgic. He makes the reader also feel sad at the loss of the rituals that connected the present to the past – not just the past in Trinidad but also the past in Africa.

4 Diction: The two most remarkable features of this passage are listing and detailed description. Not only do we learn about the little boys but also that they wear old dresses, carry brooms, blow whistles and beat drums. This enables the reader to visualize very clearly what is happening. The repetition can be found in the grammatical features seen in the use of words ending in "ing": "blowing", "beating", "sweeping", "heralding", "clearing", "announcing", "affirming". This gives the feeling of constant movement that is happening now. In the second paragraph, the two sentences beginning with "Once" and two others with "They moved" and "They threatened" emphasize the past events which Aldrick misses. Also the repetition of "alone" near the end isolates Aldrick from the rest of the Carnival. The language used contains many adjectives which help add visual and aural details to the scene but the overwhelming effect is of being battered with images, in the same way as one would feel if one was actually present at the Carnival.

5 Theme: What central point is Lovelace trying to convey? He does not just wish to describe the Carnival and allow readers to enjoy and appreciate its magnificence. He wants to convey to us its importance in the lives of the people who are descended from African slaves; to show that they were a warlike, but lively people bursting with energy and rebellion; to show how pagan rituals were still echoed in the activities of the Carnival participants; but above all to indicate how sad it is that the Carnival has become tamed. It now has "fancy robbers" not real ones, and "fantasy presentations", which are empty parodies of what was once real, vibrant and meaningful.

Now write your own commentary on the following extract from *Chocolat* by Joanne Harris. Some guiding questions have been given, which are like those given to Standard Level candidates in the Paper 1 exam.

The passage is followed by a student response. After you have finished writing your own response, read the student's commentary carefully, together with the examiner's comments that follow.

● What do you learn about the narrator and the young girl?

● In what ways does the writer appeal to the senses?

● How is the atmosphere conveyed?

● What is the importance of the carnival?

February 11, Shrove Tuesday

We came on the wind of the carnival. A warm wind for February, laden with the hot greasy scents of frying pancakes and sausages and powdery-sweet waffles cooked on the hotplate right there by the roadside, with the confetti sleeting down collars and cuffs and rolling in the gutters like an idiot antidote to winter. There is a febrile excitement in the crowds which line the narrow street, necks craning to catch sight of the crêpe-covered *char* with its trailing ribbons and paper rosettes. Anouk watches, eyes wide, a yellow balloon in one hand and a toy trumpet in the other, from between a shopping-basket and a sad brown dog. We have seen carnivals before, she and I; a procession of two hundred and fifty of the decorated *chars* in Paris last Mardi Gras, a hundred and eighty in New York, two dozen marching bands in Vienna, clowns on stilts, the *Grosses Têtes* with their lolling papier-mâché heads, drum majorettes with batons spinning and sparkling. But at six the world retains a special lustre. A wooden cart, hastily decorated with gilt and crêpe and scenes from fairy tales. A dragon's head on a shield, Rapunzel in a woollen wig, a mermaid with a Cellophane tail, a gingerbread house all icing and gilded cardboard, a witch in the doorway, waggling extravagant green fingernails at a group of silent children... At six it is possible to perceive subtleties which a year later are already out of reach. Behind the papier-mâché, the icing, the plastic, she can still see the real witch, the real magic. She looks up at me, her eyes, which are the blue-green of the Earth seen from a great height, shining.

'Are we staying? Are we staying here?' I have to remind her to speak French. 'But are we? Are we?' She clings to my sleeve. Her hair is a candyfloss tangle in the wind.

I consider. It's as good a place as any. Lansquenet-sous-Tannes, two hundred souls at most, no more than a blip on the fast road between Toulouse and Bordeaux. Blink once and it's gone. One main street, a double row of dun-coloured half-timbered houses leaning secretively together, a few laterals running parallel like the tines of a bent fork. A church, aggressively whitewashed, in a square of little shops. Farms scattered across the watchful land. Orchards, vineyards, strips of earth enclosed and regimented according to the strict apartheid of country farming: here apples, there kiwis, melons, endives beneath their black plastic shells, vines looking blighted and dead in the thin February sun but awaiting triumphant resurrection by March... Behind that, the Tannes, small tributary of the Garonne, fingers its way across the marshy pasture. And the people? They look much like all others we have known; a little pale perhaps in the unaccustomed sunlight, a little drab. Headscarves and berets are the colour of the hair beneath, brown, black or grey. Faces are lined like last summer's apples, eyes pushed into wrinkled flesh like marbles into old dough. A few children, flying colours of red and lime-green and yellow, seem like a different race. As the *char* advances ponderously along the street behind the old tractor which pulls it, a large woman with a square, unhappy face clutches a tartan coat about her shoulders and shouts something in the half-comprehensible local dialect; on the wagon a squat Santa Claus, out-of-season amongst the fairies and sirens and goblins, hurls sweets at the crowd with barely restrained aggression. An elderly small-featured man, wearing a felt hat rather than the round beret more common to the region, picks up the sad brown dog from between my legs with a look of polite apology. I see his thin graceful fingers moving in the dog's fur; the dog whines; the master's expression becomes complex with love, concern, guilt. No-one looks at us. We might as well be invisible; our clothing marks us as strangers, transients. They are polite, so polite; no-one stares at us. The woman, her long silk scarf fluttering at her throat; the child in yellow wellingtons and sky-blue mac. Their colouring marks them. Their clothes are exotic, their faces – are they too pale or too dark? – their hair marks them other, foreign, indefinably strange. The people of Lansquenet have learned the art of observation without eye contact. I feel their gaze like a breath on the nape of my neck, strangely without hostility but cold nevertheless. We are a curiosity to them, a part of the carnival, a whiff of the outlands. I feel their eyes upon us as I turn to buy a *galette* from the vendor. The paper is hot and greasy, the dark wheat pancake crispy at the edges but thick and good in the centre. I break off a piece and give it to Anouk, wiping melted butter from her chin. The vendor is a plump, balding man with thick glasses, his face slick with the steam from the hot plate. He winks at her. With the other eye he takes in every detail, knowing there will be questions later.

'On holiday, Madame?' Village etiquette allows him to ask; behind his tradesman's indifference I see a real hunger. Knowledge is currency here; with Agen and Montauban so close, tourists are a rarity.

'For a while.'

'From Paris, then?' It must be our clothes. In this garish land the people are drab. Colour is a luxury; it wears badly. The bright blossoms of the roadside are weeds, invasive, useless.

'No, no, not Paris.'

The *char* is almost at the end of the street. A small band – two fifes, two trumpets, a trombone and a side drum – follows it, playing a thin unidentifiable march. A dozen children scamper in its wake, picking up the unclaimed sweets. Some are in costume; I see Little Red Riding Hood and a shaggy person who might be the wolf squabbling companionably over possession of a handful of streamers.

A black figure brings up the rear. At first I take him for a part of the parade – the Plague Doctor, maybe – but as he approaches I recognize the old-fashioned soutane of the country priest. He is in his thirties, though from a distance his rigid stance makes him seem older. He turns towards me, and I see that he too is a stranger, with the high cheekbones and pale eyes of the North and long pianist's fingers resting on the silver cross which hangs from his neck. Perhaps this is what gives him the right to stare at me, this alienness; but I see no welcome in his cold, light eyes. Only the measuring, feline look of one who is uncertain of his territory. I smile at him; he looks away, startled, beckons the two children towards him. A gesture indicates the litter which now lines the road; reluctantly the pair begin to clear it, scooping up spent streamers and sweet-wrappers in their arms and into a nearby bin. I catch the priest staring at me again as I turn away, a look which in another man might have been of appraisal.

There is no police station at Lansquenet-sous-Tannes, therefore no crime. I try to be like Anouk, to see beneath the disguise to the truth, but for now everything is blurred.

'Are we staying? Are we, *Maman*?' she tugs at my arm, insistently. "I like it, I like it here. Are we staying?'

I catch her up into my arms and kiss the top of her head. She smells of smoke and frying pancakes and warm bedclothes on a winter's morning.

Why not? It's as good a place as any.

'Yes, of course,' I tell her, my mouth in her hair. "Of course we are.'

Not quite a lie. This time it may even be true.

Joanne Harris

Commentary

This extract, the opening of the novel *Chocolat* by Joanne Harris, tells how a mother and her young daughter, Anouk, arrive at a small rural town in France with a possibility that they might settle there.

In the town, Lansquenet-sous-Tannes, a carnival is taking place when the two arrive and it is interesting to see how some of the participants are described: "Rapunzel in a woollen wig, a mermaid with a Cellophane tail, a gingerbread house all icing and gilded cardboard…" These descriptions are a mixture of the fantasy and the ordinary, even the carnival float is merely "A wooden cart, hastily decorated with gilt and crêpe". They suggest a strong degree of transparency – perhaps a symbolic indication of what is to come further in the novel. Indeed, the carnival itself appears to be a weak attempt to impress when compared, by Anouk's mother, with other carnivals both she and her daughter have seen: "a procession of two hundred and fifty of the decorated chars in Paris, a hundred and eighty in New York, two dozen marching bands in Vienna, clowns on stilts… drum majorettes with batons spinning and sparkling".

The small town itself is described in a less than favourable light. Some of the descriptions used, such as "a blip on the fast road…", "Blink once and it's gone", rather than implying a quaint rural village appear to emphasize its insignificance. There is also the suggestion of something secretive and sinister about the place. For example, the "main street" is described as a "double row of dun-coloured houses leaning secretively together" and this is surrounded by "Farms scattered across the watchful land". These descriptions are not only effective in portraying an isolated, tight-knit community but they also arouse a degree of curiosity in the reader as to why they might be considering settling there.

There is obviously a strong religious presence within the community, although from the way both the church and the priest are described, this appears to be a restricting, dominating force in the town. For instance, the church is described as being "aggressively whitewashed" and the priest himself, "a black figure" who could be mistaken for a character from the procession, "the Plague Doctor", appears to be not only a spoilsport but a dominant figure as he insists on making the playing children clean up carnival debris by just "a gesture". Later in the piece the priest is described in greater detail, which reinforces the idea that he is a dominant but unpleasant figure, with a "rigid stance", "pale eyes", and his "high cheekbones" suggest a degree of superciliousness, especially with his "fingers resting on the silver cross which hangs from his neck". In addition, his look is described as "measuring", which implies that he is somewhat judgemental in an unchristian way.

The adult residents are also described in an unfavourable manner, which contrasts markedly with the descriptions of the children of the village. For instance, the adults are described as being somewhat insignificant: "They look much like all others we have known" and are "a little drab", and the colours used to describe their clothing and hair project "dull" images: "brown, black or grey". Their faces are described as being "lined like last summer's apples", which gives a wizened impression and suggests a sense of lifelessness which is also emphasized by their eyes being "pushed into wrinkled flesh like marbles into old dough". The descriptions of the children, on the other hand, contain life and vivid colour: "A few children, flying colours of red and lime-green and yellow". Indeed, they "seem like a different race" and they appear to inject a degree of energy in a town where even the dog is described as "sad".

The residents seem to be quite insular and suspicious of "outsiders", and although the mother in the story tells us that "No-one looks at us" she gets the impression that "We are a curiosity to them". This seems not to be surprising considering how the mother's appearance contrasts with that of the villagers, "her long silk scarf fluttering at her throat..." and with her "exotic" clothes. However, it is interesting to see that the daughter's appearance, although she too wears "exotic" clothes, is as colourful as the other children in the village. Perhaps this is an indication that she will be accepted more easily than her mother. Indeed the daughter appears to like the place: "I like it, I like it here. Are we staying?"

There is an indication that the unwelcoming feel of the place might alter later in the novel, in the line "Vines looking blighted and dead... but awaiting triumphant resurrection by March". This appears to be supported by the sense of magic induced into the writing in the opening line "We came on the wind of the carnival", the phrase being reminiscent of "the winds of change". Indeed, it would appear that magic is needed if the rural town with its "strips of earth enclosed and regimented according to the strict apartheid of country farming" is to become anything else but "drab".

Harris uses language to great effect in this piece. The many sensory inclusions, such as "hot greasy scents of frying pancakes and sausages and powdery-sweet waffles", helps us to share the carnival experience, and the simile used to describe the confetti falling is particularly effective here: "like an idiot antidote to winter", especially considering the weak attempts made to dress up for the carnival. She also uses an abundance of adjectives in her similes, which add a richness to the narrative. For instance, she describes her daughter's eyes as being "the blue-green of the Earth seen from a great height, shining". Harris also includes a degree of ambiguity which succeeds in arousing curiosity. For example, at the beginning of this piece, the line "but at six the world retains a special lustre' seems a little out of place and its meaning is unclear. A little later, the line "At six it is possible to perceive subtleties which a year later are already out of reach" also appears to be unconnected, but the meaning will become clear later in the novel. In addition, some of the words are written in French and their meaning can be tentatively assumed. For example, the word "char" is unusual but, through the reading of the passage, can be assumed to be a carnival float. This technique adds a degree of interest and colour to the extract.

The piece is definitely an effective opening. The ambiguity created and the curiosity raised by Harris makes the reader want to find out whether such a well-travelled pair who have visited Paris, New York, and Vienna will stay in such a "drab" town – indeed, why they have ever gone there in the first place.

Examiner's comments

This is a perceptive commentary in which the student pays attention to:

- the vocabulary used by the writer
- the effects of imagery in conveying the atmosphere of the town
- the sensual descriptions
- the contrast between the visitors and the people of Lansquenet-sous-Tannes
- the narrative technique which makes one wonder what will happen next
- the hints of conflict – perhaps between the narrator and the priest.

Activity

You have now read two accounts of carnivals. With a partner make a comparison between the descriptions. List the similarities and differences. Do you think one description is more effective than the other?

The next passage is a short story. Read it carefully and write a commentary on it.

A Gift

I am gifting you an experience, were your parting words. You ultimate egoist. Whichever way I look at it that sentiment yields no other meaning. And who are you to make this gift? In an artist, such detachment might be forgivable, an act of generosity even.

My experience is of my own making, thank you, my own perceptions. You can impinge on it only if I will it. Will-power, that limp uninflatable thing that hung around my self-hood, making its presence felt as the missing dimension... from the moment that you first entered that crowded room and diminished everyone by your appearance, your personality clearing a path for you. I thought at the time that I noticed you because you had such a fiery commitment to your politics, because you spoke not fluently but in a rush as if you had a pact with silence, and because somewhere deep down stirred an old memory about the romance of a French accent.

The party, to which we owed varying degrees of loyalty, threw us together with a determinism that left no room for dialectics. You had entered my consciousness like air in my lungs – essential but unfelt, gossamer like, even insubstantial. And when you entered again and again, my skin thinned, like a balloon overblown, replete at the point of rupture.

We found ourselves together on the same Saturday morning outside the same supermarkets to get guilty shoppers to help prolong the miners' strike, distributing leaflets outside the same tube stations to advertise a public meeting, holding either pole of the same banner at the same demo and rolling cigarettes for each other with fingers turned to stone by the February chill. Was it surprising then that we took turns to buy each other drinks when the day's work was done? And that the emptiness of our stomachs drove us to the fish and chips shop or a sit down Chinese meal, depending on the fullness of our pockets.

I enjoyed your presence like an old and deep friendship with an affection which made up in intensity what it lacked in maturity. And from the political, we moved to the personal. You asked, if your nose was prominent? (Do you really care?) How can I tell? Each time my eyes travel to make a judgement, they are drawn upwards by the power of your eyes and consumed, slithering sideways and away to a confused middle distance. I could not trust myself on personal grounds. And yet I could not keep politics forever on the agenda. So I tried to counter that by asking, do you like the shape of my shoulders? From where you stand, you have to look at them so often that you must have an opinion about them. Your eyes admitted the frivolity of your concern with your nose. Touché. I won that round. Now maybe we can go back into the safer waters of the impersonal.

But again, you chose to discuss the political implications of one person's passion for another. Studying the hairs on the barman's fingers, I talked passionately about the destructiveness of passion and how I would personally choose to steer clear. And you agreed and said you were good at that too. We stopped talking. We were interrupted by the silence that fell around us.

Your loyalty to silence proved to be your preservation. Being uncomfortable with silence, became my undoing – my self-respect lay in shreds like a soaring kite grounded. Only on Sunday afternoons, when you liked to unwind by playing Scrabble, would words that choked on your vocal chords come pouring out of your fingers. On one such afternoon, my words shrank on the Scrabble board as they grew and rioted inside my mouth, tumbling from my lips in cascades of incoherence. You must've known then. I wiped my mouth. Perhaps I had overcreamed my lips to preserve them from winter's chafing touch and words ungripped slipped out or was it, pure and simple, nervousness? I talked about how you filled the room, about my mother, about my past loves and the present vacuum as I placed the word "cue' on the board.

Your turn, I said. You continued to shuffle and clink the letters, the noise crowding out your silence. It was the first time your silence felt cold, a refusal to communicate. This was the first time I had been first to make a declaration of love. My incoherence and your silence. My head began to ache with an infinite series of interpretations. My heart throbbed through my eyes and my vision came in diastolic and systolic rhythms.

Through your lowered lids, your eyes bounced off the board and reduced my confusion to cinders. Then, grasping their victory for one split second, they smiled warmly. I don't believe in possession, she said, but basically I am a one-woman woman. I met her last summer. But don't let this put you off, she said, allowing her fingers to stray off the board and locking my hand in hers, "loving women is much better for your sanity than loving men'. She swept all my crumbling certainties aside in that fleeting touch which brought heaven vibrating through my blood. I had never been attracted to other women and never would be again. Never, she mocked, tchtu, tchtu, that's a dangerous word. I felt myself drowning and tried to hold on to some understanding of the situation. I was trying to elicit the essence of it, I was writing about it even as I was living it – men, power, etiquette, women, warmth, arrogance, honesty, conquest, bitterness, humiliation – words asserting their identity, refusing to come together and make sense.

Our game of Scrabble was to remain unfinished. It had become too internalised, I reflected as the letters rattled back into the box – some face up, some hiding their mystery. Misreading the signals – a painful self-reckoning.

Loss and desire merged when I kissed her goodbye, my lips scrambling across her face unfocused. This experience is yours for the keeping, she said. Make good use of it.

Rahila Gupta

Part 2 Literary genres

Objectives

- To find ways of gaining an overview when studying a novel, short story, and other prose writing
- To discuss approaches to analysing aspects of novels, short stories, and other prose writing
- To develop your own responses to novels, short stories, and other prose writing
- To prepare for studying a set text

As part of your IB Diploma you will study a number of novels and possibly some short stories and other prose writings, depending on the choices that have been made for your English A1 syllabus. You will also encounter prose passages as part of your work for the unseen commentary. This chapter will indicate some of the ways you can approach a variety of prose works.

"Yes – oh dear yes – the novel tells a story."
E.M. Forster

Studying novels

What is a novel?

The Penguin *Dictionary of Literary Terms* defines the novel as: "a form of story or prose narrative containing characters, action and incident, and, perhaps a plot". It goes on to say that it is almost impossible to have no plot as readers will always try to impose one on a work, even when none was intended. The subject matter can cover practically anything and, despite the cry that regularly goes out that the novel is dead, it has shown enormous durability. The works can vary in length and complexity from novellas of barely 100 pages to weighty tomes of 1000 or more pages which contain a huge cast of characters and several interweaving, complex plots.

The word "novel" is derived from the Italian "novella" meaning "a tale or piece of news", and the word was applied to the novel when it was a new form of writing. The earliest novels were written in Japan in the ninth century but it was not until the sixteenth century that works which could be securely identified as novels were written in Europe. Apart from John Bunyan's *Pilgrim's Progress* (1678), which is an allegorical novel, the first novel written in English is usually thought to be *Robinson Crusoe* (1719) by Daniel Defoe.

Jane Austen (1775–1817), one of England's greatest novelists, commented that a novel could be a "work in which the greatest powers of the mind are displayed, in which the most thorough knowledge of human nature, the happiest delineation of its varieties, the liveliest effusions of wit and humour, are conveyed to the world in the best chosen language". These expectations would not be fulfilled in many works that are today confidently proclaimed as novels. A distinction is made between popular fiction and literary novels, though it is not always easy to draw a clear line between them. You will normally be studying literary novels, though it is often salutary to compare a popular novel with a more literary one.

Aspects of the novel

At the outset, studying a novel which is a set text can appear a daunting prospect. If yours happens to be Dickens's *Great Expectations* or Hardy's *Tess of the D'Urbervilles*, it may be the longest book you have ever read. It is likely to contain much more sophisticated vocabulary than most of the books you will have come across. If it is a twentieth-century novel which does not follow familiar conventions, or a novel from an earlier period, where both syntax and vocabulary are complex, you may struggle to master it. But if the novel is good enough you will find that the struggle is worthwhile. Once you have read the first few chapters and become used to the writer's style, you will often find that you become interested in both the characters and the plot. Most great novels are also a "great read". In this chapter we will look at the elements of a novel which you need to identify and understand.

It is very easy, when studying a novel, to get into the habit of talking about the situations and the characters as if they were real. After all, one of the writer's intentions is to create convincing characters which the reader can believe in and have sympathy for; and a writer deliberately sets out to create a world that you can enter through your imagination. However, when studying literature it is important to see the novel as an artificial "text" constructed as a created work of art, which you can look at objectively in an analytical way. Characters are devices which the author uses and manipulates to create a particular effect. They only exist within the novel, so statements such as: "If only Jane had not fallen in love with a worthless layabout, how much happier her life would have been" are not relevant. The author decided who Jane would fall in love with, and that is all that should be considered.

There are several aspects that can be found in most novels. Most examination questions will focus on one or more of these.

Story and plot: E.M. Forster, in his work *Aspects of the Novel*, defines a story as "a narrative of events arranged in their time sequence", while a plot is "also a narrative of events, the emphasis falling on causality". The example he gives is: "'The king died and then the queen died', is a story. 'The king died and then the queen died of grief', is a plot."

When studying a novel it is necessary to look at the structure and time sequencing. Is it organized chronologically? Are there flashbacks? Is the development linear or circular? How does the structure affect the reader's response?

Point of view: Who tells the story – the writer, a persona outside the story or one of the characters? Is it told from a first- or third-person perspective? Why does the writer choose to write from this viewpoint? Would *Jane Eyre* be a different book if it had been written from Rochester's viewpoint? Jean Rhys rewrote the story from the viewpoint of Bertha Mason, Rochester's mad wife, in a work called *The Wide Sargasso Sea*. You have only to read the first few pages of both novels to realize how different they are.

Sometimes a novel can be written in the third person but remain centred on one character only. What advantages do you think this could have?

Characters: Does the writer concentrate on a few characters or is there a cast of hundreds? Are the characters presented in great detail so that you know more about them than you would about almost anyone you know in real life? Or are they caricatures who always appear the same? Do the characters change throughout the novel, and if so what factors make them change? How are they presented? Negatively, positively or objectively? Do you empathize with them, and if so why? Does the author openly tell you what they are like or do you have to work that out by interpreting their speech and actions?

Theme: What is the author trying to tell us about people or life? What messages are conveyed through the characters and the events? Themes often concern the relationships between characters and the societies they live in.

Setting: Where is the novel set? Is the setting a vital element, or would it not matter where the work was set?

Language: A book can be written in a formal or informal style. The language can be poetic, complex or very basic. It can be designed to make you laugh or weep or make you angry or sentimental. You need to consider the effects caused by the choice of one writing style instead of another.

Where to begin

With a long text like a novel, we need to learn to find our way around it easily so we can locate important passages or incidents fairly quickly. Here are some strategies that will help you gain familiarity.

- If you have time, read through the novel fairly quickly before you begin to study it. This gives you the opportunity to gain an overall impression of the novel and to read it, as it was intended, just for enjoyment. It will also help you to see how different aspects of the novel fit together when you study it in depth. The first read will give you an idea of how the plot is constructed and of the type of novel it is.
- Do some research, especially if the novel is set, or was written, in the past. Knowing something about the historical and social background and about the conventions and beliefs of the time can help you to understand things which may otherwise seem strange and incomprehensible.
- Keep a separate journal or "log" for each text. Try dividing a notebook into sections, one for each important aspect of the novel. As you study the novel, jot down your observations about each aspect in the appropriate places. Include important quotations and page references. Then when you need the information for a discussion or for writing an essay, it will be easy to locate.

> *"My way is to begin at the beginning."*
> Lord Byron

- If you have your own copy of the text it is helpful to annotate it by marking significant passages so that it is easy to find them again.

We will now look closely at passages from three very different novels:

- *Waiting for the Barbarians* by J.M. Coetzee
- *Hard Times* by Charles Dickens
- *The Handmaid's Tale* by Margaret Atwood.

Activity

Using reference books or other sources, find out what you can about the authors and their eras.

Opening pages

Usually we can learn a lot about a novel by looking closely at the opening pages where the writer wants to engage our attention so we will read on. It is quite likely that some of the important characters or themes will be presented right at the start. It is also likely that we will learn about the setting.

Activity

Here are the opening pages of the three novels listed above. Read them carefully.

Working with a partner, look at all three openings and discuss them in detail, making notes on the following points.

- Who is the narrator and what, if anything, do you find out about him or her? Is the narrative written in the third or the first person?

- Apart from the narrator, what other characters are introduced? What do you learn about them?

- What is the setting? How is it described? What is the atmosphere like?

- Does the story begin at the beginning? The middle? Or near the end?

- Is the writing simple, complex, straightforward or mysterious? Look at imagery, diction and syntax.

- Do you have any idea what the novel is going to be about? Are there any hints as to what the theme will be?

- Do you want to read further? If so, how has the author aroused your curiosity?

Waiting for the Barbarians

Chapter 1

I have never seen anything like it: two little discs of glass suspended in front of his eyes in loops of wire. Is he blind? I could understand it if he wanted to hide blind eyes. But he is not blind. The discs are dark, they look opaque from the outside, but he can see through them. He tells me they are a new invention. 'They protect one's eyes against the glare of the sun,' he says. 'You would find them useful out here in the desert. They save one from squinting all the time. One has

---

fewer headaches. Look.' He touches the corners of his eyes lightly. 'No wrinkles.' He replaces the glasses. It is true. He has the skin of a younger man. 'At home everyone wears them.'

We sit in the best room of the inn with a flask between us and a bowl of nuts. We do not discuss the reason for his being here. He is here under the emergency powers, that is enough. Instead we talk about hunting. He tells me about the last great drive he rode in, when thousands of deer, pigs, bears were slain, so many that a mountain of carcases had to be left to rot ('Which was a pity'). I tell him about the great flocks of geese and ducks that descend on the lake every year in their migrations and about native ways of trapping them. I suggest that I take him out fishing by night in a native boat. 'That is an experience not to be missed,' I say; 'the fishermen carry flaming torches and beat drums over the water to drive the fish towards the nets they have laid.' He nods. He tells me about a visit he paid elsewhere on the frontier where people eat certain snakes as a delicacy, and about a huge antelope he shot.

He picks his way uncertainly among the strange furniture but does not remove the dark glasses. He retires early. He is quartered here at the inn because this is the best accommodation the town provides. I have impressed it on the staff that he is an important visitor. 'Colonel Joll is from the Third Bureau,' I tell them. 'The Third Bureau is the most important division of the Civil Guard nowadays.' That is what we hear, anyhow, in gossip that reaches us long out of date from the capital. The proprietor nods, the maids duck their heads. 'We must make a good impression on him.'

J.M. Coetzee

Hard Times

Chapter 1

The One Thing Needful

'Now what I want is, Facts. Teach these boys and girls nothing but Facts. Facts alone are wanted in life. Plant nothing else, and root out everything else. You can only form the minds of reasoning animals upon Facts: nothing else will ever be of any service to them. This is the principle on which I bring up these children. Stick to Facts, sir.'

The scene was a plain, bare, monotonous vault of a schoolroom, and the speaker's square forefinger emphasized his observations by underscoring every sentence with a line on the schoolmaster's sleeve. The emphasis was helped by the speaker's square wall of a forehead, which had his eyebrows for its base, while his eyes found commodious cellarage in two dark caves, overshadowed by the wall. The emphasis was helped by the speaker's mouth, which was wide, thin, and hard set. The emphasis was helped by the speaker's voice, which was inflexible, dry, and dictatorial. The emphasis was helped by the speaker's hair, which bristled on the skirts of his bald head, a plantation of firs to keep the wind from its shining surface, all covered with knobs, like the crust of a plum pie, as if the head had scarcely warehouse-room for the hard facts stored inside. The speaker's obstinate carriage, square coat, square legs, square shoulders – nay, his very neckcloth, trained to take him by the throat with an unaccommodating grasp, like a stubborn fact, as it was – all helped the emphasis.

'In this life, we want nothing but Facts, sir; nothing but Facts!'

The speaker, and the schoolmaster, and the third grown person present, all backed a little, and swept with their eyes the inclined plane of little vessels then and there arranged in order, ready to have imperial gallons of facts poured into them until they were full to the brim.

Charles Dickens

Activity

You could discuss with a partner, or in a group, whether you agree with the speaker's view that education concerns only facts.

The Handmaid's Tale

Chapter 1

We slept in what had once been the gymnasium. The floor was of varnished wood, with stripes and circles painted on it, for the games that were formerly played there; the hoops for the basketball nets were still in place, though the nets were gone. A balcony ran around the room, for the spectators, and I thought I could smell, faintly like an after image, the pungent scent of sweat, shot through with the sweet taste of chewing gum and perfume from the watching girls, felt-skirted as I knew from pictures, later in mini-skirts, then pants, then in one earring, spiky green-streaked hair. Dances would have been held there; the music lingered, a palimpsest of unheard sound, style upon style, an undercurrent of drums, a forlorn wail, garlands made of tissue-paper flowers, cardboard devils, a revolving ball of mirrors, powdering the dancers with a snow of light.

There was old sex in the room and loneliness, and expectation, of something without a shape or name. I remember that yearning, for something that was always about to happen and was never the same as the hands that were on us there and then, in the small of the back, or out back, in the parking lot, or in the television room with the sound turned down and only the pictures flickering over lifting flesh.

We yearned for the future. How did we learn it, that talent for insatiability? It was in the air; and it was still in the air, an afterthought, as we tried to sleep, in the army cots that had been set up in rows, with spaces between so we could not talk. We had flannelette sheets, like children's, and army-issue blankets, old ones that still said U.S. We folded our clothes neatly and laid them on the stools at the ends of the beds. The lights were turned down but not out. Aunt Sara and Aunt Elizabeth patrolled; they had electric cattle prods slung on thongs from their leather belts.

Margaret Atwood

Narrative viewpoint

You will have noticed that in *Waiting for the Barbarians* and in *The Handmaid's Tale* the authors have chosen to use the first-person narrative, while Dickens uses the third person. There are advantages and disadvantages to each.

Writing in the first person, the author takes on the role of one of the characters (or of more than one character) and tells the story from "the inside". This can strengthen the illusion that the novel is "real", by making the reader feel involved and able to empathize with the character. However, this also limits the reader's perspective to this one character's perceptions: you only see other characters through his or her eyes. You can only know about events the narrator does not witness when they are reported by another character. Sometimes this is done through letters. As you have only this narrator's words to go on, you need to ask how far you can trust him or her. He or she might be biased, deluded or blind to the true significance of events, or may be deliberately deceiving the reader. This can add interest to the story.

In the third person the writer can be the omniscient narrator who knows everything and can show the reader what is happening anywhere in the story. Again, of course, the writer can deliberately keep information from the reader in order to provide surprises or keep the reader guessing. Sometimes the narrative is written in the third person but remains with one character so that the reader knows all that character does or thinks. Dickens will often move from omniscient narrator to over-the-shoulder of one character and later move to over-the-shoulder of another one. This enables the reader to know what the characters are thinking and feeling as well as what they are doing.

The narrator in *The Handmaid's Tale* is Offred, a woman living in a future society in which people are restricted to very narrow, specific roles. Offred is a handmaid whose role is to "breed" to ensure the survival of her nation. Other women are responsible for domestic chores while some carry out the formal duties of a wife. Much of her narrative is in the style known as "stream of consciousness", where the writer aims to convey an impression of the multitudinous thoughts and feelings that pass through the mind. We have to gradually piece together our impressions of Offred and our knowledge of her circumstances from the seemingly haphazard way she reveals her thoughts, feelings, and attitudes to other characters.

> **Activity**
>
> Here, early in the novel, Offred describes her living quarters and ponders her situation. Read the extract and make notes on everything you learn about her as a person and as a storyteller. How does Atwood try to engage your sympathy for Offred? Is she successful?

The Handmaid's Tale

Chapter 2

A window, two white curtains. Under the window, a window seat with a little cushion. When the window is partly open – it only opens partly – the air can come in and make the curtains move. I can sit in the chair, or on the window seat, hands folded, and watch this. Sunlight comes in through the window too, and falls on the floor, which is made of wood, in narrow strips, highly polished. I can smell the polish. There's a rug on the floor, oval, of braided rags. This is the kind of touch they like: folk art, archaic, made by women, in their spare time, from things that have no further use. A return to traditional values. Waste not want not. I am not being wasted. Why do I want?

A bed. Single, mattress medium-hard, covered with a flocked white spread. Nothing takes place in the bed but sleep; or no sleep. I try not to think too much. Like other things now, thought must be rationed. There's a lot that doesn't bear thinking about. Thinking can hurt your chances, and I intend to last. I know why there is no glass, in front of the water-colour picture of blue irises, and why the window only opens partly and why the glass in it is shatterproof. It isn't running away they're afraid of. We wouldn't get far. It's those other escapes, the ones you can open in yourself, given a cutting edge.

So. Apart from these details, this could be a college guest room, for the less distinguished visitors; or a room in a rooming-house, of former times, for ladies in reduced circumstances. That is what we are now. The circumstances have been reduced; for those of us who still have circumstances.

But a chair, sunlight, flowers: these are not to be dismissed. I am alive, I live, I breathe, I put my hand out, unfolded, into the sunlight. Where I am is not a prison but a privilege, as Aunt Lydia said, who was in love with either/or.

Margaret Atwood

Probably you will have noted the following points:

- She notices and describes her surroundings in detail and specific details spark off trains of thought about her life in an interior monologue. She pays attention to these things because there is plenty of time to do so and nothing else to occupy her.

- She separates herself from the people in authority by referring rather anonymously to "they" and "them".

- She feels limited by her life and is not satisfied living by the maxims she has been taught. She longs for something more – "Waste not want not. I am not being wasted. Why do I want?"

- She is determined to survive, even if this means denying the truth sometimes – "Thinking can hurt your chances, and I intend to last."

- She is optimistic enough to recognize what is good in her surroundings – "But a chair, sunlight, flowers: these are not to be dismissed."

- Her language is usually simple and she does not use specific imagery. Many of her sentences are short or incomplete. Their confiding quality suggests we already know what she is talking about and who "they" are, when in fact we know nothing about the regime in which she lives. She likes to play with words and double meanings in a wry, humorous way – "The circumstances have been reduced; for those of us who still have circumstances."

Third-person narrative offers different possibilities. The author or narrator adopts a position which is "godlike", or becomes a "fly on the wall" reporting everything to us, the readers. This omniscient (all-knowing) narrator, from a vantage point outside the action, can relate events which may occur in different places, at different times, or even simultaneously. Often we are told how different characters feel so we see things from more than one perspective.

Sometimes the author might tell the story dispassionately, without commenting or judging. Usually, however, authors make their presence felt through obvious authorial intrusion. This happens when the writer openly enters into the narrative to express an opinion or comment on a situation. It might be more subtle: for example, a character may be described in language we recognize as being sarcastic, "tongue-in-cheek" or ironic, making it clear that the author is critical or mocking; or positive or negative judgements may simply be revealed by the writer's choice of vocabulary.

We can easily detect Dickens's attitude to the speaker (Mr Gradgrind) at the beginning of *Hard Times*. He describes his forehead as a "square wall" and his voice as "inflexible, dry, and dictatorial". All these words imply that the speaker is rigid and unlikely to consider any other point of view. Think of beating your head against a brick wall and the implication of "square wall" comes through. A few pages later, when he is concluding his description of Mr Gradgrind's house, which significantly is called "Stone Lodge", Dickens's sarcasm is clear: "Iron clamps and girders... mechanical lifts... everything that the heart could wish for". Shortly after, Dickens intrudes with his own voice to express his doubts: "Everything? Well, I suppose so."

This question of the writer's stance towards characters or situation can be quite complex. Even in third-person narrative, things can often be filtered through the perception of one particular character. George Orwell does this in *1984* where the whole story is seen only from Winston Smith's viewpoint. Readers tend to trust Winston and accept his views, though we do learn that he can be disastrously mistaken, especially when it comes to judging other people's characters.

Characters

Much of the interest of a novel depends on the characters whose lives we enter and whose worlds we learn about. We usually regard them as people who share characteristics with ourselves and with others we know. The closer they are to us, the more successful we tend to think they are and the more we either empathize with or disapprove of them. However, we do need to remember that they only live in the pages of a book and so it is rarely useful to speculate about their past or future lives. It is, however, important to look at how the author presents them.

Sometimes authors describe characters directly, so that from the moment they are introduced you know what they look like and what kind of person they are. Dickens does this with Mr Bounderby. Other writers let you gradually come to see what the character is like. You have to work harder at interpreting actions, dialogue and thoughts, before you really understand them.

As you read through a novel it is a good idea to note in your journal key passages and quotations that reveal what important characters are like.

> *"You can tell a lot about a fellow's character by his way of eating jelly-beans."*
> Ronald Reagan

Characters are revealed to us in various ways:

- **Description:** The author provides us with an introductory pen-portrait and later gives us information directly when they change or we need to know more about them.

- **Dialogue:** We can often learn a lot about characters from how they speak or how others talk to them or about them.

- **Thoughts and feelings:** The "inner life" of a character can be revealed directly, especially in a first-person narrative.

- **Actions and reactions:** How characters behave in certain situations influences our view of them.

- **Imagery and symbolism:** Many authors use imagery to help establish characters. For example, a character may always be presented with fire somewhere in the scene, thus implying that their character may be warm, passionate or even angry, depending on the nature of the fire. In *Jane Eyre*, Rochester is often associated with fire in some form, as is his mad wife, Bertha Mason. Sometimes colours are used, or symbols such as a lion or a bird can indicate bravery or freedom.

Part 2 Literary genres

Activity

Here are some character sketches from *The Handmaid's Tale, Hard Times* and *Waiting for the Barbarians*. Working alone or in small groups, make notes about the following aspects.

- Is the information about appearances, behaviour or about characters' inner thoughts and feelings?

- Look at language, syntax, structure and imagery to indicate how the characters are presented.

- Is it possible to detect what the author's attitude is to the character? Sometimes names are a clue.

1   The Commander has on his black uniform, in which he looks like a museum guard. A semi-retired man, genial but wary, killing time. But only at first glance. After that he looks like a midwestern bank president, with his straight neatly brushed silver hair, his sober posture, shoulders a little stooped. And after that there is his moustache, silver also, and after that his chin, which really you can't miss. When you get down as far as the chin he looks like a vodka ad, in a glossy magazine, of times gone by.

His manner is mild, his hands large, with thick fingers and acquisitive thumbs, his blue eyes uncommunicative, falsely innocuous.

Margaret Atwood

2   [Mr Bounderby] was a rich man: a banker, merchant, manufacturer, and what not. A big, loud man, with a stare and a metallic laugh. A man made out of a coarse material, which seemed to have been stretched to make so much of him. A man with a great puffed head and forehead, swelled veins in his temples, and such a strained skin to his face that it seemed to hold his eyes open and lift his eyebrows up. A man with a pervading appearance on

him of being inflated like a balloon, and ready to start. A man who could never sufficiently vaunt himself a self-made man. A man who was always proclaiming, through that brassy speaking-trumpet of a voice of his, his old ignorance and his old poverty. A man who was the Bully of humility.

Charles Dickens

3   She kneels in the shade of the barracks wall a few yards from the gate, muffled in a coat too large for her, a fur cap open before her on the ground. She has the straight black eyebrows, the glossy black hair of the barbarians. What is a barbarian woman doing in town begging? There are no more than a few pennies in the cap.

Twice more during the day I pass her. Each time she gives me a strange regard, staring straight ahead of her until I am near, then very slowly turning her head away from me. The second time I drop a coin into the cap. 'It is cold and late to be outdoors,' I say. She nods. The sun is setting behind a strip of black cloud; the wind from the north already carries a hint of snow; the square is empty; I pass on.

The next day she is not there. I speak to the gatekeeper: 'There was a woman sitting over there all of yesterday, begging. Where does she come from?' The woman is blind, he replies. She is one of the barbarians the Colonel brought in. She was left behind.

A few days later I see her crossing the square, walking slowly and awkwardly with two sticks, the sheepskin coat trailing behind her in the dust. I give orders; she is brought to my rooms, where she stands before me propped on her sticks. 'Take off your cap,' I say. The soldier who has brought her in lifts off the cap. It is the same girl, the same black hair cut in a fringe across the forehead, the same broad mouth, the black eyes that look through and past me.

'They tell me you are blind.'

'I can see,' she says.

J.M. Coetzee

Development of character

Obviously one brief introduction to a character is not enough to tell us all we need to know. Some characters remain the same all the way through the novel while others change, often after some kind of traumatic event. In *Hard Times*, both Mr Gradgrind and his daughter Louisa change, but Mr Bounderby remains the same. Some people think that if a character does not change, he or she is not believable, but that is not necessarily so. We all know people who remain the same wherever they are. Characters can be caricatures (where they are exaggerated), stereotypes (where they behave according to a set pattern, for example always being strong and brave) or rounded (where we see various aspects of them so they may behave differently at different times or even appear to be inconsistent). Dickens is well known for his caricatures but this does not necessarily mean that his characters are unbelievable. The effect is often comic but they can enable Dickens to make serious points about a person or situation. Caricatures are often recognizable by their names (such as Bounderby) which indicate their characters, while more sympathetic characters are given ordinary names, such as Louisa.

Activity

In *Hard Times* we first meet Louisa when her father is appalled to have discovered that she and her brother Tom have been spying on the local circus, which Gradgrind regards with disgust. Study the passage closely and make notes on how Dickens reveals her character through her relationships with her father and her brother.

Hard Times

Chapter 3

'In the name of wonder, idleness, and folly!' said Mr Gradgrind, leading each away by the hand; 'what do you do here?'

'Wanted to see what it was like,' returned Louisa shortly.

'What it was like?'

'Yes, father.'

There was an air of jaded sullenness in them both, and particularly in the girl: yet, struggling through the dissatisfaction of her face, there was a light with nothing to rest upon, a fire with nothing to burn, a starved imagination keeping life in itself somehow, which brightened its expression. Not with the brightness natural to cheerful youth, but with uncertain, eager, doubtful flashes, which had something painful in them, analogous to the changes on a blind face groping its way.

She was a child now, of fifteen or sixteen; but at no distant day would seem to become a woman all at once. Her father thought so as he looked at her. She was pretty. Would have been self-willed (he thought in his eminently practical way), but for her bringing-up.

'Thomas, though I have the fact before me, I find it difficult to believe that you, with your education and resources, should have brought your sister to a scene like this.'

'I brought him, father,' said Louisa quickly. 'I asked him to come.'

'I am sorry to hear it. I am very sorry indeed to hear it. It makes Thomas no better, and it makes you worse, Louisa.'

She looked at her father again, but no tear fell down her cheek.

'You! Thomas and you, to whom the circle of the sciences is open; Thomas and you, who may be said to be replete with facts; Thomas and you, who have been trained to mathematical exactness; Thomas and you here!' cried Mr Gradgrind.

'In this degraded position! I am amazed.'

'I was tired. I have been tired a long time,' said Louisa.

'Tired? Of what?' asked the astonished father.

'I don't know of what – of everything I think.'

'Say not another word,' returned Mr Gradgrind. 'You are childish. I will hear no more.'

Charles Dickens

Louisa is presented in opposition to her father and his world of facts, but as yet the conflict is mostly within her, as her thwarted imagination fights for life. The images of light and an inward "fire with nothing to burn" will recur frequently. She often gazes at the smoking chimneys of the Coketown factories which she knows must contain flames which have been suppressed, like her own imagination, and which burst out when darkness falls.

The dialogue reveals just how little capacity Gradgrind has for understanding his children. Notice the contrast between Louisa's short answers and her father's pompous, wordy style. She seems sullen, but also honest and very self-controlled. Her dry education has rendered her incapable of tears or emotional displays. His final accusation, that she is childish, is ironic. She has never been allowed to be a child. The passage does mark the first time Gradgrind is surprised by his children. Later it will be Louisa's tragedy which jolts him out of his complacency.

Activity

Choose a character from a novel you are studying and select three or four passages from different parts of the novel which show "key" moments for the character.

Analyse these passages carefully, paying close attention to how language and imagery are used to present the character at different times.

Using examples from the chosen passages, write a short essay about the development of the chosen character.

The setting

The imaginary "world" of a novel, into which the reader is invited, is often more than simply "the place where the story happens". The physical environment may be important in itself or as a backdrop to the action but can also be used to reflect the characters and their experiences. It can also be symbolic of the ideas the writer wishes to convey. However, the "world" of a novel will also portray a society with its own culture, politics, and values. Characters may exist comfortably in their worlds, but often, the whole thrust of a novel depends on the central character being a misfit, or being in conflict with some aspect of their "society", whether this is their family, their social class, a religious group, or a state.

The world of a novel can be as small as a household or as large as a nation. In *Hard Times*, the world Dickens creates is that of a northern English industrial town. Like some of his characters, the setting is a caricature. It is based on a real town, but has exaggerated features. His intention of protesting against the deadening effect of Utilitarianism is never clearer than when he introduces us to Coketown. He presents us with an environment where the physical surroundings reflect the social conditions. Read his description and then consider it through the activity which follows.

Hard Times

Chapter 5. The Key-note

Coketown, to which Messrs Bounderby and Gradgrind now walked, was a triumph of fact; it had no greater taint of fancy in it than Mrs Gradgrind herself. Let us strike the key-note, Coketown, before pursuing our tune.

It was a town of red brick, or of brick that would have been red if the smoke and ashes had allowed it; but, as matters stood it was a town of unnatural red and black like the painted face of a savage. It was a town of machinery and tall chimneys, out of which interminable serpents of smoke trailed themselves for ever and ever, and never got uncoiled. It had a black canal in it, and a river that ran purple with ill-smelling dye, and vast piles of building full of windows where there was a rattling and a trembling all day long, and where the piston of the steam-engine worked monotonously up and down, like the head of an elephant in a state of melancholy madness. It contained several large streets all very like one another, and many small streets still more like one another, inhabited by people equally like one another, who all went in and out at the same hours, with the same sound upon the same pavements, to do the same work, and to whom every day was the same as yesterday and tomorrow, and every year the counterpart of the last and the next.

Charles Dickens

The world of *The Handmaid's Tale* is very different. It is set in the future, in an imaginary state in America, the Republic of Gilead. Fearful about declining population, due to man-made environmental disaster, a dictatorship has assigned roles to all people, but particularly to women. Wives are idealized, non-sexual beings. They wear virginal blue, while those women capable of the all-important child-bearing are assigned to men as handmaids or breeders, dressed in red. This symbolizes blood, sex, and childbirth. It marks them out as "fallen women". Gilead is a state ruled by terror, in which it is highly dangerous to ask questions or to assert one's individuality in any way. We do not even discover the narrator's real name: she is merely the handmaid "Of-Fred".

None of this is made clear to us at the start of the novel. Only gradually, as we read Offred's stream-of-consciousness narrative, do we piece together enough information to understand what is going

Activity

How does Dickens present Coketown? Make notes on his use of:

- simile and metaphor
- colour and the senses
- the rhythm of the passage
- sentence construction.

on. It is quite a way into the text before we are provided with some "historical background". Here, Offred, waiting to assist at a birth, remembers some of the teaching she received at the Red Centre, where the handmaids are trained.

Part 2 Literary genres

The Handmaid's Tale

Chapter 19

The siren goes on and on. That used to be the sound of death, for ambulances or fires. Possibly it will be the sound of death today also. We will soon know. What will Ofwarren give birth to? A baby, as we all hope? Or something else, an Unbaby, with a pinhead or a snout like a dog's, or two bodies, or a hole in its heart or no arms, or webbed hands and feet? There's no telling. They could tell once, with machines, but that is now outlawed. What would be the point of knowing, anyway? You can't have them taken out; whatever it is must be carried to term. The chances are one in four, we learned that at the Centre. The air got too full, once, of chemicals, rays, radiation, the water swarmed with toxic molecules, all of that takes years to clean up, and meanwhile they creep into your body, camp out in your fatty cells. Who knows, your very flesh may be polluted, dirty as an oily beach, sure death to shore birds and unborn babies. Maybe a vulture would die of eating you. Maybe you light up in the dark, like an old-fashioned watch. Death-watch. That's a kind of beetle, it buries carrion.

I can't think of myself, my body, sometimes, without seeing the skeleton: how I must appear to an electron. A cradle of life, made of bones; and within, hazards, warped proteins, bad crystals, jagged as glass. Women took medicines, pills, men sprayed trees, cows ate grass, all that souped-up piss flowed into the rivers. Not to mention the exploding atomic power plants, along the San Andreas fault, nobody's fault, during the earthquakes, and the mutant strain of syphilis no mould could touch. Some did it themselves, had themselves tied shut with catgut or scarred with chemicals. How could they, said Aunt Lydia, O how could they have done such a thing? Jezebels! Scorning God's gifts! Wringing her hands.

It's a risk you're taking, said Aunt Lydia, but you are the shock troops, you will march out in advance, into dangerous territory. The greater the risk, the greater the glory. She clasped her hands, radiant with our phony courage. We looked down at the tops of our desks. To go through all that and give birth to a shredder: it wasn't a fine thought. We didn't know exactly what would happen to the babies that didn't get passed, that were declared Unbabies. But we knew they were put somewhere, quickly, away.

Margaret Atwood

Activity

Read the passage carefully and discuss in a small group the answers to the following points:

- What has happened in Gilead in the past?
- What are conditions like in Gilead now?
- What are the laws and customs in Gilead in respect to pregnancy and childbirth, and how does Atwood present this information?
- How are the women treated to make sure that they do what they are told?

In *Hard Times* and *The Handmaid's Tale*, the settings are very
important. In both cases the writers have presented aspects they
dislike about their own societies in an exaggerated form. This
enables them to draw attention to these and to protest in an indirect
way while being thought-provoking and entertaining. While
Dickens demonstrates in Coketown the terrible results of extreme
Utilitarianism, Margaret Atwood writes as a feminist, concerned
about the environment and about women being defined and limited
by their traditional roles. Both writers create worlds where people
are reduced to particular functions. However, both have a hopeful
note in that the "human spirit" is not entirely crushed despite such
repressive regimes. "Fancy" and imagination may be buried and
distorted in *Hard Times*, but they do not die completely. Similarly,
through the very telling of her story we know that Offred is far
more than just her "viable ovaries".

Activity

Study and make notes on the setting of the novel you are studying.

- What sort of world is it? How large or small, open or restrictive?
- What are its rules, values, beliefs and customs?
- Locate passages where the author describes the physical surroundings.
- Do the characters represent their society or rebel against it?

Language and style

Unless you are studying linguistics, you do not usually discuss a
writer's use of language in isolation from the content. What is being
looked at now is how effectively language is used to create worlds,
or present characters, situations, and ideas. You will have noticed
that as you have looked at each of these aspects of the novel,
you have always examined the writer's language and style at the
same time.

The next writer, David Malouf, presents a different world. Here
is how he describes the unexpected arrival of an unknown man
at a farm in Australia. Notice how Malouf presents the children's
reactions to this sudden appearance.

Remembering Babylon

Chapter 1

One day in the middle of the nineteenth century, when settlement in Queensland
had advanced little more than halfway up the coast, three children were playing
at the edge of a paddock when they saw something extraordinary. They were two
little girls in patched gingham and a boy, their cousin, in short pants and braces,
all three barefooted farm children not easily scared.

They had little opportunity for play but had been engaged for the past hour in a
game of the boy's devising: the paddock, all clay-packed stones and ant trails, was
a forest in Russia – they were hunters on the track of wolves.

The boy had elaborated this scrap of make-believe out of a story in the fourth grade Reader; he was lost in it. Cold air burned his nostrils, snow squeaked underfoot; the gun he carried, a good sized stick, hung heavy on his arm. But the girls, especially Janet, who was older than he was and half a head taller, were bored. They had no experience of snow, and wolves did not interest them. They complained and dawdled and he had to exert all his gift for fantasy, his will too, which was stubborn, to keep them in the game.

They had a blue kelpie with them. He bounced along with his tongue lolling, excited by the boy's solemn concentration but puzzled too that he could get no sense of what they were after: the idea of wolf had not been transmitted to him. He danced around the little party, sometimes in front, sometimes to the side, sniffing close to the earth, raising his moist eyes in hope of instruction, and every now and then, since he was young and easily distracted, bounding away after the clippered insects that sprang up as they approached, or a grasshopper that rose with a ponderous whirring and rolled sideways from his jaws. Then suddenly he did get the scent. With a yelp of pure delight he shot off in the direction of their boundary fence, and the children, all three, turned away to see what he had found.

Lachlan Beattie felt the snow melt at his feet. He heard a faint far-off rushing, like wind rolling down a tunnel, and it took him a moment to understand that it was coming from inside him.

In the intense heat that made everything you looked at warp and glare, a fragment of ti-tree swamp, some bit of the land over there that was forbidden to them, had detached itself from the band of grey that made up the far side of the swamp, and in a shape more like a watery, heat-struck mirage than a thing of substance, elongated and airily indistinct, was bowling, leaping, flying towards them.

A black! That was the boy's first thought. We're being raided by blacks. After so many false alarms it had come.

The two little girls stood spellbound. They had given a gasp, one sharp intake of breath, then forgotten to breathe out. The boy too was struck but had begun to recover. Though he was very pale about the mouth, he did what his manhood required him to do. Holding fast to the stick, he stepped resolutely in front.

But it wasn't a raid, there was just one of them; and the thing, as far as he could make it out through the sweat in his eyes and its flamelike flickering, was not even, maybe, human. The stick-like legs, all knobbed at the joints, suggested a wounded waterbird, a brolga, or a human that in the manner of the tales they told one another, all spells and curses, had been *changed* into a bird, but only halfway, and now, neither one thing nor the other, was hopping and flapping towards them out of a world over there, beyond the no-man's-land of the swamp, that was the abode of everything savage and fearsome, and since it lay so far beyond experience, not just their own but their parents' too, of nightmare rumours, superstitions and all that belonged to Absolute Dark.

A bit of blue rag was at its middle from which sleeves hung down. They swung and signalled. But the sticks of arms above its head were also signalling, or beating off flies, or licks of invisible flame. Ah, that was it. It was a scarecrow that had somehow caught the spark of life, got down from its pole, and now, in a raggedy, rough-headed way, was stumbling about over the blazing earth, its leathery face scorched black, but with hair, they saw, as it bore down upon them, as sun-bleached and pale-straw coloured as their own.

Whatever it was, it was the boy's intention to confront it. Very sturdy and purposeful, two paces in front of his cousins, though it might have been a hundred yards in the tremendous isolation he felt, and with a belief in the power of the weapon he held that he knew was impossible and might not endure, he pushed the stick into his shoulder and took his stance.

The creature, almost upon them now and with Flash at its heels, came to a halt, gave a kind of squawk, and leaping up onto the top rail of the fence, hung there, its arms outflung as if prepared for flight. Then the ragged mouth gapped.

'Do not shoot,' it shouted. 'I am a B-b-british object.'

David Malouf

Activity

Discuss with a partner the answers to the following questions:

● From whose point of view is the story told?

● Why does Malouf always refer to the stranger as "it"?

● What have you learned about the characters of the children so far? How does Malouf present the characters?

● Many sentences are quite long, though broken up by commas. What is the effect of this technique?

● Look at the bird imagery and the references to flames and comment on their effects.

● Where do you think the novel is set? What words give you clues to the setting?

There are interesting similarities and contrasts between the meeting of the children and the stranger they think is an aborigine in the extract above, and the meeting of Robinson Crusoe with Man Friday.

Activity

Read this brief passage from Daniel Defoe's *Robinson Crusoe* and list both similarities and differences.

Robinson Crusoe has rescued a man from two others who were chasing him; one runs away and the other is shot by Crusoe, who has been waiting for a chance to get himself both a companion and a servant.

> ## Robinson Crusoe
>
> I beckoned him again to come to me, and gave him all the signs of encouragement that I could think of, and he came nearer and nearer, kneeling down every ten or twelve steps in token of acknowledgement for my saving his life. I smiled at him and looked pleasantly, and beckoned to him to come still nearer; at length he came close to me, and then he kneeled down again, kissed the ground, and laid his head upon the ground, and taking me by the foot, set my foot upon his head; this it seems was in token of swearing to be my slave for ever; I took him up, and made much of him, and encouraged him all I could.
>
> *Daniel Defoe*

Here are some points you may have noted:

- Both Malouf and Defoe present a white male who is intimidating a black man, even though later both are condescendingly gracious. Malouf writes in the third person but mainly from Lachlan Beattie's point of view. *Robinson Crusoe* is written in the first person so we only have Crusoe's point of view.

- Both Crusoe and Lachlan have a weapon, one a gun and the other a strong stick. These weapons are used to maintain their dominance of the situation.

- Both writers use long sentences, broken up by commas and semi-colons, but Malouf also uses many short sentences, especially when he is describing actions and feelings.

- Defoe's language is more formal; you may think it is old-fashioned. Malouf, by not mentioning who or what the creature is until the end of the section, keeps up suspense. Malouf uses more metaphorical language compared with Defoe's very spare prose. This has the effect of making the atmosphere in *Remembering Babylon* more frightening.

The short story

What is a short story?

In one sense the answer to this question is so obvious it hardly seems worth a thought. A "short story" is clearly a story that is short! Perhaps we need to rephrase the question and pose the one that the critic, Norman Friedman, once asked – "What makes a short story?"

Friedman answers this question by identifying two key features.

- A short story may be short because the material itself is narrow in its range or area of interest.
- A short story may be short because although the material has a potentially broad range, the writer cuts it down to focus on one aspect and maximize the story's impact or artistic effect.

Edgar Alan Poe is often credited with being the inventor of the short story but there were others, for example Sir Walter Scott and Nathaniel Hawthorne, who had already written short stories.

Many short stories do focus on a single incident, moment in time, or experience, but that is not always the case. Not all short stories are deliberately crafted by the writer as a vehicle for a single effect. In fact some stories gain their impact because they do not operate on a "single effect" structure. Indeed, in some instances the "single effect" type of story can appear contrived.

For many years the short story suffered a good deal of critical neglect and it has been regarded as an academically lightweight genre when measured against the much "weightier" and prestigious novel form. However, in more recent years there has been a recognition that the short story is something more than the novel's poor relation, and a number of different short story authors are included on the English A1 Prescribed Book List. If you are studying a short story text there are a number of areas that you will need to have some ideas about. Examination questions can be phrased in different ways, but it is likely that they will focus on one or more of the following.

- **Plot and structure:** You will need a clear understanding of what happens in the story, the basic ideas that it deals with, how it is structured, and how the various elements of it relate to one another. How the story is structured can be of particular interest if it varies from a straightforward chronological pattern.
- **Narrative viewpoint:** The question of who is telling the story is a very important one and raises questions about why the writer has chosen to present the story from this particular viewpoint and what effect this has on the reader's response.
- **Characters:** Questions often focus on one or more of the characters in the story or stories and may ask you to examine how the writer presents or develops the characters or to explore how they relate to each other.
- **Language and style:** You will also need a clear idea about the distinctive qualities of the writer's style. This will involve focusing closely on the specific detail and the writer's choice of language (the way this is used, and the effects that it creates).

Plot and structure

One thing you may have noted about short stories is that very often the story focuses on a single character in a single situation rather than tracing a range of characters through a variety of situations and phases of development, as novels often do. However, often the focus for the story is a moment at which one or more of the central characters undergo some important experience which represents a significant moment in their personal development. It can be seen as a "moment of truth" (or "epiphany", as James Joyce calls it) in which something or some perception, large or small, changes within the character. In some stories, though, this "moment of truth" is evident only to the reader and not the character(s).

Not all stories reach a climax. Some stories may offer a kind of "snapshot" of a period of time or an experience – a "day in the life of..." story might be like this. Other stories end inconclusively, leaving the reader with feelings of uncertainty, while yet other stories do not seem to have a discernible plot at all. This may lead the reader to feel completely baffled by what he or she has

Activity

Think carefully about the short stories that you have read. Make a list of the differences between these stories and novels that you have studied (apart from the obvious point to do with length!).

Activity

Think carefully about a short story that you have read and make a list of the features that you think are important in terms of making this story "work".

read and subsequently to tentatively explore a range of possible interpretations in his or her head. This might, of course, have been exactly the response that the writer intended.

This diagram presents one way of thinking about how alternative plots and structures of short stories work:

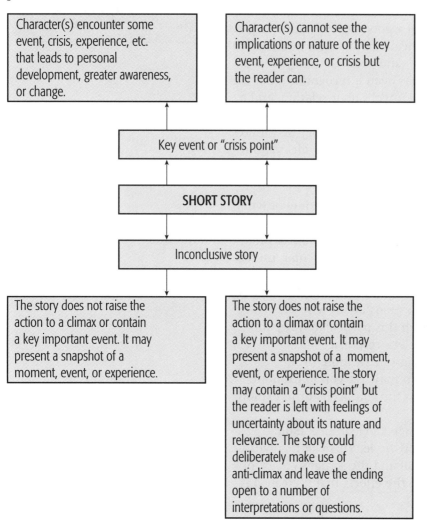

Beginnings

Our very earliest experiences of stories (the fairy tales we listen to, and then the vast range of stories that we hear, read, and see presented in film and television) teach us one thing – stories have a "beginning", a "middle", and an "end". Strictly speaking, however, that is not entirely true. There are stories that do not seem to have a beginning or an ending in the conventional sense. The vast majority of stories, however, do have some kind of beginning or opening section; a middle, where the characters, situation, and ideas are developed; and an ending that draws the story to a conclusion.

Here are some possible ways in which stories can open:

- the writer launches straight into the narrative
- the writer sets the scene by giving explicit background information
- the writer informs the reader using suggestion or implication rather than direct description
- the opening is direct and holds the reader's attention, perhaps capturing attention with a word or short phrase.

Activity

Read the following openings to three short stories. Then, on your own or in a small group, consider your responses to them. Think carefully about how each writer approaches the opening to the story and try to identify the techniques used. Make a list of what you learn about setting and characters from each opening.

1 Indian Camp

At the lake shore there was another rowboat drawn up. The two Indians stood waiting.

Nick and his father got in the stern of the boat and the Indians shoved it off and one of them got in to row. Uncle George sat in the stern of the camp rowboat. The young Indian shoved the camp boat off and got in to row Uncle George.

The two boats started off in the dark. Nick heard the oar-locks of the other boat quite a way ahead of them in the mist. The Indians rowed with quick choppy strokes. Nick lay back with his father's arm around him. It was cold on the water. The Indian who was rowing them was working very hard, but the other boat moved further ahead in the mist all the time.

'Where are we going, Dad?' Nick asked.

'Over to the Indian camp. There is an old Indian lady very sick.'

'Oh,' said Nick.

Across the bay they found the other boat beached. Uncle George was smoking a cigar in the dark. The young Indian pulled the boat way up on the beach. Uncle George gave both the Indians cigars.

They walked up from the beach through a meadow that was soaking wet with dew, following the young Indian who carried a lantern. Then they went into the woods and followed a trail that led to the logging road that ran back into the hills. It was much lighter on the logging road as the timber was cut away on both sides. The young Indian stopped and blew out his lantern and they all walked on along the road.

Ernest Hemingway

2 In the Park

Vivi's mother was taking her to the Park to see the flowers and the birds in cages. Vivi had been to the Park before; but it was a long way, right to the other side of town in the bus, and it was a long time ago. She remembered the bus but not the birds; she remembered the lake and that she mustn't get her feet wet.

Her mother put Vivi's new white sandals on for her, and tied a blue bow in her hair. Outside the summer was shrilling like the noise in the sawmill down the road; the day was so hot that Gran lay in her cane long-chair and fanned herself.

'Why you should want to take the poor child to the Park on a day like this I can't see. That long hot ride in the bus! But you get these notions in your head, and I know very well it wouldn't matter what I said, I can't talk you out of it.'

'There'll be a cool breeze out there; and she needs a bit of a change now and then. Our room isn't all that nice for a kid on a day like this, with the sun coming straight in like it does; and you don't like her messing up the rest of the house. I'd rather not see her playing in the street with those little Gardners all the time.'

Her mother called Gran sometimes Gran and sometimes Mrs Coleman. Today she had been calling her Mrs Coleman; it was something about the breakfast washing-up. Those days their voices made Vivi wince when they spoke to one another, as though she had tasted one of the little green mangoes that plumped on the grass in the garden.

Gran closed up her mouth, the little brown hairs round it bright with tiny drops from the heat; then she looked at Vivi and smiled, and tapped her leg with the fan. 'Anyway, Vivi, you look nice in those new shoes. Here's three pence for lollies.'

Vivi sat on the bus seat, her legs uncomfortable. She couldn't lean back unless her legs stuck straight out in front of her, and if she sat on the edge of the seat, she fell off when the bus turned a corner. She tried it, and slid sideways and clutched at her mother. Her mother brushed her hand away with an annoyed sound.

'Stop it, can't you? You'll crush my dress.'

Judith Wright

3 Studies in the Park

– Turn it off, turn it off, turn it off! First he listens to the news in Hindi. Directly after, in English. Broom – brroom – brrroom – the voice of doom roars. Next, in Tamil. Then in Punjabi. In Gujarati. What next, my god, what next? Turn it off before I smash it onto his head, fling it out of the window, do nothing of the sort of course, nothing of the sort.

– And my mother. She cuts and fries, cuts and fries. All day I hear her chopping and slicing and the pan of oil hissing. What all does she find to fry and feed us on, for God's sake? Eggplants, potatoes, spinach, shoe soles, newspapers, finally she'll slice me and feed me to my brothers and sisters. Ah, now she's turned on the tap. It's roaring and pouring, pouring and roaring into a bucket without a bottom.

– The bell rings. Voices clash, clatter and break. The tin-and-bottle man? The neighbours? The police? The Help-the-Blind man? Thieves and burglars? All of them, all of them, ten or twenty or a hundred of them, marching up the stairs, hammering at the door, breaking in and climbing over me – ten, twenty or a hundred of them.

– Then, worst of all, the milk arrives. In the tallest glass in the house. 'Suno, drink your milk. Good for you, Suno. You need it. Now, before the exams. Must have it, Suno. Drink.' The voice wheedles its way into my ear like a worm. I shudder.

The table tips over. The milk runs. The tumbler clangs on the floor. 'Suno, Suno, how will you do your exams?'

– That is precisely what I ask myself. All very well to give me a room – Uncle's been pushed off on a pilgrimage to Hardwar to clear a room for me – and to bring me milk and say, 'Study, Suno, study for your exam.' What about the uproar around me? These people don't know the meaning of the word Quiet. When my mother fills buckets, sloshes the kitchen floor, fries and sizzles things in the pan, she thinks she is being Quiet. The children have never even heard the word, it amazes and puzzles them.

Anita Desai

Obviously the opening of a story is vital. If readers' attention is not captured immediately the story contains no initial impact to encourage them to continue, or to draw them into the story. However, bearing in mind the constraints of length under which the short story operates, it is also important that the opening compresses information that might have taken some time to explain, so that the reader quickly and effectively gains a picture of what is going on. Short story writers are often faced with this question of how much they can omit while at the same time creating the impression of completeness and continuity in their stories.

Going back to the extracts you have just discussed, you may have noticed that Extract 2 launches straight into the narrative. Vivi, the young child, is going to go to the park with her mother. From the dialogue one realizes that there is more to this visit to the park than the mother is admitting.

In Extract 3, on the other hand, we are told very little directly and we have to work out for ourselves what is happening. This approach can provide us with just as much information as straightforward description. In this instance we learn about the sounds in the house. They are obviously important as they are described at great length. The story is told in the first person by someone called Suno, who is supposed to be studying for exams.

In contrast, Extract 1 begins with a straightforward narrative style in which Hemingway simply describes the action without any use of imagery or overly descriptive language. After the narrative opening he then introduces direct speech, which both gives further information and allows the reader to begin to get a sense of the characters involved.

Activity

In both Extract 1 and Extract 2, the story is told from the point of view of a young child. Why do you think the authors chose to do this? Can you rely on the children's observations? The third extract is told from the viewpoint of a young man. What is the effect of beginning with a description of loud noises?

From the beginnings of these short stories, do you get any idea about what may happen next?

Narrative line

Short stories, like other fictional works, order the events that they describe in a particular way. Through the story-line the writer can create a wide range of effects, such as creating suspense, raising the action to a climax point, resolving problems, leading (or misleading) the reader in particular ways, and leaving endings open to a variety of interpretations.

Very often the narrative structure is a straightforward progression with one event following another and moving towards a conclusion where all is resolved. However, sometimes a writer might play around with this structure to create particular effects. Here are some points to consider when you focus on the narrative structure of a story.

- Make a list of the key events in the story.
- Look at the order in which these events are related by the writer.
- Look at the time structure of the story – is it told in simple chronological order or is there use of flashbacks or cutting back and forth?
- Are there any details or pieces of information that the writer omits or particular points that are emphasized?

Short stories often have a moment in the plot upon which the whole structure of the story turns and which affects the outcome of the tale. Sometimes this trigger can be a quite trivial incident or experience but it signifies a moment of revelation to the central character. *Hassan's Tower* by Margaret Drabble contains just such a moment for newly married Kenneth on honeymoon with his wife, Chloë, in Morocco. They are a wealthy couple who appear to have everything that they could want in life but Kenneth is disappointed in his new wife and disillusioned with life in general. He is ill-at-ease in Morocco and goes about in constant fear of being robbed. Against his will his wife takes him to Hassan's Tower and wants to climb to the top to see the view. Reluctantly, he accompanies her and during the course of this seemingly unremarkable excursion he experiences a revelation that changes his whole outlook on his wife, his life, and those around him.

> Hassan's Tower
>
> The more he looked, the more he realized that the people on top of the tower were in their own way as astonishing a view as the more evidently panoramic vistas. The whole of the top of the tower was thick and covered with people: small children were crawling about, mothers were feeding their babies, young men were holding the hands of girls and indeed the hands of other young men, boys were sitting on the very edge and dangling their feet into space, and old women who would need a day to recover from the climb were lying back in the sun, for all the world as though they were grandmothers on a beach in England... and as he gazed he felt growing within him a sense of extraordinary familiarity that was in its own way a kind of illumination... He saw these people, quite suddenly, for what they were, for people, for nothing other than people; their clothes filled out with bodies, their faces took on expression, their relations became dazzlingly

clear, as though the details of their strangeness had dropped away, as though the terms of common humanity (always before credited in principle, but never before perceived) had become facts before his eyes.

Margaret Drabble

Endings

There are as many ways of ending a story as there are of beginning it, and the ending is clearly a very important element in the overall structure of a piece. In a short story it is often the ending which reveals meaning, points up a significant theme, or provides a resolution. This kind of ending should leave the reader contented and satisfied with a sense of a tale completed.

Equally, a writer might create an "open" ending, one that does not provide answers, an ending that might leave the reader pondering on what it all means, or unsettle him or her. This could be, of course, just the kind of response that the writer is aiming for.

The ending with "a sting in the tail", a technique often used by Maupassant, has become very popular in recent years, being popularized through the short stories of Roald Dahl. It is worth noting, however, that with this kind of ending we need to distinguish between a device which is merely used as a kind of "trick", and a twist at the end which causes us to see something fundamental in the story as a whole. When you read the ending of *A Message From the Pig-man* by John Wain on pages 84–86, decide what type of ending it has.

Activity

Choose three short stories that you know and reread them. Discuss the ending of each with a partner, thinking about the following questions.

● Does the story have what you would recognize as a definite ending?

● How does the ending relate to the rest of the story?

● Does the writer draw attention to any specific points in the ending?

● How would you have ended the story?

Narrative viewpoint

You will already be familiar with the term "viewpoint" in the sense of "from whose point of view we see the events of the story". However, it is perhaps worth bearing in mind that this term can encompass two related but distinct ideas. In addressing viewpoint we need to consider the question of who is actually seeing the events described and who is narrating them. They may be one and the same or quite separate, and the question is rather more complex than it might first appear. For example, in Judith Wright's story *In the Park*, there is a third-person narrator, but everything is seen through the eyes of Vivi.

It may be possible to approach the question of viewpoint by distinguishing between narrators who seem to address the reader directly from within the story (**internal narrators**) and those who have a more "external" narrative viewpoint. As a reader you need to be aware of how writers use viewpoint within their stories, be sensitive to subtle shifts and aware of the effects this can have on the narrative and your perception of it.

Activity

Look at the following three extracts and identify the narrative viewpoints used in each.

---

1 A Tradition of Eighteen Hundred and Four, Christmas 1882

The widely discussed possibility of an invasion of England through a Channel Tunnel has more than once recalled old Solomon Selby's story to my mind.

The occasion on which I numbered myself among his audience was one evening when he was sitting in the yawning chimney-corner of the inn-kitchen, with some others who had gathered there, and I entered for shelter from the rain. Withdrawing the stem of his pipe from the dental notch in which it habitually rested, he leaned back in the recess behind him and smiled into the fire. The smile was neither mirthful nor sad, not precisely humorous nor altogether thoughtful. We who knew him recognized it in a moment: it was his narrative smile. Breaking off our few desultory remarks we drew up closer, and he thus began:

'My father, as you mid know, was a shepherd all his life, and lived out by the Cove four miles yonder, where I was born and lived likewise, till I moved here shortly afore I was married...'

Thomas Hardy

---

2 Her First Ball

Exactly when the ball began Leila would have found it hard to say. Perhaps her first real partner was the cab. It did not matter that she shared the cab with the Sheridan girls and their brother. She sat back in her own little corner of it, and the bolster on which her hand rested felt like the sleeve of an unknown young man's suit; and away they bowled, past waltzing lamp-posts and houses and fences and trees.

'Have you really never been to a ball before, Leila? But, my child, how too weird – ' cried the Sheridan girls.

'Our nearest neighbour was fifteen miles,' said Leila softly, gently opening and shutting her fan.

Oh, dear, how hard it was to be indifferent like the others! She tried not to smile too much; she tried not to care. But every single thing was so new and exciting... Meg's tuberoses, Jose's long loop of amber, Laura's little dark head, pushing above her white fur like a flower through snow. She would remember for ever. It even gave her a pang to see her cousin Laurie throw away the wisps of tissue paper he pulled from the fastenings of his new gloves. She would like to have kept those wisps as a keepsake, as a remembrance. Laurie leaned forward and put his hand on Laura's knee.

Katherine Mansfield

3 Missy

'There you are, Mrs Ebbs, hold the cup steady. Can you manage, dear? Whoops! That's it. Now sit up properly, you'll slip down in the bed again, sit up against your pillows. That's it. Don't nod off again, will you? Now careful, Mrs Ebbs, I haven't got all day, dear. That's it, good girl.'

The voice came roaring towards her. The face was bland as suet. The face was a cow's face. An ox.

'Ox-face,' she said, but she had not said it.

She tipped the spoon and sucked in her soup, little bits of carrot and soft lentil sieving through the spaces between her teeth.

'All right now, Mrs Ebbs?'

Ox-face.

'I'm not deaf.'

Was she?

Susan Hill

In Extract 1 you will notice immediately that Hardy is writing in the first person here. He is recounting a particular evening when he heard a story told by Solomon Selby. You obviously cannot tell from this brief opening but the bulk of the story is told as if by Solomon Selby as reported by Hardy. Think about what effect this has on the narrative. Notice too how Hardy economically sets the context of the story through implication – the title providing the date, 1804, which coupled with the idea of an invasion through a "Channel Tunnel" clearly sets the story against the background of the Napoleonic Wars. Hardy also economically sets the story in its more immediate context – the cosy inn of 1882, sheltering from the rain with others gathered round the fire, and the anticipation of a good story well told. All these details help to set the mood and draw the reader into the narrative.

In Extract 2 Mansfield writes in the third person, which allows her to reveal the thoughts and feelings that run through the mind of her character. The third-person narrative is interspersed with direct speech, which allows Mansfield to begin to build up a sense of her characters and encourage the reader to engage with them.

Compare this with the approach adopted by Hill in Extract 3. She chooses a quite different way of telling her story. It is written in the third person and we are launched, without any preamble, into a "situation". It is not immediately clear what that situation is, but it seems that someone, perhaps a nurse, is feeding soup to Mrs Ebbs. Although Hill partially adopts the stance of external narrator, some of the narrative views the scene through the eyes of Mrs Ebbs as she sees the face of the nurse peering towards her.

> **Activity**
>
> Look at two or three short stories that you have studied. With a partner, discuss the narrative viewpoint that the writer adopts in each. Now write a short essay, illustrated by examples, on the way in which narrative viewpoint contributes to the overall effect of these stories.

Character

Although some critics argue that it is absurd to consider fictitious characters as if they were "real" people, on the other hand when we read stories we do create our own mental image of them based on our experiences of real life. However, we must not lose sight of the fact that they are creations of the writer and do not have an existence outside the text. In many cases writers create their characters to serve particular functions within the narrative and present them in ways that give particular impressions. Therefore, we should look carefully at the kinds of characters the writer portrays, how they are presented, which of their features are stressed, and what role they perform. We must also think about how the characters interlock with all the other elements of the story to create a unified whole, and how we respond to them as readers.

In *A Message From the Pig-man* by John Wain, Eric's father is no longer living with him and his mother. Instead, Donald is living with them. Eric does not mind Donald being there but he cannot understand why his father is not still living with them. After all, there is a spare room with no one sleeping there. He is also curious about a man his mother calls the Pig-man who regularly calls at the house. Eric thinks the man must look like a pig and that makes him feel frightened. One day, however, he is forced to go out and give him some food. Now read how the story ends.

A Message From the Pig-man

Eric was outside the door and running. This was a technique he knew. It was the same as getting into icy-cold water. If it was the end, if the Pig-man seized him by the hand and dragged him off to his hut, well, so much the worse. Swinging the paper carrier in his hand, he ran fast through the dusk.

The back view of the Pig-man was much as he had expected it to be. A slow, rather lurching gait, hunched shoulders, an old hat crushed down on his head (to hide his ears?), and the pail in his hand. Plod, plod, as if he were tired. Perhaps this was just a ruse, though; probably he could pounce quickly enough when his wicked little eyes saw a nice tasty little boy or something... did the Pig-man eat birds? Or cats?

Eric stopped. He opened his mouth to call to the Pig-man, but the first time he tried nothing came out except a small rasping squeak. His heart was banging like fireworks going off. He could hardly hear anything.

'Mr Pig-man!' he called, and this time the words came out clear and rather high.

The jogging old figure stopped, turned, and looked at him. Eric could not see properly from where he stood. But he had to see. Everything, even his fear, sank and drowned in the raging tide of his curiosity. He moved forward. With each step he saw more clearly. The Pig-man was just an ordinary old man.

'Hello, sonny. Got some stuff there for the old grunters?'

Eric nodded, mutely, and held out his offering. What old grunters? What did he mean?

The Pig-man put down his bucket. He had ordinary hands, ordinary arms. He took the lid off. Eric held out the paper carrier, and the Pig-man's hand actually touched his own for a second. A flood of gratitude rose up inside him. The Pig-man tipped the scraps into the bucket and handed the carrier back.

'Thanks, sonny,' he said.

'Who's it for?' Eric asked, with another rush of articulateness. His voice seemed to have a life of its own.

The Pig-man straightened up, puzzled. Then he laughed, in a gurgling sort of way, but not like a pig at all.

'Arh Aarh Harh Harh,' the Pig-man went. 'Not for me, if that's whatcher mean, arh harh.'

He put the lid back on the bucket. 'It's for the old grunters,' he said. 'The old porkers. Just what they likes. Only not fruit skins. I leaves a note, sometimes, about what not to put in. Never fruit skins. It gives 'em the belly-ache.'

He was called the Pig-man because he had some pigs that he looked after.

'Thank you,' said Eric. 'Good night'. He ran back towards the house, hearing the Pig-man, the ordinary old man, the ordinary, usual, normal old man, say in his just ordinary old man's voice, 'Good night, sonny.'

So that was how you did it. You just went straight ahead, not worrying about this or that. Like getting into cold water. You just *did* it.

He slowed down as he got to the gate. For instance, if there was a question you wanted to know the answer to, and you had always just felt you couldn't ask, the thing to do was to ask it. Just straight out, like going up to the Pig-man. Difficult things, troubles, questions, you just treated them like the Pig-man.

So that was it!

The warm light shone through the crack of the door. He opened it and went in. His mother was standing at the table, her hands still working the cake mixture about. She would let him scrape out the basin, and the spoon – he would ask for the spoon, too. But not straight away. There was a more important thing first.

He put the paper carrier down and went up to her. 'Mum,' he said. 'Why can't Dad be with us even if Donald *is* here? I mean, why can't he live with us as well as Donald?'

His mother turned and went to the sink. She put the tap on and held her hands under it.

'Darling,' she called.

'Yes,' came Donald's voice.

'D'you know what he's just said?'

'What?'

'He's just asked...' She turned the tap off and dried her hands, not looking at Eric. 'He wants to know why we can't have Jack to live with us.'

There was a silence, then Donald said, quietly, so that his voice only just reached Eric's ears, 'That's a hard one.'

'You can scrape out the basin,' his mother said to Eric. She lifted him up and kissed him. Then she rubbed her cheek along his, leaving a wet smear. 'Poor little Ekky,' she said in a funny voice.

She put him down and he began to scrape out the pudding-basin, certain at least of one thing, that grown-ups were mad and silly and he hated them all, all, *all*.

John Wain

Activity

In the passage above by John Wain, there are two main characters, Eric and the Pig-man. What do we learn about each one and how do we learn it? From what they do? From what they say and how they say it? From what they think? Or from what the narrator tells us about them?

We have a brief view of Eric's mother. How is she presented? Is Eric justified in hating all grown-ups?

Notice that although there is a third-person narrator, nearly everything is presented from Eric's viewpoint. What is the effect of doing this?

Language and imagery

The style in which the story is written – the choices that writers make in the language they use and the ways in which they use it – is a key element in the overall effect that is created by a story in the mind of the reader. It might be written quite plainly using little figurative language, or the writer might use imagery to help create the desired effect.

Activity

1 In *A Message From the Pig-man*, Wain differentiates between the language of the narrator ("This was a technique he knew"; "Eric nodded, mutely"; "with another rush of articulateness") and the speech of Eric ("when his wicked little eyes saw a nice tasty little boy or something"; "Why can't Dad be with us..."; "grown-ups were mad and silly...") and the way the Pig-man speaks ("Not for me, if that's whatcher mean, arh harh"). Comment on what these differences tell us about Eric and the Pig-man.

2 Wain uses imagery to present the situation. How do the following images work?

- "slow, rather lurching gait"

- "hunched shoulders"

- "plod"

- "pounce"

- "wicked little eyes".

The use of water imagery: "getting into icy-cold water", "sank and drowned", "flood of gratitude", "gurgling sort of way" all help to suggest that Eric was out of his depth at first but having plunged into the water, managed to reach safety. This helps to increase our sympathy for Eric because we realize what a trial the whole affair has been for him.

Theme

Activity

What is Wain's message to us in his story about the Pig-man? At first we think it is that if we have the courage to face our fears they will go away, but the ending suggests a different interpretation. Has the mother responded in the best way to her son's question? Is this story a condemnation of how adults mistakenly try to protect children from the truth?

Prose other than the novel and short story

As part of your A1 English programme you will also have to read a non-fiction prose text. Non-fiction works can take many forms, such as essays, biographies, autobiographies and travel books. Many of the techniques used by non-fiction writers are the same as those used by fiction writers. For example, characters can often be found in non-fiction works and although these characters have existed in real life they still need to be recreated in words. Similarly, non-fiction often contains descriptions of scenes and settings, creates moods and atmospheres, and includes themes and messages that the writers want to convey to their readers. Some texts combine factual information with speculation or with imaginative passages.

The greatest difference could be said to be that non-fiction is about events that really happen or, in the case of essays, about the ideas of people who exist. The problem is that the differences are not so clear cut as they might seem. A Japanese writer once said that if you want fiction you should read history or autobiography, and if you want truth you should read novels, plays or poetry. This is an idea you might like to discuss with others.

One genre to consider in your discussion is autobiography. Will someone writing about his or her own life always tell the truth? Or will writers be influenced by an image they want to create of themselves? How good is their memory? How good are they as writers? You might think that travel writers would be more truthful but are they, too, not influenced by their own subjectivity? Or even by their mood or state of health? When studying non-fiction texts, then, your approach need not necessarily be very different from how you study novels, drama or poetry.

We still need to ask some key questions:

- What is the text about?
- How has the author chosen to write about it?
- What is the purpose in writing it?

You may also want to try to judge the degree of reality that is conveyed by the author.

Here are some forms of non-fiction writing you might encounter:

- essays
- autobiographies or biographies
- diaries
- documentaries
- journalism.

Now look at the following extract taken from *Testament of Youth* by Vera Brittain. She left Oxford University in 1916, during World War I, in order to go to France as a V.A.D. (Voluntary Aid Detachment) nurse. Here she describes her arrival at a camp hospital in Etaples.

Testament of Youth

A heavy shower had only just ceased as I arrived at Etaples with three other V.A.D.s ordered to the same hospital, and the roads were liquid with such mud as only wartime France could produce after a few days of rain.

Leaving our camp-kit to be picked up by an ambulance, we squelched through the littered, grimy square and along a narrow, straggling street where the sole repositories for household rubbish appeared to be the pavement and the gutter. We finally emerged into open country and the huge area of camps, in which, at one time or another, practically every soldier in the British Army was dumped to await further orders for a still less agreeable destination. The main railway line from Boulogne to Paris ran between the hospitals and the distant sea, and amongst the camps, and along the sides of the road to Camiers, the humped sandhills bristled with tufts of spiky grass.

The noise of the distant guns was a sense rather than a sound; sometimes a quiver shook the earth, a vibration trembled upon the wind, when I could actually hear nothing. But that sense made any feeling of complete peace impossible; in the atmosphere was always the tenseness, the restlessness, the slight rustling, that comes before an earthquake or with imminent thunder. The glamour of the place was even more compelling, though less delirious, than the enchantment of Malta's beauty; it could not be banished though one feared and resisted it, knowing that it had to be bought at the cost of loss and frustration. France was the scene of titanic, illimitable death, and for this very reason it had become the heart of the fiercest living ever known to any generation. Nothing was permanent; everyone and everything was always on the move; friendships were temporary, appointments were temporary, life itself was the most temporary of all. Never, in any time or place, had been so appropriate the lament of 'James Lee's Wife';

> *To draw one beauty into our heart's core,*
>
> *And keep it changeless! Such our claim;*
>
> *So answered, – Never more!*

Whenever I think of the War today, it is not as summer but always as winter; always as cold and darkness and discomfort, and an intermittent warmth

---

of exhilarating excitement which made us irrationally exult in all three. Its permanent symbol, for me, is a candle stuck in the neck of a bottle, the tiny flame flickering in an ice-cold draught, yet creating a miniature illusion of light against an opaque infinity of blackness.

Vera Brittain

Activity

Look at the extract carefully and answer the following questions:

1   What techniques does Brittain use to give her readers an impression of her surroundings?

2   Do her methods have anything in common with those of novelists? Are there any differences?

3   Count the number of sentences where you could be sure that she is recording what actually happened.

Brittain uses vivid and detailed description to give the reader an impression of her surroundings. Note how she brings in the various senses to strengthen the impression of the place. For example: "The noise of the distant guns"; "a quiver shook the earth"; "we squelched through the littered, grimy square". You can see that she is using the same techniques as a novelist to set the scene and convey the atmosphere. We know that Brittain was writing from first-hand experience here, but it could equally be a piece of prose written in the first person and created from a writer's imagination.

Activity

Now read this extract from Brian Keenan's *An Evil Cradling*. It recounts his experiences of being kidnapped and held hostage by terrorists in Beirut.

1   How does he draw you into the narrative at the beginning of the passage?

2   How does he convey to you what his life was like?

3   Pick out particular details that he uses and comment on their effectiveness.

4   How does he convey his thoughts?

5   How truthful do you think his writing is? Give reasons for your answer.

6   How effective do you think his writing is overall? Why?

An Evil Cradling

Come now into the cell with me and stay here and feel if you can and if you will that time, whatever time it was, for however long, for time means nothing in this cell. Come, come in.

I am back from my daily ablutions. I hear the padlock slam behind me and I lift the towel which has draped my head from my face. I look at the food on the floor. The round of Arab bread, a boiled egg, the jam I will not eat, the slice or two of processed cheese and perhaps some houmus. Every day I look to see if it will change, if there will be some new morsel of food that will make this day different from all the other days, but there is no change. This day is the same as all the days in the past and as all the days to come. It will always be the same food sitting on the floor in the same place.

I set down my plastic bottle of drinking water and the other empty bottle. From bottle to bottle, through me, this fluid will daily run. I set the urine bottle at the far corner away from the food. This I put in a plastic bag to keep it fresh. In this heat the bread rapidly turns stale and hard. It is like eating cardboard. I pace my four paces backwards and forwards, slowly feeling my mind empty, wondering where it will go today. Will I go with it or will I try to hold it back, like a father and an unruly child? There is a greasy patch on the wall where I lay my head. Like a dog I sniff it.

I begin as I have always begun these days to think of something, anything upon which I can concentrate. Something I can think about and so try to push away the crushing emptiness of this tiny, tiny cell and the day's long silence. I try with desperation to recall the dream of the night before or perhaps to push away the horror of it. The nights are filled with dreaming. The cinema of the mind, the reels flashing and flashing by and suddenly stopping at some point when with strange contortions it throws up some absurd drama that I cannot understand. I try to block it out. Strange how in the daytime the dreams that we do not wish to remember come flickering back into the conscious mind. Those dreams that we desperately want to have with us in the daylight will not come to us but have gone and cannot be enticed back. It is as if we are running down a long empty tunnel looking for something that we left behind but cannot see in the blackness.

The guards are gone. I have not heard a noise for several hours now. It must be time to eat. I tear off a quarter of the unleavened bread and begin to peel the shell from the egg. The word 'albumen' intrigues me for a while and I wonder where the name came from. How someone decided once to call that part of the egg 'albumen'. The shape of an egg has lost its fascination for me. I have exhausted thinking about the form of an egg. A boiled egg with dry bread is doubly tasteless. I make this meaningless remark to myself every day and don't know why.

I must ration my drinking water for I am always fearful that I might finish it and then wake in the middle of the night with a raging thirst that I cannot satiate. I think of rabies and the raging thirst of mad dogs and I know how easy it would be to go mad from thirst. Now I know the full meaning of the expression so frequently used in our daily lives: 'He was mad with thirst.' If I were to knock over this water-bottle there would be nothing I could do because there is no-one here. Until tomorrow there will be silence in this tomb of a place so far down under the ground.

Then it begins, I feel it coming from out of nowhere. I recognize it now, and I shrink into the corner to await its pleasure. What will it be today? That slow down-dragging slide and pull into hopeless depression and weariness. The waters of the sea of despair are heavy and thick and I think I cannot swim through them. But today is a day of euphoria. A day in which I will not walk my four paces but in which I will glide, my feet hardly touching the ground. Up snakes and down ladders my mind is manically playing games with me and I cannot escape. Today it is teasing me, threatening me, so far without the full blast of its fury. I squat and rock backwards and forwards reciting a half-remembered nursery rhyme like a religious mantra. I am determined I will make myself more mad than my mind.

Blackness, the light has gone. There will be none for ten hours. They have given me candles. Small, stubby candles. I will not light them. I fear the dark so I save the candles. It's stupid, it's ridiculous. There are a dozen or so hidden in my bed. I will not light them, yet I hate the dark and cannot abide its thick palpable blackness. I can feel it against my skin.

I am going crazier by the day. In the thick sticky darkness I lie naked on the mattress. The blanket reeks, full of filth. It is pointless to try to shield myself from the mosquitoes drooling and humming, their constant buzz, buzz, buzz everywhere, as if it is inside my ears and inside my head. In the thick black invisibility it is foolishness to hope to kill what you cannot see but only feel when it is too late, upon your flesh.

Always in the morning I see the marks of the night's battle. Red lumps like chicken pox, all raging to be itched and scratched. I sit trying to prevent myself from scratching. The more I try to resist, the more difficult it becomes and the more demanding is my body for the exquisite pain of my nails tearing my own flesh. For some reason I do not understand, the feet and the backs of my fingers suffer the most from these insistent fleas. The pain of the bites on these tender areas can be excruciating. At times I exchange one pain for another. Deciding feverishly to tear and scratch the skin from my feet, and with it the pain of the bite, knowing that in the morning my feet will be a bloody mess and I will be unable to walk on this filthy floor. It's all so purposeless. I am naked in the dark and I try to wipe the perspiration from my skin. The night noise of these insects is insidious. I cannot bear much more. I thrust my body back upon the mattress and pull the filthy curtain over it to keep these things from feeding on my flesh. I cannot bear the heat and smell of this rag over my body like a shroud. I must content myself, let the mosquitoes feed and hope that having had a fill of me they will leave me alone to find some sleep.

Brian Keenan

DETAILED STUDY

Joseph Conrad

Joseph Conrad, whose real name was Joseph Teodor Konrad Nalecz Korzeniowski, was born in Poland in 1857 into an aristocratic family. His parents died when he was a child and he was brought up by his uncle. As a Polish aristocrat, Conrad's cultural background was Western and he spoke and read in French. However, his father, who had himself been a poet and dramatist, had been a great admirer of English literature and so, as a child, Conrad read much Shakespeare and Dickens in translation. Formal schooling did not appeal to him and by 1872 he wanted to go to sea. He was finally allowed to go at the age of 17, although his family were not happy with the idea of his becoming an ordinary sailor or with what seemed, to them, the rejection of his cultural and social background. During the years that followed he led a colourful and adventurous life. He came to England when he was 21. At that time he knew very little English and taught himself the language. He spent the next 20 years or so at sea and rose to the rank of Captain. In 1886 he became a British citizen.

As a writer, Conrad acknowledged his debt to the French author Guy de Maupassant, but he wrote his own stories in English, attracted by the quality and potential of that language. He began writing as early as 1886 and continued until his death in 1924, producing a total of 31 books as well as a large number of letters. His novels and stories include: *The Nigger of the "Narcissus"* (1897), *Lord Jim* (1900), *Typhoon* (1902), *Heart of Darkness* (1902), *Nostromo* (1904), and *The Secret Agent* (1907).

For the purpose of this Detailed Study we will focus on one of Conrad's best-known and most studied novels, *Heart of Darkness*.

In this short novel Conrad reveals the depths of human corruptibility, as the central character, Marlow (a seaman), voyages up the Congo river, in search of the enigmatic Kurtz, a European and a man of many talents. Travelling into the heart of Africa, Marlow discovers how Kurtz has gained his power and influence over the local people – a discovery which leads him to "the heart of darkness".

Themes and ideas

Heart of Darkness is a novel which contains a complex mesh of themes and ideas concerning the individual, social, political, and metaphorical aspects of human existence. Aspects covered are:

- civilization/savagery
- colonialism/imperialism
- the journey
- the self and the unconscious.

Activity

Read the following extract taken from early in the novel. In the opening part of the novel Conrad introduces, in a symbolic or metaphorical way, some of the key themes that he goes on to explore in the book. Look carefully at the extract and see if you can see in it suggestions of any of the themes mentioned above. Marlow is speaking.

'I was thinking of very old times, when the Romans first came here, nineteen hundred years ago – the other day... Light came out of this river since – you say Knights? Yes; but it is like a running blaze on a plain, like a flash of lightning in the clouds. We live in the flicker – may it last as long as the old earth keeps rolling! But darkness was here yesterday. Imagine the feelings of a commander of a fine – what d'ye call 'em? – trireme in the Mediterranean, ordered suddenly to the north; run overland across the Gauls in a hurry; put in charge of one of these craft the legionaries – a wonderful lot of handy men they must have been too

– used to build, apparently by the hundred, in a month or two, if we may believe what we read. Imagine him here – the very end of the world, a sea the colour of lead, a sky the colour of smoke, a kind of ship about as rigid as a concertina – and going up this river with stores, or orders, or what you like. Sandbanks, marshes, forests, savages – precious little to eat fit for a civilized man, nothing but Thames water to drink. No Falernian wine here, no going ashore. Here and there a military camp lost in a wilderness, like a needle in a bundle of hay – cold, fog, tempests, disease, exile, and death – death skulking in the air, in the water, in the bush. They must have been dying like flies here. Oh yes – he did it. Did it very well, too, no doubt, and without thinking much about it either, except afterwards to brag of what he had gone through in his time, perhaps. They were men enough to face the darkness. And perhaps he was cheered by keeping his eye on a chance of promotion to the fleet at Ravenna by and by, if he had good friends in Rome and survived the awful climate. Or think of a decent young citizen in a toga – perhaps too much dice, you know – coming out here in the train of some prefect, or tax-gatherer, or trader, even, to mend his fortunes. Land in a swamp, march through the woods, and in some inland post feel the savagery, the utter savagery, had closed round him – all that mysterious life of the wilderness that stirs in the forest, in the jungles, in the hearts of wild men. There's no initiation either into such mysteries. He has to live in the midst of the incomprehensible, which is also detestable. And it has a fascination, too, that goes to work upon him. The fascination of the abomination – you know, imagine the growing regrets, the longing to escape, the powerless disgust, the surrender, the hate.'

He paused.

'Mind,' he began again, lifting one arm from the elbow, the palm of the hand outwards, so that, with his legs folded before him, he had the pose of a Buddha preaching in European clothes and without a lotus-flower – 'Mind, none of us would feel exactly like this. What saves us is efficiency – the devotion to efficiency. But these chaps were not much account, really. They were no colonists; their administration was merely a squeeze, and nothing more, I suspect. They were conquerors, and for that you want only brute force – nothing to boast of, when you have it, since your strength is just an accident arising from the weakness of others. They grabbed what they could get for the sake of what was to be got. It was just robbery with violence, aggravated murder on a great scale, and men going at it blind – as is very proper for those who tackle a darkness. The conquest of the earth, which mostly means the taking it away from those who have a different complexion or slightly flatter noses than ourselves, is not a pretty thing when you look into it too much. What redeems it is the idea only. An idea at the back of it; not a sentimental pretence but an idea; and an unselfish belief in the idea – something you can set up, and bow down before, and offer a sacrifice to...'

Here are some possible ideas:

- The theme of imperialism can be seen in the reference to the Roman invasion of Britain and the "conquest of the earth". Notice how negatively he presents this invasion.

- His reference to the "growing regrets, the longing to escape, the powerless disgust, the surrender, the hate" that the Roman invaders experienced can be seen to have parallels in the journey that Kurtz undertakes in the novel.

- The reference to the Roman invasion also creates a sense of contrast between the "civilization" that their empire represented and the "savagery" which surrounded the Roman soldier – "Land in a swamp, march through the woods, and in some inland post feel the savagery, the utter savagery, had closed round him – all that mysterious life of the wilderness that stirs in the forest, in the jungles, in the hearts of wild men."

- The words in the previous quotation foreshadow later descriptions of Marlow's experiences as he travels up the Congo.

- The reference to the Roman invasion up the River Thames suggests the idea that they have made a journey, again paralleling Marlow's journey up the Congo.

- Although the novel is mainly set in the Congo, which was a Belgian colony, the book starts in London, thereby associating the British Empire with both the Roman Empire and Belgian colonial policies.

Conrad's use of symbols and motifs

Symbols are objects, colours, or characters that are used to represent ideas or themes or concepts. Motifs are recurring images, symbols, structures or patterns which are repeated at various points in the novel in order to create particular effects or to emphasize major themes. In this novel Conrad uses a number of symbols and motifs such as:

- The title itself, which holds a symbolic meaning in that it represents both the heart of the wilderness and the central darkness within Kurtz himself.
- The image of the journey, which metaphorically represents a journey into the unconscious part of the human mind.
- The characters, who can hold symbolic meanings – for example, Marlow can be seen as a shadow of Kurtz.
- The derelict machinery at the outer station, which can represent the destructive influence of white "civilization" on Africa.
- Light and darkness, which are referred to frequently throughout the novel. Normally we associate "light" and "white" with good, and "black" and "darkness" with evil. However, Conrad often uses these images in a different way. For example he sometimes gives "light" the connotation of destruction, and "white" connotations of death.
- Fog, which is used to suggest distorting or obscuring the truth. For example, Marlow's steamer is caught in the fog, meaning that he has no idea where he is going or whether danger or safety lie ahead.

Activity

Read the following passage, which describes Marlow's journey up the river to Kurtz's station. Examine the ways in which Conrad uses language here to achieve his effects. Pay particular attention to his use of imagery, and symbolism. Make a note of any images you can identify, and analyse the effects that Conrad creates through their use.

'Towards the evening of the second day we judged ourselves about eight miles from Kurtz's station. I wanted to push on; but the manager looked grave, and told me the navigation up there was so dangerous that it would be advisable, the sun being very low already, to wait where we were till next morning. Moreover, he pointed out that if the warning to approach cautiously were to be followed, we must approach in daylight – not at dusk, or in the dark. This was sensible enough. Eight miles meant nearly three hours' steaming for us, and I could also see suspicious ripples at the upper end of the reach. Nevertheless, I was annoyed beyond expression at the delay, and most unreasonably too, since one night more could not matter much after so many months. As we had plenty of wood, and caution was the word, I brought up in the middle of the stream. The reach was narrow, straight, with high sides like a railway cutting. The dusk came gliding into it long before the sun had set. The current ran smooth and swift, but a dumb immobility sat on the banks. The living trees, lashed together by the creepers and every living bush of the undergrowth, might have been changed into stone, even to the slenderest twig, to the lightest leaf. It was not sleep – it seemed unnatural, like a state of trance. Not the faintest sound of any kind could be heard. You looked on amazed, and began to suspect yourself of being deaf – then the night came suddenly, and struck you blind as well. About three in the morning some large fish leaped, and the loud splash made me jump as though a gun had been fired. When the sun rose there was a white fog, very warm and clammy, and more blinding than the night. It did not shift or drive; it was just there, standing all around you like something solid. At eight or nine, perhaps, it lifted as a shutter lifts. We had a glimpse of the towering multitude of trees, of the immense matted jungle, with the blazing little ball of the sun hanging over it – all perfectly still – and then the white shutter came down again, smoothly, as if sliding in greased grooves. I ordered the chain, which we had begun to heave in, to be paid out again. Before it stopped running with a muffled rattle, a cry, a very loud cry, as of infinite desolation, soared slowly in the opaque air. It ceased. A complaining clamour, modulated in savage discords, filled our ears. The sheer unexpectedness of it made my hair stir under my cap. I don't know how it struck the others; to me it seemed as though the mist itself had screamed, so suddenly, and apparently from all sides at once, did this tumultuous and mournful uproar arise. It culminated in a hurried outbreak of almost intolerably excessive shrieking, which stopped short, leaving us stiffened in a variety of silly attitudes, and obstinately listening to the nearly as appalling and excessive silence. "Good God! What is the meaning – ?" stammered at my elbow one of the pilgrims – a little fat man, with sandy hair and red whiskers, who wore side-spring boots, and pink pyjamas tucked into his socks. Two others remained open-mouthed a whole minute, then dashed into the little cabin, to rush out incontinently and stand darting scared glances, with Winchesters at "ready" in their hands. What we could see was just the steamer we were on, her outlines blurred as though she had been on the point of dissolving, and a misty strip of water, perhaps two feet broad, around her – and that was all. The rest of the world was nowhere, as far as our eyes and ears were concerned. Just nowhere. Gone, disappeared; swept off without leaving a whisper or a shadow behind.'

Here are some points you might have noted:

● The dusk makes it dangerous to go on – they must continue in daylight.

● When daylight comes, their vision is obscured by fog, which carries with it a psychological as well as a practical effect.

● There is a striking description of the forest on either side of the river, the "living trees" and "every living bush of the undergrowth, might have been changed into stone, even to the slenderest twig, to the lightest leaf. It was not sleep – it seemed unnatural, like a state of trance." Conrad suggests here that nature, usually thought of as living and vibrant, has become dead, like stone. This can be seen as symbolic of the deadness of the sensibilities of the white men as they approach the Inner Station.

● The next sentences – "not the faintest sound of any kind could be heard. You looked on amazed, and began to suspect yourself of being deaf – then the night came suddenly, and struck you blind as well" – emphasize the symbolic importance of this.

● This idea of blindness connects with the image of the fog, which is "more blinding than the night".

Activity

Now read this section from towards the end of the novel. Kurtz is dead and Marlow thinks about his own attitude towards death compared with the moment of truth experienced by Kurtz just before he dies.

Analyse this passage, commenting on its content and on the ways in which Conrad uses language here to achieve his effects.

'However, as you see, I did not go to join Kurtz there and then. I did not. I remained to dream the nightmare out to the end, and to show my loyalty to Kurtz once more. Destiny. My destiny! Droll thing life is – that mysterious arrangement of merciless logic for a futile purpose. The most you can hope for from it is some knowledge of yourself – that comes too late – a crop of unextinguishable regrets. I have wrestled with death. It is the most unexciting contest you can imagine. It takes place in an impalpable greyness, with nothing underfoot, with nothing around, without spectators, without clamour, without glory, without the great desire of victory, without the great fear of defeat, in a sickly atmosphere of tepid scepticism, without much belief in your own right, and still less in that of your adversary. If such is the form of ultimate wisdom, then life is a greater riddle than some of us think it to be. I was within a hair's breadth of the last opportunity for pronouncement, and I found with humiliation that probably I would have nothing to say. This is the reason why I affirm that Kurtz was a remarkable man. He had something to say. He said it. Since I had peeped over the edge myself, I understand better the meaning of his stare, that could not see the flame of the candle, but was wide enough to embrace the whole universe, piercing enough to penetrate all the hearts that beat in the darkness. He had summed up – he had judged. "The horror!" He was a remarkable man. After all, this was the expression of some sort of belief; it had candour, it had conviction, it had a vibrating note of revolt in its whisper, it had the appalling face of a glimpsed truth – the strange commingling of desire and hate. And it is not my own extremity I remember best – a vision of greyness without form filled with physical pain, and a careless contempt for the evanescence of all things – even of this pain itself. No! It is his extremity that I seem to have lived through. True, he had made that last stride, he had stepped over the edge, while I had been permitted to draw back my hesitating foot. And perhaps in this is the whole difference; perhaps all the wisdom, and all truth, and all sincerity, are just compressed into that inappreciable moment of time in which we step over the threshold of the invisible. Perhaps! I like to think my summing-up would not have been a word of careless contempt. Better his cry – much better. It was an affirmation, a moral victory paid for by innumerable defeats, by abominable terrors, by abominable satisfactions. But it was a victory! That is why I have remained loyal to Kurtz to the last, and even beyond, when a long time after I heard once more, not his own voice, but the echo of his magnificent eloquence thrown to me from a soul as translucently pure as a cliff of crystal.'

Cultural and thematic issues

Colonialism

The colonization of the Congo and the brutality which accompanied this is a key element in the book. In recent years there has been increasing interest in the nature and effects of early imperialism. Conrad's presentation of colonization in *Heart of Darkness* not only examines its effects but raises fundamental questions about the nature of "white" civilization and its imposition on what were then considered "primitive" cultures. We have already seen how the novel opens with a consideration of the impact of colonialism from early times, through reference to the Roman conquest of Britain. Conrad's exploration extends beyond that of the political to look at the impact of colonization in terms of its cultural, social, and economic aspects as well as the consequences of an individual's lust for power.

In examining the novel in terms of its presentation of colonialism, you should look at various critical views. Not all regard Conrad's presentation favourably, and it is worth reading one of the best-known negative responses, which was written by Chinua Achebe in 1977. In his article "An Image of Africa", he makes reference to the derogatory images of Africans presented in the novel. He reaches the conclusion that Conrad was a racist and that *Heart of Darkness* is full of the prejudices that for many years and in many ways called into question the very humanity of black people. Other critics, however, express different views. You should try to read as many views as you can in order to inform your own judgement. Another work that sheds light on what Conrad knew about the Congo is *King Leopold's Ghost* by Adam Hochschild. This book gives a devastating account of the way in which the Congo was treated by King Leopold of Belgium.

Self-discovery

As well as the socio-political theme, the novel also explores a more personal theme as it traces Marlow's journey through the Congo and his journey to discover himself. Marlow is confronted by the reality of colonialism but also experiences another kind of journey, through his own mind. He embarks on his travels feeling distanced from Africa and with vague ideas of "adventure". He witnesses the destruction that the Europeans have brought to Africa. He is repelled by the greed he sees in the white men, and the brutality that they display towards their fellow human beings, but at the same time he wants to find evidence that the Europeans can act as agents of good in Africa. His journey of self-discovery leads him not to the discovery of a compassionate and benign influence, however, but to the realization that there is nothing morally substantial behind the colonization of Africa. At its heart, all he finds is "darkness".

Any study you undertake of the novel should recognize that Conrad presents the physical and metaphorical journey Marlow undertakes not as separate issues but as integral to one another. In a sense, the novel is not simply about what people do, but addresses the idea that their collective actions express what each person is individually and inwardly.

5 Studying poetry

Objectives
- To identify ways in which you can approach the reading of poetry
- To explore ways of writing about poetry
- To consider some of the features to look for in analysing poems
- To prepare for studying set poetry texts
- To prepare for encountering "unseen" poetry texts

The nature of poetry

Like prose, poetry cannot be neatly categorized, and the question of what exactly poetry is – what it is that marks it out as being different from prose – is a question that has tested writers, critics, philosophers, and all concerned with literature for centuries. Certainly poets can choose from a whole range of different forms, structures, techniques, and styles when writing their poetry. They can play with language and manipulate it, even invent a "new" language to express their feelings, ideas, and themselves. Because, generally, the ideas in poems are expressed in fewer words than are used in prose, the messages or ideas in a poem are sometimes more difficult to understand than if they were written in prose.

Also, the poet may be expressing himself or herself in a unique way – it is more acceptable for the language of poetry to deviate from generally observed rules. This "poetic licence"(freedom) allows poets to experiment with language, perhaps playing around with word order, or using dialectal forms, or using different kinds of patterning to create or reinforce meaning.

Of course, prose writers can use these techniques too, but they will be much more frequently found in the language of poetry.

Throughout your life you will probably have encountered various kinds of poetry – at school, college, in reading for pleasure, on the radio, television, etc.

Reading poetry

The study of poetry is an important part of your Diploma programme. Whether you are studying a poetry set text for the Individual Oral Commentary or preparing for the commentary examination involving "unseen" texts, you will need to engage in detailed study of various poems. Even though the outcome of your work might be presented in different forms, the skills, techniques, and approaches that you need to use are essentially the same.

It is true that poetry can present particular challenges. For a number of reasons, some poetry is only fully accessible to us today if we carry out a certain amount of research such as looking up difficult words, phrases, and references. However, "responding to poetry"

> *"We make out of our quarrel with others, rhetoric, but of the quarrel with ourselves, poetry."*
> William Butler Yeats

Activity

Based on your experience of poetry, write down all the features you can think of that make poetry different from other kinds of writing. If you are working with a group, discuss your findings with others.

> *"All poets adore explosions, thunderstorms, tornadoes, conflagrations, ruins, scenes of spectacular carnage. The poetic imagination is therefore not at all a desirable quality in a chief of state."*
> W.H. Auden, *Poets at Work*

cannot be "taught" (or learned, for that matter) in the same way that some subjects can. It is no good looking for some kind of "secret formula" that you can apply to any poem. Although most poetry is written to be read by others, and in that sense carries a "public" voice, it can also be an intensely individual medium of communication and the responses it can evoke can be equally intense and individual. Much poetry works in a very personal way and your response to a particular poem might not be the same as another person's. Words and images carry with them connotations (suggestions or associations) that might trigger different responses in the minds of different people. So while it is often possible to say what a poem "is about" in general terms, the only really genuine response is that "personal response" that an individual reader feels.

This does not mean that "anything goes", of course. For example, comments like "I haven't a clue about this" or "This means nothing to me" may be personal responses but they are not much good in terms of a "literary" response. You need to give your personal analysis, and show your personal engagement with a text. In your Diploma studies you will be required to show what the programme objectives describe as "an ability to engage in independent literary criticism in a manner which reveals a personal response to literature" (Higher Level) or "an ability to approach works in an independent manner which reveals a personal response to literature" (Standard Level).

In this unit we will look at some of the things that you can do to find your way into and through a poem. Here are some general strategies for improving your understanding of poetry.

- Read widely – become as familiar as possible with as wide a range of poetry as possible.
- Think about how language is used and make a note of any interesting features, lines, images, etc. that you come across in your reading of poetry.
- Think about the ideas contained in the poems you read.
- Read other people's responses to poetry – not as a substitute for forming your own views but as a "broadening" influence. (These responses could be found in various study guides, articles in literary journals, or reviews in newspapers or critical works.) They might suggest things that had not occurred to you or they might stimulate your own thoughts if you disagree with their view.
- Read poems aloud – either in company or alone. Very often reading a poem aloud helps deepen understanding and it certainly gives you a greater insight into features such as tone and rhythm.
- Try writing poems, experimenting with different forms, and playing with rhythm and rhyme.
- Adopt a questioning attitude. Whenever you read a poem ask yourself such questions as: "What is this poem about?"; "How is it written?"; "Why has the poet chosen to write the poem in this particular way?"
- If you are studying the work of an individual poet, reading beyond the set poems will help you to understand the particular poems you are working on.

Although there is no set formula that can be applied to poetry to produce the required response, there are certain features of poetry that you will need to be aware of in order to begin to appreciate how a poem "works" – what the poet does to achieve the desired effect on the reader. Different critical books may refer to them in slightly different terms but basically these are the key elements that combine to create the overall effect of a poem. You will, no doubt, be familiar with some or all of these already.

Activity

Consider each of these aspects of poetry. Think about them for yourself or discuss your ideas in a small group and write brief notes explaining what each means. The goal here is to acquire a comfortable grasp of the terms. The following exercises should help you.

Features of poetry

Poetry is an extremely varied genre in every respect – in content, structure, style, intention, and every other way. Some poems present narratives that tell stories; some are written to be performed; some explore philosophical, emotional, or spiritual concepts and ideas; some are amusing, some are sad. In fact, it is probably safe to say that in one way or another poetry covers the whole range of human experience, and the features that it possesses can be many and varied. Poems can rhyme or not, they can use figurative language or not, they can be organized in stanzas or not, they can be written in conventional English or they can break all the rules of grammar. In other words every poem is an individual piece of work with a range of features peculiar to itself. When you are reading a poem for the first time, therefore, it is important to establish what the poet is saying to the reader – in other words, what the **purpose** of the poem is. Having identified that, you can then go on to examine *how* the poet says whatever it is that he or she wishes to say.

The purpose of poetry

In poetry, language is used in both poetic and expressive ways to convey meaning to the reader, and the purpose of the poem could be to serve any one of a wide range of functions. For example, a poem could:

● entertain
● describe
● arouse emotions
● tell a story
● provoke thought
● inform

● console
● celebrate
● express grief

or any combination of these things.

Of course the choices of vocabulary, style, form, and other features that a poet makes are closely linked to the purpose of the poem, and all provide useful clues as to what the poet's intentions are.

In order to comprehend fully any message that a poem might carry for us, it is important to look at all the features of the poem. Poets can draw upon many varied features and it is not possible to consider them all in detail here, but we will now look at some of these features.

Tone, mood, and atmosphere

The overall effect that a poem creates in the mind of the reader is very closely linked to the mood and tone that it evokes. Think of the tones and moods created in a piece of music. The "voice" of the poem can create a **tone** that conveys to the reader certain messages about the poem itself. Obviously there are many different kinds of tone. Tone is the attitude shown by the writer (or speaker) towards the material in the poem and sometimes towards the receiver or hearer of the poem.

Tone can be difficult to delineate exactly, but there are many words that can be used to describe it. This is not an exhaustive list – add any more you have on your own list. Looking at these lists may help you when you are uncertain as to how to describe a particular tone. (Make sure you know what all the words mean.)

> **Activity**
>
> Think of as many words as you can to describe tone.

Playful	Ironic	Assertive	Frivolous	Gloomy
Humorous	Sarcastic	Cynical	Calm	Heavy
Melancholy	Sardonic	Dogmatic	Serious	Personal
Mocking	Light-hearted	Dramatic	Impersonal	Angry
Sad	Philosophical	Flat	Intimate	Wistful
Evaluative	Clinical	Sharp	Solemn	Religious

Just as you might pick up clues as to how a friend feels through the tone of voice that he or she uses, so you can pick up clues from the "voice" of the poem.

The **mood** of the poem, although closely linked to the tone, is a slightly different thing – it refers to the atmosphere that the poem creates. Very often tone and mood are closely linked and a certain tone produces a certain mood. For example, if a poet uses a lively, humorous tone it is far more likely to produce a light atmosphere than a melancholy one. In your studies for the IB Diploma you will not only need to recognize the tone, mood, and atmosphere of poems but you will also need to examine the ways in which poets use language to create their tones, moods, and atmosphere.

Activity

Read the following poems carefully and think about the manner in which they are written. What kind of relationship do you think each poet wishes to establish with the reader? Comment on the tone, mood, and atmosphere created in each poem and the ways in which the poets use language to create it.

Hey There Now!
(For Lesley)

Hey there now
my brownwater flower
   my sunchild branching
from my mountain river
   hey there now!
my young stream
   headlong
     rushing
I love to watch you
   when you're
     sleeping
       blushing

Grace Nichols

Advent

Earth grown old, yet still so green,
   Deep beneath her crust of cold
Nurses fire unfelt, unseen;
   Earth grown old.

   We who live are quickly told;
Millions more lie hid between
   Inner swathings of her fold.

When will fire break up her screen?
   When will life burst through her mould?
Earth, earth, earth, thy cold is keen.
   Earth grown old.

Christina Rossetti

I Say I Say I Say

Anyone here had a go at themselves
for a laugh? Anyone opened their wrists
with a blade in the bath? Those in the dark

at the back, listen hard. Those at the front
in the know, those of us who have, hands up,
let's show that inch of lacerated skin
between the forearm and the fist. Let's tell it
like it is: strong drink, a crimson tidemark
round the tub, a yard of lint, white towels
washed a dozen times, still pink. Tough luck.
A passion then for watches, bangles, cuffs.
A likely story: you were lashed by brambles
picking berries from the woods. Come clean, come good,
repeat with me the punch line 'Just like blood'
when those at the back rush forward to say
how a little love goes a long long long way.

Simon Armitage

Activity

One student had clear ideas about what these poems meant to her. Read her responses through carefully. How close are her responses to your own thoughts on these poems? Remember, responses to poetry can be very individual.

Commentary

Grace Nichols appears to have written the poem "Hey There Now!" in celebration of someone she loves very dearly. Writing in an informal manner, she appears to invite the reader into sharing in this celebration. The poem has a loving tone which Nichols has created through the sentiments she expresses and which is enhanced by her use of language. For example, Nichols repeats the personal pronoun "my" when referring to the subject of the poem, emphasizing ownership of the subject. In addition, the subject is described in affectionate terms, "my sunchild", "my brownwater flower". The vitality of her love for the subject is complemented by Nichols's use of natural imagery which also adds to the celebratory mood. "Flower", "stream", "river", and "mountain" are all natural images included in the poem and they present the idea of a "forever" love which is natural and pure. The sense of "forever", as in an unending love, is further enhanced by the use of present continuous verb forms: "branching", "rushing", "sleeping", "blushing". These verb endings give the poem movement and add to the lively tone. The repetition of the exclamatory phrase, "Hey there now!" also adds to the lively tone, enhancing the celebratory mood of the poem as a whole.

Although natural imagery is contained in Christina Rossetti's poem, "Advent", the mood of the poem is somewhat sorrowful. Writing in a formal manner, the poet adopts a melancholy tone in her presentation of "Earth grown old". The language that Rossetti uses helps to create a mood of sadness. For instance, the earth is described as "cold", "earth, earth, thy cold is keen", which suggests that it is an unwelcoming, uncomfortable place to be. The formal manner in which the poem is written further enhances the detachment from her surroundings that the poet feels. Rather than seeing Advent as a time which precedes the warmth of spring, Rossetti presents the near-end of the year as a time of unfulfilment and decay and this is evident in the poem's vocabulary: "unseen", "unfelt", "mould". The hope of spring, a "better" time, is questionable and uncertain in this poem: "when will fire break up her screen?" adding to the melancholy tone by creating a sense of despair. The unyielding nature of the earth, as seen by the poet, is expressed and enhanced by the apparent rigidity and restrictiveness of the rhyme sequence.

The disturbing content of the poem "I Say I Say I Say" is made more so as it places us in a context in which we would expect to be in a "happy" environment. As readers, we are placed in the audience of the poet as a stand-up comedian. The poem uses informal words and phrases such as we would expect to hear in light-hearted humour from the comedian on stage: "Anyone here had a go at themselves for a laugh?", "Those in the dark at the back", "Those at the front". However, the poet shocks the audience with his subject of attempted suicide. An uncomfortable atmosphere is therefore created as a sad, solitary act, an attempted suicide, is given centre stage, the poem acting as an exposé: "Let's tell it like it is". However, the poet expresses the difficulty of "telling it like it is" through various means and use of language in the poem. For instance, he describes how one would cover up the marks on the wrists left after a suicide attempt by developing a "passion then for watches, bangles, cuffs". In addition, he includes a "cover story", a "likely story" in which "you were lashed by brambles/ picking berries from the woods". Indeed, the whole poem avoids "telling it like it is" as it fronts the disturbing act of attempted suicide with a light-hearted, comical approach: "I Say I Say I Say". Individual phrases in the poem are also seen to avoid directness. For instance, by writing, "between the forearm and the fist", which almost sounds like a comical attempt at Cockney rhyming slang, the poet avoids using the word "wrist". When people are faced with uncomfortable situations, it is often difficult to know what to say and they often resort to using clichés. Consequently, Armitage concludes the poem with a clichéd response from "those at the back", those who are not "in the know". This clichéd response confirms and enhances the uncomfortable, disturbing mood of the poem, "A little loving goes a long long long way". The unsuitability of this expected response is further stressed as an extra "long" has been inserted into this well-known cliché.

Vocabulary and word order

The choice of vocabulary (sometimes called diction) refers to the decisions about language that a poet has made when writing his or her poem. The choices that are made will depend on the poet's intentions and the effect that the piece is intended to have on the reader.

Of the various aspects to consider in looking at vocabulary, probably the most important is thinking about the connotations of words (the particular ideas, feelings or associations suggested by a word). This can be something quite separate from its denotation, or dictionary definition. Words can carry with them many connotations that might bring suggested meanings quite different from the dictionary definition of the word. Connotations can be acquired by words depending on the tone they create, the ideas or images they bring to the reader's mind, and how they have been used in the past.

There are occasions when writers choose words which have the clearest meaning or denotation, without complicating connotations. It all depends on the effects that the writer wishes to achieve – words are chosen to suit the audience and purpose. Sometimes a writer or poet might choose words that are particularly colloquial or particularly formal, according to context. Sometimes archaisms are used to give a sense of the past or add a sense of dignity and solemnity to the language. Some poetry from different cultures, rather than using Standard English, uses the non-standard English and/or dialect forms of the particular cultural background it comes from. Read the opening of *The Song of the Banana Man* by Evan Jones, a poem set in Jamaica.

> **Activity**
>
> Look at the following list of words. Although they share a common basic meaning, they have very different connotations. Use each of the words in a sentence, to show the difference in connotation between them.
>
> cunning; sly; devious; crafty; wily; artful; shifty; subtle; guileful.

The Song of the Banana Man

Touris, white man, wipin his face,
Met me in Golden Grove market place.
He looked at m'ol' clothes brown wid stain,
And soaked right through wid de Portlan rain,
He cas his eye, turn up his nose,
He says, 'You're a beggar man, I suppose?'
He says, 'Boy, get some occupation,
Be of some value to your nation.'
     I said, 'By God and dis big right han
     You mus recognize a banana man.

'Up in de hills, where de streams are cool,
An mullet an janga swim in de pool,
I have ten acres of mountain side,
An a dainty-foot donkey dat I ride,
Four Gros Mitchel, and four Lacatan,
Some coconut trees, and some hills of yam,
An I pasture on dat very same lan
Five she-goats an a big black ram,
     Dat, by God an dis big right han
     Is de property of a banana man.'

Evan Jones

> **Activity**
>
> Read Jones's poem carefully.
> 1   Try writing a Standard English version of it.
> 2   What are the differences between the two versions?
> 3   Why do you think Jones chose to write this in dialect form?

Poets can make their vocabulary very modern by using **neologisms** (invented words), which can add a sense of individuality to the poem. Sometimes a word may be chosen because it is incongruous and doesn't fit in with the rest of the vocabulary. It may jar or shock the reader, or defy the reader's expectations.

Activity

Look at the following extracts from various poems.
Fill each blank with one word from the selection given beneath, and explain why you have made your choice.

1 __a__ the spring onions,
   She made this mental note:
   You can tell it's love, the real thing,
   When you __b__ of slitting his throat.
   Wendy Cope

   a slicing, decapitating, washing
   b think, talk, dream

2 On shallow straw, in __a__ glass,
   Huddled by empty bowls, they sleep:
   No dark, no dam, no __b__, no grass –
   Mam, get us one of them to keep.
   Philip Larkin

a transparent, glaring, shadeless
b water, earth, food

3 Wild, wild the storm, and the sea __a__ running,
   Steady the __b__ of the gale, with incessant
       undertone __c__,
   Shouts of demoniac __d__ fitfully piercing and
       pealing,
   Waves, air, midnight, their savagest trinity lashing
   Walt Whitman

   a fast, high, violently
   b wail, crash, roar
   c muttering, flowing, moaning
   d screams, laughter, cackling

Now we will look at the vocabulary (or diction) in a complete poem.

The Bean Eaters

They eat beans mostly, this old yellow pair.
Dinner is a casual affair.
Plain chipware on a plain and creaking wood,
Tin flatware.

Two who are Mostly Good.
Two who have lived their day,
But keep on putting on their clothes
And putting things away.

And remembering...
Remembering, with twinklings and twinges,
As they lean over the beans in their rented back room
    that is full of beads and receipts and dolls and cloths,
    tobacco crumbs, vases and fringes.

Gwendolyn Brooks

Activity

1 What language helps to convey a precise sense of the old couple's lives?
2 What is the role of repeated and rhyming words?
3 How do the many nouns in the last two lines underscore the poem's attitude to the old couple?

Sometimes poets use vocabulary in non-standard or ungrammatical ways in order to achieve the effects they want.

Some poets might deliberately disrupt our expectations to create their effects, and sometimes they go further still in breaking the conventions of grammar. For example, E. E. Cummings is well known for the unconventional ways in which he uses language in his poems. Here is the first stanza from one of his poems. Some of the words have been removed.

__a__ lived in a pretty __b__ town

(with __c__ so floating many bells __d__)

spring summer autumn winter

he sang his __e__ he danced his __f__ .

Activity

Fill in the blanks in this stanza choosing words from the appropriate lists below.

a	b	c	d	e	f
someone	small	light	din	song	jig
Bill	quiet	gleaming	down	didn't	round
she	how	up	bright	turn	dance
they	hot	down	clamour	notes	did
anyone	slow	chimes	clash	solo	favourite

Now check your version against the original. Here are Cummings's words:

a anyone   **b** how   **c** up   **d** down   **e** didn't   **f** did

You probably found some or all of these choices rather surprising – not least because they apparently produce lines that seem nonsensical. This is because Cummings breaks the grammatical rules for combining the parts of speech or units of structure together.

Now have a look at the whole poem.

> ### Anyone lived in a pretty how town
>
> anyone lived in a pretty how town
> (with up so floating many bells down)
> spring summer autumn winter
> he sang his didn't he danced his did.
>
> Women and men(both little and small)
> cared for anyone not at all
> they sowed their isn't they reaped their same
> sun moon stars rain

children guessed(but only a few
and down they forgot as up they grew
autumn winter spring summer)
that noone loved him more by more

when by now and tree and leaf
she laughed his joy she cried his grief
bird by snow and stir by still
anyone's any was all to her

someones married their everyones
laughed their cryings and did their dance
(sleep wake hope and then)they
said their nevers they slept their dream

stars rain sun moon
(and only the snow can begin to explain
how children are apt to forget to remember
with up so floating many bells down)

one day anyone died i guess
(and noone stooped to kiss his face)
busy folk buried them side by side
little by little and was by was

all by all and deep by deep
and more by more they dream their sleep
noone and anyone earth by april
wish by spirit and if by yes.

Women and men(both dong and ding)
summer autumn winter spring
reaped their sowing and went their came
sun moon stars rain

E. E. Cummings

Activity

Now you have read the whole poem, answer the following questions:

1   Does the poet's use of the word "anyone" mean more to you now in the context of the whole poem? How do you think we are meant to interpret "anyone" and "someone"?

2   How does Cummings use pairings of words, such as "up/down", "did/didn't"? Have you found any more such pairings of opposites?

3   How does Cummings make use of repetition in the poem?

4   Now write a brief summary of what the poem is about.

5   The key question is why Cummings chooses to break the conventions of grammar and write his poem in this way. What effects do you think he achieves by this?

Part 2 Literary genres

When dealing with poems such as this one where the meaning is not necessarily immediately apparent, your initial responses may well be quite tentative. Don't worry about this, and don't worry about putting things down on paper that you feel unsure about. It is all part of the process of unravelling meaning from the text.

Here are the initial, tentative responses of two students as they work towards finding their meaning of *Anyone lived in a pretty how town*.

Commentary: Student A

1   The word "Anyone" is used to describe the people in the town. It also indicates that it is informal and impersonal, making the poem a story open to interpretation. A trivial tale about two or three people, yet the words indicate he's talking about mankind. "Anyone" and "Someone" are opposite words and the poet contrasts these types of words throughout the poem. They are meant to be interpreted as words which create a larger scale to the environment it is set in. The word "Anyone" throws the poem open to a wider scale of people and "Someone" is specific to one person. Anyone – male, Someone – female – gives it a universal theme.

2   He uses pairs of words such as "did" and "didn't", and "up" and "down", to describe how objects did things (in place of an adjective). Examples of pairing of words are: did/didn't, down/up, joy/grief, sun/moon, rain/snow – gives a pattern to the words.

3   He uses repetition to emphasize his points, for example about sleep he says "all by all" and "more by more". The repetition of the seasons indicates people moving on, living and then dying.

4   The poem describes what happens to anyone in a certain town. Through the seasons and through the weather how the men and women dance, sleep, and live.

Commentary: Student B

1   The poet uses the words "Anyone" and "Someone" throughout the poem. This could be to give the poem a more universal and wider meaning than would have been achieved if the characters had been named. "Anyone" and "Someone" could mean that the poem would be meant to apply to the reader. It stops stereotyping. Anyone is male + Someone is female.

2   Cummings uses pairings of words and opposites throughout the poem such as "up/down", "did/didn't", "joy/grief", "little/small", "dong/ding". This gives some degree of logic to often illogical sentences. It also means there is some rhyme in the verses. It leaves quite a lot open to interpretation.

3   Some words and lines are repeated throughout the poem. Although in a different order, "spring, summer, autumn, winter" and "reaped" and "sowed" are repeated to show a sense of passing of time. There is also the sense of people moving on and a cyclical element – closely tied in with environment.

4   This poem seems to tell a life story of a person. The fact that there are no names or characters generalizes the story, so it could apply to anyone. The repetition of "spring, summer, autumn, winter" suggests that life is the same every year. The inclusion of "sun, moon, stars" and "rain", especially at the end, shows that things go on and everybody is the same, as the sun, moon, stars, and rain are a constant for everyone. It seems to trivialize life

as everyone is there, they do their thing ("reaped their sowing and went their came") and then die, and it is no big deal.

Although these comments are initial and tentative, they are also exploratory. Both students have begun the process of coming to terms with a tricky brief. There are quite a number of points here that could be picked up and examined in more detail – some ideas are very perceptive, and already the students are beginning to identify the effects of such features as word pairings and repetition.

Imagery

Very often the language of poetry is made more intense through the use of images, which can add layers of meaning to a poem beyond the literal sense of the words on the page. Images can be created in various ways and language used in this way is sometime called "figurative language".

"Oh, wow! I always thought that was just a figure of speech."

Old English poets used a device of figurative language called the "kenning" which consisted of a word or phrase made up to identify a particular object or thing without naming it directly. They had a large selection of kennings for their most frequently used nouns. For example, instead of 'ocean' they could say "swan's road" or "foaming field" or "realm of monsters"; for "ship" they might say "sea goer" or "sea wood"; for a "lord" a "dispenser of rings" or "treasure giver"; for "the sun", "candle of the world".

Look at this poem by John Updike.

Winter Ocean

Many-maned scud-thumper, tub
of male whales, maker of worn wood, shrub-
ruster, sky-mocker, rave!
portly pusher of waves, wind slave.

John Updike

Activity

1 How many kennings can you identify here?
2 What is the effect of the use of kennings in this poem?
3 Make up three or four kennings of your own.

In this use of kennings, the Old English poets were using a kind of imagery to describe their particular subject. Images can work in several ways in the mind of the reader. For example, an image can be used literally to describe something, as in Wordsworth's description of taking a boat out onto the lake at night. The boat moves forward:

> Leaving behind her still, on either side,
> Small circles glittering idly in the moon,
> Until they melted all into one track
> Of sparkling light...

William Wordsworth

This creates a **literal image** as we can picture the scene in our minds from the way in which Wordsworth describes it. Non-literal, figurative or representational images can be created when the thing being described is compared to something else. You will probably already be familiar with the **simile**, in which the comparison is made very clear by the poet using the words "like" or "as". Often the elements being compared are essentially different in nature, but they come together in the poet's perception and ultimately in the reader's perception. For example, look at these lines from Anne Sexton's retelling of *Snow White and the Seven Dwarfs*:

> ...the queen dressed herself in rags
> and went out like a peddler to trap Snow White.
> She went across seven mountains.
> She came to the dwarf house
> and Snow White opened the door
> and bought a bit of lacing.
> The queen fastened it tightly
> around her bodice,
> as tight as an Ace bandage,
> so tight that Snow White swooned.
> She lay on the floor, a plucked daisy.
> When the dwarfs came home they undid the lace
> and she revived miraculously.
> She was as full of life as soda pop.

Activity

Now look at the following poem by Sylvia Plath.
1   Identify the similes that Plath uses here.
2   Describe the effect created by each simile.

Blackberrying

Nobody in the lane, and nothing, nothing but blackberries,
Blackberries on either side, though on the right mainly,
A blackberry alley, going down in hooks, and a sea

Somewhere at the end of it, heaving. Blackberries
Big as the ball of my thumb, and dumb as eyes
Ebon in the hedges, fat
With blue-red juices. These they squander on my fingers.
I had not asked for such a blood sisterhood; they must love me.
They accommodate themselves to my milkbottle, flattening their sides.

Overhead go the choughs in black, cacophonous flocks –
Bits of burnt paper wheeling in a blown sky.
Theirs is the only voice, protesting, protesting.
I do not think the sea will appear at all.
The high, green meadows are glowing, as if lit from within.
I come to one bush of berries so ripe it is a bush of flies,
Hanging their bluegreen bellies and their wing panes in a Chinese screen.
The honey-feast of the berries has stunned them; they believe in heaven.
One more hook and the berries and bushes end.

The only thing to come now is the sea.
From between two hills a sudden wind funnels at me,
Slapping its phantom laundry in my face.
These hills are too green and sweet to have tasted salt.
I follow the sheep path between them. A last hook brings me
To the hills' northern face, and the face is orange rock
That looks out on nothing, nothing but a great space
Of white and pewter lights, and a din like silversmiths
Beating and beating at an intractable metal.

Sylvia Plath

The **metaphor** is another feature that poets often use, and with which you will probably be familiar. In some ways a metaphor is like a simile in that it too creates a comparison. However, the comparison is less direct than the simile in that it does not include the terms "like" or "as", but often describes the subject as *being* the thing to which it is compared. For example, in the poem you have just examined, Plath describes the choughs (large black birds rather like crows) in this way:

Overhead go the choughs in black, cacophonous flocks –
Bits of burnt paper wheeling in a blown sky.

Of course, Plath does not literally mean that the choughs are bits of burnt paper – it is meant metaphorically. The look of the black birds wheeling in the sky reminds her of the way bits of burnt paper can float around in the air.

Another kind of feature frequently used by poets is **personification**. This is really a kind of metaphor in which the attributes of a person are given to either abstract or non-human things. Plath makes use of personification in *Blackberrying*. For example, she describes the juices which the blackberries:

... squander on my fingers.
I had not asked for such a blood sisterhood; they must love me.
They accommodate themselves to my milkbottle, flattening their sides.

Here the blackberries are described as having human feelings and doing what they can to help her collect them.

Poets often use **symbolism**, too, to help to create the effects they want, sometimes drawing on commonly recognized symbols and sometimes inventing their own. In basic terms a symbol is simply a feature whereby a word or phrase represents something else – for example, the colour white could be used to represent peace. Symbolism in poetry can be very complex, with some poems operating on two levels, the literal and the symbolic. Sometimes in order to fully understand the significance of a poem it is necessary to understand the symbolic importance of some of the ideas or images used.

Activity

Read this poem by Donald Hall and see how far you can follow the meanings Hall has invested in the relation between father and son.

My Son, My Executioner

My son, my executioner,
    I take you in my arms,
Quiet and small and just astir,
    And whom my body warms.

Sweet death, small son, our instrument
    Of immortality,
Your cries and hungers document
    Our bodily decay.

We twenty-five and twenty-two,
    Who seemed to live forever,
Observe enduring life in you
    And start to die together.

Donald Hall

Aural imagery
Some kinds of images rely not on the "pictures" they create in the mind of the reader, but on the effects they have on the ear, or a combination of both.

Alliteration
This involves the repetition of the same consonant sound, usually at the beginning of each word, over two or more words together, as in Shakespeare's lines from *The Tempest*:

Full **f**athom **f**ive thy **f**ather lies,
Of his bones are coral made.

The repeated "f" sounds create a sense of solemnity and give an incantatory feel to the line.

Assonance
Assonance is a feature similar to alliteration, but instead of consonants it involves the repetition of vowel sounds to achieve a

particular effect. An example is the long, drawn-out "o" sounds in the first line of Sylvia Plath's *Frog Autumn*:

Summer grows **old**, **cold-blooded mother**

This creates an impression of lethargy and lack of life as summer passes and winter approaches.

Onomatopoeia

Onomatopoeia refers to words that, by their sound, reflect their meaning – "bang" or "ping" are simple examples that sound like the noises they describe. Here is a more sophisticated example, from Coleridge's *The Rime of the Ancient Mariner*.

The ice was here, the ice was there,
The ice was all around;
It **cracked** and **growled**, and **roared** and **howled**,
Like noises in a swound

The words "cracked", "growled", "roared", and "howled" suggest the sounds of the icebergs grinding around the ship, and therefore make the description more graphic in an aural as well as visual way. It is perhaps worth noting also that Coleridge makes use of repetition here, emphasizing the fact that ice was everywhere.

It is very important to bear in mind when writing about poetry that there is little value in simply identifying the features unless you explain the effects they create in the poem and on the reader.

Now read the following poem by Sylvia Plath.

Mirror

I am silver and exact. I have no preconceptions.
Whatever I see I swallow immediately
Just as it is, unmisted by love or dislike.
I am not cruel, only truthful –
The eye of a little god, four-cornered.
Most of the time I meditate on the opposite wall.
It is pink, with speckles. I have looked at it so long
I think it is part of my heart. But it flickers.
Faces and darkness separate us over and over.
Now I am a lake. A woman bends over me,
Searching my reaches for what she really is.
Then she turns to those liars, the candles or the moon.
I see her back, and reflect it faithfully.
She rewards me with tears and an agitation of hands.
I am important to her. She comes and goes.
Each morning it is her face that replaces the darkness.
In me she has drowned a young girl, and in me an old woman
Rises towards her day after day, like a terrible fish.

Sylvia Plath

> **Activity**
>
> Remind yourself of *My Son, My Executioner* by Donald Hall (opposite page). Write a detailed analysis comparing the way Plath uses imagery in *The Mirror* with the ways in which Hall uses it in *My Son, My Executioner*.

Form and structure

Form and **structure** can also tell the reader something about the poet's intentions. The way that the language of the poem is laid out will have been carefully chosen by the poet to enhance or reflect the meaning of the poem. There are many different ways in which poems can be structured, and in looking at the particular structure of a poem we must ask ourselves why a poet has chosen to use a particular form.

Form can refer to the way that the poem is written on the page, or the way that the lines are organized or grouped. Basically, poetry can be divided into general categories. First there is the kind where the lines follow on from each other continuously without breaks. Long narrative poems often take this form, and poems such as Frost's *Out, Out* or Keats's *Lamia*. The technical term for this kind of poetic form is **stichic** poetry.

The other kind of poetry is that where the lines are arranged in groups, which are sometimes incorrectly called "verses". The correct term for these groups of lines is **stanzas**. This kind of poetic form is called **strophic** poetry and examples of its use are in poems such as Margaret Atwood's *Late Night* or Sylvia Plath's *Crossing the Water*.

Stanzas can be organized in many different ways. Here are some examples.

The sonnet

The sonnet is a very popular form in English poetry, and one that poets have used for centuries. Basically a sonnet consists of 14 lines with a structured rhyme scheme and a definite rhythm pattern (usually iambic pentameter, see page 122). There are two main kinds of sonnet. The Petrarchan or Italian sonnet is so called because it is named after the medieval Italian writer, Petrarch. The Petrarchan sonnet divides the 14 lines into an octave (eight lines) and a sestet (six lines). The rhyme scheme can vary but generally the pattern is *abbaabba cdecde* or *abbaabba cdcdcd*. The octave sets out the theme or key idea of the poem and the sestet provides some kind of response to it.

The other main kind of sonnet is the Shakespearean or English sonnet. In this kind of sonnet the lines are divided into three quatrains (of four lines each) and end with a couplet (two lines). The rhyme scheme in this kind of sonnet generally follows the pattern *abab cdcd efef gg*. The theme or idea is developed through the quatrains, and summed up or answered in the couplet.

Now read the following two sonnets.

> ## To My Brothers
>
> Small, busy flames play through the fresh laid coals,
>   And their faint cracklings o'er our silence creep
>   Like whispers of the household gods that keep
> A gentle empire o'er fraternal souls.

And while, for rhymes, I search around the poles,
  Your eyes are fix'd, as in poetic sleep,
  Upon the lore so voluble and deep,
That aye at fall of night our care condoles.

This is your birth-day Tom, and I rejoice
  That thus it passes smoothly, quietly.
Many such eves of gently whisp'ring noise
  May we together pass, and calmly try
What are this world's true joys, – ere the great voice,
  From its fair face, shall bid our spirits fly.

John Keats

Sonnet XVIII

Shall I compare thee to a Summers day?
Thou art more lovely and more temperate:
Rough windes do shake the darling buds of Maie,
And Sommers lease hath all too short a date:
Sometime too hot the eye of heaven shines,
And often is his gold complexion dim'd,
And every faire from faire some-time declines,
By chance, or natures changing course untrim'd:
But thy eternall Sommer shall not fade,
Nor loose possession of that faire thou ow'st,
Nor shall death brag thou wandr'st in his shade,
When in eternall lines to time thou grow'st,
  So long as men can breath or eyes can see,
  So long lives this, and this gives life to thee.

William Shakespeare

Activity

1 Examine the form each sonnet is written in and the rhyme scheme each poet has employed.

2 What are the key ideas each sonnet deals with? Examine the language each poet has used to express his ideas.

3 How does the language combine with the structure of each sonnet to fulfil the poets' intentions?

Other forms which you may come across in your studies include the following.

Ballads

Ballads date back to the oral tradition of the late Middle Ages and originally were often set to music. They are poems that tell a story, and therefore the focus tends to be on action and dialogue rather than the contemplative exploration of some kind of theme. The structure of the ballad normally consists of rhyming quatrains, sometimes using dialect forms or repetition to create effects.

Odes

Odes are lyrical poems, often elaborate, addressed to a particular person or thing or an abstract idea. They can present straightforward praise or they can develop complex philosophical ideas, and they can focus on positive or negative feelings with, perhaps, involved arguments. They are complex poems – the language often reflects the complexity of the content and many images may be contained within the poem. Odes are often organized into stanzas, but as in the following ode by the Chilean poet Pablo Neruda, they can take other forms. Below is an excerpt from one of his "common odes".

Ode to the Clothes

Every morning you wait,
clothes, over a chair,
for my vanity,
my love,
my hope, my body
to fill you,
I have scarcely
left sleep,
I say goodbye to the water
and enter your sleeves,
my legs look for
the hollow of your legs,
and thus embraced
by your unwearying fidelity
I go out to tread the fodder,
I move into poetry,
I look through windows,
at things,
men, women,
actions and struggles
keep making me what I am,
opposing me,
employing my hands,
opening my eyes,
putting taste in my mouth,
and thus,
clothes,
I make you what you are,
pushing out your elbows,
bursting the seams,
and so your life swells
the image of my life...

Pablo Neruda

Activity

We all have things both common and elevated about which we could write an ode. Try your hand at composing one. Start by listing all the things that excite you or that you love about a particular idea or thing. Then see what you can do with this kind of poem. Just remember what Mark Twain said in a letter to George Bainton, 15 October 1888: "The difference between the almost right word and the right word is really a large matter – it's the difference between the lightning bug and the lightning." (A lightning bug is another name for a firefly or glow worm.)

Free verse

Another form of verse that we should mention here is **free verse**. Although modern poets also write in forms which adhere to strict patterns and forms, some of which we have already looked at, it is true that in the twentieth century there was a move towards poetry that does not have constraints of form, structure, rhyme, or rhythm. Sometimes this type of verse does not even have regular lines, and the flexibility of free verse allows poets to use language in whatever ways seem appropriate to their purpose, and to create the effects they desire in their work.

Here is a poem written in free verse. Read it carefully.

To Women, As Far As I'm Concerned

The feelings I don't have I don't have.
The feelings I don't have I won't say I have.
The feelings you say you have, you don't have.
The feelings you would like us both to have, we neither of us have.
The feelings people ought to have, they never have.
If people say they've got feelings, you may be pretty sure
    They haven't got them.
So if you want either of us to feel anything at all
You'd better abandon all ideas of feelings altogether.

D.H. Lawrence

Activity

1   From the evidence of the way Lawrence uses language here, what do you think are the main features of free verse?

2   How do you think it differs from most other kinds of poetry?

You might have noted some of the following:

- Free verse does not follow any regular syllabic, metrical, or rhyming pattern.
- It tends to follow speech rhythms of language.
- The line is the basic unit of rhythm.
- Spaces on the page can indicate pauses in the movement of the poem.
- Free verse may rely on effects such as alliteration, or repetition, to provide unity.

Other poetic techniques

There are a range of other techniques in using language that poets can draw on in writing their poetry. For the most part these techniques, like the use of imagery for example, are common to all kinds of literary writing. However, some are generally only found in poetry. Here are some of the main ones.

Enjambment

Enjambment is the term used to describe an instance where, because of its grammatical structure, verse runs on from one line to another. This can sometimes take the reader by surprise, as the meaning is not complete at the end of the line. Often, punctuation elsewhere in the line reinforces the need to run on at the end of the line.

End stop

End stop, in contrast, describes an instance where the grammatical break coincides with the end of a line. The break is often marked by a punctuation mark, and the meaning of the line is complete in itself.

Caesura

A caesura is simply a break or a pause in a line of verse, but it can be very important in influencing the rhythm of the poem.

> I never had noticed it until
> Twas gone, – the narrow copse,
>
> **Edward Thomas**

Now read *Postcard* by Margaret Atwood.

Postcard

I'm thinking about you. What else can I say?
The palm trees on the reverse
are a delusion; so is the pink sand.
What we have are the usual
fractured coke bottles and the smell
of backed-up drains, too sweet,
like a mango on the verge
of rot, which we have also.
The air clear sweat, mosquitoes
& their tracks; birds, blue & elusive.

Time comes in waves here, a sickness, one
day after the other rolling on;
I move up, it's called
awake, then down into the uneasy
nights but never
forward. The roosters crow
for hours before dawn, and a prodded
child howls & howls
on the pocked road to school.
In the hold with the baggage
there are two prisoners,
their heads shaved by bayonets, & ten crates
of queasy chicks. Each spring
there's a race of cripples, from the store
to the church. This is the sort of junk

I carry with me; and a clipping
about democracy from the local paper.

Outside the window
they're building the damn hotel,
nail by nail, someone's
crumbling dream. A universe that includes you
can't be all bad, but
does it? At this distance
you're a mirage, a glossy image
fixed in the posture
of the last time I saw you.
Turn you over, there's the place
for the address. Wish you were
here. Love comes
in waves like the ocean, a sickness which goes on
& on, a hollow cave
in the head, filling & pounding, a kicked ear.

Margaret Atwood

> ### Activity
>
> 1 Look at the poem carefully
>   and make a note of where
>   lines are end-stopped
>   and where Atwood uses
>   enjambment. What effect
>   does this have on the poem?
>
> 2 Notice how Atwood's
>   punctuation often forces you
>   to pause in the middle of a
>   line rather than at the end.
>   What effect do you think this
>   has?

Rhythm

Rhythm can be an important element in poetry and some of the poems you remember from your earliest childhood, such as nursery rhymes, have very strong rhythms. It is these strong rhythms, along with the sounds of the words themselves and the rhymes, that give them such appeal to young children.

However, the influence of rhythm is not something exclusively reserved for nursery rhymes – a sense of rhythm can exert a profound influence on the overall effect of any poem. The rhythm can help to create mood and influence the tone and atmosphere of a poem. It is this rhythm that can give a poem its feeling of movement and life, and the poet can use rhythm to create a whole variety of effects within the poem.

Syllable stress

Poets can create rhythms in poetry in various ways. Language has natural rhythms built into it, which we use automatically every time we pronounce words. For example, with the word "randomly" we naturally stress the first syllable and not the second. Poets use these natural stresses and in-built rhythm patterns to contribute to the overall rhythmic effect.

Emphatic stress

Poets often deliberately place the emphasis on a particular word or part of the word in order to achieve a particular effect. The stress could be shifted to emphasize a particular meaning or reinforce a point, or even change meaning.

Phrasing and punctuation

The rhythm of poetry, along with other kinds of writing, can be influenced by factors such as word order, length of phrases, or the choice of punctuation marks, line and stanza breaks, and use of repetition.

Metre

Poetic metre is the pattern of stressed and unstressed syllables in a line of poetry, and as such is very closely linked to the idea of rhythm. The concept originated from the principles of classical Greek and Latin verse and was adopted by English poets from early times. These principles stated that each line of verse should follow a precise and regular pattern in terms of how many syllables it contained and the stress pattern used. These regular patterns of stressed and unstressed syllables are called **metres**. By analysing the metre, the reader can see how the poet is using the stress patterns within the language as one of the ways by which the meaning of the poem is conveyed. Variations in the pattern could mark changes in mood or tone, or signify a change of direction in the movement of the poem.

In identifying the metre of a poem, the first thing to do is to establish how the rhythm pattern is created. The syllables can be divided into groups of two or three (depending on the particular pattern). Each of these groups is called a **foot**. The number of **feet** in a line can vary.

Here are the main patterns:

One foot	monometer
Two feet	dimeter
Three feet	trimeter
Four feet	tetrameter
Five feet	pentameter
Six feet	hexameter
Seven feet	heptameter
Eight feet	octameter

The process of identifying the metre is called **scansion**. Stressed syllables are marked $^/$ while unstressed syllables are marked $^\smile$ and the feet are divided up using vertical lines |. A double vertical line ‖ indicates a caesura.

There are five basic patterns of stress. These are:

● **Iambic:** one unstressed syllable followed by a stressed one (iamb)

When I | have fears | that I | may cease | to be

Before | my pen | hath glean'd | my teem | ing brain,

Keats

- **Trochaic:** one stressed syllable followed by one unstressed (trochee)

  / ˘   / ˘   /   ˘   /
  Tyger! | Tyger! | Burning | bright
  /   ˘   /   ˘   /   ˘   /
  In the | forests | of the | night

  Blake

- **Dactylic:** one stressed syllable followed by two unstressed syllables (dactyl)

  /   ˘   ˘   /   ˘   ˘
  Half a league, | Half a league,
  /   ˘   ˘   /   ˘
  Half a league, | onward

  Tennyson

- **Anapaestic:** two unstressed syllables followed by one stressed syllable (anapaest)

  /   ˘   ˘   /   ˘   ˘   /   ˘   ˘   /
  Will's | at the dance | in the Club | -room below,
  /   ˘   ˘   /   ˘   ˘   /
  Where | the tall liqu | or cups foam;

  Hardy

- **Spondaic:** two stressed syllables (spondee)

  /   /
  One, two
  /   ˘   ˘   /
  Buckle my shoe.

  Anon

For example, look at these lines from Keats's *When I have fears*.

> ## When I have fears
>
> When I have fears that I may cease to be
>   Before my pen hath glean'd my teeming brain
> Before high-piled books, in charact'ry,
>   Hold like rich garners the full-ripen'd grain:
> When I behold, upon the night's starr'd face,
>   Huge cloudy symbols of a high romance,
> And think that I may never live to trace
>   Their shadows, with the magic hand of chance;
> And when I feel, fair creature of an hour!
>   That I shall never look upon thee more,
> Never have relish in the faery power
>   Of unreflecting love! – then on the shore
> Of the wide world I stand alone, and think
>   Till love and fame to nothingness do sink.
>
> *John Keats*

The first two lines were scanned for you on the opposite page. Now scan the remainder of the poem. How many metrical feet are there per line? What is the metrical pattern? Look at the poem again. What effect does the metrical pattern have on the overall effect of the poem?

Rhyme

Rhyme can make an important contribution to the musical quality of a poem and, like rhythm, it affects the sound and the overall effectiveness. The system of rhyme within a poem, or rhyme scheme, can influence this effect in a variety of ways. The rhyme scheme could help to unify the poem and draw it together; it could give it an incantatory quality or add emphasis to particular elements of the vocabulary. There are various kinds of rhymes and rhyme schemes. The most common rhymes work on the basis of a rhyme occurring at the end of a line and are called **complete rhymes**, as in "free" rhyming with "tree", or "feel" with "seal".

Sometimes rhymes occur within the line itself. These are called **internal rhymes**. Coleridge makes use of this kind of rhyme in *The Rime of the Ancient Mariner*.

> The fair breeze blew, the white foam flew,
> The furrow followed free;
> We were the first that ever burst
> Into that silent sea.

In this case, the rhyming of "blew" and "flew" stresses these words and adds emphasis to the image of the ship's speed and movement.

A rhyme may appear incomplete or inaccurate in various ways. The vowels may not be pronounced in the same way, for example "love" and "move" or "plough" and "rough". These are called **eye rhymes** or **sight rhymes**. Some poets choose deliberately to weaken the force of the rhyme by making either the consonant or vowel different. Wilfred Owen frequently uses this technique, as here for example:

> Like twitching agonies of men among its brambles
> Northward, incessantly, the flickering gunnery rumbles

Or:

> We only know war lasts, rain soaks, and clouds sag stormy
> Dawn massing in the east her melancholy army
> Attacks once more in ranks on shivering ranks of gray

This kind of rhyme is called **half rhyme**, **slant rhyme** or **para-rhyme**.

In the same way that the rhythm in a poem often follows a recognized pattern, so can rhyme. The important thing in looking at the rhyme scheme of a poem, however, is not spotting the rhymes or working out the scheme but being able to identify what effect the rhyme scheme has on the poem. In other words you need to be able to explain why the poet has chosen to use language in this particular way, and what the overall effects of those language choices are.

Here are some of the effects that the use of rhyme might have on a poem.

- It can make a poem sound musical and pleasing to the ear.
- It can create a jarring, discordant effect.
- It can add emphasis to certain words and give particular words an added prominence.

- It can act as a unifying influence on the poem, drawing it together through the rhyme patterns.
- It can give the poem a rhythmic, incantatory, or ritualistic feel.
- It can influence the rhythm of the verse.
- It can provide a sense of finality – the rhyming couplet, for example, is often used to give a sense of "ending".
- It can exert a subconscious effect on the reader, drawing together certain words or images, affecting the sound, or adding emphasis in some way.

Now read the following two poems carefully.

The Spirit Fox

The cattle of the spirit move slowly
along the borders of your sleep,
dark behemoths of warmth, valleys
of their backs and shoulders
damp with dew.

Then there is the spirit fox,
red and lean as fire turned into muscle.

The cattle are always there, just
beyond your dreams, your body
heavy with the thought of them,
but you see the fox only
in the way you see your breath
on a cold clear day,
that surprise of the invisible
where your mouth meets the air.

The cattle graze in winter pastures,
look up with great calm eyes
as if they do not know you,
as if you make no difference.

Their insouciance, the soothing bigness
of the hips and udders of the cows
startles you
as if it all comes down to birth.

Paws hushed by snow,
by prairie wool, the fox
steps just behind you. You feel
its gaze on the back of your neck

and you're afraid to turn
into the green flint of its stare
you know will see too much of you
and leave nothing out.

Lorna Crozier

Season

Rust is ripeness, rust,
And the wilted corn-plume.
Pollen is mating-time when swallows
Weave a dance
Of feathered arrows
Thread corn-stalks in winged
Streaks of light. And we loved to hear
Spliced phrases of the wind, to hear
Rasps in the field, where corn-leaves
Pierce like bamboo slivers.

Now, garnerers we,
Awaiting rust on tassles, draw
Long shadows from the dusk, wreathe
The thatch in wood-smoke. Laden stalks
Ride the germ's decay – we await
The promise of the rust.

Wole Soyinka

Activity

Compare the techniques used by Crozier and Soyinka and the effects that they achieve in these two poems. How do they manage to engage the reader's interest?

DETAILED STUDY

Carol Ann Duffy

Carol Ann Duffy was born in Glasgow in 1955. She grew up in Stafford and later moved to Liverpool. She graduated from Liverpool University with a degree in Philosophy and now lives in London where she works as a freelance writer. In 1977, she embarked on a career as a playwright and two of her plays were performed at Liverpool Playhouse. This led her into television where she worked as a freelance scriptwriter. However, it is for her poetry that Carol Ann Duffy is best known and has gained acclaim, winning the Dylan Thomas Award in 1989 and the Whitbread Poetry Award in 1993. She is regarded now as one of Britain's leading contemporary poets, her work dealing with themes that have universal significance touching on the concerns of all people. Although it is easy to see some of her poetry reflecting her own life, in reading her work it is a mistake to see it as autobiographical and to look for clues to its significance in Duffy's own life. The poems should be viewed in a much wider context than this and the voice of the poems should be seen as expressing concerns, experiences and emotions that lie deep within us all.

She has written several anthologies of poetry, perhaps the best known being her fourth, "Mean Time". In this Detailed Study we will focus on poems from this collection to illustrate the nature of her poetry and the ideas, themes, and issues that she explores through it. Remember, when you are thinking and writing about her poetry, examiners are not interested in students "spotting" features of language such as the use of similes or metaphors or alliteration. Just identifying such features really tells us nothing about how a poem works or the effect that it might create in the mind of the reader. What examiners really want you to look at is how poets use language and why they make the language choices that they do. In other words you need to be aware of the language choices the poet has made, be sensitive to why the poet has chosen a particular form of words, and explain the effect that is created by the words that have been chosen.

Themes and issues in Duffy's poetry

Carol Ann Duffy has said that the title of her collection, "Mean Time", can have a variety of interpretations.

> **Activity**
>
> Think about this title and write down the different ideas that can be associated with the phrase "Mean Time".

Here are some ideas that you may have thought about:

- the passage of time – "in the mean time"
- time is "mean" – hard and unforgiving
- time is "mean" – we don't get enough of it
- time means something – the "meaning" of time
- Greenwich Mean Time – this sets standard time for the world.

Here is the title poem of the collection:

Mean Time

The clocks slid back an hour
and stole light from my life
as I walked through the wrong part of town,
mourning our love.

Part 2 Literary genres

And, of course, unmendable rain
fell to the bleak streets
where I felt my heart gnaw
at all our mistakes.

If the darkening sky could lift
more than one hour from this day
there are words I would never have said
nor have heard you say.

But we will be dead, as we know,
beyond all light.
These are the shortened days
and the endless nights.

Activity

Read the poem through carefully several times. What is it about, and why do you think Duffy chose this particular poem to provide the title for the whole anthology?

Here are some ideas you might have thought of:

- The poem opens with the clocks being "put back" one hour, referring to the adjustment we make to our clocks in the autumn, which in Britain changes them from BST (British Summer Time) to GMT (Greenwich Mean Time). One obvious result when we do this is that it gets dark an hour earlier in the evenings. Note how she uses this image of "stealing light" to reveal the poet's emotional state at the breakdown of a relationship. This darkness/loss idea is further reinforced by connotations of death introduced through her use of "mourning". The sense of disorientation the poet feels at this loss is emphasized in "I walked through the wrong part of town".

- The second stanza continues this sense of despair and darkness with images such as "unmendable rain", and "bleak streets/ where I felt my heart gnaw/ at all our mistakes". The word "gnaw" here is particularly powerful, implying a constant, insidious eating away at

the mistakes that cannot be changed. This heightens the sense of destructive pain the poet endures.

- In the third stanza we return to the idea of "time" and again the mood is darkened, this time through the image of the "darkening sky", which reinforces the sense of hopelessness and resignation. Even the possibility of metaphorically "turning back the clocks" could provide no solution.

- The finality of the situation is evoked in the last stanza through the bleak image of death. The poet uses this in both a literal sense (one day they will be dead) and a metaphorical sense (they are dead in the sense that they have lost the light in their lives). The poem ends with a return to the image of the taking away of light and the ensuing darkness.

- This poem encapsulates all the central themes that Duffy explores in the poems in this selection and, as such, can be seen as a poem that sounds the "key note" of the anthology as a whole.

Activity

Write a list of the central themes that you think the poem explores.

Here is our list:
- the breakdown of a relationship
- loss
- time
- change
- emotional darkness
- pain
- love and the loss of it.

Now read *Havisham*, another poem by Duffy.

This will, perhaps, mean more to you if you have read Charles Dickens's *Great Expectations*. In that novel, Miss Havisham is an old woman who, many years previously, had been deserted by her fiancé on her wedding day. This experience leaves her a bitter and lonely woman who spends the rest of her life in solitude, shut off from the world.

Havisham

Beloved sweetheart bastard. Not a day since then
I haven't wished him dead. Prayed for it
so hard I've dark green pebbles for eyes,
ropes on the back of my hands I could strangle with.

Spinster. I stink and remember. Whole days
in bed cawing Nooooo at the wall; the dress
yellowing, trembling if I open the wardrobe;
the slewed mirror, full-length, her, myself, who did this

to me? Puce curses that are sounds not words.
Some nights better, the lost body over me,
my fluent tongue in its mouth in its ear
then down till I suddenly bite awake. Love's

hate behind a white veil; a red balloon bursting
in my face. Bang. I stabbed at a wedding-cake.
Give me a male corpse for a long slow honeymoon.
Don't think it's only the heart that b-b-b-breaks.

Activity

What does this poem have in common with *Mean Time*? What message do you think Duffy wants to convey to her readers?

The language of "Mean Time"
When we examine Duffy's use of language in her poetry, every poem needs to be looked at individually. However, in talking about what she hopes to achieve through her writing she has drawn attention to several specific features that you might like to keep in mind when looking in detail at her work. These features include:

- her use of rhyme
- her use of "echoes" and assonance
- the form of her poetry – the ways in which stanzas are organized to give an ordered shape to the poems
- the use of imagery
- the use of a language and vocabulary of her time.

Now read the following poem carefully.

Confession

Come away into this dark cell and tell
your sins to a hidden man your guardian angel
works your conscience like a glove-puppet It
smells in here doesn't it does it smell
like a coffin how would you know C'mon
out with them sins those little maggoty things
that wriggle in the soul... *Bless me Father...*

Just how bad have you been there's no water
in hell merely to think of a wrong's as evil
as doing it... *For I have sinned...* Penance
will cleanse you like a bar of good soap so
say the words into the musty gloom aye
on your knees let's hear that wee voice
recite transgression in the manner approved... *Forgive me...*

You do well to stammer A proper respect
for eternal damnation see the flicker
of your white hands clasping each other like
Hansel and Gretel in the big black wood
cross yourself Remember the vinegar and sponge
there's light on the other side of the door... *Mother
of God...* if you can only reach it Jesus loves you.

Activity

Look carefully at the form and structure and the poet's use of imagery here. What effect do the poet's choice of imagery and the overall form and structure create? (Note particularly the effect on the reader of the lack of punctuation.)

Here are some points that you might have noticed:

- The poem opens with a rather threatening image as the poet is invited to "Come away into this dark cell and tell/ your sins to a hidden man". Normally the religious idea of the confessional is associated with a comforting spiritual cleansing, but here the image is sinister and threatening. This feeling is increased through the image of the priest working "your conscience like a glove-puppet", which implies that the priest has total control, and the poet is helpless in his grip. The lack of punctuation here merges the voice of the priest and the voice of the poet into one, almost as if they have no separate identity. The image of sins as "maggoty things/ that wriggle in the soul" creates an unpleasant image of them eating away at the individual.

- Stanza 2 opens with what seems to be the voice of the priest again drawing the poet into the act of confession by evoking an image of hell and damnation. Penance, which is usually seen as an act of spiritual cleansing, is compared to being cleansed by a bar of soap. Through this imagery, Duffy is criticizing the narrow, limited, and perhaps shallow nature of the ritual of the confessional.

- The final stanza begins with the priest's reference to the poet's "stammering" through the confessional. Again punctuation marks are omitted, although capital letters are used to denote when the priest begins a new point. Again the poet's fear is played on, this time through the image of Hansel and Gretel alone "in the big black wood". This creates a sense of insecurity and alienation which is used to reinforce the need to "cross yourself". The image of the vinegar and the sponge brings to mind the crucifixion of Christ and complements the image of there being light on the other side of the door. However, the final line – "... if you can only reach it Jesus loves you" – leaves the unresolved question of whether the "light" is attainable and, if it is, is the confession box the way to attain it?

Now read the following two poems.

First Love

Waking, with a dream of first love forming real words,
as close to my lips as lipstick, I speak your name,
after a silence of years, into the pillow, and the power
of your name brings me here to the window, naked,
to say it again to a garden shaking with light.

This was a child's love, and yet I clench my eyes
till the pictures return, unfocused at first, then
almost clear, an old film played at a slow speed.
All day I will glimpse it, in windows of changing sky,
in mirrors, my lover's eyes, wherever you are.

And later a star, long dead, here, seems precisely
the size of a tear. Tonight, a love-letter out of a dream
stammers itself in my heart. Such faithfulness.
You smile in my head on the last evening. Unseen
flowers suddenly pierce and sweeten the air.

Stuffed

I put two yellow peepers in an owl.
Wow. I fix the grin of Crocodile.
Spiv. I sew the slither of an eel.

I jerk, kick-start, the back hooves of a mule.
Wild. I hold a red rag to a bull.
Mad. I spread the feathers of a gull.

I screw a tight snarl to a weasel.
Fierce. I stitch the flippers on a seal.
Splayed. I pierce the heartbeat of a quail.

I like her to be naked and to kneel.
Tame. My motionless, my living doll.
Mute. And afterwards I like her not to tell.

Activity

Compare and contrast these two poems examining the following:

- the ways in which Duffy uses imagery
- the form and structure of the poems
- the themes and issues she examines through these poems.

6 Studying drama

Part 2 Literary genres

Objectives
- To prepare yourself for writing and talking about drama
- To consider some of the features to look for in evaluating drama texts
- To prepare for studying drama texts

What is drama?

A dictionary definition will state that: "Drama is something intended specifically for performance on stage in front of an audience".

Drama is written to be seen rather than read, and its meaning can only be fully appreciated when seen in performance. This makes it a much more "public" form than prose or poetry, in that the experience of the play in performance is a shared experience. This essential aspect of drama is easy to lose sight of when sitting in a classroom, or on your own, grappling with the language of a drama text.

The two elements of study: script and performance

It is essential, then, that you are aware in approaching a play that you are dealing with a work that is very different from, say, a novel and that you will need to employ quite different strategies to handle it. You must be able to visualize the play in your head – be able to bring the play alive in your mind and see and hear the action as if you were at the theatre. Developing the ability to do this can be difficult simply by reading from the printed page. However, there are things you can do, from the outset, to help.

- Recognize that reading a play is essentially a group activity and so work with others as much as possible.
- Go and see plays performed as often as possible. (Do not restrict yourself to the ones you are studying, or just to professional productions.)
- Keep a notebook or journal of plays that you see, noting your responses – thoughts and feelings about performances and ideas on production.
- Take part in "acting out" parts of a play – this will help you to appreciate the staging implications of a text in a way that straight reading never can.
- Listen to audio tapes or watch video recordings of plays. (These do not replace seeing the play "live" but they are better than only reading the scripts.)
- Remember that words leap to life when given performance, and that each live performance alters the play in some slight or significant way.

With this key point in mind, let us consider some aspects of plays that you will need to examine in the texts that you study. Some of these aspects may be more familiar to you from television or film productions.

> "*It is in our nature to dramatise.*"
> David Mamet,
> American playwright,
> in *Three Uses of the Knife*

Opening scenes

The way that a play opens is obviously crucial to engaging the audience's attention and writers can take many options here depending on the effects that they wish to achieve. In looking at an opening scene there are some key questions that are worth asking. The central questions are: "What effect does the writer want this scene to have on the audience?" and "What purpose does the scene serve in the play as a whole?" Here are some possible answers to these questions.

● The scene provides an explanation of the situation, background information, and details the audience needs in order to understand what is going on. This is sometimes called **exposition** (see page 146). An example would be the opening of Chekhov's *Uncle Vanya*, where significant characters explain the current situation and some important background.

● The scene creates a setting or background against which the play is set, as in Williams's *A Streetcar Named Desire*.

● The scene creates a mood or creates tension which captures the audience's attention immediately (the opening scene of *Hamlet* is a good example of this).

● The scene introduces characters, situations, and relationships, as in Shakespeare's *King Lear*.

● The scene provokes a sense of intrigue which captures the audience's attention and makes them want to know more, as in Shakespeare's *Macbeth*.

Activity

1 Read carefully the opening to Brian Friel's *Making History*. Think about what Friel hopes to achieve here and what effect it would have on the audience.

2 Discuss this opening with a partner or think about it on your own, focusing on these aspects:

● your impression of the two characters and their concerns

● the information conveyed to the audience here and the techniques that Friel uses to put it across

● the kind of atmosphere created and how Friel creates it.

Making History

by Brian Friel

Act I Scene 1

(*A large living room in* **O'Neill's** *home in Dungannon, County Tyrone, Ireland. Late August in 1591. The room is spacious and scantily furnished: a large, refectory-type table; some chairs and stools; a sideboard. No attempt at decoration.*

O'Neill *moves around this comfortless room quickly and energetically, inexpertly cutting the stems off flowers, thrusting the flowers into various vases and then adding water. He is not listening to* **Harry Hoveden** *who consults and reads from various papers on the table.*

O'Neill *is forty-one. A private, sharp-minded man at this moment uncharacteristically outgoing and talkative. He always speaks in an upper-class English accent except on those occasions specifically scripted.* **Harry Hoveden**, *his personal secretary, is about the same age as* **O'Neill**. **O'Neill** *describes him as a man 'who has a comforting and a soothing effect'.*)

Harry	That takes care of Friday. Saturday you're free all day – so far. Then on Sunday – that'll be the fourteenth – O'Hagan's place at Tullyogue. A big christening party. The invitation came the day you left. I've said you'll be there. All right? *(Pause)* It's young Brian's first child – you were at his wedding last year. It'll be a good day. *(Pause)* Hugh?
O'Neill	Yes?
Harry	O'Hagan's – where you were fostered.
O'Neill	Tell me the name of these again.
Harry	Broom.
O'Neill	Broom. That's it.
Harry	The Latin name is genista. Virgil mentions it somewhere.
O'Neill	Does he really?
Harry	Actually that genista comes from Spain. (**O'Neill** *looks at the flowers in amazement.*)
O'Neill	Good Lord – does it? Spanish broom – magnificent name, isn't it?
Harry	Give them plenty of water.
O'Neill	Magnificent colour, isn't it?
Harry	A letter from the Lord Deputy –
O'Neill	They really transform the room. Splendid idea of yours, Harry. Thank you. (**O'Neill** *silently mouths the word* Genista *again and then continues distributing the flowers.*)
Harry	A letter from the Lord Deputy 'vigorously urging you to have your eldest son attend the newly established College of the Holy and Undivided Trinity in Dublin founded by the Most Serene Queen Elizabeth'. That 'vigorously urging' sounds ominous, doesn't it?
O'Neill	Sorry?
Harry	Sir William Fitzwilliam wants you to send young Hugh to the new Trinity College. I'm told he's trying to get all the big Gaelic families to send their children there. He would like an early response.
O'Neill	This jacket – what do you think, Harry? It's not a bit... excessive, is it?
Harry	Excessive?
O'Neill	You know... a little too – too strident?
Harry	Strident?
O'Neill	All right, damn it, too bloody young?
Harry	*(Looking at his papers)* It's very becoming, Hugh.
O'Neill	Do you think so? Maybe I should have got it in maroon. *(He goes off to get more flowers.)*
Harry	A reminder that the Annual Festival of Harpers takes place next month in

Roscommon. They've changed the venue to Roosky. You're Patron of the Festival and they would be very honoured if you would open the event with a short –
(He now sees that he is alone. He looks through his papers. Pause. **O'Neill** *enters again with an armful of flowers.)*

This opening scene starts the play off in quite a private and intimate setting. The stage directions at the beginning describe the setting and what is going on and this will help you to visualize the scene in your mind. Although the audience will not be so fully aware of what is happening here the activity taking place will capture their attention. The two characters, O'Neill and Harry, seem to have very different concerns at the opening of the play. O'Neill is immersed in the domestic – arranging the flowers in the room and seeking Harry's opinion about his attire. Harry, on the other hand, is concerned with imparting business and political news to O'Neill. Within this apparently low-key opening Friel makes it clear that O'Neill is a prominent public figure from the details that are mentioned – his presence being requested at important domestic and public occasions and the letter from the Lord Deputy trying to persuade him to send his son to Trinity College confirm this.

Notice how Friel's economical technique allows him to give the audience a good deal of information and establishes the central character of O'Neill right at the outset. If you were to study the whole of this play you would find that Friel also establishes one of the central themes of the play here – that of the conflict between O'Neill the private man and O'Neill the public figure. He is also able to give a clear indication of O'Neill's stature and importance, both as a political figure and as a man with pastoral responsibilities towards his people.

> *"The hero story is about a person undergoing a test that he or she didn't choose… The theatre is about the hero journey; the hero and the heroine are those people who do not give in to temptation."*
> David Mamet

Activity

1 Read the following extract, which is the opening scene from Shakespeare's tragedy *Hamlet*.

2 Think about the scene for yourself or discuss it with a partner and consider these points:

   - the effect of the opening on the audience
   - the intention of the playwright
   - the techniques used
   - the purpose of any stage directions.

Hamlet

Act I Scene 1
(Enter **Barnardo** *and* **Francisco***, two sentinels)*

Barnardo	Who's there?
Francisco	Nay, answer me. Stand and unfold yourself.
Barnardo	Long live the King.
Francisco	Barnardo?

Barnardo	He.
Francisco	You come most carefully upon your hour.
Barnardo	Tis now struck twelve. Get thee to bed, Francisco.
Francisco	For this relief much thanks. 'Tis bitter cold, And I am sick at heart.
Barnardo	Have you had quiet guard?
Francisco	Not a mouse stirring.
Barnardo	Well, good night. If you do meet Horatio and Marcellus, The rivals of my watch, bid them make haste.

*(Enter **Horatio** and **Marcellus**)*

Francisco	I think I hear them. Stand, ho! Who is there?
Horatio	Friends to this ground.
Marcellus	And liegemen to the Dane.
Francisco	Give you good night.
Marcellus	O, farewell honest soldier, Who hath relieved you?
Francisco	Barnardo hath my place. Give you good night. *(Exit)*
Marcellus	Holla, Barnardo!
Barnardo	Say, What, is Horatio there?
Horatio	A piece of him.
Barnardo	Welcome, Horatio. Welcome, good Marcellus.
Marcellus	What, has this thing appeared again tonight?
Barnardo	I have seen nothing.
Marcellus	Horatio says 'tis but our fantasy, And will not let belief take hold of him Touching this dreaded sight, twice seen of us. Therefore I have intreated him along With us to watch the minutes of this night, That, if again this apparition come, He may approve our eyes and speak to it.
Horatio	Tush, tush, 'twill not appear.
Barnardo	Sit down awhile, And let us once again assail your ears, That are so fortified against our story, What we have two nights seen.
Horatio	Well, sit we down, And let us hear Barnardo speak of this.

Barnardo	Last night of all,
	When yon same star that's westward from the pole,
	Had made his course t'illume that part of heaven
	Where now it burns, Marcellus and myself,
	The bell then beating one –

(Enter **Ghost***)*

Marcellus	Peace, break thee off. Look where it comes again!
Barnardo	In the same figure like the King that's dead.
Marcellus	Thou art a scholar, speak to it, Horatio.
Barnardo	Looks 'a not like the King? Mark it, Horatio.
Horatio	Most like. It harrows me with fear and wonder.
Barnardo	It would be spoke to.
Marcellus	Question it Horatio.
Horatio	What art thou that usurp'st this time of night,
	Together with that fair and warlike form
	In which the majesty of buried Denmark
	Did sometimes march? By heaven I charge thee speak.
Marcellus	It is offended.
Barnardo	See, it stalks away.
Horatio	Stay, speak, speak, I charge thee speak.
	(Exit **Ghost***)*

Presenting character

A key element in the impact of a dramatic production is the extent to which the playwright achieves a convincing sense of character. However, the nature of drama is such that the playwright employs very different methods of characterization from those employed by a novelist. Novelists can provide the reader with as much background information as they wish. They can enter the minds of the characters, let their readers know what characters think, feel, and are planning to do. A playwright does not have all these options.

Perhaps the most straightforward way in which a playwright can define exactly how he or she intends a character to appear to the audience is through detailed and explicit stage directions. So it is important that when you begin to study a play you pay close attention to this information. When watching the play on the stage, of course, you will not be reading stage directions but you will be seeing them in performance.

Some playwrights give a great deal of information through their descriptions of how characters are meant to appear. Look carefully at the following two examples from Tennessee Williams's *A Streetcar Named Desire*: the first one describes Blanche as she appears in the play for the first time. She has come to New Orleans to visit her younger

Activity

Focusing on a play that you are studying, think carefully about the ways the characters are presented to the audience to give a full and rounded impression of them. Make a list of these methods and devices.

sister, Stella, who lives in a rather "down-market" part of the city. The second one describes the entrance of Stanley, Stella's husband.

1 Blanche *comes round the corner, carrying a valise. She looks at the slip of paper, then at the building, then again at the slip and again at the building. Her expression is one of shocked disbelief. Her appearance is incongruous to this setting. She is daintily dressed in a white suit with a fluffy bodice, necklace and earrings of pearl, white gloves and hat, looking as if she were arriving at a summer tea or cocktail party in the garden district. She is above five years older than* **Stella**. *Her delicate beauty must avoid strong light. There is something about her uncertain manner, as well as her white clothes, that suggests a moth.*

2 Stanley *throws the screen door of the kitchen open and comes in. He is of medium height, about five feet eight or nine, and strongly, compactly built. Animal joy in his being is implicit in all his movements and attitudes. Since earliest manhood the centre of his life has been pleasure with women, the giving and the taking of it, not with weak indulgence, dependently, but with the power and pride of a richly feathered male bird among hens. Branching out from this complete and satisfying centre are all the auxiliary channels of his life, such as his heartiness with men, his appreciation of rough humour, his love of good drink and food and games, his car, his radio, everything that is his, that bears his emblem of the gaudy seed-bearer. He sizes women up at a glance, with sexual classifications, crude images flashing into his mind and determining the way he smiles at them.*

Tennessee Williams here presents anyone reading the text with a good deal of guidance not only on how to visualize the characters but on their deeper aspects. Some playwrights provide little or no such direct guidance on how to interpret their characters, but rely on other methods to convey a sense of character. These include:

- how characters speak (also sometimes embedded in stage directions)
- how characters are described by other characters
- what the characters say and do
- how other characters respond to or interact with them.

Most playwrights (including Williams) use a combination of all these methods in order to give a sense of fully developed characters, although in some cases playwrights deliberately create stereotypical characters in order to achieve their particular effect. Some of the "stock" characters to be found in Restoration comedy, such as *The Way of the World*, or a comedy of manners, such as *The Rivals*, are examples of this.

Activity

On your own or in a small group, read these stage directions carefully. Imagine you are a producer and a team of actors discussing preliminary views of these characters. Think about their appearances and personalities.

Activity

Look at the following extract from *A Streetcar Named Desire*. The annotations are on the opening stage directions of the scene followed by an excerpt from a little later in the scene.

Blanche Dubois, a complex woman with much to hide, is staying with her sister Stella and Stella's husband Stanley in New Orleans. Their life is very different from the unrealistic expectations she carries from her girlhood as a "Southern Belle". Here, she and Stella return from an evening out to find Stanley playing poker with his friends.

Make a note of the impression you form of the characters and how Williams conveys that impression.

Then write as fully as you can about Scene 3 of *A Streetcar Named Desire*, focusing on the way the male and female characters are presented.

A Streetcar Named Desire

by Tennessee Williams

Scene 3
The Poker Night
(There is a picture of Van Gogh's of a billiard parlour at night. The kitchen now suggests that sort of nocturnal brilliance, the raw colours of childhood's spectrum. Over the yellow linoleum of the kitchen table hangs an electric bulb with a vivid green glass shade. The poker players – **Stanley, Steve, Mitch,** *and* **Pablo** *– wear coloured shirts, solid blues, a purple, a red-and-white check, a light green, and they are men at the peak of their physical manhood, as coarse and direct and powerful as the primary colours. There are vivid slices of water melon on the table, whisky bottles, and glasses. The bedroom is relatively dim with only the light that spills between the portières and through the wide window on the street. The sisters appear around the corner of the next building.)…*

Colours bold, bright, simple, modern

Colour of water melon could suggest raw flesh

'Raw' suggests uncultivated

(Brilliant light where the men are)

(Where the women will be is 'dim': only light from outside)

Stella	The game is still going on.
Blanche	How do I look?
Stella	Lovely, Blanche.
Blanche	I feel so hot and frazzled. Wait till I powder before you open the door. Do I look done in?
Stella	Why no. You are as fresh as a daisy. *(Stella opens the door and they enter.)*
Stella	Well, well, well. I see you boys are still at it!
Stanley	Where you been?
Stella	Blanche and I took in a show. Blanche, this is Mr Gonzales and Mr Hubbel.
Blanche	Please don't get up.
Stanley	Nobody's going to get up, so don't be worried.
Stella	How much longer is this game going to continue?
Stanley	Till we get ready to quit.
Blanche	Poker is so fascinating. Could I kibitz?
Stanley	You could not. Why don't you women go up and sit with Eunice?
Stella	Because it is nearly two-thirty. *(Blanche crosses into the bedroom and partially closes the portières.)*
Stella	Couldn't you call it quits after one more hand? *(A chair scrapes. Stanley gives a loud whack of his hand on Stella's thigh.)*
Stella	*(Sharply)* That's not fun, Stanley. *(The men laugh. Stella goes into the bedroom.)*

Blanche concerned with her appearance. Stella gives the answers she needs to hear

Old-fashioned – she expects courtesy

She doesn't get it!

Trying to get 'in' with the men

Stan takes no account of Stella's wishes. His responses to both women are abrupt, rude.

= Look over someone's shoulder and sit in on their hand of cards

Derogatory tone

He wants them out of the way – poker is a man's world. Women excluded

Stan will have none of it

'loud whack' – Stanley is solid, boisterousness

Chauvinistic reaction – treats Stella roughly, disrespectfully, as his possession

She dislikes this; at least she expresses her anger – but she gets no support – the men think her annoyance is funny. All she can do is walk out

Stella trying to be reasonable

Here are some brief ideas.
Men: dominant, forceful, violent
Poker: a man's world – women excluded
Women: feminine – much less powerful

Blanche: nervous, flirtatious
Setting: men – "lurid" kitchen; women – "dim" bedroom
Colours: men – bold; women – white, delicate

We know that the central theme for discussion is the contrast between the male characters – presented as dominant, hard, and forceful – and the female characters – portrayed as gentler and less powerful. Yet, in the course of the essay, we are likely to explore several side issues, some of which will contribute to the main argument, while others offer exceptions to it or alternative views. It is important to find ways of incorporating these while maintaining a strong sense of direction and flow in the writing. Using connecting devices like the ones shown in the following examples can help achieve this successfully.

Commentary: A

One aspect of Williams's presentation in the scene, which contributes to our sense that the men are more powerful than the women, is the way in which he uses colours...

[... discussion of the use of colour and its effect..]

Having examined the use of colours in the scene, we can see that it reinforces the impression that the men are dominant here.

B

The relative powerlessness of the female characters is demonstrated by the fact that neither Blanche nor Stella commands any respect from the poker players. However, the two women are different in the ways in which they respond to the men...

[... comparison of the behaviour of Blanche and Stella...]

Although the female characters differ in the ways they react to the situation, they are presented in general as less forceful than the male characters.

C

Although we have seen that for the most part the men are harder and more forceful than the women, there are some exceptions...

[First... discussion of Mitch's character...

Second... examine how Stanley becomes like a pathetic small boy in his need for Stella once she has left...

Third... example of Eunice shouting roughly and angrily...]

There are, therefore, some occasions when male characters seem weaker. On the whole, however, they are presented as powerful.

In each of these examples the writer moves temporarily away from the central line of argument to discuss a side issue, but each time returns to the central question, pointing out how the side issue relates to it. This leaves the writer back on track, ready either to continue the main argument or to explore another "byway".

> ### Activity
>
> With a partner, look at how one student answers the question on Scene 3, *The Poker Night*. The student has written on the whole scene and not just the extract printed here. As you read, take note of the annotations written by an examiner and discuss how the student has structured his work.

A fair introductory paragraph which refers to the question and leads into his discussion of the characters

It has been said that Scene 3, which is the poker scene, actually represents the whole play and acts as a miniature version of the play. *The Poker Night* is an important scene because it shows how the male and female characters are presented by Tennessee Williams. The male characters as a group are presented as dominant and forceful because they have ordered the women out for the night so they can play poker and enjoy themselves. The group of men, Stanley, Steve, Mitch, and Pablo are presented as strong, powerful, and coarse. This is said in the stage directions:

An interesting point in this opening sentence which could do with more explanation

"They are men at the peak of their physical manhood, as coarse and direct as the primary colours."

"The primary colours" are the colours of the shirts the men are wearing. The colours are "solid blues, a purple, a red-and-white check, a light green". Also from these colours and the shirts being worn these are modern men unlike the type Stella and Blanche would have been used to in their past.

The group of men are seen as brutes of men as they sit around the poker table. Here the men start to "argue hotly":

Several good points about the men as a group, including some discussion of the significance of the colours they wear. Next the student focuses on individual male characters, which makes good sense

"I didn't hear you name it."

"Didn't I name it, Mitch?"

The group of men argue over a simple game of cards. This is almost like a children's squabble.

Stanley is the prime example of a forceful modern man in a world where Stella and Blanche must do as he says. He is the most dominating male character in the group of four. Here, Stella comes in and complains to Stanley about the time they are still playing poker at. Stanley shows he isn't respectful of Stella's wishes.

"A chair scrapes. Stanley gives a loud whack of his hand on her thigh."

The structure works quite well here. The student conveys a sense of how the men behave as a group and also draws a contrast between them

Stanley shows his masculinity and authority over Stella by slapping her thigh in a manly way. Stanley is showing off around his friends, proving how much of a man he is. Stanley again shows his dominance over the females when he demands Blanche turns the radio off and when she doesn't do so on his word he becomes fierce.

"Stanley stalks fiercely through the portières into the bedroom. He crosses to the small white radio and snatches it off the table. With a shouted oath, he tosses the instrument out of the window."

He uses appropriate quotations and attempts more detailed analysis in places (for example, where he comments on the significance of individual words such as 'stalks')

Even the way Stanley approaches the radio before he acts presents him in a fierce and forceful light. The words "stalks", as if he was a primitive caveman stalking his prey, and "fiercely", which is his anger, show how Stanley is going to act before he acts. Stanley acts more like a modern barbarian around women than a modern gentleman. Mitch is the only exception to the group. Mitch is sympathetic and much more considerate to what Blanche and Stella want than Stanley. Mitch shows he is more gentle in these stage directions:

"... coughing a little shyly. He realizes he still has the towel in his hands and with an embarrassed laugh hands it to Stella."

Quotations usually introduced quite neatly, providing enough information to place them in context, but he fails to do this

This is the first time we see Mitch around females and he shows he is different to the other men around him by the way he embarrassedly laughs at his little mistake. This shows a kinder and gentler side to the male populace and is a contrast to Stanley's hard, rough and ready nature. Mitch is

The student also slightly misreads Mitch's character here, not picking up that, although he is relatively gentle, he is also rather naïve and undignified in the way he responds to Blanche's flirtation

This section is less successful: the first sentence is ambiguous. Does he mean that the women are similar to each other, or to the men? He needs to round off his discussion of the men and then lead into his discussion of the women, like this: 'Although Mitch seems different from Stanley and the others, on the whole the men are strong and rough and form a powerful group. On the other hand, the women, although different from each other, seem much less forceful…'

presented as a fine character who is more suitable to Blanche and Stella and is more like the men they once knew. Here Blanche waltzes to the music with romantic gestures to Mitch.

"Mitch is delighted and moves in awkward imitation like a dancing bear."

The point here is although Mitch didn't know how to waltz he gladly made a fool of himself dancing strangely just to please Blanche. Stanley, from what we know of him, would have laughed and walked away.

The female characters are quite similar in the way they are presented. Stella is presented as strong by the way she stands up to Stanley over the card game:

"Drunk – drunk – animal thing you! All of you – please go home! If any of you have one spark of decency in you…"

Stella confronts the group of males playing poker and challenges them. Also, Stella is shown as wanting to be treated with respect.

Stanley slaps Stella's thigh and she reacts sharply and then tells Blanche:

"It makes me so mad when he does that in front of people."

Stella is showing how she wants to look as if she is respected in front of people.

Stella may be presented as strong and brave and trying to gain respect, but she is also weak when it comes down to what Stanley wants. After Stanley hits her and she and Blanche go up to Eunice's, when Stanley stands downstairs crying, she gives in and goes to Stanley, showing she needs him no matter what he's done. Blanche shows or presents another image of the female which is provocative, flirty and deceitful…

… Blanche is easily older than Stella and has blatantly lied about her age so that Mitch will become more interested in her. Blanche always tries to present herself in a better light:

"I can't stand a naked light bulb, any more than I can a rude remark or a vulgar action."

Blanche is trying to sound much more refined than she actually is. She is being provocative and flirtatious, exactly as she was in the previous scene when she was alone with Stanley.

The student has not really made use of opportunities to analyse details in his later paragraphs. For example, Blanche's statement that she 'can't stand a naked light bulb' deserves much more attention. As the student has pointed out, she is deceitful. The naked light bulb would reveal too much literally – she lies about her age – and metaphorically – it also represents the fact that she has a lot more to hide

when he quotes Mitch's moment of embarrassment. To make the situation fully clear to the reader, he needs to say: '… in these stage directions when he comes out of the bathroom and has to pass the women, who are in the bedroom…'

The essay continues with a discussion of Blanche's character and actions and concludes like this… This is rather disappointing. The essay just stops, without a conclusion to draw the ideas together. The mention of the previous scene is a red herring – not relevant to the question here

Activity

1 Swap answers to a recent essay on drama with a partner. Assess the structure of your partner's essay. Annotate it to show where the structure is clear and informative and where it could be improved. (Use the notes around the essay above as models for your own.)

2 Hand back the annotated essay and discuss your comments on it with your partner.

Asides and soliloquies

To succeed in creating a convincing character, the dramatist needs to give the audience some sense of deeper, inner thoughts and feelings. Unlike the novelist, however, who can describe these as fully as desired to the reader, the dramatist has much more limited means at his or her disposal.

Two methods that are often used to provide some insight into characters' minds are the aside and the soliloquy. The **aside** is a kind of "stage whisper", a behind-the-hand comment. Sometimes it is directed to another character but often it is aimed at the audience, or characters "speak to themselves". Asides tend to be short, often a single sentence, sometimes a single word. They are used by the playwright to convey small pieces of information concerning the plot or character to the audience.

In Shakespeare's *Othello*, for example, there is substantial use of both long and short asides. They reveal to the audience what is going on in the mind of the speaker. Below is a particularly long aside from *Othello*. Iago watches his enemy, Cassio, take the hand of Othello's wife, Desdemona. Read it through carefully.

Othello

Act II Scene 1

Iago   (*Aside*) He takes her by the palm. Ay, well said, whisper. With as little web as this will I ensnare as great a fly as Cassio. Ay, smile upon her, do. I will gyve thee in thine own courtship. You say true, 'tis so indeed. If such tricks as these strip you out of your lieutenantry, it had been better you had not kissed your three fingers so oft, which now again you are most apt to play the sir in. Very good: well kissed, an excellent courtesy! 'Tis so indeed. Yet again your fingers to your lips? Would they were clyster-pipes for your sake!

The repeated use of asides also give us an insight into Othello's growing torment. For example, in the following extract Iago urges him to secretly observe his conversation with Cassio, to convince Othello (quite wrongly) that Cassio and Desdemona are having an affair. In fact, he and Cassio are talking about Bianca.

> **Activity**
>
> Look carefully at these asides. Why do you think Shakespeare used them in this way and what effects does he achieve through their use?

Act IV Scene 1

Othello   (*Aside*) Look, how he laughs already!

Iago   I never knew a woman love man so.

Cassio   Alas, poor rogue! I think i'faith she loves me.

Othello   (*Aside*) Now he denies it faintly, and laughs it out.

Iago   Do you hear, Cassio?

Othello   (*Aside*) Now he importunes him to tell it o'er. Go to, well said, well said!

Iago   She gives it out that you shall marry her. Do you intend it?

Cassio   Ha, ha, ha!

Othello   (*Aside*) Do you triumph, Roman? Do you triumph?

Cassio	I marry her! What! A customer! Prithee bear some charity to my wit: do not think it so unwholesome. Ha, ha, ha!
Othello	*(Aside)* So, so, so, so: they laugh that win.

Soliloquies, too, are also often used by playwrights to convey both information and inward emotion to the audience. The soliloquy is one key way in which Shakespeare lets us, the audience, know what a character is really like. Through a soliloquy characters tell us directly about themselves and can inform us about a whole range of issues, such as what is in their minds, why they are acting as they are, and what they intend to do in the future.

Othello

Act I Scene 3

Iago	Thus do I ever make my fool my purse:
	For I mine own gained knowledge should profane
	If I would time expend with such a snipe
	But for my sport and profit. I hate the Moor,
	And it is thought abroad that 'twixt my sheets
	He's done my office. I know not if't be true
	But I, for mere suspicion in that kind,
	Will do as if for surety. He holds me well:
	The better shall my purpose work on him.
	Cassio's a proper man: let me see now;
	To get his place and to plume up my will
	In double knavery. How? How? Let's see.
	After some time, to abuse Othello's ear
	That he is too familiar with his wife;
	He hath a person and a smooth dispose
	To be suspected, framed to make women false.
	The Moor is of a free and open nature,
	That thinks men honest that but seem to be so,
	And will as tenderly be led by th'nose
	As asses are.
	I have't. It is engendered. Hell and night
	Must bring this monstrous birth to the world's light.
	(Exit)

> **Activity**
>
> This soliloquy is taken from *Othello*, and in it Iago reveals a good deal about his own attitudes. Read it carefully and make a list of the key points that Iago reveals about himself here.

> **Activity**
>
> Now look at the play you are studying. Make a list of the soliloquies in it and what those soliloquies tell you about the characters who speak them. Make a note of the following details:
>
> ● who is speaking
>
> ● the context of the soliloquy
>
> ● what is being said
>
> ● why the playwright uses a soliloquy at that point in the drama.

Soliloquies are frequently used at some special moment in the play or when a character is undergoing some kind of emotionally or psychologically heightened experience – for example, when a character is distressed or suffering some kind of confusion of mind or alternatively when a character is feeling exultant or wants to work through his or her own thoughts and feelings.

It has often been noted that both the aside and the soliloquy are artificial devices and that in "real life" people do not go around delivering speeches to themselves. In fact, they are just two of many conventions that we accept when watching a play which can be termed "dramatic licence". In the context of the theatre we forget their artificiality and accept them quite naturally.

Issues and themes

Complex though the formation and development of characters may be, they are themselves part of a more complex web that makes up the play as a whole. Within this web the playwright will have interwoven certain themes and issues. In studying a play, you will need to be able to identify these and to look at how the playwright explores them through the drama. Such ideas can be presented to the audience in two key ways. First, we can detect ideas, issues, thoughts, etc. expressed by the characters in a play. Secondly, we can detect themes, issues, or ideas that the playwright wants the play as a whole to project.

Sometimes a playwright will have major characters hold views or follow a philosophy that ultimately is shown to be counter to the message that the play as a whole conveys. This is often done to show the problems caused by or shortcomings of certain courses of action or philosophies. The issues that a play might raise can be many and varied but they are almost always presented via action centring on human relationships and conflicts.

Activity

List the major characters in a play that you are studying. Draw up a chart which shows briefly the ideas, philosophies, values etc. held by each character, as shown through the action of the play. Then think about these ideas and against each jot down the dramatist's view.

LATE NIGHT WITH DAVID MAMET

Plot and structure

Obviously plot is central to most plays, although there are certain kinds of play (some of Samuel Beckett's, for example) where the very lack of a plot, or at least something that we would ordinarily recognize as a plot, is essential for the effect. At its simplest the **plot** is the story of the play – what actually happens. Having said that, there is much more to plot than a simple "story-line". The whole notion of plot and its development is bound up with the way that the play is put together, with its structure. The creation of an order or pattern needs careful planning and the playwright needs to consider a number of factors. Generally speaking an effective plot should:

- maintain the interest of the audience from beginning to end
- move the action on from one episode to the next
- arouse the interest of the audience in character and situation
- create high points or moments of crisis at intervals
- create expectation and surprise.

Usually, the structure of a play follows a basic pattern which consists of a number of identifiable elements.

1 **Exposition:** this opens the play and often introduces the main characters and provides background information.
2 **Dramatic incitement:** the incident which provides the starting point for the main action of the play, and causes some type of conflict to arise.
3 **Complication:** this usually forms the main action of the play – the characters respond to the dramatic incitement and other developments that stem from it.
4 **Crisis:** the climax of the play.
5 **Resolution:** this is the final section of the play where things are worked out, conflicts are resolved, and some kind of conclusion is arrived at.

Let us look at this structure as applied to Arthur Miller's *The Crucible* to see how it works out.

1 **Exposition:** The opening of the first act is an example of an exposition, as we see the Reverend Parris, minister of religion in Salem, praying beside the bed of his ten-year-old daughter Betty. We learn that rumours of witchcraft are widespread in Salem and that some believe that his daughter's illness is the result of such unnatural causes. The previous night Parris had found his daughter, niece Abigail, and their friends dancing in the woods and the black slave, Tituba, was swaying and making strange noises.
2 **Dramatic incitement:** Another clergyman, the Reverend Hale, a specialist in witchcraft and its detection, is brought to Salem. He secures from Tituba a "confession" that she has conjured up the devil. A local farmer, John Proctor, is outspokenly sceptical of the claims of witchcraft.
3 **Complication:** The girls are credited with the power to identify all those who are witches and they denounce many people. The ringleader is Parris's niece, Abigail. She has had sexual relations with Proctor and when Abigail denounces his wife, Elizabeth

"Dramatic structure is, similarly, an exercise of a naturally occurring need or disposition to structure the world as thesis/ thesis/ synthesis."
David Mamet

Proctor suspects that she has been denounced because if she is hanged he will marry Abigail.

4   **Crisis:** Proctor himself is arrested but Hale, who now begins to suspect the truth and regret his involvement in the proceedings, tries to persuade Proctor to "confess" and so be pardoned. Although tempted, in the end Proctor goes to his death rather than "confess" and therefore lie.

5   **Resolution:** Although the play ends with the death of Proctor there is a kind of resolution because the authorities now realize how Abigail has misled them and there is a suggestion that Proctor's death strengthens others to stand up for the truth and once again restore peace and sanity to Salem.

Activity

Examine carefully the structure of a play that you are studying. Draw a diagram to represent the way that the play develops, making brief notes of key moments.

Approaching your script

There are a number of things you can do to deepen your understanding of your drama text. Here are some suggestions.

Plays in performance
- Read your drama text thoroughly prior to seeing it performed.
- See a live performance of the play.
- If you cannot see a live performance, watch a video recording or a film of it.
- Make notes on performances in a play log book to help you to remember those important initial impressions.
- Listen to the play on audio tape.
- See as many other plays as you can to broaden your experience of drama and the theatre.

Directing the text
- Work with others, dramatizing for yourselves scenes from the text.
- Talk to others about staging implications.
- Imagine you are a director – plan carefully how you would stage a production of the play, the kind of actors you would cast, how you would bring your own interpretation out on the stage, etc.
- Use diagrams, drawings, and models to work out sets, stage layout, and props for selected scenes.

Studying the text
- Think about the characters – look at key speeches, look for shifts in focus, different ways of interpreting what they do and say.
- Look for various possible "meanings" and "patterns" in the play.
- Consider how/if the theatrical effects are signalled.
- Think about the pace and variety of the action.
- Think about the overall shape and structure of the play and the impact that this could have on an audience.

- Consider the particular characteristics and qualities of the play you are studying.
- Think about relationships between these various elements of the play and how together they present a whole.
- Apply the broader knowledge you have about the nature of plays and drama.

All these activities will help you to formulate and develop your own informed critical response to the play and therefore fulfil the objectives which lie at the heart of your study of drama.

Shakespeare and dramatic study

Since Shakespeare is a dramatist, it follows that his plays have a great deal in common with those of other dramatists. They follow the clear structural pattern that we discussed in some detail earlier:

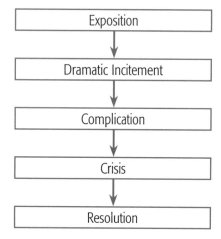

Approaching a Shakespeare text

In approaching the text you are studying, make use of the knowledge you already possess as to the nature of drama generally. This can help you understand the plot of your Shakespeare text when reading it for the first time. For example, it will help if you know that Shakespeare's plays follow this pattern:

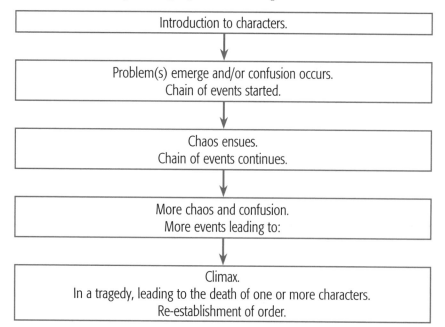

Knowledge of this general structure can help you to follow the storyline of any play, but more than this, it can provide you with a framework for your analysis of the play as a whole. One of the problems that students frequently encounter when studying a Shakespeare text is that they focus so closely on detailed summaries of scene, character, and theme that they sometimes lose sight of the fact that the play is an integrated whole. Being able to see the play in terms of its overall framework can help you to appreciate the broad pattern of the text, thus helping you to make sense of the detail when it emerges through close study.

The tragedies

The idea of disorder lies at the heart of Shakespeare's tragedies. The Roman history plays are often included in the list of tragedies. The four plays that are regarded as "the great" tragedies are *Hamlet, King Lear, Othello,* and *Macbeth*. At the heart of each of these plays is the central character after whom the play is named – the **eponymous hero**, to give the technical term – and the action focuses very much on this character. However, other characters are important too, and often several innocent victims are claimed before the play reaches its end.

Overall, Shakespeare's tragedies have many of the key features we associate with the concept of dramatic tragedy in general.

- At the beginning of the play something occurs that disrupts the normal order of things.
- Chaos or disorder in society results.
- Extreme emotions are involved.
- Social restraint disintegrates.
- A climax is reached, usually with the death of the main character (and several others), before order is restored. The purging of emotions that affects the audience at the end of a tragedy is sometimes referred to as **catharsis**.

Activity

If you are studying one of Shakespeare's tragedies think about how the play fits this general pattern. Note down one thing that happens in the play which corresponds to each of the above features.

Shakespeare's plots

As we have seen, the plots of Shakespeare's plays adhere to a general pattern common to many plays. However, when studying your text one of the first things you will need to do is to get to grips with the details of the plot. Very often your first encounter with the play will be through a reading, perhaps in class, with students taking the various parts. When reading the play either to yourself or as part of a group, however, it is easy to lose sight of the fact that you are studying a drama. The text you are reading was written to be performed and therefore brought to life on the stage. Although we now read Shakespeare's plays as "literary texts", we must not forget this central fact, and you should view the "text" as a "script". A "script" suggests something that in itself is incomplete because it needs a dramatic enactment to achieve its purpose. This opens up the whole question of how the play is to be enacted, and touches on the fact that the play has many meanings rather than a single meaning.

In coming to terms with the plot of a Shakespeare play, therefore, you first need to understand generally what is happening, and then think about ways in which this could be enacted on the stage. To help you appreciate the variety of ways that a play can be interpreted, you should try to see as many performances of it (live in the theatre, on film, or video, etc.) as you can.

Activity

In **ten** sentences, summarize the plot of the Shakespeare play you are studying. Then take the opening scene of that play and describe two possible, but contrasting, ways in which that scene could be enacted on the stage.

Structure

The structure of each play is integral to the way in which Shakespeare develops its central issues. The structure of his plays (or any play) can be viewed in two ways. What is sometimes called the **dynamic structure** of the play consists of the sequence of events which builds up in a "cause and effect" fashion to create the plot of the play, and so drives the play forward.

Underlying this obvious structure, however, it is often possible to detect another that is less prominent but just as important. This second structure consists of various parallels and cross-references, or repeated images, symbols, and language that create a network of threads running through the play. This kind of structure is sometimes called the **symmetric structure**, and it can exert a powerful influence on the overall effect of a play.

In *Hamlet*, for example, the repeated parallels between Hamlet and Laertes as avenging sons, and Hamlet's repeated contemplation of death with its associated imagery, are just two elements that help to form a web of patterning developed throughout the play. Similarly, in *King Lear*, the theme of "blindness" to the truth as well as physical blindness, presented through Gloucester and Lear, create parallels that give another kind of structure to the play.

Activity

Draw two diagrams, one to represent the dynamic structure of the Shakespeare play you are studying, the other to represent the symmetric structure.

Shakespeare's themes and ideas

Each of Shakespeare's plays is concerned with certain ideas or issues that recur and develop as the play progresses. These topics with which the play is preoccupied are the play's "themes". They are the subject that Shakespeare explores through the events, characters, and language of the play. It is the themes that give a shape and pattern to the play and give it a significance beyond the events it describes.

The themes are developed through the language of the play, and often Shakespeare creates powerful images. For example, in *Othello* one of the themes of the play is "honesty" and Iago's "dishonesty". The language itself draws attention to this theme in a variety of ways, one of which is the repetition of the word 'honest' to emphasize Othello's complete belief in Iago's "honesty" and Desdemona's "dishonesty".

It has often been said that one of the reasons that Shakespeare's plays have remained so popular for so long is that they deal with great and universal themes that were of concern to people in Shakespeare's time, and are of no less significance to us today. His plays often deal with themes such as love, hate, envy, jealousy, death, revenge, guilt, corruption, destiny.

Certain themes seem to have particularly interested Shakespeare and can be seen in one form or another in all of his plays. These themes are:

- conflict
- appearance and reality
- order and disorder
- change
- love.

Conflict

Conflict, of one type or another, is the starting point for many dramas, and it can take many forms. In *Othello*, for example, we have the conflict between Iago and Othello (a conflict that Othello is unaware of until it is too late), and the inner conflict that Othello experiences as he battles to control his growing jealousy. In *Macbeth*, conflict exists externally at the beginning of the play, as Duncan faces rebellion and invasion.

Appearance and reality

In all of Shakespeare's plays there is a mis-match between how things seem to be and how they actually are. In *Othello*, for example, everyone thinks Iago is "honest" but in fact he is completely the opposite. In *Twelfth Night*, Viola disguises herself as a boy, while in *Hamlet* the apparently popular and effective King, Claudius, is in reality guilty of the murder of his brother and seduction of his brother's wife. *Measure for Measure* is closely concerned with "seeming", as the Duke leaves his apparently incorruptible deputy, Angelo, in charge of the state, to see "If power change purpose, what our seemers be". He certainly finds out, when it is revealed that Angelo attempted to seduce the innocent Isabella.

Order and disorder

In all of Shakespeare's plays there is some kind of breakdown in order, and some form of confusion temporarily gains the upper hand. Sometimes the breakdown is in the order of the state, as in *Macbeth*, where the murder of Duncan plunges the state into turmoil and war. In *Henry IV* (Parts 1 and 2), King Henry faces rebellion and civil war, while *Twelfth Night* begins with Olivia's rejection of Orsino's suit and Viola shipwrecked on the coast of Illyria. The causes of the disruption vary from play to play, but they tend to include key causes such as jealousy, love, hate, and ambition. Very often the protagonist undergoes some kind of learning process during the course of the play before order is re-established.

Change

In all Shakespeare plays the characters undergo some kind of change. Sometimes the ultimate result of this change is death, as in *Othello*, where Othello changes from a respected military leader to a man eaten away by jealousy who murders his wife and then, realizing the terrible mistake he has made, takes his own life. In *Twelfth Night*, Malvolio changes from a puritan figure into a foolish lover.

Love

For Shakespeare, one of the instruments of change is love, which has a transforming power and is often at the heart of his plays. *Twelfth Night* begins with the words "If music be the food of love, play on." It goes on to present a world of romantic love. In *A Midsummer Night's Dream* we see young men and women who love each other but who also have to endure crosses and frustrations in love. In *Othello* we see a quite different portrayal of love, as Othello's love for Desdemona is corrupted into jealousy and hate by the scheming Iago.

Development of themes

Of course, there are many specific themes that can be traced in individual plays, but in one way or another they will relate to the five key areas discussed above.

The themes in Shakespeare's plays often develop in one of three ways:

- An individual character or characters experience some personal difficulties or inner turmoil, perhaps moral or spiritual, that causes some mental conflict. For example, Hamlet struggles to come to terms with events and revenge his father.
- The family, society, or the country is affected by turmoil. For example, the feuding Capulets and Montagues disrupt Verona in *Romeo and Juliet*, and Rome is at war with Egypt in *Antony and Cleopatra*.
- Nature or the universe may be disordered, or supernatural events may be involved. Examples are the appearance of the witches and Banquo's ghost in *Macbeth*, or the storm imagery in *King Lear*.

At the heart of the development of the themes of a play is Shakespeare's rich and complex use of language.

Shakespeare's language

Often students encounter difficulties when first studying a Shakespeare play because they find the language of Shakespeare different in a number of ways from the kind of English they are used to. This difficulty is particularly evident when reading the text rather than watching the play being performed, when actions are brought to life and give the words much more meaning.

At first, concentrate on arriving at a broad understanding of what is happening, in terms of the plot of the play. Once this basic knowledge has been established, you will very soon progress to a more detailed study of the language of the play and the effects that it creates to bring the drama to life.

Below are some of the uses to which Shakespeare puts language.

Creating atmosphere

You should remember that in Shakespeare's time theatres did not have the elaborate scenery, backdrops, and the sophisticated technology that is used to create effects in modern theatres. If you have ever visited Shakespeare's Globe in London or seen drawings of the Elizabethan theatre, you will know that they had little more than a bare stage, and in that sense theatregoers went to "hear" a play rather than to "see" a play as we would say today. The plays would also usually take place in daylight, without the elaborate lighting effects we are used to today.

Apart from all its other important functions, language was therefore essential to the creation of setting and atmosphere. In a Shakespeare play the atmosphere and setting are created through words.

Shakespeare's imagery

The use of imagery, designed to conjure up vivid images in the mind, is a very important aspect of the way in which Shakespeare works with language. Such imagery plays a key part in every Shakespeare play and very often it is closely linked to central themes of the play. For example, as Othello becomes convinced of Desdemona's infidelity, his jealousy is expressed in increasingly unpleasant animal imagery.

In *King Lear*, certain images recur time and again. Here, too, there is an abundance of animal imagery, often used to stress the inhuman behaviour of Lear's daughters. Here, Lear complains to Regan about the treatment he has received from Goneril.

King Lear

Act II Scene 4

Regan Good sir, no more; these are unsightly tricks.
Return you to my sister.

Lear (*Rising*) Never, Regan.
She hath abated me of half my train;
Looked black upon me; struck me with her tongue,
Most serpent-like, upon the very heart.
All the stored vengeances of Heaven fall
On her ungrateful top! Strike her young bones,
You taking airs, with lameness!

Cornwall Fie, sir, fie!

Lear You nimble lightnings, dart your blinding flames
Into her scornful eyes! Infect her beauty,
You fen-sucked fogs, drawn by the pow'rful sun,
To fall and blister her!

Regan	O the blest Gods! so will you wish on me, When the rash mood is on.
Lear	No, Regan, thou shalt never have my curse: Thy tender-hefted nature shall not give Thee o'er to harshness: her eyes are fierce, but thine Do comfort and not burn. 'Tis not in thee To grudge my pleasures, to cut off my train, To bandy hasty words, to scant my sizes, And, in conclusion to oppose the bolt Against my coming in:

Storm imagery also plays an important part in the language of the play, reflecting the chaos and breakdown caused to society and the mental chaos created within Lear's mind.

King Lear

Act III Scene 2
Another part of the heath. Storm still.
*Enter **Lear** and **Fool**.*

Lear	Blow, winds, and crack your cheeks! rage! blow! You cataracts and hurricanoes, spout Till you have drenched our steeples, drowned the cocks! You sulph'rous and thought-executing fires, Vaunt-couriers of oak-cleaving thunderbolts, Singe my white head! And thou, all-shaking thunder, Strike flat the thick rotundity o'th'world! Crack Nature's moulds, all germens spill at once That makes ungrateful man!
Fool	O Nuncle, court holy-water in a dry house is better than this rain-water out o'door. Good Nuncle, in, ask thy daughters blessing; here's a night pities neither wise men nor Fools.
Lear	Rumble thy bellyful! Spit, fire! spout, rain! Nor rain, wind, thunder, fire, are my daughters: I tax you not, you elements, with unkindness; I never gave you kingdom, called you children, You owe me no subscription: then let fall Your horrible pleasure; here I stand, your slave, A poor, infirm, weak, and despised old man. But yet I call you servile ministers, That will with two pernicious daughters join Your high-engendered battles 'gainst a head So old and white as this. O, ho! 'tis foul.

Activity

1 Find examples of vivid imagery in the play you are studying.

2 Are there any links between the kind of imagery the play contains and the themes of the play?

3 Pick **two** examples of imagery and analyse the ways in which Shakespeare uses language to achieve his effects.

4 Now write an essay in which you analyse the imagery patterns in the play you are studying.

Verse and prose

It has often been said that Shakespeare's greatness is rooted in his ability to use language to suit all moods, occasions, and characters. Much of his work is written in **blank verse** (without rhymes and in iambic pentameter, see page 122) – a flexible form which he adapts to suit many purposes, from moments of intense passion to bawdy bantering. However, we must not lose sight of the fact that Shakespeare makes substantial use of prose, too, which prompts the question "Why does he switch between verse and prose in his plays?"

A common answer to this question is that the "high" characters use poetry, in keeping with their elevated natures and the substance of their dialogue, while the "low" or comic characters use the more plebeian prose. An alternative answer is that Shakespeare uses prose for sub-plots, or to indicate madness or a highly wrought emotional state in a character. It is easy to find examples to support these ideas, but it is also easy to find examples to disprove them. The truth is that all these explanations are too general and simplistic to help us much, and the real explanation is rather more complex.

For example, *Hamlet* begins with the guards, Francisco and Barnardo, who are "ordinary" and minor characters, speaking in verse (see page 116). This helps to create a solemn and dignified tone with which to open the play, in keeping with the serious events that are about to unfold with the appearance of the Ghost. When Ophelia becomes mad she speaks prose but she also speaks prose in the "play-within-the-play" scene where she is perfectly sane. Hamlet himself speaks both prose and verse depending on the situation and who he is speaking to. The Players speak prose when they are not performing and verse when they are in role.

In looking at Shakespeare's use of verse and prose, therefore, you need to look at the context of the specific episode to determine why Shakespeare has chosen to use language in the form he has. In every instance there will be a good dramatic reason on which his decision is based. Remember also that Shakespeare's prose is not an unplanned, casual form of writing. It is as much an art-form as his verse, and is just as carefully structured and organized.

Make a note of where switches between verse and prose occur in the text you are studying. Choose four of these points. Give reasons why you think the switch is made in each case.

Part 2 Literary genres

DETAILED STUDY

Shakespearean comedy

There are three categories that we might use to describe Shakespearean comedy:

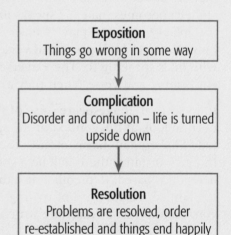

- the romantic comedies, which include *The Taming of the Shrew*, *Love's Labour's Lost*, *A Midsummer Night's Dream*, *Much Ado About Nothing*, *The Merchant of Venice*, *As You Like It*, and *Twelfth Night*
- the romances – *Cymbeline*, *The Winter's Tale*, *The Tempest*
- the problem comedies – *Troilus and Cressida*, *All's Well that Ends Well*, *Measure for Measure*.

In this Detailed Study we will focus on romantic comedy, illustrated through extracts from *Twelfth Night*.

Very often the romantic comedies are looked on as the "lightweights" of Shakespearean drama, and it is true that they do not deal with serious issues in the way that the tragedies focus on them. However, it is important to realize that despite their apparently light nature and their comic characters and situations, they are "serious" plays with real substance.

Thinking about the nature of Shakespeare's comedies will help you to understand what he is doing with this kind of drama. In many ways the structure follows the general structure of drama, which we discussed earlier:

The pattern of the comedies, then, follows the pattern of other Shakespearean drama, but there are key differences to do with how things work out within the general pattern.

- The actions of the characters create chaos and confusion, but whereas in a tragedy this chaos disturbs the audience, in romantic comedy the audience laughs at it.
- The perspective on events is one that focuses on comic rather than tragic views. A tragedy could very easily be changed into a comedy, and vice versa, by changing this perspective.

| **Exposition** |
| Things go wrong in some way |

↓

| **Complication** |
| Disorder and confusion – life is turned upside down |

↓

| **Resolution** |
| Problems are resolved, order re-established and things end happily |

Activity

Think about the last statement carefully. Choose one tragedy and one comedy that you know. Now write a brief synopsis showing how you would convert the tragedy into a comedy and the comedy into a tragedy.

The following brief plot summary will show you how the plot structure works out in *Twelfth Night*.

The play opens with Orsino, the Duke of Illyria, in love with Olivia but she does not return his love. Twins Viola and Sebastian are shipwrecked off the coast of Illyria. Viola believes Sebastian drowned.	The exposition
Viola disguises herself as a boy (Cesario) and is welcomed at Orsino's court. Orsino sends Cesario to woo Olivia on his behalf. Olivia is not moved by Orsino's declaration of love sent via Cesario, but she does feel attracted to Cesario.	Complications
Sebastian has been saved from the shipwreck by Antonio and is on his way to Orsino's court. Antonio, though, is an enemy of Orsino's. Orsino is very unhappy at Olivia's rejection and it is clear that she is in love with Cesario. However, her love is rejected by Cesario.	Complications
There then follows a variety of incidents involving the mistaking of Viola (Cesario) for Sebastian and vice versa. Olivia mistakes Sebastian for Cesario – Sebastian in turn is amazed to be invited home by a beautiful woman. She gives him a jewel and proposes marriage to him and he agrees.	Complications
Orsino confronts Antonio, who tells him he has only come to Illyria to be with his friend. Olivia enters and thinks she has just married Cesario. Viola is amazed as she knows nothing of this. The comic confusion reaches its height when Sebastian enters. Slowly the confusion begins to unravel.	Complications
All is resolved at last as Orsino realizes he is in love with Viola and he declares a double celebration when he will marry Viola, and celebrate Olivia's marriage to Sebastian.	Resolution

The sub-plot involving Sir Toby Belch, Malvolio, and various other characters also forms an integral part of the main action, and is central to the thematic development of the play.

Activity

If you are studying a different Shakespeare comedy, work out a brief synopsis of the plot to see in what ways it follows this pattern.

Shakespeare and the fantasy world

One of the features often found in Shakespeare's comedies is that the action takes place in an imaginary world. This is certainly true in *Twelfth Night*, which is set in the fictional land of Illyria. The fantasy setting allows the audience more readily to suspend their disbelief and enter a world where characters act in curious ways, and where events are not governed by the normal rules that regulate our society. There are, of course, points in the play where the characters experience sadness and pain, and they have to deal with realistic emotions. But the play is very much a fantasy in a number of ways:

- adults behave like unruly children
- the behaviour of the lovers as they fall in and out of love is not rational
- the storyline of the play is basically absurd – there are many unlikely events and coincidences that do not bear close scrutiny
- Malvolio, the one apparently serious person, is made a complete fool of.

It is worth noting that Feste's song at the end of the play recognizes that while the audience has temporarily escaped from reality into a fantasy world, they will have to emerge from the theatre into a less happy world.

Act V Scene 1

Feste   *(Sings)* When that I was and a little tiny boy
          With hey, ho, the wind and the rain,
A foolish thing was but a toy,
          For the rain it raineth every day.

But when I came to man's estate,
          With hey, ho, the wind and the rain,
'Gainst knaves and thieves men shut their gate,
          For the rain it raineth every day.

But when I came, alas, to wive,
          With hey, ho, the wind and the rain,
By swaggering could I never thrive,
          For the rain it raineth every day.

But when I came unto my beds,
          With hey, ho, the wind and the rain,
With toss-pots still had drunken heads,
          For the rain it raineth every day.

A great while ago the world begun,
          With hey, ho, the wind and the rain,
But that's all one, our play is done,
          And we'll strive to please you every day.
(Exit)

Openings

In the tragedies the opening scenes prepare us for what to expect. For example, in *Romeo and Juliet* the servants of the Capulet and Montague families come into conflict, which foreshadows the deeper conflict that is to come. Similarly, the openings of *Macbeth* and *Hamlet* prepare us for the troubling events that are to be portrayed.

Part 2 Literary genres

The openings of comedies work in much the same way, in that they prepare the audience for what is to come. The opening of *Twelfth Night* prepares us, but in this case the things that are about to happen come about through coincidence, mistaken identity, disguise, and strange adventures.

Now look at the opening of the play.

Act I Scene 1
(The Duke's Palace
Music. Enter **Orsino**, *Duke of Illyria*, **Curio**, *and other Lords)*

Duke
If music be the food of love, play on,
Give me excess of it; that, surfeiting,
The appetite may sicken, and so die.
That strain again – it had a dying fall.
O, it came o'er my ear like the sweet sound
That breathes upon a bank of violets,
Stealing and giving odour. Enough, no more,
'Tis not so sweet now as it was before.
O spirit of love, how quick and fresh art thou,
That, notwithstanding thy capacity
Receiveth as the sea, nought enters there,
Of what validity and pitch soe'er,
But falls into abatement and low price,
Even in a minute! So full of shapes is fancy,
That it alone is high fantastical.

Curio
Will you go hunt, my lord?

Duke
What, Curio?

Curio
The hart.

Duke
Why so I do, the noblest that I have.
O when mine eyes did see Olivia first,
Methought she purged the air of pestilence.
That instant was I turned into a hart,
And my desires, like fell and cruel hounds,
E'er since pursue me.

(Enter **Valentine***)*

How now, what news from her?

Valentine
So please my lord, I might not be admitted,
But from her handmaid do return this answer:
The element itself, till seven years' heat,
Shall not behold her face at ample view;
But like a cloistress she will veiled walk,
And water once a day her chamber round
With eye-offending brine; all this to season
A brother's dead love, which she would keep fresh
And lasting, in her sad remembrance.

Duke	O she that hath a heart of that fine frame
	To pay this debt of love but to a brother,
	How will she love, when the rich golden shaft
	Hath killed the flock of all affections else
	That live in her; when liver, brain, and heart,
	These sovereign thrones, are all supplied and filled,
	Her sweet perfections, with one self king.
	Away before me to sweet beds of flowers:
	Love-thoughts lie rich when canopied with bowers.

Activity

Look at the opening of *Twelfth Night*.

1   What do you make of Orsino's profession of love here?

2   What sort of mood does the play open with?

3   What power does music have?

4   Olivia, the woman Orsino is love-sick for, has said that she will not stop mourning for her brother for seven years. What effect does this have on the opening of the play?

5   What comfort does Orsino draw from this?

Now look at the opening of the second scene.

Act I Scene 2
(A Sea Coast
*Enter **Viola**, a **Captain**, and Sailors)*

Viola	What country, friends, is this?
Captain	This is Illyria, lady.
Viola	And what should I do in Illyria?
	My brother he is in Elysium.
	Perchance he is not drowned – what think you, sailors?
Captain	It is perchance that you yourself were saved.
Viola	O my poor brother, and so perchance may he be.
Captain	True, madam, and to comfort you with chance,
	Assure yourself, after our ship did split,
	When you and those poor number saved with you
	Hung on our driving boat, I saw your brother,
	Most provident in peril, bind himself –
	Courage and hope both teaching him the practice –
	To a strong mast that lived upon the sea;
	Where, like Arion on the dolphin's back,
	I saw him hold acquaintance with the waves
	So long as I could see.
Viola	For saying so, there's gold.
	Mine own escape unfoldeth to my hope,
	Whereto thy speech serves for authority,
	The like of him. Know'st thou this country?
Captain	Ay, madam, well, for I was bred and born
	Not three hours' travel from this very place.
Viola	Who governs here?
Captain	A noble duke, in nature as in name.

Viola	What is his name?
Captain	Orsino.
Viola	Orsino – I have heard my father name him. He was a bachelor then.
Captain	And so is now, or was so very late; For but a month ago I went from hence, And then 'twas fresh in murmur – as, you know, What great ones do the less will prattle of – That he did seek the love of fair Olivia.
Viola	What's she?
Captain	A virtuous maid, the daughter of a count That died some twelvemonth since, then leaving her In the protection of his son, her brother, Who shortly also died; for whose dear love, They say, she hath abjured the company And sight of men.
Viola	O that I served that lady And might not be delivered to the world, Till I had made mine own occasion mellow What my estate is.
Captain	That were hard to compass, Because she will admit no kind of suit, No, not the Duke's.
Viola	There is a fair behaviour in thee, captain, And though that nature with a beauteous wall Doth oft close in pollution, yet of thee I will believe thou hast a mind that suits With this thy fair and outward character. I prithee – and I'll pay thee bounteously – Conceal me what I am, and be my aid For such disguise as haply shall become The form of my intent. I'll serve this duke; Thou shalt present me as an eunuch to him. It may be worth thy pains, for I can sing And speak to him in many sorts of music That will allow me very worth his service. Only shape thou thy silence to my wit.
Captain	Be you his eunuch, and your mute I'll be. When my tongue blabs, then let mine eyes not see.
Viola	I thank thee. Lead me on.
	(Exeunt)

Activity

What information do you draw from this scene? What clues do you get from these opening two scenes as to what might happen later? Use the information you gain about the characters, as well as the clues from the dialogue.

Thematic development

As the plot of *Twelfth Night* develops, various themes begin to emerge. These echo some of Shakespeare's central concerns in many of his plays:

● love
● appearance and reality
● order and disorder.

In *Twelfth Night* Viola is disguised as a boy in the service of Orsino. He sends her to try to woo Olivia for him. Viola has by this time fallen in love with Orsino. However, Viola now begins to realize that Olivia has fallen in love with her, believing her to be a man. Look carefully at this extract.

Act II Scene 2

Viola   Poor lady, she were better love a dream.
Disguise, I see thou art a wickedness
Wherein the pregnant enemy does much.
How easy is it for the proper false
In women's waxen hearts to set their forms.
Alas, our frailty is the cause, not we.
For such as we are made of, such we be.
How will this fadge? My master loves her dearly.
And I, poor monster, fond as much of him;
And she, mistaken, seems to dote on me.
What will become of this? As I am man,
My state is desperate for my master's love;
As I am woman, – now alas the day –
What thriftless sighs shall poor Olivia breathe.
O time, thou must untangle this, not I;
It is too hard a knot for me t'untie.
(Exit)

Activity

1 What does Viola have to say in this soliloquy?
2 How does what she says relate to the theme of appearance and reality?

As noted earlier, another thematic strand that is commonly found in the plays of Shakespeare is that of order and disorder. In *King Lear* or *Macbeth* this disruption of order has far-reaching and ultimately tragic consequences. In a comedy such as *Twelfth Night* the disruption of order ultimately adds to the comedy.

Sir Toby Belch is a key character associated with disorder. However, the sense of disorder within the play is much more deeply embedded in the play than merely in the superficial disruption of Sir Toby. The whole essence of *Twelfth Night* implies a relaxation of order and a liberal, "festive" attitude. This is reinforced by the play's subtitle – "What You Will". In more subtle ways Feste, the clown, subverts order and even Viola and Sebastian play roles that contribute to disorder, in that through them conventional distinctions are broken down.

Activity

Think about the play that you are studying and write about the ways in which the theme of order/disorder is relevant to it.

Endings

At the end of a Shakespearean comedy there is always some kind of resolution, a sorting out of the confusions and misunderstandings that have developed through the action. In *Twelfth Night* the long, single closing scene of Act V resolves all the problems of the play. In this lengthy concluding scene all the various plot entanglements are disentangled and the confusions of identity are sorted out.

Even in a comedy there may be some bitter moments to be endured during this period of resolution. For example, read this extract from the closing of *Twelfth Night*.

	Act V Scene 1
Duke	Is this the madman?
Olivia	Ay, my lord, this same. How now, Malvolio?
Malvolio	Madam, you have done me wrong, Notorious wrong.
Olivia	Have I, Malvolio? No.
Malvolio	Lady, you have. Pray you peruse that letter. You must not now deny it is your hand; Write from it if you can, in hand or phrase; Or say 'tis not your seal, not your invention; You can say none of this. Well, grant it then, And tell me, in the modesty of honour, Why you have given me such clear lights of favour, Bade me come smiling and cross-gartered to you, To put on yellow stockings and to frown Upon Sir Toby and the lighter people; And, acting this in an obedient hope, Why have you suffered me to be imprisoned, Kept in a dark house, visited by the priest, And made the most notorious geck and gull That e'er invention played on? Tell me why.
Olivia	Alas, Malvolio, this is not my writing, Though, I confess, much like the character; But out of question 'tis Maria's hand. And now I do bethink me, it was she First told me thou wast mad; then cam'st in smiling, And in such forms which here were presupposed Upon thee in the letter. Prithee be content, This practice hath most shrewdly passed upon thee. But when we know the grounds and authors of it, Thou shalt be both the plaintiff and the judge Of thine own cause.
Fabian	Good madam, hear me speak, And let no quarrel nor no brawl to come Taint the condition of this present hour, Which I have wondered at. In hope it shall not, Most freely I confess myself and Toby

Set this device against Malvolio here,
Upon some stubborn and uncourteous parts
We had conceived against him. Maria writ
The letter at Sir Toby's great importance,
In recompense whereof he hath married her.
How with a sportful malice it was followed
May rather pluck on laughter than revenge,
If that the injuries be justly weighed
That have on both sides passed.

Olivia   Alas, poor fool, how have they baffled thee!

Feste   Why, 'Some are born great, some achieve greatness, and some have greatness
thrown upon them.' I was one, sir, in this interlude, one Sir Topas, sir; but that's
all one. 'By the Lord, fool, I am not mad.' But do you remember? – 'Madam, why
laugh you at such a barren rascal? An you smile not he's gagged.' And thus the
whirligig of time brings in his revenges.

Malvolio   I'll be revenged on the whole pack of you.
            (Exit)

Olivia   He hath been most notoriously abused.

Duke   Pursue him, and entreat him to a peace;
            He hath not told us of the captain yet.
            *(Exit **Fabian** or some other)*

Activity

Think about the comedy that you are studying or one
that you have studied in the past. How does it end?
Make notes on the ways in which it fits in with the
patterns we have seen with *Twelfth Night*.

Now write an essay on the nature of Shakespearean
comedy, based on two plays that you have read or seen.

"Good, but not immortal."

7 Comparative study

Objectives

- To establish a strategy of approaching world literature assignments
- To read texts with a sense of their value to you, personally, as someone with a growing international consciousness
- To practise constructing literary arguments involving two texts
- To explore various ways of interpreting and conveying appreciation for texts from all over the world

If you are studying at Higher Level you will complete **two** World Literature Assignments for your Language A1 English course. If you are studying at Standard Level you will complete **one**.

All students, Standard and Higher Level, must complete Assignment 1, which involves a comparative study of at least two of the three World Literature works studied in Part 1 of the programme. Although you can, if you wish, base your assignment on three works studied in Part 1, most students write better assignments using two works. Having said that, some very good assignments have been written based on three works, especially when the topic is very narrow, for example "The authors' use of nicknames in…", or "How the chapter titles are used as metaphors by three writers".

Here are some general points to bear in mind:

- You are required to study independently, under the supervision of a teacher, and to submit your written work for external assessment.
- You are expected to use your own sense of the texts and your own inventiveness in choosing the type and title of the assignment, although you **must** check your direction with your teacher, either in discussion or through some written format.
- You should select any aspect of the World Literature works studied in your programme for the assignment.

- Where another student has chosen to write about the same topic or aspect, you must work independently of one another and the content of your assignments must be different.
- Your assignment must be written in English.
- Your assignment must be 1000–1500 words in length and the number of words used must be stated at the end of each assignment. Quotations from works must be included in the word count, but footnotes and bibliographies are not to be included. You should **not**, however, include textual references to the two or three works discussed in the footnotes.

Assignment 1: Comparative study

Assignment 1 must be a comparative study, based on at **least two** of the three World Literature works studied in Part 1 of the programme. It must be between 1000 and 1500 words in length.

Aspects

You must select an aspect of the Part 1 World Literature works for your assignment. The aspect selected must focus on some relevant link between the two or three works used for the assignment, and may reflect your own interests.

You may choose, for your assignment, a topic which focuses on aspects such as:

- narrative technique
- characterization
- patterns of imagery
- dramatic structure
- techniques of dialogue.

Approach

Candidates often fail to choose an approach that will convey their views as an argument. You will need to decide on a position, for example, "Fyodor Dostoevsky's techniques of characterization create portrayals that are much more sympathetic than Mikhail Lermontov's". You will then need to provide details from the two novels that **show** the reader of your essay that you can construct a persuasive case for this view.

Structure

Standard features of essays, such as introduction, main body and conclusion, are expected in this exercise.

The **introduction** should tell the reader the nature of the topic and how it is to be approached. It could be, for example, a brief statement of the aims of the assignment.

The **main body** should reveal your insight into the works and your appreciation of the chosen link between the works. A variety of methods is acceptable including, for example, Socratic dialogue, interview, or a formal development of ideas as in an essay.

The **conclusion** could be, for example, a brief summary and personal evaluation of the discussion or the particular achievement of the writing.

Approaching the comparison

Before you can really get to grips with the comparison, of course, you must study each of the texts carefully, looking at all the relevant features that we have discussed in earlier units. However, when you have developed a sound knowledge of the two texts you are studying, you will need to begin to think carefully about them as a pair.

At this point it is often helpful to make a visual aid for yourself in which you create a heading for each work and list *all* the possible links you can see between them. Don't forget to include very precise aspects such as names, or terms used to describe emotions, or precise details of a setting, as well as larger aspects, such as convincing or unconvincing techniques of characterization, biased or unbiased narrators, or the role of setting in novels.

The following model is one way in which you could approach your comparative study.

Plan

- Identify and think about comparative areas and issues in your texts.

- Identify and list aspects of comparison. Push yourself to think of as many as you can, since the first one you choose may not be one you will want to pursue.
- Test one or two of these. Set out the topic and see how many details you can find that relate to that topic.
- Survey your list of details and see what might be interesting to discuss. For example, the use of images of fire in one novel may possibly be comparable to the use of water images in another text. At this point you might be ready to see what is interesting about the two sets of images; for example, one writer uses images of fire to more fully characterize the protagonist, while images of water are used to convey a changing emotional atmosphere in the other novel.

Other examples of comparisons might include:

- How food is used to provide character revelation in *Madame Bovary* and *Anna Karenina*.
- The way the playwright uses choric figures in *Accidental Death of an Anarchist* and *Antigone*.
- The effect of point of view on how readers view women in *The House of the Spirits* and *Like Water for Chocolate*.
- The different uses of irony in the poetry of Wislawa Szymborska and Bei Dao.

Finding a topic that truly interests you is the single most important step in writing this comparative essay, and the next is adopting a position or thesis that can be argued based on detailed references found in the texts.

We will now look at some approaches to the comparison of the texts.

The two novels discussed here are *The Outsider* by Albert Camus, a French writer, and *Metamorphosis* by Franz Kafka, a writer born in Prague. The two works are treated in their English translations. A short plot summary is given in case you are not familiar with these works.

The Outsider

In *The Outsider* Meursault, the protagonist and also narrator of the novel, is a young shipping clerk living in Algiers. The book opens as Meursault recalls his mother's death. The day after his mother's funeral Meursault meets a beautiful young woman, Marie Cardona, and the two spend the day together. They later return to Meursault's apartment where they make love. Meursault returns to his mundane life and becomes friendly with a neighbour, Raymond Sintès. One day Raymond takes Meursault and Marie to the beach to visit his friend, Masson. During this excursion they fight with a group of Arabs who then run off. After the three men return to Masson's cottage Meursault goes back to the beach with Raymond's gun. Here he meets one of the Arabs they had fought with earlier. The Arab draws a knife and Meursault shoots him once, and then fires four more bullets into his body.

He is arrested and put in jail to await trial. Several months later when his trial begins, the prosecution makes much of his apparent indifference to the death of his mother. Marie also tells the court that they began their relationship immediately after his mother's funeral. The jury and the judges are convinced that Meursault is a callous, unfeeling monster. He is convicted of premeditated murder and sentenced to be executed in public by guillotine. While awaiting his execution he thinks over his life and what he has done, but his indifference does not change. The chaplain tries to offer him comfort but Meursault does not believe in God and rejects his offers of help. Finally, as he approaches his own death he realizes how his mother must have felt when at the point of death herself – a kind of liberation and readiness to live her life again.

Metamorphosis

In *Metamorphosis*, Gregor Samsa is a young travelling salesman who lives with and selflessly supports his parents and younger sister. One morning he awakes to discover that he has turned into an insect during the night. To begin with he is concerned with the practical everyday problems of how to move about with his newly acquired multiple legs, and how he will get to work on time.

As he has not arrived at work the chief clerk arrives at Gregor's house to find him still shut in his bedroom unable to show himself to his family. His family think that he is unwell and they try to persuade him to open the door.

The chief clerk suggests that Gregor's strange behaviour has something to do with some cash payments which had recently been entrusted to him. Gregor is obviously dismayed at this slur on his previously unblemished reputation and tries even harder to get up and move about. And eventually, after great efforts, he manages to unlock the door and reveals himself to the others. Understandably his family is terrified and the chief clerk runs away. Finally Gregor's father pushes him back into the room and locks the door.

In Chapter 2 the family has calmed down to some extent and Gregor stays hidden away in his room. His sister takes him food and cleans up after him. His parents ignore him and try to pretend he is not there. Gregor can hear them talking about their money worries now that Gregor is not working to support them. His parents do not enter his room or see him for the first two weeks, and he is looked after entirely by his sister. However, his mother does eventually enter his room and accidentally catches sight of him and faints. When Gregor's father comes in he blames Gregor for everything and in his disgust throws apples at Gregor. One of them lodges in his back, wounding him and driving him back into his room.

In the third chapter the family's resentment of Gregor grows and even his sister stops caring for him very well. The wound on his back caused by the apple begins to fester and slowly he becomes weaker and weaker. In the end Gregor, thinking how much he loves his sister, finds that he is rejected by her and retreats into his room for a third time, where he dies. His body is cleared away by the maid. In the end the family prepare to start a new life, forgetting all about Gregor.

Now read the following passage taken from the opening of *Metamorphosis*. Think about these questions and write down your responses:

1 What is the impact of Kafka's opening sentence?

2 How is this impact reinforced in the remainder of the opening paragraph?

3 What effect is created by the details that you are given in the second paragraph?

4 What is your response to the rest of the extract? Think about the ideas it contains, the ways in which Kafka uses language, and the effects he achieves.

Metamorphosis

As Gregor Samsa awoke one morning from uneasy dreams he found himself transformed in his bed into a gigantic insect. He was lying on his hard, as if it were armour-plated, back and when he lifted his head a little he could see his dome-like brown belly divided into stiff, arched segments on top of which the bed-quilt could hardly keep in position and was about to slide off completely. His numerous legs, which were pitifully thin compared to the rest of his bulk, waved helplessly before his eyes.

What has happened to me? he thought. It was no dream. His room, a regular human bedroom, only rather too small, lay quiet between the four familiar walls. Above the table on which a collection of cloth samples was unpacked and spread out – Samsa was a commercial traveller – hung the picture which he had recently cut out of an illustrated magazine and put into a pretty gilt frame. It showed a lady, with a fur cap on and a fur stole, sitting upright and holding out to the spectator a huge fur muff into which the whole of her forearm had vanished.

Gregor's eyes turned next to the window, and the overcast sky – one could hear the raindrops beating on the window gutter – made him quite melancholy. What about sleeping a little longer and forgetting all this nonsense, he thought, but it could not be done, for he was accustomed to sleep on his right side and in his present condition he could not turn himself over. However violently he forced himself towards his right side he always rolled onto his back again. He tried it at least a hundred times, shutting his eyes to keep from seeing his struggling legs, and only desisted when he began to feel in his side a faint dull ache he had never experienced before.

Oh God, he thought, what an exhausting job I've picked on! Travelling about day in, day out. It's much more irritating work than doing the actual business in the warehouse, and on top of that there's the trouble of constant travelling, of worrying about train connexions, the bed and the irregular meals, casual acquaintances that are always new and never become intimate friends. The devil take it all! He felt a slight itching up on his belly; slowly pushed himself on his back nearer to the top of the bed so that he could lift his head more easily; identified the itching place which was surrounded by many small white spots the nature of which he could not understand, and made to touch it with a leg, but drew the leg back immediately, for the contact made a cold shiver run through him.

Franz Kafka

Here are some notes made by a student on these activities. Read them through and compare her ideas with your own.

Commentary

1 ● The contrast between the "normal" and the "absurd" in the opening sentence is very striking.

● The image of the "gigantic insect" is somewhat disturbing.

● The inclusion of the words "uneasy dreams" suggests an air of foreboding.

2 ● Detailed descriptions such as: "his hard... armour-plated back", "his dome-like brown belly", "His numerous legs... waved helplessly before his eyes", reinforce the disturbing opening.

● The image of a gigantic insect lying underneath a "bed-quilt" reinforces the absurd nature of the opening.

● The matter-of-fact way in which Gregor is described makes the images appear all the more startling.

3 ● Realization that "It was no dream".

● Inclusion of materialistic elements which portray images of extravagance: "gilt frame", "fur cap", "fur stole", and "a huge fur muff into which the whole of her forearm had vanished".

● These extravagant images contrast with the comparatively meagre "regular... bedroom" which is "rather too small".

4 ● The "overcast sky" reasserts the sense of foreboding.

● A sense of his helplessness and despair is created through the line "What about sleeping a little longer and forgetting all this nonsense, he thought, but it could not be done". This is also true of Gregor's exclamation: "The devil take it all!" Although, it is unclear whether he is thinking about his physical condition or his job.

● The twist in the phrase "Oh God, he thought, what an exhausting job I've picked on!" One assumes he is referring to the effort he is putting into turning over – "He tried it at least a hundred times"– but here he is actually referring to his job as a commercial traveller.

● His dissatisfaction with his job is shown through descriptions of it as "irritating work", with "constant travelling" and "irregular meals".

● A sense of his solitary existence is achieved through "casual acquaintances that are always new and never become intimate friends".

● A suggestion of how, in his job, time is an added pressure is given in "worrying about train connexions".

● Additional details describe his transformation. He now has "small white spots".

● "He felt a slight itching up on his belly" because of the spots; this suggests that the transformation will not be a positive change or a pleasant experience.

Activity

Now read the second part of this opening section of the story.

1 What do you learn about the nature of Gregor's life and daily routine prior to his change into an insect?

2 How does Kafka present this picture of his life?

3 Look back over the whole of this opening section of the story and make notes on the following

aspects of it:

● the ideas it contains

● the ways in which the characters are presented

● the tone of the writing

● the language that Kafka uses and the effects he creates.

Metamorphosis

He slid down again into his former position. This getting up early, he thought, makes one quite stupid. A man needs his sleep. Other commercials live like harem women. For instance, when I come back to the hotel of a morning to write up the orders I've got, these others are only sitting down to breakfast. Let me just try that on with my chief; I'd be sacked on the spot. Anyhow, that might be quite a good thing for me, who can tell? If I didn't have to hold my hand because of my parents I'd have given notice long ago, I'd have gone to the chief and told him exactly what I think of him. That would knock him endways from his desk! It's a queer way of acting, too, this sitting on high at a desk and talking down to employees, especially when they have to come quite near because the chief is hard of hearing. Well, there's still hope; once I've saved enough money to pay back my parents' debts to him – that should take another five or six years – I'll do it without fail. I'll cut myself completely loose then. For the moment, though, I'd better get up, since my train goes at five.

He looked at the alarm-clock ticking on the chest. Heavenly Father! he thought. It was half past six o'clock and the hands were quietly moving on, it was even past the half hour, it was getting on for a quarter to seven. Had the alarm-clock not gone off? From the bed one could see that it had been properly set for four o'clock; of course it must have gone off. Yes, but was it possible to sleep quietly through that ear-splitting noise? Well, he had not slept quietly, yet apparently all the more soundly for that. But what was he to do now? The next train went at seven o'clock; to catch that he would need to hurry like mad and his samples weren't even packed up, and he himself wasn't feeling particularly fresh and active. And even if he did catch the train he wouldn't avoid a row with the chief, since the warehouse porter would have been waiting for the five o'clock train and would have long since reported his failure to turn up. The porter was a creature of the chief's, spineless and stupid. Well, supposing he were to say he was sick? But that would be most unpleasant and would look suspicious, since during his five years' employment he had not been ill once. The chief himself would be sure to come with the sick-insurance doctor, would reproach his parents with their son's laziness, and would cut all excuses short by referring to the insurance doctor, who of course regarded all mankind as perfectly healthy malingerers. And would he be so far wrong on this occasion? Gregor really felt quite well, apart from a drowsiness that was utterly superfluous after such a long sleep, and he was even unusually hungry.

As all this was running through his mind at top speed without his being able to decide to leave his bed – the alarm-clock had just struck a quarter to seven – there came a cautious tap at the door behind the head of his bed. 'Gregor,' said a voice – it was his mother's – 'it's a quarter to seven. Hadn't you a train to catch?' That gentle voice! Gregor had a shock as he heard his own voice answering hers, unmistakably his own voice, it was true, but with a persistent horrible twittering squeak behind it like an undertone, that left the words in their clear shape only for the first moment and then rose up reverberating round them to destroy their sense, so that one could not be sure one had heard them rightly. Gregor wanted to answer at length and explain everything, but in the circumstances he confined himself to saying: 'Yes, yes, thank you, mother, I'm getting up now.' The wooden door between them must have kept the change in his voice from being noticeable outside, for his mother contented herself with this statement and shuffled away. Yet this brief exchange of words had made the other members of the family aware that Gregor was still in the house, as they had not expected, and at one of the side-doors his father was already knocking, gently, yet with his fist. 'Gregor, Gregor,' he called, 'what's the matter with you?' And after a little while he called again in a deeper voice: 'Gregor! Gregor!' At the other side-door his sister was saying in a low, plaintive tone: 'Gregor? Aren't you well? Are you needing anything?' He answered them both at once: 'I'm just ready,' and did his best to make his voice sound as normal as possible by enunciating the words very clearly and leaving long pauses between them. So his father went back to his breakfast, but his sister whispered: 'Gregor, open the door, do.' However, he was not thinking of opening the door, and felt thankful for the prudent habit he had acquired in travelling of locking all doors during the night, even at home.

Franz Kafka

Activity

Now look at the following extract. It is taken from the opening of *The Outsider* by Albert Camus.

1 What effect does Camus create in his opening paragraph?

2 What attitude does Meursault show towards the death of his mother?

3 Summarize Meursault's relationship with his mother before she died.

4 What techniques does Camus use to give us a sense of this relationship?

5 What is your response to this opening of the novel? Make notes on the following aspects of it:

- the ideas it contains

- the ways in which the central character is presented

- the tone of the writing

- the language that Camus uses and the effects he creates.

The Outsider

Mother died today. Or maybe yesterday, I don't know. I had a telegram from the home: 'Mother passed away. Funeral tomorrow. Yours sincerely.' That doesn't mean anything. It may have been yesterday.

The old people's home is at Marengo, fifty miles from Algiers. I'll catch the two o'clock bus and get there in the afternoon. Then I can keep the vigil and I'll come back tomorrow night. I asked my boss for two days off and he couldn't refuse under the circumstances. But he didn't seem pleased. I even said, 'It's not my fault.' He didn't answer. Then I thought maybe I shouldn't have said that. After all, it wasn't for me to apologize. It was more up to him to offer me his condolences. But he probably will do the day after tomorrow, when he sees me in mourning. For the moment it's almost as if mother were still alive. After the funeral though, the death will be a classified fact and the whole thing will have assumed a more official aura.

I caught the two o'clock bus. It was very hot. I ate at Céleste's restaurant, as usual. They all felt very sorry for me and Céleste told me, 'There's no one like a mother.' When I left, they came to the door with me. I was in a bit of a daze because I had to go up to Emmanuel's place to borrow a black tie and armband. He lost his uncle, a few months ago.

I had to run for the bus. It was probably all this dashing about and then the jolting and the smell of petrol and the glare of the sky reflecting off the road that made me doze off. I slept almost all the way. And when I woke up, I found myself cramped up against a soldier who smiled at me and asked me if I'd come far. I said, 'Yes' so as not to have to talk any more.

The home is just over a mile from the village. I walked it. I wanted to see mother straight away. But the caretaker told me I had to meet the warden. He was busy, so I waited a bit. The caretaker talked the whole time and then he showed me into the warden's office. He was a small, elderly man with the Legion of Honour. He looked at me with bright eyes. Then he shook my hand and held it for so long that I didn't quite know how to take it back again. He consulted a file and told me, 'Mrs Meursault came here three years ago. You were her only means of support.' I felt as if he was reproaching me for something and I started to explain. But he interrupted me, 'You've no need to justify yourself, my dear boy. I've read your mother's file. You weren't able to look after her properly. She needed a nurse. You only have a modest income. And all things considered, she was happier here.' I said, 'Yes, sir.' He added, 'You see, she had friends here, people of her own age. She could share her interests with them. You're a young man, a different generation, and she must have been bored living with you.'

It was true. When she was at home, mother used to spend all her time just watching me in silence. She cried a lot the first few days at the old people's home. But that was only because she wasn't used to it. That's partly why during this last year I hardly ever went to see her any more. And also because it meant giving up my Sunday – let alone making the effort of going to the bus stop, buying tickets and spending two hours travelling.

The warden spoke to me again. But I wasn't really listening any more. Then he said, 'I expect you'd like to see your mother.' I stood up without saying anything and he led the way to the door. On our way downstairs he explained, 'We've transferred her to our little mortuary. So as not to upset the others. Every time one of the inmates dies the others feel uneasy for two or three days. And that makes it difficult for the staff.' We crossed a courtyard where there were lots of old people, chatting in little groups. They'd stop talking as we went by, then behind us the conversations would start up again. It was like the muted chatter of budgerigars. At the door of a small building the warden stopped. 'I'll leave you now, Mr Meursault. If you need me for anything, I'll be in my office. We've arranged the funeral as usual for ten o'clock in the morning. We thought that that would enable you to watch over the departed tonight. One other thing: your mother apparently often mentioned to her friends that she wished to have a religious funeral. I've taken it upon myself to make the necessary arrangements.

But I thought I should let you know.' I thanked him. Though she wasn't an atheist, mother had never given a thought to religion in her life.

I went in. It was a very bright room, with whitewashed walls and a glass roof. The furniture consisted of some chairs and some cross-shaped trestles. Two of these, in the centre of the room, were supporting a coffin. The lid was on, but a row of shiny screws, which hadn't yet been tightened down, stood out against the walnut-stained wood. Near the coffin there was an Arab nurse in a white overall, with a brightly coloured scarf on her head.

At that point the caretaker came in behind me. He must have been running. He stuttered a bit. 'We covered her up. But I was to unscrew the coffin to let you see her.' He was just going up to the coffin when I stopped him. He said, 'Don't you want to?' I answered, 'No.' He didn't say anything and I was embarrassed because I felt I shouldn't have said that. After a moment he looked at me and asked, 'Why not?' but not reproachfully, just as if he wanted to know. I said, 'I don't know.' He began twiddling his white moustache and then, without looking at me, he announced, 'I understand.' He had beautiful bright blue eyes and a reddish complexion. He offered me a chair and then he sat down just behind me. The nurse stood up and went towards the door. At that point the caretaker said to me, 'It's a chancre she's got.' I didn't understand, so I looked at the nurse and saw that she had a bandage round her head just below the eyes. Where her nose should have been, the bandage was flat. Her face seemed to be nothing but a white bandage.

Albert Camus

Here are the notes a student made in response to the questions. Read them through carefully and compare them to your own ideas. Remember, however, that very often a text can be interpreted in more than one way. There is often no "right" answer. What matters is that you can support your ideas with reference to the text.

Commentary

1 ● Emotionless statement opens the novel: "Mother died today".
  ● Confusion is created through the telegram "Funeral tomorrow".
  ● Camus's short sentences mirror the emotionless, uncaring wording in the telegram.

2 ● Meursault appears to exhibit a degree of indifference: "Mother died today".
  ● He appears to lack any emotional attachment to his mother and this can be seen through the calm, calculated manner in which he plans his attendance at her funeral: "I'll catch the two o'clock bus... get there in the afternoon... keep the vigil and I'll come back tomorrow night."
  ● The phrase Meursault uses to describe his mother's death as a "classified fact" emphasizes the suggestion that he is unaffected by it and is somewhat cold in his manner.
  ● He is somewhat cold and detached as he appears to concentrate more on the coffin than his mother inside: "The lid was on, but a row of shiny screws, which hadn't yet been tightened down, stood out against the walnut-stained wood."
  ● He refuses to see his mother in the coffin.

3 ● Suggestion that their relationship was a distant one through the line "That doesn't mean anything". This could relate to the confusion in the telegram or Meursault's feelings towards his mother's death.
 ● He appears to lack compassion in his explanation of why his mother cried when she was first placed in the home "... that was only because she wasn't used to it".
 ● This idea is developed further as he states that visiting his mother in the home meant "giving up my Sunday".
 ● His lack of interest in his mother, and lack of knowledge about her, is suggested in his response to being told that she had asked for a religious funeral: "Though she wasn't an atheist, mother had never given a thought to religion in her life".

4 ● Camus's use of first-person narrative emphasizes the fact that Meursault's indifferent reaction to his mother's death is an honest one and not merely the assessment of an observer.
 ● Camus also includes minor characters through which Meursault's detachment from his mother can be recognized. This can be seen quite clearly through his interactions with the caretaker when asked if he wishes to see his mother's body.
 ● Through the line "But the caretaker told me I had to meet the warden" Camus gives another indication that Meursault's relationship with his mother was not close, as one might expect that he himself would request to see the warden.

5 Ideas:
 ● attitude towards death
 ● mother/son relationship
 ● the guilt associated with putting a relative in a nursing home
 ● the attitude towards other cultures through the distinction of race: "an Arab nurse"
 ● the lack of concern by employers for their employees.

Central character:
● Meursault is presented as cold and unfeeling with regard to his relationship with, and the death of, his mother.
● His concentration on the physical environment and physical attributes of people rather than emotional involvement reasserts the idea that he is cold and indifferent.
● He displays a characteristic attention to detail both through his observations of other characters and the environment, and through the attentive planning of his journey.
● He is in a subordinate position in his place of work.
● He is unsure how to react in social situations: "I said, 'Yes' so as not to have to talk any more"; "he shook my hand and held it for so long that I didn't quite know how to take it back again".

Tone of the writing:
● An uneasy tone is created through Meursault's indifference at the death of his mother.
● A sense of foreboding is created through the somewhat misplaced comment directed towards his boss when Meursault is asking for time off work: "It's not my fault".
● A degree of sadness is created through the presentation of an old lady weeping while in the nursing home.

Part 3 World literature

Language:

- The inclusion of the comment that the nursing home is "fifty miles from Algiers" emphasizes the distance evident in the relationship between the mother and son.
- The piece is largely constructed of short sentences, which inhibits reader engagement. This mirrors the lack of engagement between mother and son.
- His omission of emotional references gives the piece a somewhat "clinical" feel – this also supports the idea of their relationship being unfeeling and distant.
- The description of the residents as "inmates" connotes a prison-like environment.
- The line "... there were lots of old people, chatting in little groups" is somewhat patronizing and disrespectful.
- The contrast between the way Meursault describes his mother as being "dead" and the warden's euphemistic "departed" emphasizes the different reactions towards her death by the two.

Activity

Read over these two openings again and write an essay of approximately 500 words comparing the two extracts. You should consider the following:

- the ways in which the characters are presented
- ideas or themes that might be suggested
- the ways in which the writers use language and the effects they achieve
- any other ideas or features that you have found interesting.

Commentary: A comparison of the openings of *Metamorphosis* by Franz Kafka and *The Outsider* by Albert Camus

Activity

Here is how one student began her essay on these openings. Read it through and make a note of any points you think important.

The openings to the novels *The Outsider* and *Metamorphosis* both concentrate on the reactions of individuals to a change in circumstances. In *Metamorphosis* we see how Gregor awakes to find himself changed into "a gigantic insect" and in *The Outsider* how Meursault reacts to the death of his mother. Although these are very different circumstances, their reactions in some ways are quite similar. For instance, both display a degree of indifference to the changes that have taken place and both are related in a matter-of-fact manner.

In both openings the theme of isolation appears to be explored. For instance, both Gregor and Meursault appear to be solitary characters, though for very different reasons. Meursault appears to lack the ability to engage socially, as can be seen in his reluctance to engage with the soldier on the bus: "I said, 'Yes' so as not to have to talk any more." However, Gregor's solitary lifestyle seems to be caused by his job as a commercial traveller: "casual acquaintances that are always new and never become intimate friends". Indeed Gregor appears to be extremely dissatisfied with his job due to the restrictions it places on his life, as it involves "irritating work", with "constant travelling" and "irregular meals", etc.

It is interesting to see how both writers include elaborate descriptions in their novels. For instance, Kafka's description of the changes to Gregor's body are very detailed: "his dome-like brown belly divided into stiff, arched segments... His numerous legs... waved helplessly before his eyes." The attention to the details of the coffin in which Meursault's mother lies is similar to this: "The lid was on, but a row of shiny screws, which hadn't yet been tightened down, stood out against the walnut-stained wood." However, this level of description is reserved for physical aspects in both works, thus emphasizing the lack of emotional engagement and reasserting the idea of emotional detachment and isolation.

You might have noted some of the following features in this student's handling of the opening of this essay.

- The opening paragraph focuses on both texts and makes it clear that a comparison is being made between them.
- This paragraph indicates that there are differences but also similarities between the two, and an example is given.
- There is also a reference to the significance of the "tone" of the two texts.
- The second paragraph begins to explore a thematic link between the two, together with some detailed supporting evidence from the texts.
- A comparison is made of the writers' styles, again well-supported through reference to the text.

Although these works are very different in nature they do have some features in common. One of the key points of similarity is the themes they deal with. If you read the whole texts for yourself, you might see the following ideas emerging.

Metamorphosis
- Isolation is a key theme. After Gregor has changed into an insect he becomes increasingly isolated from his family and is ultimately rejected by them. The chief clerk runs away from him and his father throws apples at him (indirectly, therefore, being responsible for his death). Gregor's isolation is increased by the fact that physical movement and speech are difficult for him.
- Questions are raised about the purpose of existence. Before his transformation, Gregor is unhappy and dissatisfied with his work but is trapped in it because he needs to support his family. He accepts his miserable existence.
- The purpose of human lives in the modern world is questioned. Kafka symbolically portrays how far human beings can be reduced and how life's struggle can become futile.
- The absurdity of life is symbolically reflected in the absurdity of the idea that a person could change into an insect. What is Kafka trying to do with this story? It poses questions about the difference between the significant and the insignificant.

The Outsider
- Isolation is also a key theme of *The Outsider*. As the title suggests, Meursault feels himself to be alienated from the "ordinary" human life that surrounds him.
- He embodies the absurdity of life, working at a mundane job he does not enjoy and trying to fill his spare time with activity, but he often finds himself purposeless and without motivation.
- Love as an emotion has no meaning for him, and he finds no fulfilment in relationships.

● *The Outsider* is a difficult work to interpret. Is it about the meaningless of life? In the end, is Meursault's death as meaningless as his life? In a sense he welcomes death.

Part 3 World literature

Activity

The following two passages are taken from near the end of the texts. In the first one Meursault is found guilty of murder and sentenced to be executed by decapitation. The second extract describes the final rejection and death of Gregor.

Read them carefully and write an essay of 500–750 words in which you explore the two texts. You should consider the following aspects:

● the ways in which the characters are presented

● ideas or themes that might be suggested

● the ways in which the writers use language and the effects they achieve

● any other ideas or features that you have found interesting.

The Outsider

That afternoon the huge fans were still churning up the dense atmosphere in the courtroom and the jurymen were all waving their little coloured fans in the same direction. I thought my lawyer's speech was never going to end. At one point though I listened because he said, 'It's true that I killed a man.' Then he went on like that, saying 'I' every time he meant me. I was very surprised. I leant over to one of the policemen and asked him why this was. He told me to be quiet and a moment later added, 'Lawyers always do that.' It seemed to me that it was just another way of excluding me from the proceedings, reducing me to insignificance and, in a sense, substituting himself for me. But I think I was already a very long way from that courtroom. Besides, I thought my lawyer was ridiculous. He made a quick plea of provocation and then he too started talking about my soul. But he didn't seem to have nearly as much talent as the prosecutor. 'I too,' he said, 'have peered into this man's soul, but unlike my eminent colleague from the State Prosecutor's office, I did find something there and in fact I read it like an open book.' He'd read that I was an honest chap, a regular and tireless worker who was faithful to the company that employed him, popular with everyone and sympathetic to the misfortunes of others. To him I was a model son who had supported his mother for as long as he could. In the end I'd hoped that an old people's home would give the old lady the comforts which my limited means prevented me from providing for her. 'I am amazed, gentlemen,' he added, 'that such a fuss has been made of this home. For after all, if proof were needed of the importance and usefulness of these institutions, one need only say that it is the state itself which subsidizes them.' The only thing was that he didn't talk about the funeral and I felt that this was an important omission in his speech. But what with all these long sentences and the endless days and hours that people had been talking about my soul, I just had the impression that I was drowning in some sort of colourless liquid.

In the end all I remember is that, echoing towards me from out in the street and crossing the vast expanse of chambers and courtrooms as my lawyer went on talking, came the sound of an ice-seller's trumpet. I was assailed by memories of a life which was no longer mine, but in which I'd found my simplest and most lasting pleasures: the smells of summer, the part of town that I loved, the sky on certain evenings, Marie's dresses and the way she laughed. And the utter pointlessness of what I was doing here took me by the throat and all I wanted was to get it over with and to go back to my cell and sleep. I hardly even heard my lawyer exclaim finally that the jury would surely not send an honest worker to his death just because he forgot himself for a moment, and then appeal for extenuating circumstances since my surest punishment for this crime was the eternal remorse with which I was already stricken. The court was adjourned and the lawyer sat down, looking exhausted. But his colleagues came over to shake hands with him. I heard a 'magnificent, old chap'. One of them even called me to witness. 'Eh?' he said. I agreed, but it was hardly a sincere compliment, because I was too tired.

However, the sun was getting low outside and it wasn't so hot any more. From the few street noises that I could hear, I sensed the calm of evening. There we all were, waiting. And what we were all waiting for concerned no one but me. I looked round the room again. Everything was just as it had been on the first day. I met the eye of the journalist in the grey jacket and of the little robot-woman. That reminded me that I hadn't looked for Marie once during the whole trial. I hadn't forgotten her, only I'd been too busy. I saw her sitting between Céleste and Raymond. She gave me a little wave as if to say, 'At last,' and I saw a rather anxious smile on her face. But my heart felt locked and I couldn't even smile back.

The judges returned. The jury was very rapidly read a series of questions. I heard 'guilty of murder . . .', 'premeditation . . .', 'extenuating circumstances'. The jury went out and I was taken into the little room where I'd waited once already. My lawyer came to join me: he was very talkative and spoke to me in a more confident and friendly way than he'd ever done before. He thought that everything would be all right and that I'd get off with a few years of prison or hard labour. I asked him whether there was any chance of getting the sentence quashed if it was unfavourable. He said no. His tactics had been not to lodge any objections so as not to antagonize the jury. He explained that they didn't quash sentences just like that, for no reason. It seemed obvious and I accepted his argument. Looking at it coldly, it was completely natural. If the opposite were the case, there'd be far too much pointless paperwork. 'Anyway,' my lawyer told me, 'you can always appeal. But I'm convinced the outcome will be favourable.'

We waited a very long time, almost three quarters of an hour, I think. At the end of that time a bell rang. My lawyer left me, saying, 'The foreman of the jury is going to read out the verdict. You'll only be brought in for the passing of the sentence.' Some doors banged. People were running up and down stairs, but I couldn't tell how far away they were. Then I heard a muffled voice reading something out in the courtroom. When the bell rang again and the door to the dock opened, what greeted me was the silence that filled the room, the silence and that strange sensation I had when I discovered that the young journalist had looked away. I didn't look over at Marie. I didn't have time to because the judge told me in a peculiar way that I would be decapitated in a public square in the name of the French people. And I think I recognized the expression that I could see on every face. I'm quite sure it was one of respect. The policemen were very gentle with me. The lawyer placed his hand on my wrist. I'd stopped thinking altogether. But the judge asked me if I had anything to add. I thought it over. I said, 'No.' That was when they took me away.

Albert Camus

Metamorphosis

'We must try to get rid of it,' his sister now said explicitly to her father, since her mother was coughing too much to hear a word, 'it will be the death of both of you, I can see that coming. When one has to work as hard as we do, all of us, one can't stand this continual torment at home on top of it. At least I can't stand it any longer.' And she burst into such a passion of sobbing that her tears dropped on her mother's face, where she wiped them off mechanically.

'My dear,' said the old man sympathetically, and with evident understanding, 'but what can we do?'

Gregor's sister merely shrugged her shoulders to indicate the feeling of helplessness that had now over-mastered her during her weeping fit, in contrast to her former confidence.

'If he could understand us,' said her father, half questioningly; Grete, still sobbing, vehemently waved a hand to show how unthinkable that was.

'If he could understand us,' repeated the old man, shutting his eyes to consider his daughter's conviction that understanding was impossible, 'then perhaps we might come to some agreement with him. But as it is – '

'He must go,' cried Gregor's sister, 'that's the only solution, Father. You must just try to get rid of the idea that this is Gregor. The fact that we've believed it for so long is the root of all our trouble. But how can it be Gregor? If this were Gregor, he would have realized long ago that human beings can't live with such a creature, and he'd have gone away of his own accord. Then we wouldn't have any brother, but we'd be able to go on living and keep his memory in honour. As it is, this creature persecutes us, drives away our lodgers, obviously wants the whole apartment to himself and would have us all sleep in the gutter. Just look, Father,' she shrieked all at once, 'he's at it again!' And in an access of panic that was quite incomprehensible to Gregor she even quitted her mother, literally thrusting the chair from her as if she would rather sacrifice her mother than stay so near to Gregor, and rushed behind her father, who also rose up, being simply upset by her agitation, and half spread his arms out as if to protect her.

Yet Gregor had not the slightest intention of frightening anyone, far less his sister. He had only begun to turn round in order to crawl back to his room, but it was certainly a startling operation to watch, since because of his disabled condition he could not execute the difficult turning movements, except by lifting his head and then bracing it against the floor over and over again. He paused and looked round. His good intentions seemed to have been recognized; the alarm had only been momentary. Now they were all watching him in melancholy silence. His mother lay in her chair, her legs stiffly outstretched and pressed together, her eyes almost closing for sheer weariness; his father and his sister were sitting beside each other, his sister's arm around the old man's neck.

Perhaps I can go on turning round now, thought Gregor, and began his labours again. He could not stop himself from panting with the effort, and had to pause now and then to take breath. Nor did anyone harass him, he was left entirely to himself. When he had completed the turn-round he began at once to crawl straight back. He was amazed at the distance separating him from his room and could not understand how in his weak state he had managed to accomplish the same journey so recently, almost without remarking it. Intent on crawling as fast as possible, he barely noticed that not a single word, not an ejaculation from his family, interfered with his progress. Only when he was already in the doorway did he turn his head round, not completely, for his neck muscles were getting stiff, but enough to see that nothing had changed behind him except that his sister had risen to her feet. His last glance fell on his mother, who was now quite overcome by sleep.

Hardly was he well inside his room when the door was hastily pushed shut, bolted and locked. The sudden noise in his rear startled him so much that his little legs gave beneath him. It was his sister who had shown such haste. She had been standing ready waiting and had made a light spring forward, Gregor had not even heard her coming, and she cried 'At last!' to her parents as she turned the key in the lock.

'And what now?' said Gregor to himself, looking round in the darkness. Soon he made the discovery that he was now unable to stir a limb. This did not surprise him, rather it seemed unnatural that he should ever actually have been able to move on these feeble little legs. Otherwise he felt relatively comfortable. True, his whole body was aching, but it seemed that the pain was gradually growing less and would finally pass away. The rotting apple in his back and the inflamed path around it, all covered with soft dust, already hardly troubled him. He thought of his family with tenderness and love. The decision that he must disappear was one that he held to even more strongly than his sister – if that were possible. In this state of vacant and peaceful meditation he remained until the tower clock struck three in the morning. The first broadening of light in the world outside the window entered his consciousness once more. Then his head sank to the floor of its own accord and from his nostrils came the last faint flicker of his breath.

When the charwoman arrived early in the morning – what between her strength and her impatience she slammed all the doors so loudly, never mind how often she had been begged not to do so, that no one in the whole apartment could enjoy any quiet sleep after her arrival – she noticed nothing unusual as she took her customary peep into Gregor's room. She thought he was lying motionless on purpose, pretending to be in the sulks; she credited him with every kind of intelligence. Since she happened to have a long-handled broom in her hand she tried to tickle him up with it from the doorway. When that too produced no reaction she felt provoked and poked at him a little harder, and only when she had pushed him along the floor without meeting any resistance was her attention aroused. It did not take her long to establish the truth of the matter, and her eyes widened, she let out a whistle, yet did not waste much time over it but tore open the door of the Samsas' bedroom and yelled into the darkness at the top of her voice: 'Just look at this, it's dead; it's lying here dead and done for!'

Mr and Mrs Samsa started up in their double bed and before they realized the nature of the charwoman's announcement had some difficulty in overcoming the shock of it. But then they got out of bed quickly, one on either side, Mr Samsa throwing a blanket over his shoulders, Mrs Samsa in nothing but her nightgown; in this array they entered Gregor's room. Meanwhile the door of the living-room opened, too, where Grete had been sleeping since the advent of the lodgers; she was completely dressed as if she had not been to bed, which seemed to be confirmed also by the paleness of her face. 'Dead?' said Mrs Samsa, looking questioningly at the charwoman, although she could have investigated for herself, and the fact was obvious enough without investigation. 'I should say so,' said the charwoman, proving her words by pushing Gregor's corpse a long way to one side with her broomstick. Mrs Samsa made a movement as if to stop her, but checked it. 'Well,' said Mr Samsa, 'now thanks be to God.' He crossed himself, and the three women followed his example. Grete, whose eyes never left the corpse, said: 'Just see how thin he was. It's such a long time since he's eaten anything. The food came out again just as it went in.' Indeed, Gregor's body was completely flat and dry, as could only now be seen when it was no longer supported by the legs and nothing prevented one from looking closely at it.

'Come in beside us, Grete, for a little while,' said Mrs Samsa with a tremulous smile, and Grete, not without looking back at the corpse, followed her parents into their bedroom. The charwoman shut the door and opened the window wide. Although it was so early in the morning a certain softness was perceptible in the fresh air. After all, it was already the end of March.

Franz Kafka

Translation issues

In an international programme such as the IB Diploma where you are required as part of your English class to read a certain number of works in translation, it is important that we consider issues of **language**. There are certainly people who hold the view that poetry, in particular, is untranslatable. Issues of figurative language, of rhyme, of rhythm, of idiom can affect the way the meaning of the work is delivered, and some of these are regarded as "untranslatable". Ultimately, the question comes down to whether we want to read literature only in languages that we know, or whether we really do want to have some sense of the wider world through the medium of what the French call *belles lettres*.

> *"… arrogant parishes bordered by silence."*
> George Steiner, Introduction, *Penguin Book of Modern Verse Translation*

John Felstiner in *Translating Neruda*, has this to say: "A translation converts strangeness into likeness, and yet in doing so may bring home to us the strangeness of the original. We need translation in order to know what in us a poem is like or not like. Doing without translations, then, might confine us to a kind of solipsistic prison." Felstiner then cites George Steiner's description above of not accepting translations of poetry, of existing in "arrogant parishes" where we choose to be "bordered by silence". The same can be said of the need to translate plays, novels, essays and the like.

The language issues involved in translation can be both interesting and fruitful for students, both those who can work with a piece of literature in both languages and those who do not know the original language. Such work can sharpen our sense of individual words, but also of the way words work, alone and together.

We also encounter issues such as:

● the relation of language and words to culture
● how sound interacts with meaning
● the effect of language on conceptual thinking.

Sometimes a good exercise is to examine how two translators bring material from one language to another.

Activity

Compare two passages from different translations of a work you are currently studying. For example, Matthew Ward and Stuart Gilbert have both translated Camus's *The Outsider*.

Consider how tone, atmosphere, and your feelings about the situation are affected by the difference in the translators' choices.

Writing your assignment

Now that you have observed one process toward writing World Literature Assignment 1, let's review the basic steps you will need to follow to bring your own assignment to a successful conclusion.

Preparation

● First, you need to make a list of particular aspects in any of your three Part 1 works that you find interesting.
● Next, see which features appear in more than one of the works, either very directly or with some similarity, such as characters who commit acts of violence, scenes from plays that seem to be turning points in the dramatic action, political viewpoints in poems.
● Choose two or three of these topics that **link** these works, narrowing down your potential choices.
● Try out the choices, seeing in what different or similar ways these features seem to occur in the works. Look for detail, and consider how much material you have to work with. One or two similarities or differences will be unlikely to lead to a convincing 1500-word essay.
● Select one of the topics and construct a chart or list as you have seen above in the study of Camus and Kafka.

- Construct an arguable position or "thesis". You might look back to pages 178–182 and practice this crucial process by using bullet points. For example, you may choose "isolation". How have the two writers handled isolation? How significant is isolation to the whole work? Through what events or language is a sense of isolation conveyed to the reader?
- In asking these questions, you should be able to sense some interesting similarities and/or differences. It is important to remember, however, that good essays go beyond merely listing similarities and differences in the works.
- Go on to ask how these linking materials impact on the work. For example, you might show that one writer is very explicit in highlighting isolation in order to develop the main character, while the other includes isolation as one of several features used to develop the character of the protagonist.

Whatever your focus, you need to be constantly thinking about choices that the writer makes and the effect of those choices. In the preceding example, your position or thesis might be that because Camus wishes to show that no human can maintain absolute isolation, he foregrounds Meursault's isolation, whereas Kafka has several agendas, in which isolation plays only a secondary part.

Alternatively, the isolation in Kafka is consolidated by the actions of other people, whereas in Camus, Meursault is the chief agent of his own isolation. What are the effects of these two different strategies in terms of the larger meaning and effect of the two novels?

With a working thesis or position in place, you can now proceed to gather details to support your view. These details, which should be sufficiently numerous, are what make your argument persuasive.

Writing

1. Construct an outline, and discuss it with your teacher.
2. Write a first draft and also discuss this with your teacher.
3. Working with the advice you have received, write a final draft, including:
   - a clear title
   - footnotes indicating which editions of the texts you are using, and including the name of the translator in particular (after the first citation, you may use page numbers to refer to your primary sources)
   - a bibliography listing your primary sources (World Literature texts) and any secondary sources you have used
   - numbered pages with your candidate number on each one.
4. Carefully proofread your work.
5. Fill out and sign a cover sheet which your teacher will provide.

Your teacher will show you the official IB criteria for this assignment. The following summary highlights some of the most important features of the criteria.

Assessment of your work

Your work will be assessed under four separate criteria. These are:

- selection of the aspect and its treatment
- knowledge and understanding of works
- presentation
- language.

In order to achieve a good mark you will need to:

- choose an aspect appropriate to the assignment
- ensure that your chosen aspect has a relevant focus
- make sure that your ideas show independence of thought and your treatment is relevant to the aspect chosen
- show detailed knowledge of, and good insight into, the aspects of the works most relevant to the assignment
- show clear and meaningful linking of works
- show good appreciation of the cultural setting relevant to the assignment, where appropriate
- show a clear and logical structure to the assignment
- show precise and pertinent references to the works
- remain within the prescribed word limit
- use an effective register appropriate for the assignment selected
- follow closely the conventions of written work
- write fluently and clearly.

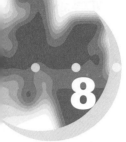

8 Comparative, creative and detailed study options

Objectives
- To establish a strategy for approaching world literature assignments
- To understand the requirements of comparative, creative, and detailed study assignments

World Literature Assignment 2

If you are studying at Higher Level you will need to complete a second World Literature assignment. For this assignment you must choose one of three alternatives. Here is an outline of what is involved in each of the choices. Remember – you choose only one option.

It is very important that you clearly label your work for World Literature Assignment 2. The reader must know from the outset whether you are presenting Assignment 2a, 2b or 2c.

Assignment 2a: Comparative study

In this assignment you have the option of choosing one of the works in your syllabus written originally in English (there are at least ten of these) and comparing it with one of the five World Literature works listed on your syllabus. The first thing you will need to do is look over the whole syllabus and identify which works you have or will have completed at the point of doing this assignment.

The only works excluded (in addition to the ones you have not yet covered in class) are the works you have used for World Literature Assignment 1 or that you plan to use. Remember, you may not repeat any works across these two assignments.

To meet the requirements of this assignment in which you compare two works, you must do some of the following:

- focus on some link or feature that shows the works to be comparable
- choose some literary feature that connects the two works
- reveal a sense of the authors making choices and the effects of these choices
- show some insight into the cultures that form the backdrop of the works, when this is relevant
- demonstrate some sense of personal engagement with the works.

In respect to the form of this assignment, you will most likely follow standard essay procedure, introducing, developing and concluding your argument, and supporting your ideas with detail from the texts you are using.

You will see below (page 190) an example of this exercise, in which you can practise with the openings of one World Literature text and one English A1 text.

Assignment 2b: Creative or imaginative assignment

This option presents you with a variety of ways to engage in creative writing in relation to either one of the World Literature works not being used for Assignment 1.

Creative or imaginative writing in relation to your World Literature texts can take two forms:

● you can work with a single World Literature text
● you can work with two texts, one from the texts labelled "World Literature" on your syllabus, i.e. one that you have already studied in class. You will write about this World Literature text in combination with one of the other ten texts on your syllabus, those called "English A1" texts.

Whichever option you choose, it is wise to understand that this option combines both a **creative** and a **critical** element.

The assignment must be preceded by a critical rationale which is called the Statement of Intent. Here you should outline *briefly* what you intend to do. You must also – and this is very important – explain *why* you have chosen this way of responding to the text or texts. This element of your Statement of Intent lets the reader know what has moved you to accomplish this creative exercise and how your doing it will illuminate some aspect of the text or texts, and enhance your appreciation of the original work(s).

Finally, you may need to identify those stylistic features of the original(s) that you plan to imitate in your new response.

This last feature is most likely to apply when you are changing, adding to or inserting some creative writing into the original text. You will find these options in the list of "Suggested approaches" below.

Other guidelines you must observe in writing your Statement of Intent are as follows.

● It must be included in the word count (1000–1500) for the whole of Assignment 2.
● It should normally be about 500 words in length. However, if you are writing a very short creative piece, of 300 or 400 words, the Statement of Intent will likely be longer in order to meet the 1000-word lower limit.
● It should go before the creative piece in order to show the reader what you are attempting to do.

Suggested approaches

● A director's letter to an actor in a play you have studied. Here it is important that an appropriate tone is achieved and understanding of the relation of directors to actors is demonstrated.
● A critic's review of a dramatic interpretation or performance.
● An editorial objecting to censorship of or exclusion of a text from a school syllabus.
● A letter to a publisher arguing for the merits of a work yet to be published.

- A transcription of an interview with the author of the work, or a conversation between two authors. It is important that the context and appropriateness of the chosen writers is considered.

Other approaches are more in the nature of "pastiche", where the style of the original writing is consciously imitated. Options of this kind include the following.

- The insertion of a new scene, or the addition of a scene or chapter to the end of the work.
- The adaptation of the "story" of the original into another form, such as dramatic monologue, scriptural narrative, folk tale, myth, or similar. Shifting the story to an entirely different cultural setting might be another option, always with attention to appropriateness.
- The creation of a dramatic monologue or a conversation between two characters from different works.
- The diary of a character. Here you must be very careful that you do not simply provide a narrative account of events told by a character. This can be a challenging assignment in which what you write must be well rationalized as adding to or illuminating some aspect of the work.

You will find some examples of the Statement of Intent and portions of some creative assignments on pages 194–196.

Assignment 2c: Detailed study

If you choose this option you will need to write a detailed study based on one World Literature work that you have studied in Part 1, Part 3, or Part 4 of the course. However, you must not use a work that you have already used for Assignment 1. Your assignment could take the form of a formal essay, or a commentary, or an analysis of one or two key passages.

If extracts are chosen for analysis or commentary, they should **not** be included in the word count, but copies must be attached to the assignment when submitted for assessment.

What differentiates this option from the ones discussed above is that you will work with only one World Literature work, and again, it must be one that you will not be using in Assignment 1. Remember also that it must be one of the works designated "World Literature" on your syllabus.

The most commonly chosen approaches to this option include the following.

- An essay on one World Literature work. Here you will select some feature of the World Literature work, preferably quite sharply focused, and discuss it. You will follow the conventional features of an essay, and very likely you will construct an argument in which you discuss a particular view of content or form in the work.
- An analytic essay called a "Key passage exercise". In this exercise you identify a passage from the work and discuss why it is central to our understanding of the work, and how it functions, for example, as a turning point in the work, or a place where

many strands of the work come together or are highlighted. You may also compare two key passages, showing how they function importantly in the whole work and what roles they play. It is best to choose fairly short extracts for this exercise, as some of your attention will be focused on the style of writing in the passage (see diagram below).

● A commentary on an extract from the passage. In this exercise, normally working with a passage of not more than 40 lines, you will need first to contextualize the passage, noting where it appears in the whole, and why you have chosen this particular passage. Then your job is to examine the passage closely, exploring the choices of words, tone, imagery, diction and so on that the author has made, and the effects of these on what is conveyed to the reader.

Often students have difficulty distinguishing between what is done in a **key passage** exercise as compared with a **commentary** exercise. The following diagram may help you to be sure of the difference. You will see the different emphasis in the direction of the arrows.

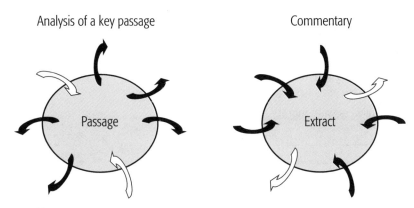

Analysis of a key passage   Commentary

Passage   Extract

Key:
The black arrows represent the main focus of the analysis or commentary. The transparent arrows represent the complementary focus.

For the **key passage** discussion, most of the arrows point outward, indicating that much of what you say will involve connecting the passage to the larger work. With the **commentary** exercise, once you have contextualized the passage, the primary focus will be on what is going on stylistically within the passage. Most of the arrows in this case point to the passage itself.

Note: You are required to attach a copy of the extract(s), whether key passage(s) or commentary, to your assignment.

The following pages show some examples of each kind of assignment.

2a Comparative study

If you choose this option for your assignment the first thing you will need to think carefully about is which texts to base your assignment on, making sure that you have plenty of scope to undertake your comparative analysis.

Having decided on your texts, you will need to think of a title for your assignment. This needs very careful thought. Your title should indicate specific, focused topics, rather than general, broad ones. For example, "A comparison of the presentation and significance of the characters of Winston Smith and Ivan Denisovich in *1984* and *One Day in the Life of Ivan Denisovich*" is better than "A comparison of Winston Smith and Ivan Denisovich in *1984* and *One Day in the Life of Ivan Denisovich*".

Activity

Read the following two extracts carefully. The first is from the opening of George Orwell's novel *1984* and the second is from Alexander Solzhenitsyn's novel *One Day in the Life of Ivan Denisovich*.

1 How does each writer capture the reader's attention in the opening paragraphs?

2 What techniques do the writers use to create a vivid picture of the scenes they describe?

3 How would you describe the tone of each piece?

4 What impression do you get of the central character in each extract? How do the writers convey these impressions?

5 What is your overall response to each extract? Give reasons for your comments.

6 Which extract do you find most effective as the opening to a novel? Why?

When you have finished your work, compare your answers with another student's and discuss your ideas.

1984

It was a bright cold day in April, and the clocks were striking thirteen. Winston Smith, his chin nuzzled into his breast in an effort to escape the vile wind, slipped quickly through the glass doors of Victory Mansions, though not quickly enough to prevent a swirl of gritty dust from entering along with him.

The hallway smelt of boiled cabbage and old rag mats. At one end of it a coloured poster, too large for indoor display, had been tacked to the wall. It depicted simply an enormous face, more than a metre wide: the face of a man of about forty-five, with a heavy black moustache and ruggedly handsome features. Winston made for the stairs. It was no use trying the lift. Even at the best of times it was seldom working, and at present the electric current was cut off during daylight hours. It was part of the economy drive in preparation for Hate Week. The flat was seven flights up, and Winston, who was thirty-nine and had a varicose ulcer above his right ankle, went slowly, resting several times on the way. On each landing, opposite the lift-shaft, the poster with the enormous face gazed from the wall. It was one of those pictures which are so contrived that the eyes follow you about when you move. BIG BROTHER IS WATCHING YOU, the caption beneath it ran.

Inside the flat a fruity voice was reading out a list of figures which had something to do with the production of pig-iron. The voice came from an oblong metal plaque like a dulled mirror which formed part of the surface of the right-hand wall. Winston turned a switch and the voice sank somewhat, though the words were still distinguishable. The instrument (the telescreen, it was called) could be dimmed, but there was no way of shutting it off completely. He moved over to the window: a smallish, frail figure, the meagreness of his body merely emphasized by the blue overalls which were the uniform of the Party. His hair was very fair, his face naturally sanguine, his skin roughened by coarse soap and blunt razor blades and the cold of the winter that had just ended.

Outside, even through the shut window-pane, the world looked cold. Down in the street little eddies of wind were whirling dust and torn paper into spirals, and though the sun was shining and the sky a harsh blue, there seemed to be no colour in anything, except the posters that were plastered everywhere. The black-moustachio'd face gazed down from every commanding corner. There was one on the house-front immediately opposite. BIG BROTHER IS WATCHING YOU, the caption said, while the dark eyes looked deep into Winston's own. Down at street level another poster, torn at one corner, flapped fitfully in the wind, alternately covering and uncovering the single word INGSOC. In the far distance a helicopter skimmed down between the roofs, hovered for an instant like a bluebottle, and darted away again with a curving flight. It was the police patrol, snooping into people's windows. The patrols did not matter, however. Only the Thought Police mattered.

Behind Winston's back the voice from the telescreen was still babbling away about pig-iron and the overfulfilment of the Ninth Three-Year Plan. The telescreen received and transmitted simultaneously. Any sound that Winston made, above the level of a very low whisper, would be picked up by it; moreover, so long as he remained within the field of vision which the metal plaque commanded, he could be seen as well as heard. There was of course no way of knowing whether you were being watched at any given moment. How often, or on what system, the Thought Police plugged in on any individual wire was guesswork. It was even conceivable that they watched everybody all the time. But at any rate they could plug in your wire whenever they wanted to. You had to live – did live, from habit that became instinct – in the assumption that every sound you made was overheard, and, except in darkness, every movement scrutinized.

Winston kept his back turned to the telescreen. It was safer; though, as he well knew, even a back can be revealing. A kilometre away the Ministry of Truth, his place of work, towered vast and white above the grimy landscape. This, he thought with a sort of vague distaste – this was London, chief city of Airstrip One, itself the third most populous of the provinces of Oceania. He tried to squeeze out some childhood memory that should tell him whether London had always been quite like this. Were there always these vistas of rotting nineteenth-century houses, their sides shored up with baulks of timber, their windows patched with cardboard and their roofs with corrugated iron, their crazy garden walls sagging in all directions? And the bombed sites where the plaster dust swirled in the air and the willow-herb straggled over the heaps of rubble; and the places where the bombs had cleared a larger patch and there had sprung up sordid colonies of wooden dwellings like chicken-houses? But it was no use, he could not remember; nothing remained of his childhood except a series of bright-lit tableaux occurring against no background and mostly unintelligible.

The Ministry of Truth – Minitrue, in Newspeak – was startlingly different from any other object in sight. It was an enormous pyramidal structure of glittering white concrete, soaring up, terrace after terrace, 300 metres into the air. From where Winston stood it was just possible to read, picked out on its white face in elegant lettering, the three slogans of the party:

WAR IS PEACE

FREEDOM IS SLAVERY

IGNORANCE IS STRENGTH

George Orwell

One Day in the Life of Ivan Denisovich

As usual, at five o'clock that morning reveille was sounded by the blows of a hammer on a length of rail hanging up near the staff quarters. The intermittent sound barely penetrated the window-panes on which the frost lay two fingers thick, and they ended almost as soon as they'd begun. It was cold outside, and the camp-guard was reluctant to go on beating out the reveille for long.

The clanging ceased, but everything outside still looked like the middle of the night when Ivan Denisovich Shukhov got up to go to the bucket. It was pitch dark except for the yellow light cast on the window by three lamps – two in the outer zone, one inside the camp itself.

And no one came to unbolt the barrack-hut door; there was no sound of the barrack-orderlies pushing a pole into place to lift the barrel of nightsoil and carry it out.

Shukhov never overslept reveille. He always got up at once, for the next ninety minutes, until they assembled for work, belonged to him, not to the authorities, and any old-timer could always earn a bit – by sewing a pair of over-mittens for someone out of old sleeve lining; or bringing some rich lag in the team his dry valenki* – right up to his bunk, so that he wouldn't have to stumble barefoot round the heaps of boots looking for his own pair; or going the rounds of the store-huts, offering to be of service, sweeping up this or fetching that; or going to the mess-hall to collect bowls from the tables and bring them stacked to the dishwashers – you're sure to be given something to eat there, though there were plenty of others at that game, more than plenty – and, what's worse, if you found a bowl with something left in it you could hardly resist licking it out. But Shukhov had never forgotten the words of his first team-leader, Kuziomin – a hard-bitten prisoner who had already been in for twelve years by 1943 – who told the newcomers, just in from the front, as they sat beside a fire in a desolate cutting in the forest:

'Here, lads, we live by the law of the taiga. But even here people manage to live. D'you know who are the ones the camps finish off? Those who lick other men's left-overs, those who set store by the doctors, and those who peach on their mates.'

As for the peachers, he was wrong there. Those people were sure to get through the camp all right. Only, they were saving their own skin at the expense of other people's blood.

Shukhov always arose at reveille. But this day he didn't. He had felt queer the evening before, feverish, with pains all over his body. He hadn't been able to get warm all through the night. Even in his sleep he had felt at one moment that he was getting seriously ill, at another that he was getting better. He had longed for the morning not to come.

But the morning came as usual.

Anyway, it wasn't surprising that he'd felt cold in the night. That ice on the window-pane! And the white cobwebs of hoar-frost all along the huge hut where the walls joined the ceiling!

He didn't get up. He lay there in his bunk on the top tier, his head buried in a blanket and a coat, his two feet stuffed into one sleeve, with the end tucked under, of his wadded jacket. He couldn't see, but his ears told him everything going on in the barrack-room and especially in the corner his team occupied. He heard the heavy tread of the orderlies carrying one of the big barrels of nightsoil along the passage outside. A light job, that was considered, a job for the infirm, but just you try and carry out the muck without spilling any. He heard some of the 75th slamming bunches of boots on to the floor from the drying-shed. Now their own lads were doing it (it was their own team's turn, too, to dry valenki). Tiurin, the team-leader, and his deputy Pavlo put on their valenki without a word but he heard their bunks creaking. Now Pavlo would be going off to the bread-stores and Tiurin to the staff quarters to see the P.P.D.†

Ah, but not simply to report as usual to the authorities who distributed the daily assignments. Shukhov remembered that this morning his fate hung in the balance: they wanted to shift the 104th from the building-shops to a new site, the 'Socialist Way of Life' settlement. It lay in open country covered with snow-drifts, and before anything else could be done there they would have to dig pits and put up posts and attach barbed wire to them. Wire themselves in, so that they wouldn't run away. Only then would they start building.

There wouldn't be a warm corner for a whole month. Not a dog-kennel. And fires were out of the question. Where was the firewood to come from? Warm up with the work, that was your only salvation.

No wonder the team-leader looked so worried, that was his responsibility – to elbow some other team, some bunch of clod-hoppers, into the assignment instead of the 104th. Of course he wouldn't get the authorities to agree if he turned up empty-handed. He'd have to take a pound of pork-fat to the senior official there, if not a couple of pounds.

There's never any harm in trying, so why not have a go at the sick-bay and get a few days off if you can? After all, he did feel as though every limb was out of joint.

Alexander Solzhenitsyn

* Knee-length felt boots for winter wear

† Production Planning Department

Activity

> Now write a comparative literary analysis of these two openings. Your response should be about 500 words in length.

2b Creative or imaginative assignment

Student sample 1

The first example assignment below is based on the poetry of the Chinese writer, Bei Dao, work that the candidate has studied in class in translation. Choosing an interview format, the candidate offers a rationale for the piece that tells the reader why this format will give a sense of the candidate's understanding and interpretation of some of Bei Dao's poems. These poems will be attached to the assignment. Only the first third of the completed assignment is included below, as the object is to give you an example of a Statement of Intent and a sample of the approach.

Commentary

An interview with an artist about her adaptation of Bei Dao's "Strangers" to visual media

Statement of Intent: This assignment is a creative, dialogic commentary of Bei Dao's "Strangers". Its format is an interview with Hannah Conklin, an imaginary artist, by a journalist for a magazine of art criticism; the premise is that Conklin has just premiered an exhibition of her adaptations of Bei Dao's poetry to visual media. The body of the assignment is a transcription of this fictional interview.

This unusual approach has a number of advantages over a conventional format. Commenting on the poem in a dialogue allows me to state and address potential challenges, and the logical steps by which it was reached. Mackenzie Lloyd, the interviewer, essentially plays the role of the audience; thus Conklin may speak clearly and directly to the audience through him. His questions are the reader's questions and this format allows me to answer them in an unambiguous way. Because I may speak through a character and in a human voice, it is possible to discuss subjective decisions made in the interpretation of the poem, which is essential to "Strangers" because it is so consciously ambiguous and nebulous that the reader must supply the meaning. Furthermore, the intimacy of colloquial speech makes it easier to express complex ideas.

Ironically, clarity is also the motivation for inventing characters, a painting, and a scenario to convey my interpretation of "Strangers". This contrived, complicated method allows me to illuminate aspects of the poem which elude a purely verbal description. By comparing esoteric elements of mood and form with imagery and technique in painting, their function within "Strangers" is revealed more clearly than words would allow. For example, I make a concept like temporal progression through imagery more tangible by associating it with a change of artistic style within a painting. Furthermore, because Hannah Conklin must discuss why an adaptation is permissible, I am better able to discuss the universality or cultural dependence of Bei Dao's poetry.

Creative assignment : *Hannah Conklin recently premiered her exhibition "Meditations on the Poetry of Bei Dao". This collection of 12 pieces covers*

a spectrum of artistic styles and media; each is an adaptation of a poem by the esteemed Chinese poet, Bei Dao. One work in particular has won her critical acclaim: a striking adaptation of the poem "Strangers". We will direct our questions towards this piece to gain an understanding of how she formulated an interpretation for this unquestionably esoteric poem. Our own correspondent Mackenzie Lloyd had the privilege of meeting her at her San Francisco home for this exclusive interview.

ML: Thank you for this opportunity. I'd like to begin by asking why you undertook this project; while many artists simply use literature as an unacknowledged muse for their art, you chose to do an actual adaptation of the written word. Some might remark that "adapting" is more a technical exercise than art because it relies on someone else's creativity and emotional impulses. Clearly this was not the case for your show, particularly the piece "Strangers". Why is that so?

HC: The obscurity and ambiguity of Bei Dao's poetry permits a lot of interpretative latitude, so I had to arrive at a meaning for the poem myself. I based it on the text, of course, but my own creativity and impulses were central to my interpretation of "Strangers". Bei Dao forces you to impress your own meaning on his poetry. In it, the implicit meanings are more profound than the denotative or connotative meanings of the words or lines themselves.

However, I did have to consider whether his poetry was so tied to Chinese culture that to adapt it to Western-style art would change its significance. I concluded that regardless of Dao's political or local inspiration for these poems, their imagery spoke to *universal* sentiments that transcend cultural boundaries. As translator Bonne McDougall says, "Their interest to Western readers… (is) in their grasp of human dilemmas present in varying degrees in all modern societies."

I paid careful attention to faithfully reproducing all the concrete aspects of "Strangers" that require less input from the reader, notably imagery and structure.

ML: Then let's discuss your interpretation of "Strangers".

HC: In as few words as possible, I'll explain: for me, "Strangers" laments a secret and unrequited love. The speaker obsesses over every memory he associates with "you", yet he is unsure whether he is even anything more than a stranger to her. "With so many chances to get to know you/ it would seem we're/ not strangers." It leaves the reader with a feeling of pity and melancholy; how can a man so obsessed with a woman be nothing more than a stranger to her? Furthermore, the diction he uses to describe himself – "seasick", "lonely", "in search" – evinces his initial sadness and fear to approach her. However, by the end of the poem there is a glimmer of hope for the speaker.

ML: Did you attempt to mimic the underlying structure of "Strangers"? The composition of the painting indicates a lot of thought.

HC: That's true. The latent structure of "Strangers" is one of its most important aspects. While at first glance the poem appears to be a shapeless, dense stream of images without a clear subject or grammatical form, there is an underlying progression. The poem is drawn along by the transition from esoteric metaphors such as "a shoe/ slid over the ice-locked river" to more explicit metaphors such as "the door knob/ has turned a little". There is also a progression in tense; from the past, "you/ took a bad fall", to the present, "it would seem we're/ not strangers, the door knob/ has turned a little". This is how Bei Dao intimates the passage of time; to create the sense that the speaker has been watching and loving his object ("you") for a long time. I adapted this structure to my art because it intensifies the sadness that the speaker has been obsessed with his love for so long and so fruitlessly. I reproduced this sense in my piece by painting on an elongated sheet that is slim at one end and fat at the other – a visual device that creates distance.

> **Activity**
>
> Taking one of your World Literature works, try creating an interview in dialogue format (using authors, characters from the work, and/or interviewers) that sheds light on your understanding of the work and its stylistic or rhetorical implications.

Student sample 2: Pastiche

A second example of the creative assignment is the following, based on the play *Art* by Yasmina Reza. Look carefully at the Statement of Intent to distinguish where the candidate has made clear why he has undertaken this task. Then consider, when reading the creative piece, how well he seems to have fulfilled his aims.

Statement of Intent

This pastiche is based on the play "Art" by Yasmina Reza. It should be placed on page 61, immediately after Serge, Marc, and Yvan leave to go to dinner. I am adding a scene to the play, consisting of the dinner at which Marc and Serge decide to repair their relationship. Yasmina leaves this scene to the imagination, concluding the play with Marc, Serge, and Yvan at Serge's house, after the dinner.

This new section is interesting for several reasons. Every other scene in the play occurs at the house of either Serge, Marc, or Yvan, in their living room, in the presence of a painting above the mantle. This scene takes the three characters out of that constant, contrived environment, and forces their interaction with other things. Whereas the focus in their homes can only be on the art that seems to stand watch over them, this new scene at the restaurant brings about a new focus, food.

There is a theme of food throughout the play. It seems that even when in heated discussion (over the topic of art), the characters are easily distracted by food. When Marc first comes over to Yvan's house on page 9, and proceeds to perform a tirade about Serge's delusions, Yvan interrupts with an offer of cashew nuts. Near the end of the play, Marc and Serge seem to gang up on Yvan in a reversal of enmity, and after Yvan breaks down and shocks Marc and Serge into solicitude, he asks for a bowl of olives, which they all pass around. For a moment, the focus turns to the snacks, away from the issues that seem to upset them so much. In an opposite way I hope to create an environment at this restaurant where the focus is food, and the three characters are sometimes distracted by art. They will maintain their respective personalities, reflected in their table manners and food choices, and with the buffer of the meal between them, Marc and Serge will decide to patch up their relationship in a way that was not possible when the source of conflict was so close to them.

(Serge, Marc, and Yvan standing to one side of the stage, facing the other side of the stage, standing in line in that order. Serge holds his hat in his hands, Yvan wears a scarf. They walk very slowly from one side of the stage to the other. When they reach the other side of the stage, they pass off as they finish their conversation.)

Serge	Where to?
Marc	The Lyonnaise.
Serge	I don't feel like going there anymore. *(Serge turns his head back, looks at Yvan)* Yvan? *(Yvan looks away, towards the ground.)*
Yvan	I don't care. Let's just eat something. *(Serge looks at Marc, Marc gives a halfway shrug. Serge faces ahead again. After several moments, Marc speaks up.)*
Marc	How about chez Emile.
Serge	Yes... chez Emile. Wonderful! idea. We always loved that place. *(At the mention of chez Emile, Yvan looks up sharply, but doesn't say anything. Then they all freeze and Yvan faces the audience.)*
Yvan	*(as if alone)* We had our first meal together, chez Emile. That was back when we were all just starting out, before I met Catherine, before Serge had the money to buy paintings. It was something of a splurge, but we all agreed it was worth it. It's pretty obvious what they're trying to say by going there. *(As Yvan stops speaking, he turns back to face the side, and they continue off the stage. Just as he exits:)*
Serge	Here we are. *(They walk back on stage, this time in the order of Marc, Yvan and Serge. Marc rolls a table towards the centre of the stage, talking as he goes. Yvan and Serge follow. Yvan carries a tablecloth, Serge carries three collapsible chairs.)*
Marc	It's good we didn't have to wait in line, we're lucky.
Serge	Yes, the Lyonnaise would have been packed. *(Marc sets up the table with Serge's help, Yvan lays a tablecloth over it. They sit down at the table. Serge cranes his neck to look around the room.)*
Serge	This place hasn't changed at all. *(Looks into space in a random direction. The others follow his example.)* Yes, thank you. I'll take [a French meal that is simple]
Marc	You've become frugal all of a sudden, Serge. You've always been a richer eater, experimenting with all those exotic delicacies...
Yvan	Jeez, Marc, can't you even stop at dinner?
Serge	No it's true. What's the point of living if don't live a little bit? But I suppose I've transferred my little excesses elsewhere.
Marc	*(Snorts)* I suppose I'll just have to make up for your lack, only this will be tasteful decadence. *(Making his order)* I'll have that [traditional yet expensive meal].
Serge	Hmm. Not very exciting, but you're right, it's better than that cheap crap you usually get. Just wait until my dessert though, I know I can scrape together enough money for something truly amazing. I haven't completely lost my flair.
Yvan	I'll take [some random French meal, neither very rich nor very distinctive]. *(Marc and Serge roll their eyes, in exasperation.)*

Marc	*(Calling out)* Just a moment, Garcon. *(To* **Yvan***)* The same thing at every restaurant we ever go to. You'd think he'd die if he ate anything else.
Yvan	I order it because I like it. What's wrong with that?
Serge	Because you've never bothered to try anything else. Where's your sense of adventure? Do something for yourself for once, instead of just doing what's easiest. Marc may not have much of an imagination, but he makes an effort.
Marc	Don't push it, Serge. Anyway, I'm not the one who usually ends up with diarrhoea after our dinners; does that mean I'm unimaginative, or does that mean I'm just smarter.
Serge	*(Laughs, gestures expansively)* What can I say, it's part of the game. You stay safe but you're boring. Keep that up and you might turn out like Yvan. (**Yvan** *turns away, upset.* **Marc** *snickers, as* **Serge** *slaps* **Yvan** *lightly on the back.)*
Serge	I, on the other hand, take risks. Sometimes I get burned, like with that Mexican food, but sometimes I strike gold, like with my painting. (**Marc** *throws his hands up in exasperation, but it's obvious he's still amused. They continue to motion and banter silently while* **Yvan** *pulls his chair away from the table a little bit and talks to the audience.)*
Yvan	So this is how the whole night seems to be going. As usual, I'm the middle man, the butt of the joke. Normally I would enjoy it, I would give just as good as I get, but I can't seem to dig up any enthusiasm tonight. The wedding is coming up, that must be it... No. Finkelzohn wouldn't like me to say that. It goes deeper, I guess. Serge and Marc seem to be getting past their problems, but I'm still the same, my problems aren't going away. *(To the others)* Alright, fine, order whatever you want for me, I'll eat it.
Serge	That's right Yvan, assert yourself. Here Marc, what should we get him? (**Marc** *and* **Serge** *lean together and whisper, then* **Marc** *pretends to whisper to the waiter.* **Marc** *and* **Serge** *laugh together, try to get* **Yvan** *to laugh with them, but he stays apart.)*
Marc	Serge, let's go back to your place after dinner. Maybe we can do something about that blank atrocity of yours. Fix it up a little bit.

Activity

Find a place in one of your World Literature texts that interests you or intrigues you; one that you think leaves questions unanswered or implications vague.

First, identify some stylistic traits of the writer that you could learn something about by attempting to imitate them. Second, construct a passage that imitates these stylistic features and that also clarifies or elaborates some elements of the original.

Reminders about the creative or imaginative assignment

- Both critical and creative work is involved.
- You must convey to the reader *why* you have chosen to present this approach.
- You need to indicate how the assignment has increased your understanding of the original work, both its content and its style.

2c Detailed study

The three most commonly chosen options here – where you will be working with one World Literature work that you have not used or will not use in Assignment 1 – are as follows.

- A formal essay, in which you discuss some significant feature of the work.
- A commentary in which you focus primarily on *how* the writer has delivered the content of the passage. Your focus here will be on authorial choices and their effects.
- The study of a key moment or passage in a larger work. This might be a moment of illumination for a character or characters, or a turning point in a work, or a climactic or culminating moment. Sometimes, candidates choose two passages; this is a more challenging exercise and the passages must be carefully selected and rationalized.

Sometimes a passage is an effective choice for either a commentary or for examination of it as a key moment in the whole work. It is important that you distinguish carefully between the two approaches and that you clearly label the assignment as "Commentary" or "Key passage exercise".

The following passage from Kafka's *Metamorphosis* could be treated in two ways. A candidate could write a commentary on it or treat it as a key passage in the whole story. It presents a significant moment in the narrative when Gregor's father drives his son, who has turned into an insect, back into his room for the first time.

Metamorphosis

'Mother, Mother,' said Gregor in a low voice and looked up at her. The chief clerk, for the moment, had quite slipped from his mind; instead, he could not resist snapping his jaws together at the sight of the creaming coffee. That made his mother scream again, she fled from the table and fell into the arms of his father, who hastened to catch her. But Gregor had now no time to spare for his parents; the chief clerk was already on the stairs; with his chin on the banisters he was taking one last backward look. Gregor made a spring, to be as sure as possible of overtaking him; the chief clerk must have divined his intention, for he leapt down several steps and vanished; he was still yelling 'Ugh!' and it echoed through the whole staircase. Unfortunately, the flight of the chief clerk seemed completely to upset Gregor's father, who had remained relatively calm until now, for instead of running after the man himself, or at least not hindering Gregor in his pursuit, he seized in his right hand the walking-stick which the chief clerk had left behind on a chair, together with a hat and great-coat, snatched in his left hand a large newspaper from the table and began stamping his feet and flourishing the stick and the newspaper to drive Gregor back into his room. No entreaty of Gregor's availed, indeed no entreaty was even understood, however humbly he bent his head his father only stamped on the floor the more loudly. Behind his father his mother had torn open a window, despite the cold weather, and was leaning far out of it with her face in her hands. A strong draught set in

---

from the street to the staircase, the window curtains blew in, the newspapers on the table fluttered, stray pages whisked over the floor. Pitilessly Gregor's father drove him back, hissing and crying 'Shoo!' like a savage. But Gregor was quite unpractised in walking backwards, it really was a slow business. If he only had a chance to turn round he could get back to his room at once, but he was afraid of exasperating his father by the slowness of such a rotation and at any moment the stick in his father's hand might hit him a fatal blow on the back or on the head. In the end, however, nothing else was left for him to do since to his horror he observed that in moving backwards he could not even control the direction he took; and so, keeping an anxious eye on his father all the time over his shoulder, he began to turn round as quickly as he could, which was in reality very slowly. Perhaps his father noted his good intentions, for he did not interfere except every now and then to help him in the manoeuvre from a distance with the point of the stick. If only he would have stopped making that unbearable hissing noise! It made Gregor quite lose his head. He had turned almost completely round when the hissing noise so distracted him that he even turned a little the wrong way again. But when at last his head was fortunately right in front of the doorway, it appeared that his body was too broad simply to get through the opening. His father, of course, in his present mood was far from thinking of such a thing as opening the other half of the door, to let Gregor have enough space. He had merely the fixed idea of driving Gregor back into his room as quickly as possible. He would never have suffered Gregor to make the circumstantial preparations for standing up on end and perhaps slipping his way through the door. Maybe he was now making more noise than ever to urge Gregor forward, as if no obstacle impeded him; to Gregor, anyhow, the noise in his rear sounded no longer like the voice of one single father; this was really no joke, and Gregor thrust himself – come what might – into the doorway. One side of his body rose up, he was tilted at an angle in the doorway, his flank was quite bruised, horrid blotches stained the white door, soon he was stuck fast and, left to himself, could not have moved at all, his legs on one side fluttered trembling in the air, those on the other were crushed painfully to the floor – when from behind his father gave him a strong push which was literally a deliverance and he flew far into the room, bleeding freely. The door was slammed behind him with the stick, and then at last there was silence.

Franz Kafka

Activity

Choose an important passage (a turning point in the action, a revelation, a reversal of fortune for a character, or something equally significant), and work through the following questions, then construct an essay based on your findings.

The questions below could assist you in choosing one or the other exercise for your chosen passage.

Key passage exercise

- Where in the whole text does this passage occur? What leads up to it and follows it?
- Why have you chosen this as a key moment in the narrative?
- What recurring features of the narrative are also in evidence here?
- How does this passage connect to those other elements? Does it bring them to a climax? Does it repeat in different ways events that have occurred elsewhere or will occur subsequently?
- Are there certain themes or smaller lines of meaning (motifs) that are in evidence here?
- Does the way the writer presents the characters here reflect or contrast with their presentation elsewhere in the text? How?
- Are there details presented here that add significantly to our grasp of events, symbols, or characters as a whole?
- What is achieved here that makes the passage one of the "key" or memorable moments in the text?
- Finally, to spur your own thinking, and not necessarily to be included in your assignment, consider what would be lost if the passage were missing from the text.

Commentary

- Where does this passage occur in the whole text?
- Why have you decided it is worth close reading?
- What, very briefly, is the content of the passage?
- What are the significant stylistic features of this particular passage?
- What is the nature of each of these stylistic features (tone, imagery, diction, and the like)?
- What is the effect of each of these features on the whole passage?
- Which of these stylistic features seem to be characteristic of the style of the whole text?

Note: Not all of the points in these two lists are included in every key passage exercise or commentary. Some elements will receive most of your attention, others will be briefly treated. For example, in the commentary, the fourth, fifth and sixth bullet points will comprise the body of your assignment.

You will find examples of commentary in Chapter 4, Studying Prose. Because commentary is a key element of English A1, it appears more than once in the whole programme as a required exercise.

Activity

Think about the assignment you are going to work on for your World Literature assessment. Make a note of all the texts you might consider basing the assignment on, and think about which approach you should adopt.

Planning and writing your assignment

The topic

When you have decided on the text you are going to use in your assignment you need to think of a suitable topic. You can discuss your ideas with your teacher and he or she can help to make sure that your topic is appropriate and well-focused, but your teacher is not allowed to set the topic for you. You must have some ideas of your own.

The title

When you have chosen your topic you will need to think of a suitable assignment title.

The outline

When you have decided on your title you then need to prepare an outline of your assignment in which you plan how you will approach it and structure your ideas. Again you should discuss your ideas with your teacher before you begin to write your first draft.

The first draft

You are now ready to write the first draft of your assignment. When you have completed this you can give it to your teacher who can read it and make general comments on it. Your teacher is not allowed to mark it or write any comments on it, however.

Further drafts

After you have completed your first draft and have had some general feedback from your teacher on it, you can go on to write further drafts or, if you feel ready, to complete a final draft of it. After the first draft stage your teacher cannot give any further feedback to you. You now need to work on the assignment on your own.

Stages to follow

Here is a summary of the stages you need to go through in producing your assignment:

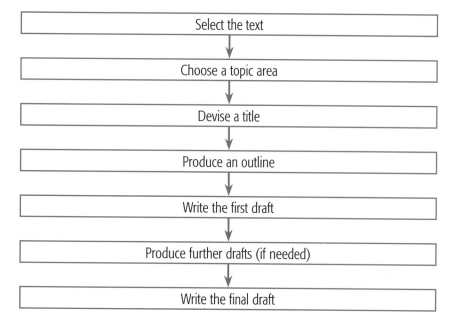

Select the text
Choose a topic area
Devise a title
Produce an outline
Write the first draft
Produce further drafts (if needed)
Write the final draft

Assessment of your work

Your work will be assessed under four separate criteria. These are:

- selection of the aspect and its treatment
- knowledge and understanding of works
- presentation
- language.

In order to achieve a good mark you will need to:

- choose an aspect appropriate to the assignment
- ensure that your chosen aspect has a relevant focus
- make sure that your ideas show independence of thought and your treatment is relevant to the aspect chosen
- show detailed knowledge of, and good insight into, the aspects of the works most relevant to the assignment
- show good appreciation of the cultural setting relevant to the assignment, where appropriate
- show a clear and logical structure to the assignment
- show precise and pertinent references to the works
- remain within the prescribed word limit
- use an effective register appropriate for the assignment selected
- follow closely the conventions of written work
- write fluently and clearly.

9 The individual oral commentary

Objectives
- To analyse the requirements of the individual oral commentary
- To prepare for the individual oral commentary by practising responding to extracts

All students studying for English A1 must complete two compulsory oral components, which are internally assessed. The first of these assessments is the individual oral commentary, and we will look at the requirements and methods of approaching this component in this chapter. The second component is the individual oral presentation, and we will look at this element in the next chapter.

The objectives of the internally assessed oral component are to:
- ensure assessment of all parts of the syllabus
- ensure an overall, balanced assessment of your proficiency in the subject by taking into account performance in teacher-assessed work during the course, as well as in the externally assessed components
- include methods which may not be practicable in the context of external assessment but which are appropriate in the classroom context
- assess your oral skills in a variety of contexts.

The individual oral commentary is based on an extract, selected by your teacher, from one of the works studied in Part 2 of the syllabus. The extract that you are given will be accompanied by guiding questions set by your teacher. You are **not** allowed to choose your own extract.

Any of the works you have studied in Part 2 may be used in the individual oral commentary and you will not be told in advance from which work the extract for the individual oral commentary will be taken.

The choice of extract
Your teacher will choose an extract which plays an important part in the text as a whole and highlights a significant aspect of it. The length of the extract you are given will depend on how complex it is, but normally it will not be longer than 40 lines. With poetry, it is likely that a single poem will be used, unless you have studied a long poem, in which case an extract may be chosen from it.

Guiding questions
Your teacher will set **one** or **two** questions for each extract or poem. The purpose of these guiding questions is to give you a starting point for organizing your commentary. These guiding questions will relate to some of the most significant aspects of the extract and help you to

focus on interpreting them. The questions should help you to look at aspects such as:

- the presentation and role of character(s)
- the presentation of relationships
- theme(s)
- the use of language
- the significance of the extract to the development of the plot or text as a whole
- the effects created by the structure, style, and techniques employed by the writer.

You should note, however, that the guiding questions will not:

- refer to specific details or to any particular interpretation of the extract
- restrict your ability to explore independently the significant features or aspects of the extract.

In the activities that follow, you will find examples of the kinds of guiding questions that you may encounter in your individual oral commentary.

The focus and structure of the commentary

The focus and emphasis of your commentary depends on the particular extract chosen. However, in all cases you should aim to identify and explore all the significant features and aspects of the extract. These include:

- placing the extract in context as precisely as you can within the work as a whole
- commenting on the effectiveness of the writer's techniques, including, if you are studying at Higher Level, the writer's use of stylistic techniques and the effects that these create for the reader.

It is important to note, however, that you must **not** be tempted to discuss everything you know about the whole text. Your commentary must **focus** on the specific extract that you are given for discussion. You should relate it to the whole work only where relevant – for example, to establish the context, or discuss its importance to the work as a whole.

Your commentary should be well-structured and your ideas should be presented in an integrated and fluent way – not as a series of separate points. You must also take care to avoid a narrative approach in which you "re-tell the story" of the text or give a line-by-line paraphrase.

Preparation and delivery

Before you give your commentary, you will be allowed 20 minutes supervised preparation time. You will be expected to use this time to:

- read the extract and the accompanying questions carefully
- identify the significant features of the extract and analyse them closely
- make notes in preparation for your commentary
- organize and structure your commentary.

Delivery of your commentary

After you have prepared your commentary you will be given
15 minutes in which to deliver it. You will be able to give your
commentary without interruption or distraction, and your teacher
should not normally intervene while you are giving your commentary.
You will be expected to speak on your own for about 10 to 12 minutes
as the entire oral commentary will conclude after 15 minutes.

After completing the commentary

After listening to your commentary your teacher will discuss it and
the extract with you. The purpose of this discussion is to allow you
to show further understanding and appreciation of the text, and to
expand or develop some of the statements made. Your teacher will
want to be sure that you have understood specific words, phrases,
references, and allusions, and that you have recognized their
importance within the extract. Your teacher will also want to be sure
that you have understood the significance of the extract within the
whole work, or, in the case of a complete poem, the relationship
between the poem and others you have studied. Higher Level
students in particular must show that they are able to comment on
the techniques that the writer uses.

Assessment of your commentary

Your commentary will be assessed against a number of criteria.
These are:

A   Knowledge and understanding of the text
B   Interpretation and personal response
C   Presentation
D   Use of language.

In order to achieve a good result you will need to show:

● good knowledge and understanding of the content of the extract
  or work(s)
● thorough knowledge of the appropriate context of the extract or
  work(s)
● a valid and detailed interpretation of the thought and feeling
  expressed in the extract or work(s), including a considered
  critical response
● a good awareness and detailed analysis of the effects of the
  literary features of the extract or work(s)
● a response supported by relevant references to the extract or
  work(s)
● a clear and logical structure to the response
● a focused response presented in a clear, coherent, effective, and
  convincing manner
● integrated supporting references
● a clear, varied, and precise use of language using an appropriate
  register and style, and relevant literary terms.

The individual oral commentary in practice

We will now look at some examples of individual oral commentary
extracts. If you have not studied these texts you will obviously not
be able to relate the extracts to the whole text, but the focus of these

activities is to give you practice in looking at and thinking about the extracts themselves.

Naturally the Foundation Will Bear Your Expenses

Hurrying to catch my Comet
  One dark November day,
Which soon would snatch me from it
  To the sunshine of Bombay,
I pondered pages Berkeley
  Not three weeks since had heard,
Perceiving Chatto darkly
  Through the mirror of the Third.

Crowds, colourless and careworn,
  Had made my taxi late,
Yet not till I was airborne
  Did I recall the date –
That day when Queen and Minister
  And Band of Guards and all
Still act their solemn-sinister
  Wreath-rubbish in Whitehall.

It used to make me throw up,
  These mawkish nursery games:
O when will England grow up?
  – But I outsoar the Thames,
And dwindle off down Auster
  To greet Professor Lal
(He once met Morgan Forster),
  My contact and my pal.

Philip Larkin

Activity

Look at this poem by Philip Larkin. Think about what you would say about it if you were asked to speak about it to the rest of your class or group. Make a note of the points you would make about the poem, the ways in which Larkin uses language, and the effects that he achieves through his use of language.

Here are some points you might have made:

- It is written in the first person and so the "voice" could be that of the poet himself speaking, but it might also be that of a persona he has created.
- The "speaker" of the poem is a narrator figure – the views that he expresses are not necessarily those of Larkin himself. In fact, the "speaker" here seems to be an English academic who jets around the world giving his papers to major universities.
- Larkin is present here too, but his attitudes and ideas lie behind the words spoken by his character.
- He satirizes his character in order to cast a critical light on the persona he has created, and the views that are expressed through him.
- He uses a range of poetic techniques to achieve his effects (imagery, alliteration, etc.).
- The poem has a clear structure.

Activity

1 Read the following poem, *Churning Day* by Seamus Heaney, and make a note of the initial features that strike you about the way Heaney writes his poem.

2 Now look at the first stanza. How does Heaney begin the poem and how does he use imagery here to create his effects?

3 The next stanza describes the stage where the milk is poured from the crocks into the churn. Make a note of any descriptions or images that strike you here.

4 Now look carefully at the third stanza. What effect is created here by the use of the verb "dance"

(line 19) to describe the butter forming, the metaphor "coagulated sunlight" (line 24) and the simile "like gilded gravel" (line 26)?

5 In the final stanza the poet describes the after-effects of churning day. The stanza opens with a shock to the senses. In what way?

6 What is the effect of the final four lines of the poem?

7 Using all the ideas you have noted, write out what you would say if you were giving an individual oral commentary on this poem.

Churning Day

A thick-crust, coarse-grained as limestone rough-cast,
hardened gradually on top of the four crocks
that stood, large pottery bombs, in the small pantry.
After the hot brewery of gland, cud and udder
cool porous earthenware fermented the buttermilk
for churning day, when the hooped churn was scoured
with plumping kettles and the busy scrubber
echoed daintily on the seasoned wood.
It stood then, purified, on the flagged kitchen floor.

Out came the four crocks, spilled their heavy lip
of cream, their white insides, into the sterile churn.
The staff, like a great whisky muddler fashioned
in deal wood, was plunged in, the lid fitted.
My mother took first turn, set up rhythms
that slugged and thumped for hours. Arms ached.
Hands blistered. Cheeks and clothes were spattered
with flabby milk.

Where finally gold flecks
began to dance. They poured hot water then,
sterilized a birchwood-bowl
and little corrugated butter-spades.
Their short stroke quickened, suddenly
a yellow curd was weighting the churned up white,
heavy and rich, coagulated sunlight
that they fished, dripping, in a wide tin strainer,
heaped up like gilded gravel in a bowl.

The house would stink long after churning day,
acrid as a sulphur mine. The empty crocks
were ranged along the wall again, the butter
in soft printed slabs was piled on pantry shelves.
And in the house we moved with gravid ease,

our brains turned crystals full of clean deal churns,
the plash and gurgle of the sour-breathed milk,
the pat and slap of small spades on wet lumps.

Seamus Heaney

1   Here are some ideas that you might have noted when working through the poem:

- Heaney uses detail to convey the sights, sounds, smells, and feelings associated with the memory he is describing.
- He uses similes and metaphors, adjectives and adverbs to make his descriptions more vivid and immediate in our minds.
- The subject – churning cream from milk to make butter – is a simple country experience.

2   The poem begins with a detailed description of the four crocks in which the buttermilk is standing, fermenting, ready for the churning process to begin. In the simile used to describe the thick crust that has formed on the milk, he likens it to "limestone rough-cast". Heaney uses a metaphor to describe the crocks as "large pottery bombs", which perhaps reflects the shape of these vessels but also gives a sense of the readiness of the milk to be churned – like a bomb ready to go off. He uses another metaphor – "the hot brewery" – to describe how the milk has formed within the cow, creating milk from grass, the "cud", in the same way as a brewery takes natural ingredients to produce beer through a fermentation process. A contrast is created by the "hot" brewery and the "cool" earthenware crocks. The poet describes all the activity that has taken place to prepare the churn for the churning. The use of the adjective "plumping" is unusual and almost has an onomatopoeic effect, imitating the sound of the kettle boiling. Finally the churn is cleaned – the word "purified" gives an almost religious sense to the rituals that have been carried out to prepare for the transforming of the milk into butter, perhaps a kind of miracle in itself.

3   - The poet personifies the crocks – the milk coming from their "white insides" as if it is part of them.
    - The churn is set up with the staff placed through the wooden lid – a simile compares this to a "whisky muddler", which is a large paddle-shaped object used to help whisky ferment.
    - The mother takes over and the hard, physical nature of the work is expressed in the phrase "slugged and thumped for hours. Arms ached./ Hands blistered".
    - Others take their turns and soon they are "spattered" with "flabby" milk as it begins to coagulate.

4   - The verb "dance" to describe the gold flecks of butter as they begin to form is suggestive of a kind of celebration, and it also suggests a quickening of pace as they prepare to form the butter into pats.

Part 4 Talking about literature

- The metaphor "coagulated sunlight" describes the coagulation of the milk into butter and brings to mind its colour and warmth and glow.
- The final simile in the stanza repeats this image of a golden colour, with the use of the word "gilded" emphasizing its richness.

5   The use of the word "stink" at the beginning of the final stanza is unexpected, but describes the lingering smell of the curd. This is emphasized further by the simile "acrid as a sulphur mine", graphically giving a sense of the permeating nature of the smell in the house.

6   The ending of the poem creates a sense of a job well done and of satisfaction. Their minds are like "crystals", the churns are clean and the onomatopoeic effect of "plash" and "gurgle", "pat" and "slap" gives a satisfying sense of the butter being slapped by the butter spades and turned into slabs.

Activity

The following extract is taken from Shakespeare's play *Hamlet*. Here Hamlet is grieving for his father, the king, who has recently died. Hamlet's mother has married his uncle, who has become king himself.

1   Read the extract carefully, and the guiding questions that follow it.

2   Spend 20 minutes preparing your ideas for an oral commentary on this extract.

3   Write notes on the extract as if you were preparing to give an oral commentary on it.

4   Write down what you would say if you were giving an individual oral commentary on this extract.

Hamlet   O that this too too solid flesh would melt,
Thaw and resolve itself into a dew,
Or that the Everlasting had not fixed
His canon 'gainst self-slaughter. O God, God,
How weary, stale, flat and unprofitable
Seem to me all the uses of this world!
Fie on 't, ah fie, 'tis an unweeded garden
That grows to seed: things rank and gross in nature
Possess it merely. That it should come to this –
But two months dead, nay not so much, not two –
So excellent a king, that was to this
Hyperion to a satyr, so loving to my mother
That he might not beteem the winds of heaven
Visit her face too roughly. Heaven and earth,
Must I remember? Why she would hang on him
As if increase of appetite had grown
By what it fed on, and yet within a month –
Let me not think on't – frailty, thy name is woman.
A little month or e'er those shoes were old
With which she followed my poor father's body,
Like Niobe all tears, why she, even she –
O God, a beast that wants discourse of reason
Would have mourned longer – married with my uncle,
My father's brother, but no more like my father
Than I to Hercules; within a month –
Ere yet the salt of most unrighteous tears

Had left the flushing in her galled eyes,
She married. O most wicked speed, to post
With such dexterity to incestuous sheets.
It is not, nor it cannot come to good:
But break, my heart, for I must hold my tongue.

Guiding question 1:	(Higher Level and Standard Level) Discuss Hamlet's state of mind as indicated by the choices made in his language.
Guiding question 2:	(Higher Level and Standard Level) What conclusions can you draw about Hamlet's view of women and of his mother in particular?

The following extract is also taken from Shakespeare's play *Hamlet*. The extract shows Hamlet – who is faced with the prospect of taking revenge for the death of his father, murdered by Hamlet's uncle, Claudius, now king – debating with himself the nature of death.

(Enter **Hamlet**)

Hamlet   To be, or not to be, that is the question:
Whether 'tis nobler in the mind to suffer
The slings and arrows of outrageous fortune,
Or to take arms against a sea of troubles,
And by opposing end them? To die, to sleep –
No more; and by a sleep to say we end
The heart-ache, and the thousand natural shocks
That flesh is heir to; 'tis a consummation
Devoutly to be wished. To die, to sleep –
To sleep, perchance to dream, ay there's the rub,
For in that sleep of death what dreams may come
When we have shuffled off this mortal coil,
Must give us pause; there's the respect
That makes calamity of so long life.
For who would bear the whips and scorns of time,
Th' oppressor's wrong, the proud man's contumely,
The pangs of despised love, the law's delay,
The insolence of office, and the spurns
That patient merit of th' unworthy takes
When he himself might his quietus make
With a bare bodkin? Who would fardels bear,
To grunt and sweat under a weary life,
But that the dread of something after death,
The undiscovered country from whose bourn
No traveller returns, puzzles the will,
And makes us rather bear those ills we have,
Than fly to others that we know not of?
Thus conscience does make cowards of us all,
And thus the native hue of resolution
Is sicklied o'er with the pale cast of thought,

Activity

1   Read the extract carefully, and the guiding questions that follow it.

2   Spend 20 minutes preparing your ideas for an oral commentary on this extract.

3   Write notes on the extract as if you were preparing to give an oral commentary on it.

4   Write down what you would say if you were giving an individual oral commentary on this extract.

Part 4 Talking about literature

And enterprises of great pitch and moment
With this regard their currents turn awry,
And lose the name of action. Soft you now,
The fair Ophelia. – Nymph, in thy orisons
Be all my sins remembered.

Guiding question 1:	(Higher Level and Standard Level) What does this extract show about Hamlet's character and his state of mind at this point in the play?
Guiding question 2:	(Higher Level) Identify the poetic techniques used in this extract. What effects do they achieve? (Standard Level) What do you think are the important themes in this extract?

This extract taken from a little later in *Hamlet* is from the point in the play where Hamlet's uncle Claudius, thinking he is alone, tries to repent of his crime of killing his brother. Hamlet sees him and is aware that this presents him with a prime opportunity to kill Claudius.

King

O my offence is rank, it smells to heaven;
It hath the primal eldest curse upon't,
A brother's murder. Pray can I not,
Though inclination be as sharp as will.
My stronger guilt defeats my strong intent,
And like a man to double business bound,
I stand in pause when I shall first begin,
And both neglect. What if this cursed hand
Were thicker than itself with brother's blood,
Is there not rain enough in the sweet heavens
To wash it white as snow? Whereto serves mercy
But to confront the visage of offence?
And what's in prayer but this two-fold force,
To be forestalled ere we come to fall,
Or pardoned being down? Then I'll look up;
My fault is past. But O what form of prayer
Can serve my turn? 'Forgive me my foul murder'?
That cannot be since I am still possessed
Of those effects for which I did the murder,
My crown, mine own ambition, and my Queen.
May one be pardoned and retain th' offence?
In the corrupted currents of this world
Offence's gilded hand may shove by justice,
And oft 'tis seen the wicked prize itself
Buys out the law. But 'tis not so above;
There is no shuffling, there the action lies
In his true nature, and we ourselves compelled,
Even to the teeth and forehead of our faults
To give in evidence. What then? What rests?

Activity

1 Read the extract carefully, and the guiding questions that follow it.

2 Spend 20 minutes preparing your ideas for an oral commentary on this extract.

3 Write notes on the extract as if you were preparing to give an oral commentary on it.

4 Write down what you would say if you were giving an individual oral commentary on this extract.

Try what repentance can – what can it not?
Yet what can it, when one can not repent?
O wretched state, O bosom black as death,
O limed soul, that struggling to be free,
Art more engaged! Help, angels, make assay.
Bow stubborn knees, and heart with strings of steel,
Be soft as sinews of the new-born babe.
All may be well.
(Kneels)

(Enter **Hamlet***)*

Hamlet   Now might I do it pat, now he is praying;
And now I'll do 't – and so he goes to heaven;
And so am I revenged. That would be scanned:
A villain kills my father, and for that,
I his sole son do this same villain send
To heaven.
Why, this is hire and salary, not revenge.
'A took my father grossly full of bread,
With all his crimes broad blown, as flush as May,
And how his audit stands who knows save heaven?
But in our circumstance and course of thought,
'Tis heavy with him; and am I then revenged,
To take him in the purging of his soul,
When he is fit and seasoned for his passage?
No.
Up sword, and know thou a more horrid hent,
When he is drunk asleep, or in his rage,
Or in th' incestuous pleasure of his bed,
At game, a-swearing, or about some act
That has no relish of salvation in't –
Then trip him that his heels may kick at heaven,
And that his soul may be as damned and black
As hell whereto it goes. My mother stays.
This physic but prolongs thy sickly days.

King   *(Rising)* My words fly up, my thoughts remain below.
Words without thoughts never to heaven go.

Guiding question 1:	(Higher Level and Standard Level) What do you think this extract reveals about the two characters?
Guiding question 2:	(Higher Level) Given the chance, how might you direct this scene to reveal the mental state of each of the characters? (Standard Level) What topics does Claudius address to show his anguish?

The unusual thing about the following extract, which is taken from Emily Brontë's novel *Wuthering Heights*, is that although the story is told in the third person there are, in fact, two narrators here. Mr Lockwood begins the narrative but then this is taken over by Nellie Dean. If you are studying this novel you will know that there are also other narrators at different points. In this extract it is clear that Lockwood has had a bad experience at Wuthering Heights and knows nothing of the history of the family. Nellie, on the other hand, is an old family servant who has a wealth of knowledge about Wuthering Heights that she is only too willing to share with him. The majority of this information is conveyed to us through the dialogue between the two of them.

Activity

1 Read the following extract carefully, and the guiding questions that follow it.

2 Spend 20 minutes preparing your ideas for an oral commentary on this extract.

3 Write notes on the extract as if you were preparing to give an oral commentary on it.

4 Write down what you would say if you were giving an individual oral commentary on this extract.

Wuthering Heights

'I see the house at Wuthering Heights has "Earnshaw" carved over the front door. Are they an old family?'

'Very old, sir; and Hareton is the last of them, as our Miss Cathy is of us – I mean, of the Lintons. Have you been to Wuthering Heights? I beg pardon for asking; but I should like to hear how she is.'

'Mrs Heathcliff? she looked very well, and very handsome; yet, I think, not very happy.'

'Oh dear, I don't wonder! And how did you like the master?'

'A rough fellow, rather, Mrs Dean. Is not that his character?'

'Rough as a saw-edge, and hard as whinstone! The less you meddle with him the better.'

'He must have had some ups and downs in life to make him such a churl. Do you know anything of his history?'

'It's a cuckoo's, sir – I know all about it; except where he was born, and who were his parents, and how he got his money, at first. And Hareton has been cast out like an unfledged dunnock! The unfortunate lad is the only one in all this parish that does not guess how he has been cheated.'

'Well, Mrs Dean, it will be a charitable deed to tell me something of my neighbours: I feel I shall not rest, if I go to bed; so be good enough to sit and chat an hour.'

'Oh, certainly, sir! I'll just fetch a little sewing, and then I'll sit as long as you please. But you've caught cold; I saw you shivering, and you must have some gruel to drive it out.'

The worthy woman bustled off, and I crouched nearer the fire; my head felt hot, and the rest of me chill: moreover I was excited, almost to a pitch of foolishness, through my nerves and brain. This caused me to feel, not uncomfortable, but rather fearful (as I am still) of serious effects from the incidents of to-day and yesterday.

She returned presently, bringing a smoking basin and a basket of work; and, having placed the former on the hob, drew in her seat, evidently pleased to find me so companionable.

Before I came to live here, she commenced – waiting no further invitation to her story – I was almost always at Wuthering Heights; because my mother had nursed Mr Hindley Earnshaw, that was Hareton's father, and I got used to playing with the children: I ran errands too, and helped to make hay, and hung about the farm ready for anything that anybody would set me to.

One fine summer morning – it was the beginning of harvest, I remember – Mr Earnshaw, the old master, came downstairs, dressed for a journey; and after he had told Joseph what was to be done during the day, he turned to Hindley, and Cathy, and me – for I sat eating my porridge with them – and he said, speaking to his son, 'Now, my bonny man, I'm going to Liverpool to-day, what shall I bring you? You may choose what you like; only let it be little, for I shall walk there and back: sixty miles each way, that is a long spell!' Hindley named a fiddle, and then he asked Miss Cathy; she was hardly six years old, but she could ride any horse in the stable, and she chose a whip.

He did not forget me: for he had a kind heart though he was rather severe sometimes. He promised to bring me a pocketful of apples and pears, and then he kissed his children good-bye and set off.

Emily Brontë

Guiding question 1:	(Higher Level and Standard Level) What do you learn about the narrators from this extract?
Guiding question 2:	(Higher Level) Identify the narrative techniques that Brontë uses here and the effects she creates through them. (Standard Level) How is information conveyed to you in this extract?

The following extract is the opening passage from *The Pickup*, a novel about South Africa by Nadine Gordimer. It introduces the young woman who is the protagonist of the novel. Her car has broken down in the middle of rush hour in the city.

Activity

1 Read the extract carefully and the guiding questions that follow it.

2 Spend 20 minutes preparing your ideas for an oral commentary on this extract.

3 Write notes on the extract in preparation for an oral commentary on it.

4 Write down what you would say if you were giving an individual oral commentary on this extract.

The Pickup

Clustered predators around a kill. It's a small car with a young woman inside it. The battery has failed and taxis, cars, minibuses, vans, motorcycles butt and challenge one another, reproach and curse her, a traffic mob mounting its own confusion. Get going. Stupid bloody woman. *Idikazana lomlongu, le*! She throws up hands, palms open, in surrender. They continue to jostle and blare their impatience. She gets out of her car and faces them. One of the unemployed black men who beg by waving vehicles into parking bays sidles his way deftly through fenders, signals with his head – Oka-ay, Oka-ay go inside, go! – and mimes control of the steering wheel. Another like him appears, and they push her and her car into a loading bay. The street hustles on. They stand, looking musingly beyond her while she fumbles for her purse. An expert's quick glance at what she has put in his hand assures the street boss that it is more than adequate. She doesn't know how to thank them enough, etc. He hitches his body to get the money stowed in trousers cut to fit somebody else and smiles with his attention on the lookout for the next vehicle seeking a place to park. A woman wearing a towel as a shawl, enthroned on a fruit-box before her stock of hair combs, razor blades, pumice stones, woollen caps and headache powders, yells out to him what must be a teasing remark in a language the young woman doesn't understand.

There. You've seen. I've seen. The gesture. A woman in a traffic jam among those that are everyday in the city, any city. You won't remember it, you won't know who she is.

But I know because from the sight of her I'll find out – as a story – what was going to happen as the consequence of that commonplace embarrassment on the streets; where it was heading her for, and what. Her hands thrown up, open.

Nadine Gordimer

Guiding question 1:	(Higher Level) What elements of the passage are constructed so as to intrigue and engage the reader?
Guiding question 2:	(Higher Level) How does sentence structure reflect the content of the passage?

Activity

1 Read the following extract from Michael Ondaatje's memoir *Running in the Family,* and the guiding questions that follow it. As the text is a memoir you need to be conscious of what a passage such as this might contribute to building a picture of Ondaatje's boyhood days in Sri Lanka.

2 Spend 20 minutes preparing your ideas for an oral commentary on this extract.

3 Write notes on the extract as if you were preparing to give an oral commentary on it.

4 Write down what you would say if you were giving an individual oral commentary on this extract.

Running in the Family

The family home of Rock Hill was littered with snakes, especially cobras. The immediate garden was not so dangerous, but one step further and you would see several. The chickens that my father kept in later years were an even greater magnet. The snakes came for the eggs. The only deterrent my father discovered was ping-pong balls. He had crates of ping-pong balls shipped to Rock Hill and distributed them among the eggs. The snake would swallow the ball whole and be unable to digest it. There are several paragraphs on this method of snake control in a pamphlet he wrote on poultry farming.

The snakes also had the habit of coming into the house and at least once a month there would be shrieks, the family would run around, the shotgun would be pulled out, and the snake would be blasted to pieces. Certain sections of the walls and floors showed the scars of shot. My stepmother found one coiled asleep on her desk and was unable to approach the drawer to get the key to open the gun case. At another time one lay sleeping on the large radio to draw its warmth and, as nobody wanted to destroy the one source of music in the house, this one was watched carefully but left alone.

Most times though there would be running footsteps, yells of fear and excitement, everybody trying to quiet everybody else, and my father or stepmother would blast away not caring what was in the background, a wall, a good ebony, a sofa, or a decanter. They killed at least thirty snakes between them.

After my father died, a grey cobra came into the house. My stepmother loaded the gun and fired at point blank range. The gun jammed. She stepped back and reloaded but by then the snake had slid out into the garden. For the next month this snake would often come into the house and each time the gun would misfire or jam, or my stepmother would miss at absurdly short range. The snake attacked no one and had a tendency to follow my younger sister Susan around. Other snakes entering the house were killed by the shotgun, lifted with a long stick and flicked into the bushes, but the old grey cobra led a charmed life. Finally one of the old workers at Rock Hill told my stepmother what had become obvious, that it was my father who had come to protect his family. And in fact, whether it was because the chicken farm closed down or because of my father's presence in the form of a snake, very few other snakes came into the house again.

Michael Ondaatje

Guiding question 1:	(Higher Level and Standard Level) What does the tone of the extract contribute to the reader's response to the extract?
Guiding question 2:	(Higher Level) How does the structure of the extract, including both repetition and sentence structure, contribute to the overall effect of the passage? (Standard Level) How are details of description important to the overall effect of this recollection of the family?

Keats's poem *To Autumn* was written about 19 September 1819, and is one of his best-known and best-loved poems. It is addressed throughout to a personified "Autumn" and in many ways is a valedictory poem which presents the fruitfulness of autumn and signals the approaching winter. It presents a vision of humanity working in close harmony with the natural processes of nature.

Activity

1 Read the poem carefully, and the guiding questions that follow it.
2 Spend 20 minutes preparing your ideas for an oral commentary on this poem.
3 Write notes on the poem as if you were preparing to give an oral commentary on it.
4 Write down what you would say if you were giving an individual oral commentary on this poem.

To Autumn

Season of mists and mellow fruitfulness,
Close bosom-friend of the maturing sun;
Conspiring with him how to load and bless
With fruit the vines that round the thatch-eaves run;
To bend with apples the moss'd cottage-trees,
And fill all fruit with ripeness to the core;
To swell the gourd, and plump the hazel shells
With a sweet kernel; to set budding more,
And still more, later flowers for the bees,
Until they think warm days will never cease,
For Summer has o'erbrimm'd their clammy cells.

Who hath not seen thee oft amid thy store?
Sometimes whoever seeks abroad may find
Thee sitting careless on a granary floor,
Thy hair soft-lifted by the winnowing wind;
Or on a half-reap'd furrow sound asleep,

Drows'd with the fume of poppies, while thy hook
Spares the next swath and all its twinèd flowers;
And sometimes like a gleaner thou dost keep
Steady thy laden head across a brook;
Or by a cider-press, with patient look,
Thou watchest the last oozings, hours by hours.

Where are the songs of Spring? Aye, where are they?
Think not of them, – thou hast thy music too,
While barrèd clouds bloom the soft-dying day,
And touch the stubble-plains with rosy hue;
Then in a wailful choir the small gnats mourn
Among the river sallows, borne aloft
Or sinking as the light wind lives or dies;
And full-grown lambs loud bleat from hilly bourn;
Hedge-crickets sing, and now with treble soft
The redbreast whistles from a garden-croft;
And gathering swallows twitter in the skies.

John Keats

Guiding question 1:	(Higher Level and Standard Level) What is your response to the opening stanza of the poem?
Guiding question 2:	(Higher Level) How does Keats use imagery in the poem? What effects does this create? (Standard Level) What is the overall effect of the poem as reflected in the final stanza?

Activity

Now read this transcript from a student's oral commentary on *To Autumn* and compare the ideas with your own.

Commentary

I feel that the first line of the poem immediately captures a sense of the essence of autumn combining the characteristics of "mists" and "mellow fruitfulness". The second line links the season to the sun – a "maturing" sun in the sense that the natural cycle of the year has reached its maturity. It also introduces the idea of the sun being an essential component of the natural process in bringing the fruits of autumn to ripeness and fruition. In this first stanza autumn is characterized by a strong reproductive force which is traditionally represented as female (in mythology, Ceres, the goddess of corn and the harvest). Just as the earth is generically female (hence phrases like "Mother Earth"), the sun is traditionally characterized as male (as in the god Apollo) and the two together produce the rich fruits of autumn. Keats describes this union as "conspiring" (line 3) which gives the impression of the two secretly and mysteriously working together to produce, almost as if by magic, the bounties of autumn. The poem is rich in imagery and here Keats uses it to create a sense of the bounty produced by this union, as in lines 5–11.

The first image in stanza 2 personifies autumn as being "amid thy store" cleaning the grain of chaff – one of the routine tasks following the harvest called "winnowing" – hence Keats's reference to the "winnowing wind" (line 15). I feel that this again has feminine connotations, created by the reference to "Thy hair soft-lifted" (line 15). He follows this with a second image, this time of the field worker asleep on a "half-reap'd furrow". The reference to "Drows'd with the fume of poppies" suggests not only sleep but a sleep that is drug-induced and therefore a state of heightened subconscious awareness. The worker's scythe is suspended, sparing the "next swath and all its twinèd flowers" (line 18).

A third image Keats uses here creates a picture of a gleaner carrying a head of corn across a brook. The "laden head" (line 20) creates the sense of plenty.

A final image in this stanza gives me a picture of a worker at the cider-press crushing the juice from the apples to make cider. This image reminds me of the richness of the apple harvest, which was created in stanza 1.

These images together present a series of mental pictures which capture some of the activities that typify autumn and the harvest. As well as reinforcing the impression of abundance, they also suggest a sense of progression – the reaper cuts the crop, the gleaner gathers it after the reaper, the winnower winnows it. The crushing of the apples marks a stage of progression from apple to cider. Each of these activities, then, brings us closer to the end of nature's annual cycle of life and prepares us for the final stanza.

In the final stanza Keats unites his images and the experiences of the first two stanzas. It presents an acceptance of autumn's passing, with its suggestion of death and the impending winter. However, the opening question with its reference to spring has a consoling effect in that it reminds us not only that the "songs of Spring" (line 23) have passed and winter is approaching, but that spring will come again too. The poet consoles himself also with the idea that although autumn signals the approaching end of the natural cycle, it too has its own beauty. The compensation for the loss of the "songs of Spring" lies in the beauty of natural maturity and it is this that the poem celebrates. There are compensations in that although autumn has no "songs" it has its own "music". There is a melancholy in this music, though: "in a wailful choir the small gnats mourn" (line 27) and the "full-grown lambs loud bleat from hilly bourn" (line 30). On the other hand the "Hedge-crickets sing" (line 31) and the "redbreast whistles" (line 32) while the swallows "twitter in the skies" as they prepare to migrate for the winter; like autumn, their stay is nearing its end. The ending of the poem, however, does not strike me as depressing but rather has a sense of optimism. I think that Keats is pointing here to the natural cycle, and although autumn is at an end and winter is drawing close, that too in its turn will be followed by another spring and another summer. In that sense I think that this poem not only celebrates the end of the natural year but also looks forward to celebrating the start of a new one.

10 The individual oral presentation

Objectives
- To analyse the requirements of the individual oral presentation
- To prepare for the individual oral presentation by practising topic work

The individual oral presentation is the second compulsory oral activity that all Language A1 students must complete and is based on a work or works studied in Part 4 of the syllabus. This presentation is based on a topic that you have chosen in consultation with your teacher.

Choice of topic
When thinking about what topic you are going to choose as the subject for your oral presentation, you should be aware that you may choose a topic which reflects your personal interests. Obviously if you choose a topic that you have some interest in you are likely to produce a more effective and interesting presentation than if you choose a topic you find boring. You have quite a wide choice as it can be based on any work or works you have studied in Part 4 of the syllabus. Your topic may be based on any aspect or aspects of the work(s) studied, including:

- cultural setting of the work(s) and related issues
- thematic focus
- characterization
- techniques and style
- author's attitude to particular elements of the works such as character(s), subject matter
- interpretation of particular elements from different perspectives.

Possible activities
The range of activities that you could choose for your individual oral presentation is very wide and the suggestions that follow are simply examples of the kinds of things you could do. You should discuss your own ideas with your teacher and select an activity that is appropriate to the topic you have chosen.

Structured discussions
These could be:

- Class discussions where you have been given special responsibilities, such as doing advance preparation, giving a short report, adopting a provocative position, etc. The whole class may participate in this kind of activity, although only the presenter will be assessed.

● The presentation of material that promotes class discussion, such as presenting opposing readings of a work. This would probably involve the presenter answering questions from the class.

● An interview conducted by the teacher on an agreed topic or work(s).

Oral exposés
These could be:

● An introduction to a writer, a work, or a particular text.

● An explanation of a particular aspect of an author's work.

● The setting of a particular writer's work against another body of material, such as details on social background or political views.

● A commentary on the use of a particular image, idea, or symbol in one text or in a writer's work.

● An imitation of a poem that you have studied. This activity should be followed by some explanation of, and discussion on, what you have tried to do and to show.

● A comparison of two passages, two characters, or two works.

● A commentary on an extract from a work you have studied in class which has been prepared at home.

● An account of your developing response to a work.

Role play
This could involve:

● A monologue by a character at an important point in the work.

● Reminiscences by a character from a point in later life.

● An author's reaction to a particular interpretation of his or her work.

If you choose to do a role play for your oral presentation, it is important that you provide a rationale explaining what you have done and what you hoped to achieve.

Focus of your individual oral presentation
The main focus of your oral presentation will depend very much on the nature and scope of the topic that you choose. However, in order to do well in your presentation you will be expected to show a good level of literary appreciation. Naturally it is expected that this will be more sophisticated at Higher Level than at Standard Level. Whatever the topic you choose you will be expected to show:

● knowledge and understanding of the work(s)

● thorough appreciation of the aspect discussed

● knowledge and use of the linguistic register appropriate for the type of presentation, which means being sensitive to your use of such elements as vocabulary, tone, sentence structure, and modes of expression, and ensuring that they are appropriate to the task.

At Higher Level, where appropriate, you should consider the effects created by the ways in which the writer(s) have explored the material you are presenting.

Structure of your individual oral presentation

Again the precise structure of your oral presentation depends, to a large extent, on the type of activity you have chosen and your topic. Some activities, such as a discussion and an oral exposé, may be suited to a more formally structured discussion approach which follows a logical sequence from one point to another. Others, such as a role play, may not be so effectively presented through a formal, structured approach. The main thing is that you should decide on the type of presentation most likely to achieve the objectives you have for your topic. Whatever you choose, however, you should bear in mind that all presentations must have some kind of coherent structure.

Preparation of your individual oral presentation

You will be expected to do the preparation work for your individual oral presentation outside class time. When you have chosen your topic it is your responsibility to:

- select appropriate material for your presentation
- organize the material into a coherent structure
- choose and rehearse the appropriate register for your presentation.

Presentation and discussion

Your presentation should last between 10 and 15 minutes. Once you have started to give your presentation you will not be interrupted and you will not be allowed any assistance.

When you have completed your presentation your teacher will discuss the material with you further to explore your knowledge and understanding of the work(s) or topic you have presented. Your teacher will want to make sure that you can justify your selection of:

- the material used in your presentation
- the activity you have chosen to present the topic
- the linguistic register you have used for the presentation of your topic.

The whole class may take part in the discussions following your presentation.

Assessment of your presentation

Your presentation will be assessed against a number of criteria. These are:

A Knowledge and understanding of the text
B Interpretation and personal response
C Presentation
D Use of language.

In order to achieve a good result you will need to show:

- good knowledge and understanding of the content of the extract or work(s)
- thorough knowledge of the appropriate context of the extract or work(s)

- a valid and detailed interpretation of the thought and feeling expressed in the extract or work(s), including a considered critical response
- a good awareness and detailed analysis of the effects of the literary features of the extract or work(s)
- a response supported by relevant references to the extract or work(s)
- a clear and logical structure to the response
- a focused response presented in a clear, coherent, effective, and convincing manner
- integrated supporting references
- a clear, varied, and precise use of language using an appropriate register and style, and relevant literary terms.

The individual oral presentation in practice

When you are preparing your presentation it is important that you approach the task in a structured and coherent way, in order to produce a structured and coherent presentation.

Activity

The following notes were made by a student in preparation for a presentation on John Steinbeck's use of language, structure, and style in his novel *Of Mice and Men*. These notes represent the first stage in the student preparing ideas that will ultimately be included in the final presentation.

Read them carefully and think about the following points:

- the range of ideas they contain
- the way they are structured
- how effectively they convey their ideas.

Commentary: Language, structure, and style in John Steinbeck's novel *Of Mice and Men*

One of the striking features of Steinbeck's story is the realistic way in which it is presented. His writing shows an interest in the lives of the poor and of the socially deprived. There are certain aspects of the way that he uses language that the reader becomes aware of when reading his novel. For example:

- The story is written in the third person. In other words, the writer seems "invisible" but readers can see everything that goes on and even what is inside people's minds. The writer of a third-person account can describe characters' thoughts, speech, and actions to the reader. In this story, however, Steinbeck does not use the technique of looking into people's minds very much. In fact, only once do we see directly into people's thoughts.

- Steinbeck uses simple language and straightforward vocabulary, which means that his story is told in a direct, plain, and uncomplicated fashion.

- The dialogue is written as it would have been spoken, and Steinbeck makes use of dialect forms.

- He uses a different kind of speech for different characters. For example, Lennie's sentences are very childlike in character. Curley's language tends to be full of pent-up aggression and anger. Slang, or colloquial language, is used in the novel, again to reflect the way that real people speak.

Style

Here are some important features of the style in which "Of Mice and Men" is written:

● The story is a blend of description and drama.

● When Steinbeck uses description, which is most notable in the first and last scenes, he creates a vivid picture of nature and the natural world. Although not vital to the development of the story, these descriptions form a background against which the story is set and also contain a symbolic importance. The events at the ranch, on the other hand, are written very economically with very little description. Everything there is designed to develop or reveal a theme or a character trait, most of which indicate the fate which is to befall Lennie and George.

● The dramatic style that Steinbeck intended from the outset consists mainly of dialogue and of short exchanges, and the story is developed through these exchanges. Originally, Steinbeck intended the story to be easily adapted for the stage, and so the writing is very similar to the way in which a play would be written.

Imagery

Imagery is the use of words to create pictures or images in the reader's mind and is used by a writer to make his or her words more effective and powerful. Although "Of Mice and Men" is written in simple and straightforward language, Steinbeck uses several images as symbols. A symbol is something which is used to represent or indicate something else. For example, he begins with the description of the river and the path and the campsite. Wildlife is referred to only in the opening and closing scenes, which are set by the river. Perhaps here Steinbeck is drawing a contrast between the ongoing cycle of nature and a human being's temporary appearance in this scene, which typifies the transient lifestyle of the itinerant workers. Although animals feature prominently in the plot, the images of them often emphasize the harshness of the workers' lives. They also feature in the descriptions of people, particularly Lennie. He is compared to a bear and a horse, and later in the first scene Steinbeck likens him to a terrier when he shows reluctance to give up his pet mouse to George. Imagery to do with hands is also used in the novel. For example, Lennie's hands are referred to several times as "paws", and the gloved fist of Curley plays an important part in the story.

The use of light

Steinbeck often refers to light and dark, or sunshine and shadow, and frequently these are used to create atmosphere.

The structure of the story

When we talk of the structure of the story we really mean the way that the story is put together. This is quite a short story but it nonetheless has a very tight and clearly defined structure and within the structure everything comes full circle. For example, the action ends in the same place as it began.

Six central scenes comprise the story

● Scene One: sets the scene and introduces the main characters

● Scene Two: we meet Curley and there is the shooting of Candy's dog

● Scene Three: the damage to Curley's hand

● Scene Four: the confrontation with Curley's wife

● Scene Five: her death

● Scene Six: Lennie's death.

Activity

The following represents the transcript of an oral presentation that a student prepared on the topic of the sonnets of John Keats. The student selected for herself a range of sonnets and prepared her presentation on them.

Read the transcript through carefully and make a note of the impression that you get of the presentation. Ask yourself the following questions:

1 How well does the student seem to know and understand the sonnets she presents?

2 How effectively has she analysed the effects of literary features such as diction, imagery, tone, structure, style, and technique?

3 How structured is the student's response?

4 How effective and convincing is her presentation?

5 How appropriately does she integrate supporting references to illustrate her ideas?

6 How accurate, clear, and precise is her use of language?

7 How appropriate is her choice of register and style for the presentation?

8 How do you think the presentation could be improved?

Commentary: The sonnets of John Keats

In this presentation I will look at a selection of sonnets written by the English Romantic poet, John Keats. The sonnets I have chosen reveal the progression in style that Keats's writing underwent as his style developed.

On First Looking into Chapman's Homer

Before studying this sonnet it may help you to know that Keats wrote it in October 1816 after reading for the first time a translation by George Chapman of Homer's Iliad and Odyssey. It is often regarded as Keats's first poem of any real significance. Keats himself could not read Greek and so his knowledge of the works of Homer was limited to the refined translation of the eighteenth-century writer Alexander Pope. However, one night his friend and teacher, Charles Cowden Clarke, introduced him to Elizabethan translator Chapman's version, which he found much more exciting and powerful than the previous versions he had read.

Probably the most immediately striking thing about the opening lines is the richness of the language. Words like "realms", "gold", "goodly", "kingdoms" give an immediate impression of one whose experience has brought him into contact with a wealth of riches. Notice too the reference to "bards" (poets) who express their "fealty" (loyalty) to their lord, Apollo (the Greek god of poetry and music).

Keats continues the metaphor of him as a traveller journeying in rich and mystical lands in the next few lines and speaks of how he had been told of a "wide expanse" that Homer, the Greek poet and writer of the Iliad and Odyssey, ruled as his kingdom. However, he says that he had never breathed the clear air ("pure serene") of Homer until he heard "Chapman speak out loud and bold". In other words, although he had heard of Homer before he had never really fully experienced his work until he read Chapman's translation.

In the closing six lines of the poem, or the sestet as it is called, Keats uses two similes. In the first he compares his excitement on reading Chapman's version with that felt by an astronomer who discovers a new planet. He then compares his feelings to those experienced by Cortez when he discovered the Pacific Ocean and looked upon it from a hill in Darien (an isthmus in Central America).

Both these similes stress the magnitude of the effect that Chapman's Homer had on Keats. It is perhaps worth noting here that many critics and writers have observed that, in fact, Balboa and not Cortez was the first European to discover the Pacific. It is known that Keats had read Robertson's "History of America" which contains descriptions of Balboa's discovery of the Pacific and Cortez's discovery of Mexico City. Some feel that Keats deliberately wrote "Cortez" because he preferred the sound of that name to that of "Balboa". However, in poetic terms the point is an insignificant one as the poetic intention here is not to present a historically accurate account but to convey a sense of Keats's experience. It could be argued that the name of "Cortez" has a more musical quality to it as well as carrying connotations of excitement and discovery that "Balboa" lacks.

In these last six lines there are a number of words or phrases that add power to the sense of the excitement of a new discovery that Keats creates. For example, "stout Cortez" and "eagle eyes" give an impression of the intrepid, observant, and sharp-eyed explorer constantly looking for new discoveries. The description of his men looking at each other "with a wild surmise" reinforces the impression of hardly being able to believe the discovery. "Silent" again reinforces this idea as Cortez's men are speechless as the enormity of their discovery sinks in.

Keats also uses the structure of the poem to develop his ideas. The poem is written in the sonnet form and in the first eight lines or octave Keats describes his experiences of reading a wealth of rich literature in the past. In the final two lines of the octave, though, Keats prepares us for the final lines of the sonnet by telling us that despite such reading he had never truly experienced its beauty and wonder until he read Chapman. The final six lines of the sonnet (the sestet) go on to describe how he felt at this exciting discovery, through the imagery of an astronomer discovering a new star or an explorer discovering a new ocean. The poem is unified through the central metaphor of the traveller and the voyage of discovery.

It is worth remembering that many critics regard this poem as being Keats's first poem of any real significance and it records, as many of his later poems do in different ways, the thrill of an aesthetic experience and the power of art to influence the human mind.

To My Brothers

This sonnet was written in November 1816 on the nineteenth birthday of Keats's youngest brother, Thomas. At that time Keats was living with his brothers George and Thomas in London.

In the octave of the sonnet the poet observes the flames playing over the coals in the fire and contemplates the quietness of the house in which he and his brothers reside, and the "household gods that keep/ A gentle empire o'er fraternal souls". He thinks of how, as he searches for poetic inspiration, his younger brother's eyes "are fix'd, as in a poetic sleep" on his learning, and how the fall of night offers comfort to their cares.

In the sestet he develops these ideas further. In these lines Keats focuses on the fact that it is his brother Tom's birthday and he expresses gladness that it has passed in such a tranquil mood. He also expresses the wish that they may pass many such quiet evenings together and to experience life's true joys before they die.

The mood of this poem is very meditative, as the poet weighs in his mind "What are the world's true joys". Overall, the tone is conversational, although there are some more elevated poetic images such as "A gentle empire o'er fraternal souls" and "I search around the poles". These help to suggest a more universal message in the poem, beyond that of the domestic scene he celebrates.

Addressed to [Haydon]

Another poem written in the sonnet form, "Addressed to [Haydon]" was also written in November 1816. The poem is addressed to Benjamin Robert Haydon, a painter whom Keats had met earlier that year.

In the octave he speaks of "Great spirits", who are staying or travelling on earth. The first of these "Great spirits", "He of the cloud, the cataract, the lake" refers to the poet William Wordsworth (Haydon's painting, "Wordsworth Musing Upon Helvellyn", is in the National Portrait Gallery – Helvellyn is a mountain in the Lake District). Keats says that the inspiration of Wordsworth's poetry came from the wing of an angel of the highest order.

"He of the rose, the violet, the spring" refers to Leigh Hunt, who was imprisoned "for Freedom's sake" and who, while in prison, turned his cell into a bower of flowers using wallpaper. The third reference is to Raphael (both the name of an archangel and the famous Renaissance painter) and is a tribute to the painter, Haydon.

In the final lines of the poem the poet ponders on the fact that other great spirits will appear from ages yet to come and these spirits too will have an important and shaping influence upon the world: "these will give the world another heart,/ And other pulses". His emphasis here is upon the shaping of humanity and imagination. He asks the reader "Hear ye not the hum/ Of mighty workings?" These are the workings of the imagination within the human spirit, and he urges all to be silent and listen to the imagination.

The structure of this sonnet is in the conventional form except for the unconventional thirteenth line, which is, in fact, half a line. Originally Keats completed this line with the words "in a distant Mart". He then decided to leave out the second part of the line. By omitting the second part of this line the poet allows the silence to take its place in a real sense in response to his question. "Hear ye not the hum/ Of might workings?"

Unlike "To My Brothers", the tone of this sonnet is elevated, in keeping with the sense of admiration Keats wants to create for Wordsworth, Leigh Hunt, and Haydon, and it is specific in its reference to the poets and the painter.

On the Sea

This sonnet was written on 16 or 17 April 1817, when Keats was staying at Carisbrooke on the Isle of Wight.

In the octave his imagery brings out the eternal nature of the sea and the use of personification adds power to this. There is little elevated language here (despite the reference to Hecate – a goddess who had power over the heavens, earth, and the sea). Notice the description here – the "desolate shores", "its mighty swell" – and the finely observed detail – "the very smallest shell" – which create a contrast between the sea's mightiest and minutest effects.

The sestet opens with an invocation to those "who have your eye-balls vexed and tired" to look upon the sea; and to those whose "ears are dinned with uproar rude" to sit near the mouth of a sea-cave and listen to the sounds of the sea. Keats captures the noise of the sea through a succession of onomatopoeic consonants, "dinned with uproar rude", for example.

The poem then reveals Keats's admiration, not only for the sea's eternal nature and awesome power, but also for its restorative effects on the human heart and mind.

On Sitting Down to Read King Lear Once Again

This sonnet was written in January 1818 and contains Keats's thoughts as he sits down to read "King Lear" again.

In the opening lines here he dismisses the idea of "Romance", which he personifies as "golden-tongued Romance, with serene lute!" He is referring here to a kind of self-indulgent writing which has lured him in the past – note the use of "Syren", in mythology a bewitching figure. He bids farewell to this kind of writing, for he must "burn through" the "fierce dispute/ Betwixt damnation and impassioned clay". The latter refers directly to the theme of the play "King Lear", while "burn through" presents the reading of the play as a kind of ordeal by fire – an image which is picked up again in the final couplet of the sonnet. Note also the image of the play as a "bitter-sweet... fruit".

In the final lines he speaks of "Albion" – the ancient name for Britain, and the setting of "King Lear" and therefore the "Begetters of our deep eternal theme". The "old oak forest" into which Keats speaks of going points to the endurance or suffering that the poet must face but his plan is that when he is consumed by fire he can be re-born with the poetic self-discipline and determination that he desires. It is worth noting that this sonnet concludes in the style of a Shakespearean sonnet with a rhyming couplet, and in that it differs from the early sonnets that we have looked at. This rhyming couplet adds a sense of finality to the ideas expressed. It is also worth noting that uncharacteristically the last line contains an extra foot, which breaks the pattern of pentameters that is established in the rest of the sonnet. It is unclear whether this was an oversight on Keats's part or a deliberate feature. An interesting effect is achieved through this lengthened final line.

When I have fears that I may cease to be

Written between 22 and 31 January 1818, this sonnet shows even more clearly than the previous one the influence of Shakespeare on Keats's writing. The 36 sonnets Keats wrote up to the beginning of 1818 are all Petrarchan in form – the pattern used by Milton and Wordsworth. This is a form which strictly follows the pattern of an octave rhyming abbaabba followed by a sestet of two tercets (three lines) rhyming either cdcdcd or cde cde. He moved away slightly from this form in "On Sitting Down to Read King Lear Once Again", which is basically Petrarchan in form but with a concluding rhyming couplet. However, "When I have fears that I may cease to be", written a day or two later, is fully Shakespearean in form.

The rhyme scheme is abab/cdcd/efef/gg. This form of three quatrains concluding with a rhyming couplet is one that Shakespeare commonly uses in his sonnets. Its lines are end-stopped and the three quatrains, although separate, are logically linked and develop one from the other. The concluding couplet links back to the whole of the rest of the poem, to give both a sense of unity and conclusion. However, the influence extends beyond the rhyme scheme: Keats's subject matter also has features that are reminiscent of Shakespeare's (and Keats's) concerns, i.e. "death", "love" and "poetic destiny".

The poet expresses the fear that death will come to him before he has been able to write all that is in his mind. He thinks of all the beauty that exists and regrets that he "may never live to trace/ Their shadows with the magic hand of chance". He thinks of the "fair creature of an hour!" (often regarded as a reference to a young woman he met briefly in a chance encounter, but transformed into a metaphor for man in quest of a rare, nameless, and unattainable beauty) and the fact that he will "never look upon thee more". At the end of the poem he is left empty and alone to face death, in the face of which "love and fame to nothingness do sink".

He uses a number of images in the poem which create a particular effect. For example, the first part of the poem is rich in harvest and cosmic imagery: "gleaned my teeming brain", "like rich garners the full-ripened grain", "the night's starred face", "Huge cloudy symbols". These images blend together the richness and fruitfulness of the poetic imagination and ambition within the context of the universe.

The imagery of the second part of the poem elevates the ephemeral experience to an importance greater than that of ambition, but this is a level that he will never attain – "Never have relish in the faery power/ Of unreflecting love!"

Images of death run throughout the poem – "fears that I may cease to be", "I may never live", "I shall never look upon thee more", "I stand alone".

Although it is perfectly possible to read this poem as an expression of a universal experience without reference to biographical overtones, the poem does possess these overtones.

The main factor here relates to the tuberculosis that ran through Keats's family. As a young man he had nursed his mother through the last stages of the disease and by January 1818 he was already becoming concerned about the state of his brother Tom's health. It is understandable, therefore, particularly bearing in mind his medical training, that he might have thought too about the prospects for his own health. He had, in fact, already begun to think that he did not have long to live himself, even though no signs of the disease had yet shown themselves. As it turned out, his own misgivings turned out to be remarkably accurate, as his death came only three years later.

Part 4 Talking about literature

> **Here are some points you might have noted about how the presentation could be improved:**
> - The student tends to deal with the sonnets individually. The presentation would be improved if links were drawn between them.
> - More developed comments could be made on Keats's style.
> - There could be more detailed analysis and evaluation.

In the next section we will look at how a student worked through a specific theme to prepare a presentation based on the literature of war. In this instance the student took as his theme: "The First World War in Literature".

He began by setting the literature in a historical context.

Activity

Read the historical context which follows. How well do you think this sets the context for the presentation?

Commentary: The historical context

The "Great War" of 1914–1918, one of the greatest catastrophes of modern times, cast a long shadow over twentieth-century Europe. This so-called "war to end wars" did nothing of the kind, but it did bring about profound changes in society, culture, and ways of thinking. It is said to have marked the true beginning of the "modern age".

You may have some knowledge of the events of the First World War, which often feature in television documentaries or history programmes. Here is a helpful summary from Paul Fussell's introduction to "The Bloody Game", a huge, fascinating anthology of the literature of modern war.

"It had all begun in June 1914, when Archduke Francis Ferdinand, heir to the throne of Austria-Hungary, was assassinated in Sarajevo, Bosnia-Herzegovina, by a Serbian patriot fed up with Austrian domination of his country. Austria-Hungary used the occasion to pick a long-desired quarrel with Serbia and to issue an ultimatum that could only produce war. At this point the system of European alliances, negotiated over many decades, had to be honored: Russia came to the aid of Serbia, whereupon Germany jumped in on the side of Austria-Hungary. France then honored her treaty with Russia, Britain hers with France. By October 1914, Turkey had joined the side of Germany and Austria-Hungary (the 'Central Powers'). By the end of the year the notorious trench system was emplaced in Belgium and France, running 400 miles from its northern anchor at the North Sea to its southern end at the Swiss border, while in the east, another front developed along the Russian border with Austria-Hungary. Italy came in on the side of the Allies in 1915, opening a front against Austria. And in April 1917, the United States, exasperated by German sinking of its ships, joined the Allies, although it took many months for an American army to be assembled, supplied, trained, shipped to Europe and installed in the line. The Americans arrived so late in the war that although they fought impressively and were generally credited with supplying the needed weight to win the war, they suffered only about one-tenth the casualties of the British, and more American soldiers died from influenza than from gas and bullets and shells."

The student went on to identify certain features which were peculiar to the First World War.

Certain features of the First World War made it different from anything that had gone before.

- The sheer number of casualties: Over 37 million people died or were wounded.

- War was a mass activity: All eligible (male) civilians were called up or conscripted to fight, where previously wars had been fought by professional armies at a distance from civilian life. The first ever air raids – from Zeppelin airships – also brought war much closer to home.

- Technology such as machine guns, tanks, barbed wire, and poison gas were used for the first time. These new weapons killed indiscriminately, regardless of whether soldiers were "brave" or not. Enemies did not have to see each other and the personal element of face-to-face combat was removed. It became easier, literally and psychologically, to kill.

- Trench warfare: Much of the war was fought in a system of deep, muddy ditches in which soldiers lived, in appalling conditions, for months on end, facing the "enemy" across fifty yards of "no man's land".

- Gender issues: Women did not participate directly in the fighting – although some did experience the war at close quarters through serving as army nurses – but the war had a drastic effect on their lives. The loss of so many men left gaps in the workforce and caused an imbalance between the genders. Some women took on roles that had never been open to them before, while many more, who had lost husbands or lovers, had no choice but to remain single.

The student then went on to set a literary context for the material he was going to discuss.

Writing the war: the literary context

The war occurred at a time when literature flourished and was highly respected, and it prompted a great outpouring of writing of all sorts. Its peculiar horrors have continued to inspire and fascinate authors to the present day.

To understand the literature of the war, you need some understanding of how people typically thought and felt about these events, both at the time and afterwards. There are recurring themes, ideas and "motifs" in First World War literature. Here are some.

- The features of First World War combat, mentioned above, are reflected in an increasing sense of depersonalization. Soldiers became mere numbers, not individuals. Literary accounts of the dehumanizing experience of the trenches became more graphic as the war went on, while contemporary authors like Pat Barker and Sebastian Faulks continue the trend. Their language and imagery reflect this.

- First World War literature is full of starkly contrasted images. The war generated a tendency to see things in "black and white", in terms of two-sided "splits" or contrasts, between for example:

  – "us" and "them" (the "enemy")
  – people who fought and people who stayed at home
  – soldiers at the front and high-ranking officials who gave their orders from safe places
  – men and women – men could not communicate the full horror of their experiences to women who had stayed at home, which caused misunderstanding and resentment
  – the horror of war and the comfort of home; the smart restaurants and theatres of London were sometimes no more than seventy miles from the trenches
  – the ugliness of the war-torn landscape and the beauty of nature.

- In 1914, people were filled with a patriotic fervour and idealism which, with hindsight, appears painfully naive. Young men, susceptible to propaganda, saw the war as a "big picnic", and dying for their country was regarded as an honour, or a religious duty. By the time the war ended, those who were left felt resigned or cynical. Religion no longer offered consolation, and soldiers had little to rely on except the comradeship they shared. British poetry before and early in the war tended to be lyrical and pastoral, or "Georgian", extolling nature and idealizing English country life. It is easy to see the contrast between the high-flown rhetoric and religious language used early in the war and the bitter realism, which doesn't mince words, of later writing.

● Away from the front, governments and the press – which was heavily censored – continued to present the war to the public in old-fashioned, idealized language. Soldiers were still "gallant warriors" and horses were "steeds". Writers like Siegfried Sassoon and Wilfred Owen wanted to expose this dishonesty, and poetry was a "safe" way of expressing protest. When Sassoon protested openly in a public statement, he was sent to a mental institution.

● Trench warfare generated a language of its own. As well as vocabulary associated with the trenches themselves ("dugouts", "funk-holes") and the technology of war ("whizz-bangs", "five-nines"), soldiers had their own codes and euphemisms to describe their activities. Some who were stationed in France also developed a kind of "pidgin" French.

Writers of the First World War
This is just a selection of those who have written significantly about the war.

Writers who experienced the war
Rupert Brooke: Poetry; also letters

Robert Graves: Memoir "Goodbye to All That"

R.C. Sherriff: Drama "Journey's End"

Wilfred Owen: Poetry; letters

David Jones: Memoir "In Parenthesis"

Siegfried Sassoon: Poetry; memoirs, especially the semi-fictional "Memoirs of an Infantry Officer" and "Sherston's Progress"; diaries

Ivor Gurney: Poetry; letters

Erich Maria Remarque: Memoir "All Quiet on the Western Front"

Charles Hamilton Sorley: Poetry

Julian Grenfell: Poetry

Vera Brittain: Memoir "Testament of Youth"; poetry; letters.

Later writings
Virginia Woolf: Her novel "Mrs Dalloway" includes a portrait of a shell-shocked soldier attempting to come to terms with his experience and the lack of understanding of the people around him

Sebastian Faulks: Novel "Birdsong"

Pat Barker: Novels "Regeneration", "The Eye in the Door", "The Ghost Road"; also "Another World".

Many other authors have written on the war, and their work is included in anthologies, which are a very useful way of seeing the variety of writing produced.

Consider what you have read so far. Do you think it provides a sound introduction to the theme "The First World War in Literature", or would you add any other details? Do you think some could be left out?

The student went on to look at some specific texts. The texts and extracts that the student chose were selected to demonstrate a range of different genres, styles, and points of view. These pieces could be approached in various ways.

One of the poems selected for the presentation was Laurence Binyon's poem *For the Fallen*, which was written very early in the war and is characteristic of the mood of religious, idealized, patriotic fervour.

For the Fallen

(September 1914)

With proud thanksgiving, a mother for her children,
England mourns for her dead across the sea.
Flesh of her flesh they were, spirit of her spirit.
Fallen in the cause of the free.

Solemn the drums thrill: Death august and royal
Sings sorrow up into immortal spheres.
There is music in the midst of desolation
And a glory that shines upon our tears.

They went with songs to the battle, they were young,
Straight of limb, true of eye, steady and aglow.
They were staunch to the end against odds uncounted,
They fell with their faces to the foe.

They shall grow not old, as we that are left grow old:
Age shall not weary them, nor the years condemn.
At the going down of the sun and in the morning
We will remember them.

They mingle not with their laughing comrades again;
They sit no more at familiar tables of home;
They have no lot in our labour of the day-time;
They sleep beyond England's foam.

But where our desires are and our hopes profound,
Felt as a well-spring that is hidden from sight,
To the innermost heart of their own land they are known
As the stars are known to the night.

As the stars that shall be bright when we are dust,
Moving in marches upon the heavenly plain,
As the stars that are starry in the time of our darkness,
To the end, to the end, they remain.

Laurence Binyon

Activity

1 Working on your own or with a partner, read the poem carefully and make notes. In particular, think about:

- how England and death are presented in the poem
- how the soldiers are described in stanza 3
- the effect of the form and rhythm of the poem
- the imagery of stars in stanzas 6 and 7
- how imagery, vocabulary, rhyme, rhythm, and sound are used to create the atmosphere or tone of the poem, and to reinforce the message Binyon wishes to convey
- Binyon's use of "we" for the voice of the poem
- whether the ideas in the poem are "concrete" (real, down to earth) or "abstract".

2 Use your notes to write a detailed account of the poem, suitable for use in an individual oral presentation. Include your own response to Binyon's view of what it means to die for your country.

Also selected for the presentation on the First World War were these two letters, in which young officer poets relate some of their experiences to loved ones at home. They illustrate the change in attitude that occurred between the excitement of the early months of the war and the disillusionment of the later years, as well as the different personalities of the writers. The first is from Rupert Brooke to his friend Katharine Cox, and was written from a transport ship in the Aegean Sea, between Greece and North Africa. At this stage, he can still describe the experience of war as "romantic". In the second letter, Wilfred Owen writes to his mother of the realities of "Flanders". Both letters show evidence of the censorship that prevented soldiers from giving away too much about their activities. Neither of these young men survived the war: Rupert Brooke died at sea and was buried on a small Greek island, and Owen was killed only days before the Armistice in 1918.

To KATHARINE COX

19–24 March [1915]
Somewhere
(some way from the front)

Dear Ka,

Your letter of the 3rd of March has just reached me. Fairly quick. There are said to be 80 bags of mail still (parcels, if anything, I suspect) at headquarters (here). But your letter is the only letter I've had since we sailed. It is fun getting letters. Tell people – Dudley and such – to write occasionally. I can't write much. There's very little I *could*, of interest. And that, as a rule, I *mayn't*. This letter is to be censored by the Brigade Chaplain... Here three quarters of the day is dullish – routine – and the society is unnatural – over a long period – all men. Anyway, it's nice to hear.

... Yes: this is romantic. (But I won't admit that Flanders isn't.) But I'm afraid I can't tell you most of the romantic things, at present.

My own lot have seen no fighting yet, and very likely won't for months. The only thing that seems almost certain is that one doesn't know from day to day what's to happen. The other day we – some of us – were told that we sailed next day to make a landing. A few thousand of us. Off we stole that night through the phosphorescent Aegean, scribbling farewell letters, and snatching periods of dream-broken, excited sleep. At four we rose, buckled on our panoply[1], hung ourselves with glasses compasses periscopes revolvers food and the rest, and had a stealthy large breakfast. *That* was a mistake. It is ruinous to load up one's belly four or five hours before it expects it: it throws the machinery out of gear for a week. I felt extremely ill the rest of that day.

We paraded in silence, under paling stars, along the sides of the ship. The darkness on the sea was full of scattered flashing lights, hinting at our fellow-transports and the rest. Slowly the day became wan and green and the sea opal. Everyone's face looked drawn and ghastly. *If* we landed, my company was to be the first to land... We made out that we were only a mile or two from a dim shore. I was seized with an agony of remorse that I hadn't taught my platoon a thousand things more energetically and competently. The light grew. The shore looked to be crammed with Fate, and most ominously silent. One man thought he saw a camel through his glasses...

There were some hours of silence.

About seven someone said 'We're going home.' We dismissed the stokers, who said, quietly, 'When's the next battle?'; and disempanoplied, and had another breakfast. If we were a 'feint', or if it was too rough to land, or, in general, what little part we blindly played, we never knew, and shall not. Still, we did our bit; not ignobly, I trust. We did not see the enemy. We did not fire at them; nor they at us. It seemed improbable they saw us. One of B Company – she was rolling very slightly – was sick on parade. Otherwise no casualties. A notable battle.

All is well. Good-bye.

Rupert

1 *Panoply*: full suit of armour (old-fashioned word; suggests what knights would wear)

To Susan Owen
Friday, 19 January 1917   *2nd Manchester Regiment,*
                                             British Expeditionary Force.

We are now a long way back in a ruined village, all huddled together in a farm. We all sleep in the same room where we eat and try to live. My bed is a hammock of rabbit-wire stuck up beside a great shell hole in the wall. Snow is deep about, and melts through the gaping roof, on to my blanket. We are wretched beyond my previous imagination – but safe.

Last night indeed I had to 'go up' with a party. We got lost in the snow. I went on ahead to scout – foolishly – alone – and when half a mile away from the party, got overtaken by

GAS

It was only tear-gas from a shell, and I got safely back (to the party) in my helmet, with nothing worse than a severe fright! And a few tears, some natural, some unnatural.

Part 4 Talking about literature

Here is an Addition to my List of Wants:

Safety Razor (in my drawer) & Blades

Socks (2 pairs)

6 handkerchiefs

Celluloid Soap Box (Boots)

Cigarette Holder (Bone, 3d. or 6d.)

Paraffin for Hair.

(I can't wash hair and have taken to washing my face with snow.)

Coal, water, candles, accommodation, everything is scarce. We have not always air! When I took my helmet off last night – O Air it was a heavenly thing!

Please thank uncle for his letter, and send the Compass. I scattered abroad some 50 Field Post Cards from the Base, which should bring forth a good harvest of letters. But nothing but a daily one from you will keep me up.

I think Colin might try a weekly letter. And Father?

We have a Gramophone, and so musical does it seem now that I shall never more disparage one. Indeed I can never disparage anything in Blighty again for a long time except certain parvenus living in a street of the same name as you take to go to the Abbey [*i.e. Westminster*].

They want to call No Man's Land 'England' because we keep supremacy there.

It is like the eternal place of gnashing of teeth; the Slough of Despond could be contained in one of its crater-holes; the fires of Sodom and Gomorrah could not light a candle to it – to find the way to Babylon the Fallen.

It is pock-marked like a body of foulest disease and its odour is the breath of cancer.

I have not seen any dead. I have done worse. In the dank air I have perceived it, and in the darkness, *felt*. Those 'Somme Pictures' are the laughing stock of the army – like the trenches on exhibition in Kensington.

No Man's Land under snow is like the face of the moon, chaotic, crater-ridden, uninhabitable, awful, the abode of madness.

To call it 'England'!

... Now I have let myself tell you more facts than I should, in the exuberance of having already done 'a Bit'. *It is done*, and we are all going still farther back for a long time. A long time. The people of England needn't hope. They must agitate. But they are not yet agitated even. Let them imagine 50 strong men trembling as with ague for 50 hours!

Dearer & stronger love than ever. W.E.O.

1 Read the letters carefully, thinking about the following questions:

- What are the main topics and concerns of each writer?
- In what ways are the letters alike? How do they differ?
- What is each writer's attitude to his experience of war?
- What are their attitudes to people at home – public figures and/or their family and friends?
- How is each letter influenced by the time at which it was written?
- How does each writer reveal that his words are subject to censorship?
- What evidence can you detect, from the ways they use language, that these two young soldiers are also poets?

2 Write as fully as you can about these two letters, in a form that you could use for an individual oral presentation. Examine the similarities and differences between the ways in which these young men portray their experience of war.

Now look at two poems in which the same writers reveal contrasting attitudes to death in battle. Brooke's five patriotic *Sonnets 1914* won huge popularity early in the war. For Owen, however, exposing the horror and the pity of war is the main concern.

The Dead

Blow out, you bugles, over the rich Dead!
    There's none of these so lonely and poor of old
    But, dying, has made us rarer gifts than gold.
These laid the world away; poured out the red
Sweet wine of youth; gave up the years to be
    Of work and joy, and that unhoped serene,
    That men call age; and those who would have been,
Their sons, they gave, their immortality.

Blow, Bugles, Blow! They brought us, for our dearth,
    Holiness, lacked so long, and Love, and Pain.
Honour has come back, as a king, to earth,
    And paid his subjects with a royal wage;
And Nobleness walks in our ways again;
    And we have come into our heritage.

Rupert Brooke

Futility

Move him into the sun –
Gently its touch awoke him once,
At home, whispering of fields unsown.
Always it woke him, even in France,
Until this morning and this snow.
If anything might rouse him now
The kind old sun will know.

Think how it wakes the seeds, –
Woke, once, the clays of cold star.
Are limbs, so dear-achieved, are sides,
Full-nerved – still warm – too hard to stir?
Was it for this the clay grew tall?
– O what made fatuous sunbeams toil
To break earth's sleep at all?

Wilfred Owen

Activity

Looking closely at the language and imagery of each poet, write a comparison of their attitudes to death and war.

These examples represent just a small range of the approaches that you can adopt for your individual oral presentation. The key things to remember are:

● Choose a topic or work that you are interested in.

● Discuss your ideas with your teacher.

● Prepare carefully and thoroughly.

● Make sure that your presentation focuses on aspects on which you will be assessed.

Objectives
- To think about appropriate ways of approaching exam essays, essay planning, and working under timed conditions
- To plan the revision of your set texts
- To understand how examiners will mark your work

Range of question topics

As part of your Language A1 Diploma programme you will need to sit two examinations. The first is the Commentary, which we looked at in Chapters 1–3. The second exam is the Essay paper, in which you will have 1 hour 30 minutes (Standard Level) or 2 hours (Higher Level) to answer **one** question based on at least **two** of the Part 3 works you have studied. You may include in your answer a discussion of a Part 2 work of the same genre if relevant. You will have a choice of answering on drama, poetry, prose: the novel and short story, or prose: other than the novel and short story.

The questions on this paper will focus on various aspects of the texts that you have studied and these require different approaches and different kinds of responses, depending on the specific question you are answering. But ultimately their objective is the same – to allow you to show to the best of your ability your knowledge, understanding, and informed critical response to the particular texts.

One way you can prepare yourself for the exam is to be fully aware of the various kinds of question topics you can be asked to respond to. Here are some of the topics that you might be asked to write about in the exam.

Drama
- how dramatists present characters and communicate to the audience their thoughts and motivations
- the structure of the plays
- the importance of conflicts in drama
- dramatic techniques and staging
- how dramatists present their ideas and thematic strands
- the use of language in plays.

Poetry
- features of different poets' writing
- the use of imagery
- use and effects of various poetic techniques
- use of poetic voice
- effects created through the use of structure, rhyme, rhythm
- presentation of ideas.

Prose: the novel and short story
● how writers create, present, and develop characters
● techniques writers use to open novels and short stories
● techniques writers use to bring their narrative to conclusions
● how writers present themes and ideas
● how writers use language to create different effects.

Prose (other than the novel or short story)
● how effective you have found the writing in various works
● what the writing has to say about the writers
● ideas, themes, and descriptions you have found effective
● ways in which ideas, views, and descriptions are presented.

A very useful way to begin to understand the kinds of things you might be asked in the exam is to spend time looking at past or specimen papers to become completely familiar with the format and phrasing that are commonly used in the questions. Your teacher may be able to provide you with specimen and past-paper questions, or you can obtain these from the IB.

Approaching questions
When you are presented with any question it is vital that you read it carefully to make sure you are perfectly clear about what it is asking of you. One useful tactic is to identify the key words and the focus of the question. Circle or underline the key words or phrases, and then jot down in a few words of your own what the question is asking you to focus on.

> **Activity**
>
> Practise this technique for yourself. Look at a selection of essay questions on the texts you have studied. You could take these from past papers, or use ones supplied by your teacher. Go through them identifying clearly the key words and the focus of each. It can be useful to work in pairs on this and to discuss your ideas with a partner.
>
> Becoming familiar with the phraseology and formats frequently used in such questions will help you to handle different types in the exam.

The use of quotation
Students often feel unsure about how much direct quotation to include in an answer. In any kind of literature exam, lengthy quotation is definitely not advisable. The two key points about any quotation are that it should be short and it should be relevant. Include a quotation only to illustrate a comment or to act as a discussion point. Do not be tempted to over-quote to illustrate your points. Remember: time is too short to waste on simply writing out quotations.

Examiners also say that the same few quotations crop up in essay after essay from a particular centre, as if students are parroting information from a common set of notes. Obviously, certain quotations will be particularly relevant to a question, but it is not likely that there will be only the same three or four! Think for yourself and use the material that best suits the points you want

> **Activity**
>
> 1 Choose two texts from one genre that you have studied as part of your course, and create a question based on those texts.
>
>   Your question should:
>
>   ● refer to a specific topic or idea
>
>   ● ask something quite specific which will involve looking in detail at the texts.
>
> 2 Exchange questions with a partner and plan an answer to each other's questions. Discuss the plans you make.

to make. Then you will be articulating informed, independent opinions and judgements.

It is important not only to choose your quotations carefully, but to weave them into the fabric of your writing so they become an essential part of what you have to say. Very short quotations of three or four words are best worked into the structure of your own sentences. For example:

> In this soliloquy Hamlet appears deeply depressed as he considers whether it is better "To be, or not to be...", and his mind dwells on what death might hold.

Longer quotations need to be set out on a separate line, but they should still be worked into the fabric of your argument. Avoid using a quotation that seems to be just inserted into the text of your essay and detached from the structure of your own writing, as in this example:

> Hamlet thinks that people carry on even though life is painful for them because they are afraid of the unknown and what death might hold.
> "But that the dread of something after death,
> The undiscovered country, from whose bourn
> No traveller returns, puzzles the will,
> And makes us rather bear those ills we have,
> Than fly to others that we know not of?"

This quotation would be more effective if it were integrated into the student's writing in a shortened form. As it is, it appears as a "chunk" of text lacking any sense of continuity with the student's own words. A more effective use of the same material would be:

> Hamlet thinks that people carry on even though life is painful for them because they have a
> "... dread of something after death,
> The undiscovered country, from whose bourn
> No traveller returns..."
> It is this fear that "... makes us rather bear those ills we have" than willingly go to others that are unknown.

It is not always necessary to use direct quotation to support your ideas. "With reference to the text" means just that – it is perfectly possible to refer to the text without quoting verbatim from it. You can explain the significance of a certain comment or draw examples from the text without using direct quotation at all. It is textual reference in support of your argument that matters, not quotation for its own sake. For example, this student makes the same point but without using direct quotation at all:

> Hamlet thinks that people carry on even though life is painful for them because of the fear of what might come after death. It is this fear that drives people to continue with life no matter how hard or painful, rather than go into the unknown, which might be even worse.

Remember that the whole point of using quotation or textual support is to reinforce a particular point or to support close analysis: in short, to add to the overall meaning or relevance of your essay.

Revising set texts

The texts you have studied obviously play a key role in your final assessment for your Diploma course, and it is essential that you revise them very carefully in readiness for the exam. Exactly how many texts you have studied will depend on your particular course, designed by your teacher. Your grade will depend on the quality and effectiveness of your preparation, and so it is well worth planning how you intend to revise your set texts in good time. This is not a matter that you should put off until the last minute; hasty, inadequate revision could well damage your chances of getting the grade that you want. Students who do well will show an independence of mind which reveals the ability to think for themselves and to think under the pressure of exam conditions. Revision is key to these skills.

Now let us have a look at some of the things you can do to help revise your set texts and prepare yourself for the exam.

Reading and re-reading

By this stage you will, no doubt, have read your texts a number of times. This reading and re-reading of the texts is essential to the development of your understanding and appreciation of them.

However, different kinds of reading are appropriate depending on why you are doing the reading. You may read a text quickly before you start to study it in detail. The next time you read it you will probably read it quite slowly and thoroughly so as to follow the plot carefully, to examine the ways in which the characters emerge, and to get used to the style and language used. Subsequent readings will be different again. You may skim through the text to quickly refresh your memory of the whole thing, or you may scan the text looking for particular references to images or ideas. These various readings are extremely important for a number of reasons.

- They help you to become very familiar with the text, not just in terms of the plot (although some books do need to be read several times just to sort out what is happening) but also in terms of picking up on the details of the text. Often when you re-read them you notice something new, something that you had not picked up the first, second, or even third time round.
- You tend to come to an understanding of a text over a period of time. You do not just read it, understand it, and that is that. The kinds of texts that you will have encountered need thinking about. You need to allow yourself this thinking time in order to reflect on what you have read, to absorb the material, and then return to it again.

Obviously this kind of reading is part of a developmental process which enhances your knowledge and understanding of your set texts and, therefore, it needs to be planned for over a period of time.

Time management

Time is a crucial factor in your revision programme. Building time into your programme for sufficient practice on a variety of tasks is vital. To make sure that you do this, it is advisable to draw up a revision programme to cover the build-up to the final exams. This can be quite loose in the initial stages but the closer you get to the exams, the tighter it needs to be. Make sure that you cover every aspect of assessment that you need to. Here are some basic principles to think about when drawing up your revision programme.

● Be realistic – do not overestimate how much you can get through in a given time. It is far better to start your revision programme earlier than to try to cram everything in at the last minute.

● Make sure that your programme gives the necessary attention to every text. Don't ever think "I know that one well enough so I needn't revise it". Often, when you come to revise a text that you studied months before, you remember things about it that you had forgotten or that had become hazy.

● Create a balance between revision activities which are based on reading and those which involve writing tasks. For example, as well as the various reading activities there are those involving written responses, such as practice on past papers, timed essays, and essay planning.

● Build into your programme some time off to relax. You will not work at your best if you spend all your time studying. Revision is best done with a fresh mind and in relatively short sessions with breaks. You can only take in so much at one sitting. One to two hours at a stretch is enough.

> **Activity**
>
> Try planning out a short revision programme for yourself lasting a week.
>
> If you are approaching examinations you could make the programme a little longer and use it to give some structure to your revision.

Past-paper and specimen paper questions

As part of your revision programme, try to look at as many questions from past papers as you can. The value of this lies in giving you the flavour of the question types that examiners set. Certainly, looking at past-paper questions on your texts will show you a range of topics that questions have focused on in the past, and sometimes similar questions do appear again. However, do not learn "model" answers and hope to be able to use these in the exam. If you come across specimen or model answers, regard them critically and as one possible way of answering, but do not take them to be the definitive answer. Remember, in the exam you will be expected to respond using your own ideas and thoughts, and examiners can spot immediately if you are parroting a "model" answer you have learned.

> **Activity**
>
> Gather as many questions as you can on the texts that you have studied. Draft out a rough essay plan for each of these questions. (Do not spend more than two or three minutes on each plan.)
>
> As well as giving you ideas of the types of things that have been asked about before, looking at past-paper questions will also give you a clear idea of how questions can be worded and the style in which they are presented. The more you know in this respect, the less likely you are to be thrown by question phrasing or terminology. Looking at past papers can also show up gaps in your knowledge of a set text and allow you to remedy them.

Timed essays

One of the main worries that students have in terms of answering on their set texts is how they are going to get all their ideas down in the time available. It is important that you get a good deal of practice in writing under timed conditions. You will, no doubt, do some timed pieces in class but there is no reason why you should not practise them at home as well. All you need are some suitable questions, a quiet place, and some time. In one sense it does not even matter if the work is not marked (although obviously you will get even more benefit from it if it is) – what really matters with this is building up your experience of writing against the clock. One thing is certain – the more you practise, the quicker you will get. It really will help you to speed up and it will also show you how much information you can deal with in a specified time and how well you can plan your work under time pressures.

Essay planning

Practice in essay planning should form another key part of your revision process. The best essays are those where students have thought about what they want to say before they start to write. By planning essays you can ensure that your argument is coherent and that you are using your knowledge and evidence to best effect. Essays that are not planned can easily drift away from the main point of the question or become rambling and jumbled.

In the exam itself you will have little time to spend on planning; you will feel an in-built pressure to start writing as soon as possible. However, what you do in that first two or three minutes after reading the question can be vital to the success of your answer. Practice in the build-up to the exam will help you to develop the skills to plan quickly and effectively. There are a number of things you can do to help.

- Read the question very carefully and make sure that you understand all parts of it.
- Identify which aspect or aspects of the text the question is about – use the key words approach already discussed.
- Analyse the question and note down the key topic areas it deals with.
- Briefly plan how you intend to deal with these areas – this may mean only three or four points each, summed up in a few words. The main thing is that you will have a checklist of the points you are going to cover before you begin writing your essay.

Immediately after reading the question it is likely that ideas will whiz through your mind very quickly. If you do not get these down on paper in the form of a rough plan, there is a chance you might miss out an important point in the finished essay.

As well as doing your timed essays it will also be useful preparation if you can make essay plans for as many questions as you can. This will help to get you into the routine of planning, but it will also give you the opportunity to think about a wide variety of issues related to your texts.

Writing your essay

Here are some things to bear in mind when writing your answers.

- Always begin your essay by addressing the question directly. It can be a very useful technique to use some of the words of the question in your introduction. Your introduction should give a general indication of your response to the question or summarize the approach you intend to take, perhaps stating your viewpoint. The introduction might consist of your basic essay plan, expanded a little. However, keep the introduction brief and never include biographical information or plot summary.
- An alternative way to begin your essay, and one that can be very effective, is to respond to the question by starting with a strong, perhaps contentious idea that captures the reader's attention immediately. This will launch you straight into points that will support your argument.
- Develop your points clearly, using evidence and references to the text to support your ideas.
- Assume that the examiner has read the text you are writing about and knows it extremely well, so there is no need to explain the plot or who the characters are.
- Make sure that your essay deals with all parts of the question.
- If your answer is similar to an essay you have written before, make sure that you are being relevant at all times and are not simply regurgitating a "set" answer that is in your mind. Also, avoid rehashing your notes as an answer to a question.
- Use quotations that are short and relevant.
- Make sure that your essay has a conclusion in which you sum up your arguments and analysis. It is often through the conclusion that the relevance of certain points you have made is brought into focus and the essay is given a sense of unity and completeness.

Throughout your revision period, bear in mind what you will be expected to show in the exam. Some factual knowledge will be required, but not much. That you know the "facts" about a text, the story-line, who the characters are, etc., will be taken for granted. The emphasis will be much more on showing judgement, analysis, sensitivity, and perception in your responses.

What the examiner looks for

An important person in the process of your assessment is the examiner who will mark your work. "Examiners" are not some special breed of people who spend their lives marking examination scripts. For the most part, they are practising teachers who work with students like yourself and help them to prepare for exams. However, they can mark only the work that you present to them, and the mark that is awarded depends solely on the quality of the work. It is a fallacy that one examiner might be more generous with you than another. Careful procedures are followed to ensure that the mark you receive from one examiner is just the same as the mark you would receive if another assessed your work. Indeed, it is not simply a case of one examiner looking at your work and giving a mark. Exam scripts go through a number of processes which involve responses being looked at by several people before a final mark is awarded. How well you do is up to you, not the examiner.

It is also worth dispelling another misconception that some students have concerning the role of the examiner. They picture him or her as some kind of merciless inquisitor who takes delight in catching them out. Examiners, so the thinking goes, look only for negative aspects in responses, and they ruthlessly dismantle every essay they come across. Questions are their tools, designed to catch students out.

In fact, nothing could be further from the truth. Questions are designed to let you show your knowledge to the best of your ability. Obviously examiners will not reward qualities which are not present in your responses, but they will look for the positive features in your work. Examiners take far more pleasure and satisfaction in reading good quality material that they can reward than they do in poor work that achieves poor marks. Think of the examiner as an interested and positive audience for your writing, who will award marks fairly and look positively on responses wherever there are positive qualities to be found.

The questions

Questions are rarely prescriptive. They are "open" so as to invite you to debate the issues and encourage you to develop informed judgements on the texts and the issues they raise. It is these judgements that the examiner is interested in seeing.

Where the question contains some kind of proposition, you are never expected to simply accept it. Acceptance or rejection needs to be supported with evidence and justification. One criticism frequently made by examiners is that some students simply agree with or reject the proposition, and then go on to write about something else entirely. This still happens with worrying regularity.

The key thing is to read the question and do what it says.

Technical accuracy

Clearly the ideas that you express in your answers are of primary importance. However, these ideas will be not presented most effectively if your writing suffers from various technical inaccuracies. It is, therefore, crucial that your answers are as free from technical errors as you can make them.

There are several points that examiners draw attention to in this respect.

- **Punctuation:** Ensure that you use full stops, commas, quotation marks, etc. where appropriate. It is easy for these things to be forgotten in the heat of the exam, but poor punctuation can mean that your ideas are communicated to the reader less effectively, and this may affect your mark.
- **Sentences:** Make sure that you write in sentences and that you avoid long, convoluted ones.
- **Paragraphing:** Few candidates fail to use paragraphs at all, but examiners often point to the inappropriate use of paragraphs. For example, one-sentence paragraphs should be avoided and so should excessively long paragraphs.

- **Vocabulary:** Try to vary your vocabulary without becoming verbose simply to make your essay sound more "impressive".
- **Spelling:** Obviously you should try to make your work free of spelling errors. However, in the heat of writing under exam conditions some errors may well creep in. You should do your best to check each answer as you complete it, to keep these to a minimum. If nothing else, make sure that you are spelling the titles of the texts, the names of the characters, and the names of the authors correctly. It does not give a good impression if, after two years' study, you are still writing about "Shakespear's play" or "Jayne Austin's novel".
- **Cliché, flattery, and slang:** Avoid the use of well-worn phrases such as "Jane Eyre is a victim of male domination" or "Lear acts like a man possessed". Flattery towards authors, such as "Shakespeare's portrayal of a man in emotional turmoil is second to none" or "It is clear that Keats is one of the giants of English poetry" are equally to be avoided; so are slang expressions, such as "Laertes goes ballistic when he hears about his father's death".
- **Quotation:** If you are using quotation, make sure it is accurate. If you are relying on memory, it is very easy to misquote. Perhaps all that needs to be said is that it is better not to use a quotation than to misquote or worse still "invent" a quote based on a rough idea of how it goes.

Model and prepared answers

There is nothing wrong with reading model answers as long as you use them wisely. They can be useful in presenting you with new ideas, but be aware that they represent just one way of answering a question. The examiner is interested in what *you* have to say on a particular topic or question, not what the writer of a prepared answer has to say.

Remember that the best responses are those in which your own voice can be heard. The whole point of the course that you are studying is to develop your ability to write confidently, relevantly, and thoughtfully about your ideas on the texts you have studied. Do not be afraid to use the pronoun "I" occasionally in your essays, and do not be afraid to respond genuinely to a question. Attempts to memorize prepared answers never work.

How the examiner will mark your work

Above all, examiners marking scripts are trained to be positive and flexible. The examiners will look for the good qualities in your work. They will not approach your response with a preconceived idea of an "ideal answer", but will have an open mind. They will evaluate your efforts to provide an informed, personal response to the question.

Answering the question

Examiners are always aware of students who do not read the questions carefully enough. You should make absolutely sure that you are well trained in studying carefully the exact wording of the question. Remember that the question should be the whole basis and framework of your answer.

Length

Examiners do not award marks on the basis of the length of your essay but they will look for what you have achieved in your writing. An essay may appear brief but on closer inspection it may be a succinct and well-argued response, and therefore worthy of a high mark. It is true to say, though, that essays that are very short often lack sufficient depth in the development of ideas. On the other hand, over-long essays can become repetitive, rambling and lacking in a coherent structure. Do your best to create a balanced answer.

Activity

The following is a student's answer to this essay question:

"What is noticed has been made more noticeable." How do writers of prose, other than the novel and short story, attract and sustain the reader's interest? Compare **two** or **three** prose works, other than the novel or short story, in your answer.

Read the essay carefully, making a note of its good points and where it might be improved.

Commentary

For the works "Down and Out in Paris and London" and "Running in the Family", the themes of overall poverty and someone searching for their family's past, respectively, have certainly been touched on before. Yet the authors of both of these works, George Orwell and Michael Ondaatje, manage to make these noticed themes much more noticeable, by outing a fresh spin on old themes to the end of attracting and sustaining the reader's interest.

In "Down and Out in Paris and London", George Orwell steers clear from many of the conventions in literature about poverty. George Orwell writes about poverty based on his own experience, but stays away from the cheapness of self pity in this work. He also limits, save for Chapter 22 and a few other spots, rhetorical comments on the nature of poverty, using this technique quite effectively but sparingly. Instead, the bulk of "Down and Out in Paris and London" is Orwell relating his personal experiences on the individual intricacies of poverty: "I should like to know people like Mario and Paddy and Bill the Moocher, not from casual encounters, but intimately. I should like to know what really goes on in the souls of plongeurs and tramps and Embankment sleepers," says Orwell. This attitude leads Orwell to fill the book with rich character sketches, like Charlie on the Rue du Coq d'or, Boris in the hotel, or Bozo in London, that enrich the text by putting a face on the poverty that Orwell speaks of. Orwell's dedication to relating the personal stories of poverty develops and sustains an interest in the reader that separates the book from others in the genre of literature about poverty.

Orwell is also very effective at using the structure of his work to sustain interest. After relating his rich personal experiences, Orwell sprinkles in generalized comments on poverty, which place the personal experience back in its grander context and sustains interest. For example, in Chapter VII, Orwell hooks the reader in by talking about hunger, and how, after two days of not eating, Orwell was too tired to go out and look for food "so [he] spent the day in bed reading The Memoirs of Sherlock Holmes". After drawing the reader in with an interesting and capturing phrase, Orwell goes on to make a point about how hunger reduces one to a vegetable state.

Orwell successfully bounces back and forth between personal experience and generalized comments to sustain the reader's interest. Because of this, "Down and Out in Paris and London" is both a good read and a pointed work with a strong message.

Like Orwell writing of poverty, someone writing of a search for their family has been done before but Michael Ondaatje, in "Running in the Family", is able to bring a freshness to that theme in which he manages to create and sustain a high level of interest. "Running in the Family" is strong because Ondaatje frees himself from the bonds of dictating a strict narrative of himself and his family history and rather focuses on conveying the mood of his family: "I must confess that this book is not a history but a portrait or 'gesture'… I can only say that in Sri Lanka a well told lie is worth a thousand facts," says Ondaatje about his work. This admission does wonders for the text in terms of sustaining interest. Ondaatje takes an approach where, yes, the anecdotes and tales do matter, but the meat of the theme is in the mood that is created by these stories. Ondaatje uses that mood very effectively to communicate the core essences of his family. It is not particularly important, per se, to Ondaatje or the reader, how many times the train from Colombo to Kegalle was sent back and forth by a drunk Mervyn Ondaatje, or for how many days Lalla hid an accused murderer under her neighbour's bed, or how many ways the family poultry farm could kill snakes; what is important is the meaning behind these stories, that Michael Ondaatje comes from an eccentric, free willed, and determined family, whether or not the events happened exactly as they were portrayed in the book. This approach keeps the theme very subtly sustained and maintains interest by keeping the reader constantly guessing, forced on their own to come up with the essence of the family.

Ondaatje does provide, though, a plethora of resources to the reader to develop their own essence of the family which greatly adds to the interest of the work. "Running in the Family" is a rich collage of different styles, different times, and different approaches that serve to communicate a central mood. The chapter "Tabula Asiae", for example, uses the motif of maps for Ondaatje to explore his family. Ondaatje has rich intertextuality in this chapter with references to Ptolemy, Mercator, and others, and Ondaatje follows the history of Ceylon through the use of strong imagery associated with the maps, a sea monster here and a Moorish king there. Then, Ondaatje is able to pull all of that back to his family, recounting how his Dutch ancestor married his Ceylonese ancestor. If that approach doesn't work for some readers, then the sensory details of Monsoon Notebook (i), (ii), and (iii), or the epigraphs, or the poetry, or the finely tuned narratives of broken down cars and wild parties will capture the reader's interest. Although Ondaatje takes such a diverse approach in terms of style to this work, it is particularly strong in that it manages to stick to a central theme. This makes what has been noticed (a man searching for his family) much more noticeable by approaching the search for family from several angles.

Both Orwell and Ondaatje put a fresh spin onto the themes that they wrote about in their respective works. I now know Boris, an odd former Russian soldier who hops around looking for work in the different hotels in Paris. Orwell's rich character sketches and devotion to experiencing poverty intimately made the book very interesting and put a face on poverty, attracting and sustaining a high level of interest. This is very similar to the way the rich and varied styles found in "Running in the Family" got me acquainted with the Ondaatje family and sustained my interest. George

Orwell and Michael Ondaatje, in "Down and Out in Paris and London" and "Running in the Family" respectively, are successful in using their writing techniques to create and keep alive interest, and thus make the noticed more noticeable in their works.

Assessment of your work

Your answer will be assessed against the following categories:

- knowledge and understanding of the works
- response to the question
- appreciation of literary features
- presentation
- formal use of language.

In order to achieve a good mark you need to show:

- a good understanding of the Part 3 (and Part 2) works used to answer the question
- detailed and appropriate references to the works
- that your ideas are relevant and include a personal response, where appropriate
- a detailed analysis of ideas illustrated by relevant examples
- analysis of the effects of the literary features of the works in relation to the question
- analysis that is appropriately illustrated by relevant examples
- a clear and logical structure to the essay
- supporting examples that are integrated into the body of the essay
- clear, varied, and precise use of language
- no significant lapses in grammar, spelling, and sentence construction
- effective and appropriately varied use of vocabulary, idiom, and style
- suitable choice of register.

In reading these descriptions you will see the key features that can bring you success in the exam, and to achieve them there are some basic things you can do. In fact if you are to achieve success there are certain things that you *must* do. You must make sure that:

- you have read your texts carefully several times
- you know your texts thoroughly
- you are fully aware of the issues, ideas, themes, etc. they contain
- you are aware of the stylistic features of the texts you have studied
- you can support your ideas and comments effectively.

Remember: The secret of success is to be well prepared. Know your material and know what you think about it. If you can show through your responses that you possess independent opinions and you can use these to express your "knowledge" and "understanding" of the works, then you will have every chance of achieving the success that you seek in your studies.

12 The extended essay

Objectives

- To identify the key features of the extended essay
- To identify ways in which you can approach your planning of the extended essay
- To prepare for researching and writing the essay

As well as taking six subjects, students studying for the IB Diploma have to write an extended essay of 4000 words, follow a course in Theory of Knowledge, and participate in CAS (Creativity, Action, Service). These extra requirements explain why the IB is a unique programme. This chapter will discuss the main features of the extended essay and give advice on how to complete this requirement successfully.

You have to write an extended essay to gain an IB Diploma but you only have to write it in one subject. In other words, not all English A1 students will choose to write an extended essay in English. The subject that you choose must be taught in your school, but it does not have to be a subject you are taking at Higher Level, or even a subject you are particularly good at. However, it should be a subject you like because you need to spend at least 40 hours working on it. It is also possible that your school has special policies relating to what subjects you can take. You should check this with your IB coordinator.

The extended essay is designed to give students an opportunity to acquire research skills, work independently, work on a topic they are particularly interested in, and produce a formally presented piece of structured writing. If you ask former IB students what was the most rewarding part of the IB programme, many will say that it was working on their extended essay.

The nature of the extended essay

The *Extended Essay Guide* defines the essay as "an in-depth study of a focused topic chosen from a list of approved Diploma Programme subjects". Your personal research is at the heart of this exercise. Your task is to research the topic and then present your results in a logical and coherent manner. When completed, the essay will be judged by certain criteria, which will be described later in this chapter.

The first two things you need to do are choose the subject you want to write about and find a teacher who is willing to supervise your essay. If you have decided to write about English literature, you need to find an English teacher in the school who will be your supervisor. It is wise to do this as quickly as possible, especially if the subject you have chosen is popular in your school.

Your supervisor will:

- help you to decide on a suitable topic
- help you formulate your research question
- give advice on where to find appropriate sources
- give advice on how to gather and analyse evidence
- show you how to set out your references and bibliography correctly
- advise you on how to write an abstract
- read your first draft and make comments on it.

An English A1 extended essay enables you to:

- study and research a literary topic which is narrow enough to be written about in 4000 words
- engage in a personal and critical analysis of literature and compare your views, where appropriate, with those of established critics
- develop the ability to put forward your views persuasively and in a well-structured manner, using the register appropriate for the study of literature.

There are several important stages that you should follow:

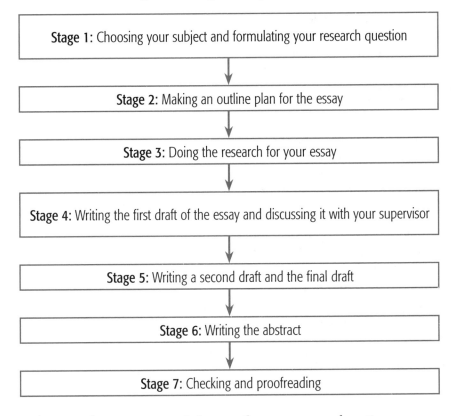

Stage 1: Choosing your subject and formulating your research question

Stage 2: Making an outline plan for the essay

Stage 3: Doing the research for your essay

Stage 4: Writing the first draft of the essay and discussing it with your supervisor

Stage 5: Writing a second draft and the final draft

Stage 6: Writing the abstract

Stage 7: Checking and proofreading

Before starting your extended essay there are several matters you need to be aware of. Most schools set up a timetable for work on extended essays, or you may devise one for yourself. It is absolutely vital that you keep to this timetable, as it is impossible to research and write your essay at the last minute. The most sensible time to do your research is during the summer holidays between the first and second years of the IB programme, as you will have time and (hopefully) access to the sources you need for research. You also need to be very sure that it will be possible for you to do the necessary research. It is very disheartening to spend a lot of time on a topic only to find that, for some reason, it is not going to result in a satisfactory outcome.

The school will have copies of the *Extended Essay Guide*. Ask your supervisor or the IB coordinator to lend you a copy so you can read for yourself the requirements and, in particular, the methods of assessment. It is also a good idea to read a few extended essays written in previous years so that you can gain some idea of the standard required.

Stage 1 The research question

An English A1 extended essay must be written in English and you must choose at least one work written in English for your research. You can write about one work or several but in practice it is not advisable to research more than three works because of the time available (40 hours) and the number of words for the essay (4000). You can compare an English work with one written in another language, but you *must* include one work written originally in English; if you don't, you will lose marks.

Having chosen English A1 as your subject, and found a teacher who is willing to be your supervisor, the next step is to decide on the topic you would like to research. The topic is the basis for your research question, and it can be indicated by a thesis statement or as a question. For example, you could choose to write about death imagery in the poetry of Sylvia Plath. This can be written as: "Sylvia Plath's poetry is saturated with images of death" or "Is Sylvia Plath's poetry always concerned with death?" By stating the topic in the form of a question, you are less likely to set about proving a thesis and (possibly) ignoring any evidence that is contradictory; you are more likely to carry out an investigation into whether your ideas are valid. The latter approach tends to result in a better essay, but both forms are acceptable.

It is vital that your choice of research topic is neither too broad, too narrow, too obvious or too difficult. To research all of Plath's poetry would be too broad; for a successful essay, it would be necessary to limit the number of poems you have to analyse. Depth is always rewarded more than breadth. Some candidates choose questions that are too obvious, For example, the question "Is *Romeo and Juliet* a love story?" is far too easy. Everyone knows the answer.

Works from any genre may be chosen for study. Works do not need to be on the Prescribed Book List which schools use to choose their syllabuses. This means that you can use a book that has been published very recently.

It is essential that the focus of your essay should be literary. This means that you should not treat fictional works as if they were giving factual evidence of social or psychological conditions. You are not writing a sociological, psychological, philosophical, political or biographical essay, though you may show how such aspects are presented. In a literary essay you must always remember that there is an author who has deliberately chosen to present ideas, characters and scenes in a certain way.

Sometimes candidates have problems distinguishing between the terms "topic", "title" and "research question". Obviously they are related, but there are slight differences. An example may help to clarify the position. A student has decided that she is interested in how judicial systems are presented in literature, and has decided to compare the court scenes in Camus's *The Outsider* with the court scenes in Harper Lee's *To Kill a Mockingbird*. The title could be: "The trials of Meursault and Tom Robinson". The topic is "Law and justice in works by Camus and Harper Lee", while the research question could be phrased as: "How are the judicial systems in *The Outsider* and *To Kill a Mockingbird* presented by their respective authors?"

Here are some points to remember.

- Choose a topic that interests you. You will be spending quite a lot of time on this essay.
- Make sure your topic is limited enough in scope to allow you to examine it in depth.
- Choose a topic where you are able to collect and research information that you can analyse and use as evidence.
- Make sure your topic is a literary one.
- Make sure that at least one of your works has been written originally in English.

For English A1 you can write under two categories.

Category 1

The essay should be based on a work or works written in English.

Here are some examples of suitable research topics in this category:

- the influences of fairy tales in the work of Angela Carter
- compare Sebastian Faulks's descriptions of battle scenes in *Birdsong* with those of Timothy Findlay in *The Wars*
- the contours of the New Zealand landscape in selected poems by James Baxter
- G.B. Shaw's presentation of class distinctions in *Pygmalion*.

Category 2

Essays in this category should be a comparison of at least one work written in English with a work or works written in another language, and probably studied in translation. Examples are:

- compare the ways in which G.B. Shaw and Jean Anouilh present Joan of Arc
- the importance of religion in *The Poisonwood Bible* by Barbara Kingsolver and in *Silence* by Shusako Endo.

Here is a summary of Stage 1:

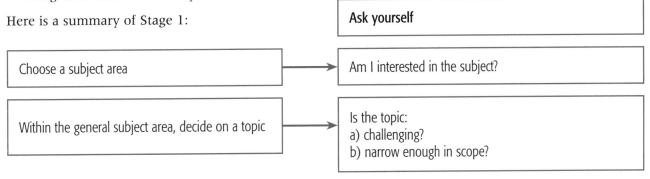

Ask yourself

Choose a subject area → Am I interested in the subject?

Within the general subject area, decide on a topic → Is the topic:
a) challenging?
b) narrow enough in scope?

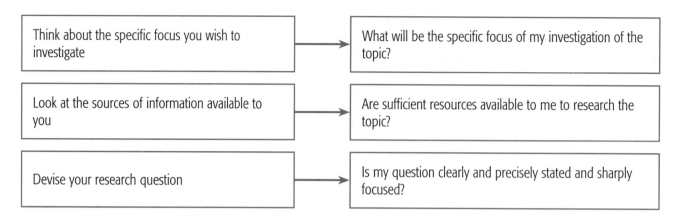

Stage 2 Making an outline plan

Having read the chosen text(s) and decided on your topic and the wording of your research question, it is important then to sketch out a plan of how you are likely to organize your essay. You do not need to keep to this plan; in fact, after you have done your research you are very likely to make changes in it, but at least you will have a working model to act as a guide. It may save you from veering off in irrelevant directions and thereby wasting your time. You should discuss the plan with your supervisor, who can advise you on whether it is likely to lead to a satisfactory essay. Your supervisor can also suggest lines of research; he or she may indicate where to start, and will, perhaps, give you a list of resources.

Activity

Make an outline plan of your essay and show it to your supervisor. You can always make amendments to this at a later stage.

Here is a summary of Stage 2:

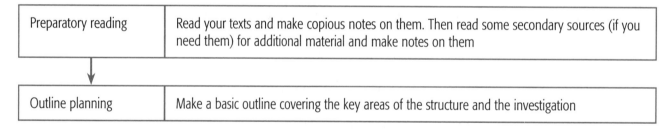

Stage 3 The research process

Re-reading: The first thing you need to do is re-read the works you will be writing about. Either during this reading, or the next, you should annotate the work to mark passages you will use as evidence for your argument. If you cannot write on the text you are researching then you will need to make separate notes on cards or in a folder.

Secondary sources: It is not essential for you to read literary critics when you are writing an English A1 essay. It all depends on your authors. Make sure you test information gained from critics, as this can be misleading. You may, however, need to read up on background material, especially if the work is set in a country or time you are unfamiliar with.

Taking notes: You will save yourself a lot of time later if you are careful about how you take notes right from the beginning. Some researchers keep their notes on cards, with a separate card for each book; others use separate sheets of paper which they keep in a folder. Using separate sheets or cards enables you to move them round or discard them if necessary. *Always* write down the author, title, publisher and date of any work you are researching; do this before you begin reading. If you don't, then months later, when you have returned the book to the library, or to a friend, or left it in some other part of the world, you will have a terrible time trying to recover this vital information for your bibliography.

Quotations: If you are recording quotations from a work, make sure you mark them clearly as quotations in your notes and write down the page numbers of the book the quotations come from. It is very easy to copy out a quotation and then write a comment of your own beside it. When you read the notes later you may not realize which are your words and which are someone else's. This can lead to your being accused of plagiarism.

Plagiarism: What is plagiarism? This is defined by the IB in a publication entitled *Academic Honesty: Guidance for Schools* as: "the representation of the ideas or work of another person as the candidate's own". This doesn't mean that you can't use other people's ideas or words. You may, as long as you acknowledge your sources. There will be more about how to present bibliographies and referencing later. It is important for you to be aware of the dangers of plagiarism, for if an examiner thinks you have plagiarized you may be accused of malpractice, which could result in your failing to gain the diploma. The IB regards plagiarism as a very serious offence.

Sources: Here is a list of sources you may possibly use.
- First and foremost, for a literary essay your main source is the text or texts you have chosen to analyse. The essay will be judged primarily on your interpretation of your chosen text(s).
- Critical works – either whole works or parts of them.
- Articles from magazines, periodicals or newspapers.
- The Internet. Be careful of this source as it can be unreliable; ask your supervisor for advice.
- Information from CD ROMs relating to your research question.

While taking notes:
1 Read the material through first; you cannot decide what is relevant until you have read the main ideas of the writer.
2 Focus on the key points; try not to be distracted by information that may be interesting but is irrelevant.
3 Use your own words for the bulk of your notes, rather than copying out the text word for word; when you read your notes again you are more likely to understand them, and this way you are less likely to be accused of plagiarism. This does not mean that you should not acknowledge your sources in your bibliography.
4 Note page references so that you can go back and check them if necessary.
5 Make a note of all the relevant details of the sources: author, title etc.

Stage 4 First draft

Students often find that starting to write their essay is quite difficult. Some are very reluctant to construct an adequate plan before starting to write their essay, but with an exercise as complex as the extended essay it is essential that you should construct an adequate, detailed plan. The outline that you made when you first started this research project could still be a workable model, or merely need some adjustment. It is possible that you may need to make an entirely different plan, depending on what you have discovered through your research.

After you have made your plan, you can start writing the essay. Don't forget that this is only a first draft. The main thing is to set out your ideas, which you can revise and edit later.

The first draft needs to have the following.

1   An introduction, in which you state the research question (either as a thesis or a question) and give reasons why you have chosen it. Lengthy biographical or historical accounts should be avoided as they do not explain the significance of your choice of topic. Many candidates think they have to include biographical details of their authors, but this is only necessary if they are directly relevant to the research question.

2   The body of the essay, consisting of an argument supported by evidence from the primary sources. This is where it is easy to go astray if you have no clear plan of what you want to say. You may have gathered a lot of material which is not easy to organize effectively. Don't worry too much at this point; it will be easier to correct after you have written the first draft.

3   A conclusion, which must be clearly linked to both the research question and the argument in the body of the essay. It should not, however, just be a repetition of what you have already stated in the introduction. It should present a new interpretation in the light of the preceding discussion.

After you have written your first draft you should give it to your supervisor, who will read it and then discuss with you how to improve it. It may need better organization, more evidence from the primary source(s), or improvements in the technical accuracy of your writing.

Stage 5 Further drafts and final draft

Once you have finished your first draft and discussed it with your supervisor, it is time to revise and edit your work. If all goes well, your second draft may be your final draft, but it is very possible that you may feel you need another rewrite. You may find you have so much material that you have written more than 4000 words. Examiners do not have to read beyond this word limit. This means that you must prune your work to 4000 words or you will lose marks.

There are different ways of approaching revision and editing, but it is useful to read through your work, marking any alterations, deletions or corrections with a range of coloured pens. Most candidates write their essays on computers, so moving sections and making alterations is relatively easy. If you want your extended essay to be an excellent one, then you need to read and reread your essay to make sure that your argument is clear and your English is correct.

Here is a summary of stages 4 and 5:

Structuring your material	Plan your work carefully so that you present your material in a logical way that develops your points from one to another

The first draft	You will certainly need to write one draft of your essay but be prepared to re-draft as much as you need to in order to produce a "polished" final piece of work

Revising and editing	Effective revising and editing is an essential part of producing a good essay. Don't be afraid to make changes if you need to

The final draft	Work on revisions and drafts until you are happy with your finished essay

Organizing your essay	Make sure that your work is organized and that all the required sections are complete

Stage 6 The abstract

Many candidates have problems writing their abstracts, because they're not sure what they should do. It is, in fact, fairly straightforward. It must not be more than 300 words in length and it has only three requirements.

1 A clear statement of your research question. You can just write, for example: "My research consists of an investigation into the use of symbolism in *1984* by George Orwell".
2 An account of the scope of the essay. This raises problems because the word "scope" can be interpreted in different ways; for English A1 you need to explain what the focus of the investigation was and what your sources were.
3 A brief summary of your conclusion.

It is important to remember that the abstract is *not* the same as the introduction, and in it you are not required to explain why you have chosen your topic. Nor are you expected to summarize the whole essay. Normally, the abstract is written last so that it reflects what you have done, rather than what you intended to do.

Stage 7 The final check

Before handing in your essay, you need to put it into the order required by the IB. The order in which the essay must be presented is as follows.

1 **The title page:** This should give the title of the essay, the research question if the wording is different, your name, your number and the name of your school.

2 **The abstract:** This should be printed on one side of a separate page and placed immediately after the title page.

3 **The contents:** This should give your main section headings with their page numbers. It should also be on a separate page.

4 **The essay:** This consists of the introduction, main body and conclusion.

5 **Footnotes or endnotes:** These will not appear at the end of the essay if they are already present within the body of the essay. See the comments under "Formal presentation" on the opposite page.

6 **The bibliography:** Include all the sources you have used for the essay.

7 **Appendix:** Literary essays do not usually require appendices. However, if you are researching the poems of a poet who is not very well known, the examiner will be grateful if you print the poems you are analysing in an appendix.

A final check should also make sure that the essay is not longer than 4000 words, that the pages are numbered, that spelling and punctuation have been checked, that all references have been acknowledged and that the general presentation and appearance of the essay are excellent. In other words, you must proofread your essay before handing it in.

Assessment criteria

Your essay is marked by an external examiner, who will use the following criteria to decide your grade. For a complete outline of the assessment criteria, consult the official IB *Extended Essay Guide*. The following is an explanation of what each criterion covers.

A: Research question

To gain full marks the research question must be stated clearly at the beginning of the essay (not just on the title page) and it must be appropriate for research for English A1. It can be stated as a question or as a proposition for discussion.

B: Introduction

The introduction should focus on the research question and give the reasons for choosing it. You do not need to give a lengthy historical or biographical background for the author(s), but you should explain why you think your research is worth doing.

C: Investigation

Marks for this criterion are given for careful planning and the use of resources. The most important resource for a literary essay is the work or works that you have chosen to write about. You may, but you do not have to, read published criticism on your author(s).

D: Knowledge and understanding of the topic studied

Your understanding of, and engagement with, your primary text or texts is the most important concern of this criterion.

E: Reasoned argument

There must be a clear argument running through the essay which is based on your analysis of the topic. You will not gain marks from merely stating unsupported personal views, or for plot summaries.

F: Application of analytical and evaluative skills

If your essay is purely descriptive or relies entirely on second-hand interpretations, you will lose marks here.

G: Use of language

You are judged as a native speaker of English, even if you are not one. Your writing style needs to be fluent, clear and accurate.

H: Conclusion

Your conclusion must be consistent with the argument of the essay. You should not just repeat what you said in the introduction. From the argument in the body of the essay you should have developed a convincing interpretation of the text(s).

I: Formal presentation

This relates to whether your essay conforms to the way academic research papers should be presented. It concerns the bibliography, references or citations, page numbers, contents page and the appearance of the whole essay. If any of these elements are missing, you will lose marks. There are a number of different styles you can use when you set out your bibliography and record your references. Your supervisor will give you help as to which one to use. Most importantly, you must be consistent.

A bibliography is an alphabetical list of every source used to research and write the essay. The author, title, date and publisher are normally required for each source.

A reference is the way in which you indicate to the reader where specific information has come from. References must be given whenever someone else's work is quoted or summarized. Whether placed as endnotes or as footnotes, references are numbered within the text of the essay. It is important to realize that footnotes are for information only. They must not be used as a way of getting around the word limitation. Quotations or explanations that are an integral part of the essay should not be put in the footnotes.

A citation is a shorthand method of making a reference in the body of an essay, which is then linked to a full reference at the end of the essay. In both a reference and a citation, you must give page numbers so the examiner can check your accuracy.

J: The abstract

Your abstract is judged on how clearly you state the three required elements (see page 259).

K: Holistic judgement

This criterion allows examiners to award marks for creativity and insight. Routine essays on well-worn subjects do not score highly here.

It is not always easy to understand what is required merely by reading about it. Below you will find an example of parts of a successful literary extended essay; these are the parts where you are most likely to make mistakes.

The title of the essay is: "The Two Emilies".

The topic is: "The poetry of Emily Brontë and Emily Dickinson".

The research question is: "Do Emily Brontë and Emily Dickinson exhibit similar attitudes to nature and death in their poetry?"

Commentary: The two Emilies

Abstract

Emily Brontë and Emily Dickinson share more than just a name. They were both female writers in the nineteenth century, a time when it was still not easy for women to have their writing published. They both wrote extensively about nature and death. My research question is: Do Emily Brontë and Emily Dickinson exhibit similar attitudes to nature and death in their poetry?

As it would be impossible to discuss all of the poetry written by the two Emilies, I have concentrated on comparing and analysing the following poems by Emily Brontë: "I said, Go, gentle singer"; "I'm happiest when most away"; "In the earth, the earth, thou shalt be laid"; "Shall earth no more inspire me"; and by Emily Dickinson: "What mystery pervades a well!"; "I felt a funeral in my brain"; "A great Hope fell"; "Death is the supple Suitor"; "Safe in their Alabaster Chambers–". I have also consulted a range of secondary sources, some of which threw light on the interweaving of nature and death that can be found in both writers.

The similarities that I found in the works of Brontë and Dickinson were surprising. The importance of nature in their lives, its magnetic force as an inspiration and the retreat it provided them from the isolation they felt from society were all too obvious. What was more striking was that just as society had failed them, so, in the end, did nature. Only in death did they feel that they would find both peace and the answers they sought to what was the meaning of life.

The abstract has been divided into three paragraphs to indicate clearly the different elements. It is not necessary to set it out in this manner.

Commentary: Introduction

Female poets in the middle of the nineteenth century, whether in England or America, were not in the most agreeable of positions. In that period it was generally accepted that the role of women was confined to the home and all its associated chores. The literary world of the time revolved round such names as Byron, Emerson, Wordsworth and Keats and poetry by women in this pre-emancipation society had difficulty in being acknowledged. Under these conditions it is not difficult for the reader to understand that the suppressed poetic genius of women who could not blossom freely outwards was likely to turn inwards and inflict considerable suffering to their minds, souls and bodies.

My original interest in Emily Brontë and Emily Dickinson arose from the fact that they had the same name, but that proved to be the least significant similarity between them. Although an ocean separated the two great literary minds, the connections between them are striking. Each lived an intimate family life, was fully absorbed in the natural world, strove to find liberty for the soul, shared a fascination with death and defied societal expectations by determinedly putting their thoughts on paper. As Paul Ferlazzo has written of Emily Dickinson: "In choosing to devote herself to the pursuit of great art, she challenged and rejected the psychic and social stereotyped images of the women of her era." (1) In this essay I investigate the similarities between the two Emilies. To what extent are their attitudes to nature and death the same?

Note that the research question appears at the end of the introduction. It can be included at any point.

Commentary: Conclusion

Not only did the subjects of nature and death bind these two introverted women closely together, but the question that seemed to tease them both was: what is the real answer to the question of the meaning of life? The answer was not to be found in society; nor could they find it within themselves, regardless of inner inspiration and heightened spiritual experiences. They turned to mysticism and away from faith in a traditional God but even this did not satisfy them. Dickinson and Brontë finally came to the realization that the answer could only be found in death. Combined with a growing curiosity about death, each was also confronted with the battle of exchanging an earth which was beautiful for the uncertainties of finding answers in a world that lay beyond. The deaths of both Emilies at an early age lead us to assume that nature could no longer satisfy the requirements of such complex minds. Both died with the belief that they were reaching a realm of higher spiritual enlightenment, as Dickinson writes in her farewell:

> Good-by to the life I used to live
> And the world I used to know;
> And kiss the hills for me, just once;
> Now I am ready to go.

13 Theory of Knowledge in the English A1 course

> **Objectives**
> - To identify areas where knowledge issues are relevant to the reading and writing you must do in this course
> - To encourage you to maintain a consciousness and appreciation of many elements that are involved in the study of language and literary art

Knowledge

The acquisition of "knowledge" is certainly on the agenda for your English A1 course. You will come to "know" texts, that is to have read and studied the works themselves. You will become acquainted with the social and historical contexts in which these works have been produced. The biographies of the writers and perhaps of some of their contemporaries are often included in your work with the texts. You will encounter many human issues, including moral dilemmas and the complexity of relationships, and you will be asked to become aware of and articulate about the artistry involved in literature.

You may also study how the texts have been received. You will be involved in knowing how people have spoken and written about these texts, and will be speaking and writing about them yourselves. The latter, especially, requires knowledge of the language of the discipline. You will need to know literary terminology and the forms in which literary knowledge is delivered: journal entries, commentaries and essays as well as novels, poems, and plays.

Always in English courses and those of other literatures, issues of **language** are implicitly and explicitly addressed, as well as issues of art – the **aesthetic** matters mentioned above. Clearly the goals of this kind of study are for you to become sensitive to what is involved in using language in artistic ways, but also in persuasive (or **rhetorical**) ways. The course, therefore, views you as a **reader**, a **writer**, and an **evaluator**.

In the International Baccalaureate, a course required for all diploma candidates is called the **Theory of Knowledge**. At the centre of this course is you, the knower or learner.

In this course you are asked to reflect on yourself as a knower and to consider the ways of knowing and the areas of knowledge. "How do I know what I know?" is a constant consideration in this course.

Consider your study of a novel in this English course. Once you have read *Great Expectations*, for example, you can say that you now "know" this novel. You know the construct that Dickens has created with language – the "world" in which Pip and Estella and Miss Havisham operate. You will be aware of how Dickens uses language, creates characters and events, raises issues about human behaviour and choices. You may also venture into how the novel is like and unlike other novels you have read, and into questions about whether this is a "good" novel and why. Clearly, you are involved here with issues of knowledge and knowledge claims, "their underlying assumptions and their implications" (*Theory of Knowledge Guide*).

What follows is not an outline of a Theory of Knowledge course – which will happen elsewhere in your programme – but a few suggestions about how some of the concerns of Theory of Knowledge are involved throughout your English course, and some examples of how these two pursuits may touch upon each other. You will see a few examples of how one of the **ways of knowing** – language – and one of the **areas of knowledge** – literary art – are implicit and can be made explicit in your study for English A1.

There are, as you will discover in your Theory of Knowledge course, many ways to view the relation of language to knowledge, to thought and to truth. In the English A1 course, one of the primary considerations is the "clothing" of thought, the ways language is used to produce the "skin" of thought. Within the language, there are almost infinite choices of words to use and ways to use them. These choices made by a writer are artistic and rhetorical decisions about language and the structuring of language – something we call **style**.

As soon as we propose the word "style" to be used in our discussions, we encounter one of the most significant problems of the literary discipline: the problem of clarity of language when we talk about literary art. The issue of **literary terminology** is a vexing one, and leads us into many of the basic issues about language that will arise in other areas of knowledge as well, particularly in the human sciences and ethics, for example.

Terms we use to talk about literary art

Language is, of course, an essential tool for conveying what we know, for checking the validity of our claims about knowledge, and is necessary to all areas of knowledge. In English A1, language is not only what we use to convey our perceptions, but also the **matter** that we study and discuss, argue about, and evaluate.

However, we discover some considerable problems when we use abstract terms such as **style**, **symbol**, **image**, or **tone**. The first problem is that when we discuss what we observe about the choices authors make, much of the language we use has counterparts in the ordinary language of everyday usage; in fact, it is often derived from such usage. For example, we may observe that a certain person has a considerable amount of **style** in the clothes he chooses to wear, or that a **style** of behaviour is not acceptable in a particular context. You may have been told to "change your **tone**" by a parent, or that the **image** you have of yourself is not the one that other people have of you.

> *"Language is the skin on my thought."*
> Arundhati Roy, quoted in
> *The God of Small Things:
> A Reader's Guide*, John Mullaney

So we find ourselves constantly working to refine and clarify our terminology for talking about literary art. If we are to understand what other people are proposing about a piece of literature, we need to have a clear understanding of the terms they use.

In the case of some terms, we can be on somewhat firmer ground. Terms that are derived from manuals of rhetoric or poetics in classical or medieval times, such as **apostrophe**, **pathos**, or **paronomasia**, are generally more precise and can be used with a common consensus about their meaning and usage.

Activity

Choose a term that you find you have used often in writing commentaries or essays about literary works, and either through your library or by using the Internet, compare several definitions, such as those in dictionaries of literary terms, or the results of web searches.

Other problems with literary terminology

Very often students will say the difficulties they have in reading a passage or poem are caused by the writing being too "abstract". While sometimes this term is used to mean "difficult", "elusive" or simply incomprehensible for a particular reader, there is some basis for using "abstract" in this very imprecise way. Abstractions are elusive, and some believe they are dangerous not only to communication but to a survivable world order. Here we come to one of the crucial points where the conversations in your Theory of Knowledge course and your English course are likely to converge.

The mathematician and semanticist Alfred Korzybski (in his book *Science and Sanity*) and the economist and engineer Stuart Chase were both troubled by the difficulties posed by what Chase identifies as a kind of curse, the widespread use of high-level abstractions. "I found it almost impossible to read philosophy," says Chase, in discussing these linguistic problems in *The Tyranny of Words*. "The great words went round and round in my head until I became dizzy. Sometime they made pleasant music, but I could rarely effect passage between them and the real world of experience."

According to Chase, in Korzybski's view abstractions are one of the factors that have "deflected straight thinking for centuries". In Chase's discussions of language, he discerns three levels of language, as follows.

1   Labels for common objects such as "pencil" or "dog". Here we are, he proposes, on pretty safe ground.
2   Labels for clusters and collections, such as "the courts" or "the white race", where we can already see the process of abstraction increasing.
3   Abstractions, such as "love", "knowledge", or "international understanding".

It is at this level 2 or 3 that we can see the connection to literary terminology and its problems, because we tend to use terms from the general vocabulary and adapt them for use in literary criticism, and many terms are level 3 words or abstractions.

"It sometimes seems to me that a pestilence has struck the human race in its most distinctive faculty – that is, the use of words. It is a plague afflicting language… an automatism that tends to level out all expression into the most generic, anonymous and abstract formulas, to dilute meanings, to blunt the edge of expressiveness, extinguishing the spark that shoots out from the collision of new words and new circumstances."
Italo Calvino, *Six Memos for the Next Millennium*

For example, what do we mean when we say that "the **style** of this writer is **tonally complex**, but the **richness** of the **imagery** is what makes the **effect** of the poem **memorable**"?

The aim must be to reduce the semantic difficulties we encounter when we read literary criticism or write it, as you are often asked to do in the English A1 course. To do this, we need to bear in mind:

- the need to work towards precision in our understanding of literary terms
- the elusiveness and ambiguity that are inherent in the terms
- the problems of the reliability of our knowledge
- the difficulty of clear communication.

This will help us to think not only about the particular terms we use, but about the way we use language in other disciplines and how our daily use of language either diminishes or contributes to our understanding of the world and of other people.

Activity

Choose a piece of your own writing for this course and discuss it with another person, first underlining some of the literary terms you have used and then investigating whether you are communicating clear meanings to the other person. See how clearly either of you can define the terms for style that you have used.

Ambiguity

One of the most interesting language issues – and there are many – that is related to the study of *belles-lettres* (an expressive French term used to describe literary art), is the issue of **determinacy/ indeterminacy** or **ambiguity**. Because literature attempts to do a good deal more than simply deliver information or plead a cause, **ambiguity** is often a planned choice on the part of writers, perhaps more frequently in poetry than in other forms such as novels or drama.

Why might that be? Since literature seeks to express emotion, personal experience or insight, and the subtleties of the human condition, often these matters do not lend themselves to straightforward, unequivocal language. So while in many kinds of discourse, such as scientific work, ambiguity is not at all desirable, this may not be the case in literature.

Again, students encountering ambiguity in a piece of literary art will often resort to asserting that it is "too abstract". Perhaps what they mean is that they find in the work a kind of **indeterminacy** which troubles or eludes them. Words tend to go well beyond their **denotative** usage in the hands of inventive writers. Does the writer mean to imply, for example, that no conclusion can be drawn about a character, or that an emotion is so complex that we have no exact terms for it? Or that there is a great deal more to this character or these events than meets the eye? That the choice that is made or the event that occurs cannot truly be named, or fully understood?

"The communicating of ideas… is not the chief and only end of language, as is commonly supposed… There are other ends, as the raising of some passion, the exciting to or deterring from some action, the putting of the mind in some particular disposition…"
Bishop George Berkeley,
Treatise Concerning the Principles of Human Knowledge (1710)

Activity

What does Kafka mean to tell us or show us in the following short parable, *An Imperial Message*? (A parable, as you know, is a story which poses or answers a question or points to a moral or message.)

The Emperor, so a parable runs, has sent a message to you, the humble subject, the insignificant shadow cowering in the remotest distance before the imperial sun; the Emperor from his deathbed has sent a message to you alone. He has commanded the messenger to kneel down by the bed, and has whispered the message to him; so much store did he lay on it that he ordered the messenger to whisper it back into his ear again. Then by a nod of the head he has confirmed that it is right. Yes, before the assembled spectators of his death – all the obstructing walls have been broken down, and on the spacious and loftily mounting open staircases stand in a ring the great princes of the Empire – before all these he has delivered his message. The messenger immediately sets out on his journey; a powerful, an indefatigable man; now pushing with his right arm, now with his left, he cleaves a way for himself through the throng; if he encounters resistance he points to his breast, where the symbol of the sun glitters; the way is made easier for him than it would be for any other man. But the multitudes are so vast; their numbers have no end. If he could reach the open fields how fast he would fly, and soon doubtless you would hear the welcome hammering of his fists on your door. But instead how vainly does he wear out his strength; still he is only making his way through the chambers of the innermost palace; never will he get to the end of them; and if he succeeded in that nothing would be gained; he must next fight his way down the stair; and if he succeeded in that nothing would be gained; the courts would still have to be crossed; and after the courts the second outer palace; and once more stairs and courts; and once more another palace; and so on for thousands of years; and if at last he should burst through the outermost gate – but never, never can that happen – the imperial capital would lie before him, the center of the world, crammed to bursting with its own sediment. Nobody could fight his way though here even with a message from a dead man. But you sit at your window when evening falls and dream it to yourself.

Franz Kafka

Often the ambiguity in literary art is frustrating to students. However, it can be argued that ambiguity produces the richness and complexity that makes literature so provocative and compelling. One literary critic, William Empson, wrote a book called *Seven Types of Ambiguity* in which he explored the many ways in which the nuances of ambiguity can enhance statements and thus the experience of the receiver or reader.

While all this may make reading literature sound like very hard work, think how many times you have watched a film without being convinced that you had grasped everything, and wanted to look at it again to sort out those ambiguities.

While often there are ambiguities in plots, or in the behaviour of characters, writers can – simply through patterning a few words –

add another dimension to a narrative that gives us both knowledge and an intriguing uncertainty. The story of the interaction of two characters in E.M. Forster's novel, *A Passage to India*, is a helpful example.

In Forster's novel, Mrs Moore is a British woman who has accompanied her daughter to India. Adela, the daughter, needs to decide whether she wants to marry a British civil servant who is stationed there. Professor Godbole, a Hindu Brahmin, is one of the few Indians that Mrs Moore meets. Early in the story, at a social occasion in the home of Fielding, an educator, Professor Godbole is asked to sing.

'I may sing now,' he replied, and did.

This thin voice rose, and gave out one sound after another. At times there seemed rhythm, at times there was the illusion of a Western melody. But the ear, baffled repeatedly, soon lost any clue, and wandered in a maze of noises, none harsh or unpleasant, none intelligible...

'Thanks so much; what was that?' asked Fielding.

'I will explain in detail. It was a religious song. I placed myself in the position of a milkmaiden. I say to Shri Krishna: "Come! Come to me only." The God refuses to come. I grow humble and say: "Do not come to me only. Multiply yourself into a hundred Krishnas, and let one go to each of my hundred companions, but one, O Lord of the Universe, come to me." He refuses to come. This is repeated several times. The song is composed in a raga appropriate to the present hour, which is the evening.'

'But He comes in some other song, I hope?' said Mrs Moore, gently.

'Oh no, He refuses to come,' repeated Godbole, perhaps not understanding her question. 'I say to Him, Come, come, come, come, come, come. He neglects to come.'

... there was a moment of absolute silence. No ripple disturbed the water, no leaf stirred.

E.M. Forster

The ambiguity here is generated certainly by cultural issues, but also by the pivot of meaning created by the word "come", and its use by the two people in dialogue. For both Mrs Moore and Adela, it seems to provoke a certain apathy; a later passage tells us:

> Ever since Professor Godbole had sung his queer little song, they had lived more or less inside cocoons, and the difference between them was that the elder lady accepted her own apathy, while the younger resented hers.

What begins here with one word evolves into a significant issue for Mrs Moore, in terms of her understanding of both Hindu spiritual culture and her own Christian faith. In a later visit to the Marabar Caves, she is caught in a crowd in one of these dark spaces, and hears a single sound – "Boum". Again a single syllable, an onomatopoeic sound, has a great impact and reverberates as a profoundly disturbing echo for Mrs Moore:

> But suddenly, at the edge of her mind, Religion appeared, poor little talkative Christianity, and she knew that all its divine words from 'Let there be light' to 'It is finished' only amounted to 'boum'.

Shortly after these experiences, Mrs Moore decides abruptly to return to England and, partly because she does so in exceptionally hot weather, dies on the voyage. Interestingly, David Lean's film version of the novel has Professor Godbole appear, framed enigmatically in an arch of the railway station, as Mrs Moore's train to the port is pulling out of the station. What might be intended by this addition to Forster's novel?

From all of this, what are we to make of Forster's combination of the words "come", "apathy", and "boum"? For most readers, Mrs Moore's experience is somewhat ambiguous. Does her desire to connect with India render her own faith meaningless? Does she experience an existential crisis? Does she fall prey to despair, or a loss of identity, having seen the behaviour of colonial Britain in India? And further, do these uncertainties diminish the novel, or does the ambiguity enhance it?

Activity

Below are two poems. After discussing each with a group, explore these questions:

- What do you think you know about the situation described?

- What do you know for certain?

- What is ambiguous about the poem?

- What has ambiguity contributed to your experience of the poem? In what ways has it diminished your enjoyment of the poem?

- What is your opinion, at this point, of the values or problems of ambiguity in literary art?

- How reliable do you find the "knowledge" arrived at in your group?

Glass

Words of a poem should be glass
But glass so simple-subtle its shape
Is nothing but the shape of what it holds.

A glass spun for itself is empty,
Brittle, at best Venetian trinket.
Embossed glass hides the poem or its absence

Words should be looked through, should be windows.
The best word were invisible.
The poem is the thing the poet thinks.

If the impossible were not
And if the glass, only the glass,
Could be removed, the poem would remain.

Robert Francis

Notes from a Nonexistent Himalayan Expedition

So these are the Himalayas.
Mountains racing to the moon.
The moment of their start recorded
on the startling, ripped canvas of the sky.
Holes punched in a desert of clouds.
Thrust into nothing.
Echo – a white mute.
Quiet.

Yeti, down there we've got Wednesday,
bread and alphabets.
Two times two is four.
Roses are red there,
and violets are blue.

Yeti, crime is not all
we're up to down there.
Yeti, not every sentence there
means death.

We've inherited hope –
the gift of forgetting.
You'll see how we give
birth among the ruins.

Yeti, we've got Shakespeare there.
Yeti, we play solitaire
and violin. At nightfall,
we turn lights on, Yeti.

Up here it's neither moon nor earth.
Tears freeze.
Oh Yeti, semi-moonman,
turn back, think again!

I called this to the Yeti
inside four walls of avalanche,
stomping my feet for warmth
on the everlasting
snow.

Wislawa Szymborska

Theory of Knowledge and the art of literature

In one section of James Joyce's novel about the evolution of the artist, Stephen Daedalus (the hero) is struggling to put into words what he perceives to be a valid theory of **aesthetics**.

There are many ways to define and discuss "aesthetics", but it is essentially a branch of philosophy which explores values in art, or the theory of beauty, or a philosophy of art. For our purposes we can focus more narrowly on something that implicitly (and sometimes explicitly) occurs in your English classroom.

The range of value judgements in your classroom may range from something as vague as "this novel is no good" to "this poem more successfully (articulately? beautifully? movingly?) expresses the experience of being rejected than the other one and here are my reasons for saying so". Whether or not we are conscious of them, we make value judgements about literary art quite regularly as we study and discuss texts.

One of the "areas of knowledge" as defined in the IB Theory of Knowledge course is "The arts", and of course literary art is one of those. The following pages are aimed at making the connection between what you do every day in your English class and the approach to the arts involved in the Theory of Knowledge course. Some of the questions that can be explored involve wondering whether art can deliver any kind of "knowledge", what is the nature of the "artful" in literature, what is the role of taste in aesthetic evaluation, and whether art includes any moral responsibility. We cannot deal with all of those questions here, but we can look at several that may occur frequently in your discussions and writings:

1 How can we tell a "good" piece of literary art from something other than good?
2 Is there such a thing as a "bad" literary work?
3 How do we know?

> "*When may we expect to have something from you on the aesthetic question?*"
> The Dean of Studies to Stephen Daedalus in *A Portrait of the Artist as a Young Man* by James Joyce

"Instead of 'It sucks' you could say, 'It doesn't speak to me.'"

In these matters we raise questions about what is subjective, and the temptations of relativism that are common in discussions of ethics, for example. People who practise the discipline of literary criticism – which includes you – usually find some theoretical grounds through which they can move beyond purely subjective judgements by basing their evaluations on some theory. These theories can range widely through structuralism, deconstructionism, archetypal or Marxist criticism and many others, some of which you will be acquainted with through your teachers or your own reading. Recently, as literary studies have acknowledged their deep connection with wider cultural issues, psychoanalytic, feminist and post-colonial studies have widened the ways in which literary works are judged.

Different cultures can have very different intentions and norms for art; in an international programme such as the IB, which includes literature from all over the world, you must try to expand your awareness in this respect as well. An account of prison life by Pramoedya Ananta Toer, an Indonesian, in *The Mute's Soliloquy* is quite a different work from Solzhenitsyn's *One Day in the Life of Ivan Denisovich*.

However, the kinds of assessment that the IB English course requires at present are largely based in formalist or New Critical principles (involving close study of the text as an aesthetic object or construct), and so that provides us with one way of exploring literature. When you are looking at something more than such responses as "I like this novel (or don't)" it should be possible for you to see some ways in which you can extend the conversation beyond expressions of liking or **taste**. **Taste** is indeed both valid and also a good place to begin to make an evaluation, but in order to have a conversation about a literary work, it's useful to get beyond it.

When we embark on a conversation that is critical, a conversation that begins "this is a good poem (or essay, or novel, or play)…" we will need to find or devise or borrow some **norms** by which we can measure "good", or "somewhat or partially good", or "not very good". These **norms** can be called your **aesthetic principles**. There are many, many views of what these norms can or should be.

In Joyce's novel, Stephen Daedalus chooses to develop his norms from the ideas of the Scholastic philosopher, Thomas Aquinas, some of whose ideas are derived in turn from Aristotle. So Stephen uses as a root of his norms the idea that "the beautiful is that which being seen pleases". For him the major norms for a "good" work of art (one that is pleasing) are then set out: wholeness, harmony and radiance. Sometimes these characteristics are called unity, complexity and intensity, as Monroe C. Beardsley labelled them. They may be helpful to you in deciding what is important for a good work of literature. If "beauty" seems a problematic term – there is surely an aesthetic of the ugly – then thinking of literature as *belles-lettres* might be useful to you.

Others would place value on art in different ways, defining its success as its potential to make you a better person, claiming that "true art is moral art", something close to the view of Horace, that the purpose of art is both to teach and to delight. Some theories consider the best art to be that which fully expresses the ideas and feelings of the artist.

To help you discover a little more of where you stand in relation to **aesthetic evaluation** of literature, you will find below an extract based on the work of the critic M.H. Abrams, who in his significant work *The Mirror and the Lamp* outlines some characteristics of four different modes of responding to art. He names four "theories" of art which can enable you to find out a little more about how you respond to works of literature and other forms of art: the **mimetic** theory, the **expressive** theory, the **pragmatic** theory, and the **objective** theory. Other people will give these different names as well as different characteristics, but you may well find that such a frame will give you a starting point for thinking about such questions as:

● What kind of art am I drawn to?
● What is the function of art for me?
● Is some kind of knowledge being provided by art?
● What is the relation of taste and judgement when it comes to art?

If you value art because art imitates life... it reflects what is out there in the 'real world'... it confirms that your perception of the world is good, authentic or 'right'... you can 'identify with it'... it presents or articulates what it may not be possible for you to express about reality... it helps you to see and better understand the world... it looks like, sounds like, what is 'really out there'... then your judgements are shaped, to some degree, by the **mimetic** theory of art... the **world** matters.

If you value art because art expresses the artist... that art is a kind of therapy for the artist... that it is spontaneous and manifests authentically what the artist feels... that it expresses the essence of 'reality' through intuition and feeling rather than logic... that it puts something new into the world rather than representing the already existing... that it springs from a deep and mysterious well of creative energy... then you probably practise the **expressive** theory of art... the **artist** matters.

If you value art because art delivers a message... sends you a message from the artist, something you can use in your daily life... refreshes and reshapes your view of the unity, dignity, variety of human experience... produces an ongoing and coherent record of artistic perception and technique... makes the world a better place to live... then you are probably influenced by or oriented to the **pragmatic** theory of art... the **value to you** matters.

If you value art because it exists as itself... it is an object or construct with its own existence, made beautiful by internal harmony and integrity... it is created to be nothing more than itself, through an artistic intention... it reveals itself, under close scrutiny, to have resilient unity in complexity... it provides an arrested or exalted moment or moments of stasis, or ecstasis when encountered, then you probably are influenced by the **objective** theory of art... the **object** matters most.

You may well find that you can work more comfortably with these ideas if you first try them out with some visual art, either in a museum or in your classroom. Once you begin to see how one of these sets of norms – or a combination of them, which is quite common – seem to reflect the way you "see" and value art, it will be interesting to discuss works with other people.

There will be many aspects to your evaluation of a piece of literature; all those features that are discussed, for example, in Part 1 of this book on commentary. These will have varying prominence in an individual work and will depend to some degree on your own interests and angle of vision.

Activity

Read and make notes for a commentary on each of the two pieces of writing below. Then see if you can construct a comparative **evaluative** paragraph in which you make some judgements about their relative success – why one might be "better" on some grounds or whether they are equally "good" pieces of writing, but for different reasons.

Additionally, you might ask yourself such questions as:

● What kind of knowledge or "truth" have I derived from reading these pieces?

● Is this valid knowledge?

● How could more sense of the context enhance my experience or enable me to better evaluate them?

● To what degree is the material here simply subjective?

● How reliable can my evaluation of a work of art be?

Happenings

What is truth? Truth is a lie told by Fernando Silva.

Fernando tells stories not only with his words but with his whole body. He can turn himself into someone else or into a flying critter or anything at all, and he does it in such a way that afterwards one hears, let us say, a mockingbird singing in a tree, and thinks:

'That bird is imitating Fernando imitating a mockingbird.'

He tells stories of the beautiful little people: newly created people still smelling of clay; and also of outrageous characters he has known – like the mirror-maker who made mirrors he would walk into and get lost in, or the volcano-snuffer whom the Devil blinded in one eye out of vengeance by spitting in it. The stories happen in places where Fernando has been: the hotel open only to ghosts, the mansion where witches died of boredom, or Ticuantepe's house, which was so dark and cool one longed to have a girlfriend waiting there.

In addition, Fernando works as a doctor. He prefers herbs to pills, and cures ulcers with cardosanto and pigeons' eggs; but prefers his own hands to herbs. For he cures by the laying on of hands – and by telling stories, which is another way of laying on hands.

Eduardo Galeano

The Colonel

What you have heard is true. I was in his house. His wife carried a tray of coffee and sugar. His daughter filed her nails, his sons went out for the night. There were daily papers, pet dogs, a pistol on the cushion beside him. The moon swung bare on its black cord over the house. On the television was a cop show. It was in English. Broken bottles were embedded in the walls around the house to scoop the kneecaps from a man's legs or cut his hands to lace. On the windows there were gratings like those in liquor stores. We had dinner, rack of lamb, good wine, a gold bell was on the table for calling the maid. The maid brought green mangoes, salt, a type of bread. I was asked how I enjoyed the country. There was a brief commercial in Spanish. His wife took everything away. There was some talk then of how difficult it had become to govern. The parrot said hello on the terrace. The colonel told it to shut up, and pushed himself from the table. My friend said to me with his eyes: say nothing. The colonel returned with a sack used to bring groceries home. He spilled many human ears on the table. They were like dried peach halves. There is no other way to say this. He took one of them in his hands, shook it in our faces, dropped it into a water glass. It came alive there. I am tired of fooling around he said. And as for the rights of anyone, tell your people they can go fuck themselves. He swept the ears to the floor with his arm and held the last of his wine in the air. Something for your poetry, no? he said. Some of the ears on the floor caught this scrap of his voice. Some of the ears on the floor were pressed to the ground.

Carolyn Forché

Glossary

Allegory a story or narrative, often told at some length, which has a deeper meaning below the surface. *The Pilgrim's Progress* by John Bunyan is a well-known allegory. A more modern example is George Orwell's *Animal Farm*, which on a surface level is about a group of animals who take over their farm but on a deeper level is an allegory of the Russian Revolution and the shortcomings of Communism.

Alliteration the repetition of the same consonant sound, especially at the beginning of words. For example, "Five miles meandering with a mazy motion" (*Kubla Khan* by S.T. Coleridge).

Allusion a reference to another event, person, place, or work of literature – the allusion is usually implied rather than explicit and often provides another layer of meaning to what is being said

Ambiguity use of language where the meaning is unclear or has two or more possible interpretations or meanings. It could be created through a weakness in the way the writer has expressed himself or herself, but often it is used by writers quite deliberately to create layers of meaning in the mind of the reader.

Ambivalence this indicates more than one possible attitude is being displayed by the writer towards a character, theme, or idea, etc.

Anachronism something that is historically inaccurate, for example the reference to a clock chiming in Shakespeare's *Julius Caesar*.

Anthropomorphism the endowment of something that is not human with human characteristics.

Antithesis contrasting ideas or words that are balanced against each other.

Apostrophe an interruption in a poem or narrative so that the speaker or writer can address a dead or absent person or particular audience directly.

Archaic language that is old-fashioned – not completely obsolete but no longer in current use.

Assonance the repetition of similar vowel sounds. For example: "There must be Gods thrown down and trumpets blown" (*Hyperion* by John Keats).

This shows the paired assonance of "must", "trum", "thrown", "blown".

Atmosphere the prevailing mood created by a piece of writing.

Ballad a narrative poem that tells a story (traditional ballads were songs) usually in a straightforward way. The theme is often tragic or contains a whimsical, supernatural, or fantastical element.

Bathos an anti-climax or sudden descent from the serious to the ridiculous – sometimes deliberate, sometimes unintentional on the part of the writer.

Blank verse unrhymed poetry that adheres to a strict pattern in that each line is an iambic pentameter (a ten-syllable line with five stresses). It is close to the natural rhythm of English speech or prose, and is used a great deal by many writers including Shakespeare and Milton.

Caesura a conscious break in a line of poetry (see Chapter 5, page 120).

Caricature a character described through the exaggeration of a small number of features that he or she possesses.

Catharsis a purging of the emotions which takes place at the end of a tragedy.

Cliché a phrase, idea, or image that has been used so much that it has lost much of its original meaning, impact, and freshness.

Colloquial ordinary, everyday speech and language.

Comedy originally simply a play or other work which ended happily. Now we use this term to describe something that is funny and which makes us laugh. In literature the comedy is not a necessarily a lightweight form. A play like Shakespeare's *Measure for Measure*, for example, is, for the most part a serious and dark play but as it ends happily, it is often described as a comedy.

Conceit an elaborate, extended, and sometimes surprising comparison between things that, at first sight, do not have much in common.

Connotation an implication or association attached to a word or phrase. A connotation is suggested or felt rather than being explicit.

Consonance the repetition of the same consonant sounds in two or more words in which the vowel sounds are different. For example: "And by his smile, I knew that sullen hall,/ By his dead smile I knew we stood in Hell" (*Strange Meeting* by Wilfred Owen). Where consonance replaces the rhyme, as here, it is called half-rhyme.

Couplet two consecutive lines of verse that rhyme.

Dénouement the ending of a play, novel, or drama where "all is revealed" and the plot is unravelled.

Diction the choice of words that a writer makes. Another term for "vocabulary".

Didactic a work that is intended to preach or teach, often containing a particular moral or political point.

Dramatic monologue a poem or prose piece in which a character addresses an audience. Often the monologue is complete in itself, as in Alan Bennett's *Talking Heads*.

Elegy a meditative poem, usually sad and reflective in nature. Sometimes, though not always, it is concerned with the theme of death.

Empathy a feeling on the part of the reader of sharing the particular experience being described by the character or writer.

End stopping a verse line with a pause or a stop at the end of it.

Enjambment a line of verse that flows on into the next line without a pause.

Epic a long narrative poem, written in an elevated style and usually dealing with a heroic theme or story. Homer's *The Iliad* and Milton's *Paradise Lost* are examples of this.

Euphemism expressing an unpleasant or unsavoury idea in a less blunt and more pleasant way.

Euphony use of pleasant or melodious sounds.

Exemplum a story that contains or illustrates a moral point put forward as an "example".

Fable a short story that presents a clear moral lesson.

Fabliau a short comic tale with a bawdy element, akin to the "dirty story". Chaucer's *The Miller's Tale* contains strong elements of the fabliau.

Farce a play that aims to entertain the audience through absurd and ridiculous characters and action.

Feminine ending an extra unstressed syllable at the end of a line of poetry. (Contrast with a stressed syllable, a masculine ending.)

Figurative language language that is symbolic or metaphorical and not meant to be taken literally.

Foot a group of syllables forming a unit of verse – the basic unit of "metre". (See Chapter 5, pages 122–123.)

Free verse verse written without any fixed structure (either in metre or rhyme).

Genre a particular type of writing, e.g. prose, poetry, drama.

Heptameter a verse line containing seven feet.

Hexameter a verse line containing six feet.

Hyperbole deliberate and extravagant exaggeration.

Iamb the most common metrical foot in English poetry, consisting of an unstressed syllable followed by a stressed syllable.

Idyll a story, often written in verse, usually concerning innocent and rustic characters in rural, idealized surroundings. This form can also deal with more heroic subjects, as in Tennyson's *Idylls of the King*. (See **Pastoral**.)

Imagery the use of words to create a picture or "image" in the mind of the reader. Images can relate to any of the senses, not just sight, but also hearing, taste, touch, and smell. "Imagery" is often used to refer to the use of descriptive language, particularly to the use of metaphors and similes.

Internal rhyme rhyming words within a line rather than at the end of lines.

Inter-textual having clear links with other texts through the themes, ideas, or issues which are explored.

Irony at its simplest level, irony means saying one thing while meaning another. It occurs where a word or phrase has one surface meaning but another contradictory, possibly opposite meaning is implied. Irony is frequently confused with sarcasm. Sarcasm is spoken, often relying on tone of voice, and is much more blunt than irony.

Lament a poem expressing intense grief.

Lyric originally a song performed to the accompaniment of a lyre (an early harp-like instrument) but now it can mean a song-like poem or a short poem expressing personal feeling.

Metaphor a comparison of one thing to another in order to make description more vivid. The metaphor actually states that one thing *is* the other. For example, a simile would be: "The huge knight stood like an impregnable tower in the ranks of the enemy", whereas the corresponding metaphor would be: "The huge knight was an impregnable tower in the ranks of the enemy". (See **Simile** and **Personification**.)

Metre the regular use of stressed and unstressed syllables in poetry. (See **Foot** and Chapter 5, pages 122–123.)

Mock heroic a poem that treats trivial subject matter in the grand and elevated style of epic poetry. The effect produced is often satirical, as in Pope's *The Rape of the Lock*.

Monometer a verse line consisting of only one metrical foot.

Motif a dominant theme, subject or idea which runs through a piece of literature. Often a "motif" can assume a symbolic importance.

Narrative a piece of writing that tells a story.

Octameter a verse line consisting of eight feet.

Octave the first eight lines of a sonnet.

Ode a verse form similar to a lyric but often more lengthy and containing more serious and elevated thoughts.

Onomatopoeia the use of words whose sound copies the sound of the thing or process that they describe. On a simple level, words like "bang", "hiss", and "splash" are onomatopoeic, but it also has more subtle uses.

Oxymoron a figure of speech which joins together words of opposite meanings, e.g. "the living dead", "bitter sweet", etc.

Paradox a statement that appears contradictory, but when considered more closely is seen to contain a good deal of truth.

Parody a work that is written in imitation of another work, very often with the intention of making fun of the original.

Pastoral generally, literature concerning rural life with idealized settings and rustic characters. Often pastorals are concerned with the lives of shepherds and shepherdesses presented in idyllic and unrealistic ways. (See **Idyll**.)

Pathos the effect in literature which makes the reader feel sadness or pity.

Pentameter a line of verse containing five feet.

Periphrasis a round-about or long-winded way of expressing something.

Personification the attribution of human feelings, emotions, or sensations to an inanimate object. Personification is a kind of metaphor where human qualities are given to things or abstract ideas, and they are described as if they were a person.

Plot the sequence of events in a poem, play, novel, or short story that make up the main storyline.

Prose any kind of writing which is not verse – usually divided into fiction and non-fiction.

Protagonist the main character or speaker in a poem, monologue, play, or story.

Pun a play on words that have similar sounds but quite different meanings.

Quatrain a stanza of four lines which can have various rhyme schemes.

Refrain repetition throughout a poem of a phrase, line, or series of lines, as in the "chorus" of a song.

Rhetoric originally, the art of speaking and writing in such a way as to persuade an audience to a particular point of view. Now this term is often used to imply grand words that have no substance to them. There are a variety of rhetorical devices, such as the rhetorical question – a question which does not require an answer as the answer is either obvious or implied in the question itself. (See **Apostrophe, Exemplum**.)

Rhyme corresponding sounds in words, usually at the end of each line but not always. (See **Internal rhyme**.)

Rhyme scheme the pattern of the rhymes in a poem.

Rhythm the "movement" of the poem as created through the metre and the way that language is stressed within the poem.

Satire the highlighting or exposing of human failings or foolishness within a society through ridiculing them. Satire can range from being gentle and light to being extremely biting and bitter in tone, e.g. Swift's *Gulliver's Travels* or *A Modest Proposal*, and George Orwell's *Animal Farm*.

Scansion the analysis of metrical patterns in poetry. (See Chapter 5, pages 122–123.)

Septet a seven-line stanza.

Sestet the last six lines of a sonnet.

Simile a comparison of one thing to another in order to make description more vivid. Similes use the words "like" or "as" in this comparison. (See **Metaphor**.)

Soliloquy a speech in which a character, alone on stage, expresses his or her thoughts and feelings aloud for the benefit of the audience, often in a revealing way.

Sonnet a fourteen-line poem, usually with ten syllables in each line. There are several ways in which the lines can be organized, but often they consist of an octave and a sestet.

Stanza the blocks of lines into which a poem is divided. (Sometimes these are, less precisely, referred to as verses, which can lead to confusion as poetry is sometimes called "verse".)

Stream of consciousness a technique in which the writer records thoughts and emotions in a "stream" as they come to mind, without giving order or structure.

Structure the way that a poem or play or other piece of writing has been put together. This can include the metre pattern, stanza arrangement, and the way the ideas are developed, etc.

Style the individual way in which a writer has used language to express his or her ideas.

Sub-plot a secondary storyline in a story or play. Often, as in some Shakespeare plays, the sub-plot can provide some comic relief from the main action, but sub-plots can also relate in quite complex ways to the main plot of a text.

Sub-text ideas, themes, or issues that are not dealt with overtly by a text but which exist below the surface meaning of it.

Symbol like images, symbols represent something else. In very simple terms a red rose is often used to symbolize love; distant thunder is often symbolic of approaching trouble. Symbols can be very subtle and multi-layered in their significance.

Syntax the way in which sentences are structured. Sentences can be structured in different ways to achieve different effects.

Tetrameter a verse line of four feet.

Theme the central idea or ideas that the writer explores through a text.

Tone the tone of a text is created through the combined effects of a number of features, such as diction, syntax, rhythm, etc. The tone is a major factor in establishing the overall impression of the piece of writing.

Trimeter a verse line consisting of three feet.

Zeugma a device that joins together two apparently incongruous things by applying a verb or adjective to both which only really applies to one of them, e.g. "Kill the boys and the luggage" (Shakespeare's *Henry V*).

Index